WITHDRAWN

Case-Based Reasoning

Experiences, Lessons,
& Future Directions

Case-Based Reasoning

Experiences, Lessons, & Future Directions

Edited by

David B. Leake

AAAI Press / The MIT Press

Menlo Park, California / Cambridge, Massachusetts / London, England

"A Tutorial Introduction to Case-Based Reasoning," was adapted by Janet Kolodner and David B. Leake from Kolodner, J., *Case-Based Reasoning,* San Francisco: Morgan Kaufmann, 1993.

"Towards More Creative Case-Based Design Systems," by Linda M. Wills and Janet L. Kolodner, was reprinted from *Proceedings of the Twelfth National Conference on Artificial Intelligence,* 50–55. Menlo Park, Calif.: AAAI Press, 1994.

"Flexible Strategy Learning Using Analogical Replay of Problem Solving Episodes," by Manuela M. Veloso, was reprinted from *Proceedings of the Twelfth National Conference on Artificial Intelligence,* 595–600. Menlo Park, Calif.: AAAI Press, 1994.

"Learning to Improve Case Adaptation by Introspective Reasoning and CBR," by David B. Leake, Andrew Kinley, and David Wilson, was reprinted with minor revisions from *Proceedings of The First International Conference on Case-Based Reasoning,* 229–240. Berlin: Springer Verlag, 1995.

To my parents

Contents

Contributors

Robin Burke is a visiting assistant professor in the department of computer science at the University of Chicago. He received his Ph.D. from Northwestern University. His research applies case-based reasoning to problems of information access, particularly in the area of educational information retrieval. His research goal is the development of active retrieval systems that seek information on the user's behalf, making use of both domain-specific knowledge and high-level retrieval strategies. His address is: Artificial Intelligence Laboratory, Department of Computer Science, The University of Chicago, 1100 East 58th Street, Chicago, IL 60637.

Eric A. Domeshek is an assistant professor of computer science in the electrical engineering and computer science department at Northwestern University, and a member of Northwestern's Institute for the Learning Sciences. He received his Ph.D. in computer science from Yale University. His work focuses on indexing unstructured information for appropriate retrieval. His research interests include artificial intelligence and cognitive science with emphases on case-based reasoning, representation design, human-computer systems, and educational applications. His address is The Institute for the Learning Sciences, Northwestern University, 1890 Maple Avenue, Evanston, IL 60201.

Anthony G. Francis, Jr. is currently a Ph.D. candidate investigating the relationship of agency, memory, and reasoning at the Georgia Institute of Technology, where he received his B.S. in information and computer science with highest honors. His other research interests include case-based reasoning, the utility problem, creativity, natural language, animal cognition, semiotics, and cognitive science. He is also a professional science fiction author. His address is: College of Computing, Georgia Institute of Technology, Atlanta, GA 30332-0280.

M. Timur Friedman is a Ph.D. candidate in computer science at the University of Massachusetts at Amherst, from which he received an M.S.; he also holds degrees from Harvard College and Stevens Institute of Technology. He is presently doing research on quality of service issues in inter-network protocols. His address is: Computer Science Department, University of Massachusetts at Amherst, Amherst, MA 01003.

Anna L. Griffith currently performs knowledge acquisition and knowledge engix CONTRIBUTORS

neering for an air campaign planning project at ISX Corporation. She received her B.S. from Allegheny College and her M.S. from the Georgia Institute of Technology, where she conducted research on case-based reasoning. Her address is: ISX Corporation, 1165 Northchase Parkway Ste 120, Marietta, GA 30067.

Kristian J. Hammond is director of the Artificial Intelligence Laboratory at The University of Chicago. He received his Ph.D. from Yale University. He is one of the developers of case-based reasoning and the developer of the first case-based planning system, CHEF. He has gone on to direct research on a wide range of case-based reasoning systems. He has recently begun developing internet-based software agents. These systems communicate via examples rather than explicit queries or questions. He chaired the 1989 DARPA Case-Based Reasoning Workshop. His address is: Artificial Intelligence Laboratory, Department of Computer Science, The University of Chicago, 1100 East 58th Street, Chicago, IL 60637.

David Hinkle is currently pursuing his Ph.D. in neuroscience at The Johns Hopkins University, focusing on computational and systems neuroscience. As a senior scientist at Lockheed Martin's Artificial Intelligence Research Center for more than seven years, his research activities included machine learning, case-based reasoning, data mining, and robotics. He received his B.S. in computer science from Syracuse University and his M.S. in computer science from Northeastern University. His address is: Department of Neuroscience, The Johns Hopkins University School of Medicine, 725 Wolfe Street, Baltimore, MD 21205-2185.

Alex Kass is associate director for research at The Institute for the Learning Sciences at Northwestern University, where he oversees numerous educational-software research and development projects. He received his Ph.D. from Yale University. His principal research focus is on computer-based education and training, particularly the construction of intelligent learning-by-doing environments, the integration of case-presentation and simulation-based training, the construction of theory-rich authoring tools for learning environments, computer-assisted creativity, and multimedia-based simulation. His address is: The Institute for the Learning Sciences, Northwestern University, 1890 Maple Avenue, Evanston, IL 60201.

Mark T. Keane holds a lectureship in artificial intelligence at the Department of Computer Science, The University of Dublin, Trinity College. He received his Ph.D. in cognitive psychology from The University of Dublin, Trinity College. He has published over 50 papers and 10 books in both cognitive psychology and artificial intelligence, mainly in the areas of analogical problem solving, insight problem solving and case-based reasoning. In 1994 he cochaired the Second European Workshop on Case-Based Reasoning. His address is: Reasoning Research Project, Department of Computer Science, Trinity College, University of Dublin, Dublin 2, Ireland.

Andrew Kinley is currently a Ph.D. candidate at Indiana University. He received his B.A. cum laude with honors in computer science at Bowdoin College and his M.S. from Indiana University. His research focuses on improving performance of case adaptation in case-based reasoning. Additional research interests include memory, planning, and cognitive science. His address is: Computer Science Department, Indiana University, Bloomington, IN 47405.

Janet L. Kolodner is professor of computing and cognitive science in the College of Computing at the Georgia Institute of Technology. She is founding director of the EduTech Institute, whose mission is to use knowledge about cognition to inform the design of educational technology and learning environments. She pioneered case-based reasoning, with her laboratory emphasizing its use in situations of real-world complexity. Her current research concentrates on the applications and implications of case-based reasoning for design, decision aiding, education, and creative problem solving. She is editor in chief of *The Journal of the Learning Sciences* and is a fellow of the American Association for Artificial Intelligence. Her address is: College of Computing, Georgia Institute of Technology, Atlanta, GA 30332-0280.

Hiroaki Kitano is a researcher at Sony Computer Science Laboratory in Tokyo and a visiting researcher at Carnegie Mellon University. He received his Ph.D. in computer science from Kyoto University. His research focuses on massively parallel artificial intelligence and on combining diverse approaches to model the emergence and evolution of intelligence. He received the 1993 Computers and Thought Award of the International Joint Conferences on Artificial Intelligence. His address is: Sony Computer Science Laboratory, 3-14-13, Higashi-Gotanda, Shinagawa, Tokyo, 141 Japan.

David B. Leake is an assistant professor of computer science and member of the cognitive science faculty at Indiana University. He received his Ph.D. in computer science from Yale University. His primary research interests are case-based reasoning, especially the use of introspective methods for refining indexing and adaptation, abductive explanation, and goal-driven learning. He has over fifty publications in these areas, including three books. He chaired the AAAI-93 Workshop on Case-Based Reasoning. In 1995 he presented the opening tutorial at the First International Conference on Case-Based Reasoning in Sesimbra, Portugal, and he is cochair of the upcoming Second International Conference on Case-Based Reasoning. His address is: Computer Science Department, Indiana University, Bloomington, IN 47405.

William Mark is director of computer science and systems at the National Semiconductor Research Laboratory. Computer science and systems is focusing on the silicon-based systems of the future, particularly in the areas of networks (wired and wireless), network access devices, and "smart devices" for homes and offices. Mark was formerly director of information and computing sciences for the Lockheed Martin Palo Alto Research Laboratories. Prior to joining Lockheed, he was a cofounder and director of Savoir, a company developing products and services for factory automation. Mark holds a software patent for user interface design, and a PhD in computer science from MIT. His personal research interests include information agents and intelligent user interfaces. Current address: National Semiconductor Research Laboratory, 2900 Semiconductor Dr. M/S E-100, Santa Clara, CA 95052.

Ashwin Ram is an associate professor of computer and cognitive science in the College of Computing of the Georgia Institute of Technology, and an adjunct professor in the School of Psychology. He received his Ph.D. degree from Yale University. His research interests lie in the areas of machine learning, case-based reasoning, natural language understanding, and cognitive science, and he has many research publications in these areas. He is a coeditor of a book on goal-driven learning and a forthcoming book on computational models of reading and understanding. He recently cochaired the Sixteenth Annual Conference of the Cognitive Science Society. His address is: College of Computing, Georgia Institute of Technology, Atlanta, GA 30332-0280.

Christopher K. Riesbeck is associate professor in the department of electrical engineering and computer science at Northwestern University, and the associate director for research at The Institute for the Learning Sciences. He received his Ph.D. in computer science from Stanford University. He is a fellow of the American Association for Artificial Intelligence. His current research focuses on case-based reasoning, memory-based language understanding, and intelligent interfaces for knowledge presentation and teaching. His address is: The Institute for the Learning Sciences, Northwestern University, 1890 Maple Avenue, Evanston, IL 60201.

Edwina L. Rissland is professor of computer science at the University of Massachusetts at Amherst and a lecturer on law at the Harvard Law School. She received her Sc.B. in applied mathematics, magna cum laude, from Brown University, M.A. in mathematics from Brandeis University, and Ph.D. in mathematics from MIT. Her research interests include case-based reasoning, CBR and information retrieval, case-based conceptual change, and AI and law. She is a fellow of the American Association for Artificial Intelligence and currently president of the International Association for AI and Law. Her address is: Department of Computer Science, University of Massachusetts at Amherst, Amherst, MA 01003.

Juan Carlos Santamaría is currently a Ph.D. candidate in artificial intelligence at the Georgia Institute of Technology. He received the B.S. degree in electronic engineering (cum laude) at the Simon Bolivar University in Venezuela and holds M.S. degrees in computer science and industrial engineering from the Georgia Institute of Technology. His research interests include learning and adaptation in autonomous agents, intelligent control, and theories of perception and action selection. His address is: College of Computing, Georgia Institute of Technology, Atlanta, GA 30332-0280.

Roger C. Schank is director of the Institute for the Learning Sciences at Northwestern University and John Evans professor of computer science, education and psychology. He received his Ph.D. from the University of Texas. He is a leader in the field of artificial intelligence and multimedia-based interactive training. He is the author of more than 125 publications. He is a fellow of the American Association for Artificial Intelligence and was the founder of the Cognitive Science Society and cofounder of the journal *Cognitive Science*. He is the president of the Learning Sciences Corporation, a company formed in partnership with Northwestern University to market the software initially developed at the Institute for the Learning Sciences. His address is: The Institute for the Learning Sciences, Northwestern University, 1890 Maple Avenue, Evanston, IL 60201.

Kathryn Schmitt received her B.S. in computer science from the University of Wisconsin-Madison. She has worked in the mathematics and computer science division of Argonne National Laboratory and as a research programmer in the Artificial Intelligence Laboratory at the University of Chicago, where she was involved in a number of projects on knowledge navigation. She has also been a software developer in the financial industry. She is now writing fiction and thinking about how stories might be experienced in the next century.

Hideo Shimazu currently manages a commercial tool development project at NEC Corporation to combine CBR with multimedia authoring. He received his B.S. and M.S. degrees in electrical engineering from Keio University and has been a visiting scholar at UCLA. After joining NEC Corporation, his work focused on the fifth generation project, computer graphics, natural language processing, computer music, and case-based reasoning. His address is: Information Technology Research Labs, NEC Corporation, 4-1-1 Miyazaki, Miyamae-ku, Kawasaki, Kanagawa, 216 Japan.

Evangelos Simoudis is the director of data mining solutions at IBM North America. He received a B.A. in physics from Grinnell College, a B.S. in electrical engineering from The California Institute of Technology, an M.S. in computer science from the University of Oregon, and a Ph.D. in computer science from Brandeis University. Prior to joining IBM, he worked at Lockheed Corporation's Research Laboratories and at Digital Equipment Corporation. His address is: IBM Almaden Research Center, Mailstop D9DB-E2, 650 Harry Road, San Jose, CA 95120.

David B. Skalak is currently a Ph.D. candidate in the Department of Computer Science at the University of Massachusetts at Amherst. He holds degrees from Union College, Dartmouth College, Harvard Law School and the University of Massachusetts. His primary research interests are in machine learning and case-based reasoning. His address is: Department of Computer Science, University of Massachusetts, Amherst, MA 01003.

Barry Smyth is a lecturer in artificial intelligence and computability theory at University College, Dublin. He received his B.Sc. in computer science from University College, has been a research scientist at Hitachi Research Laboratory, and did his doctoral studies at Trinity College in Dublin. His current research interests include case-based reasoning and computational models of problem solving and design. With coauthor Mark Keane he received the Publisher's Prize at the 1995 International Joint Conference on Artificial Intelligence and the Distinguished Paper Award at the First International Conference on Case-Based Reasoning. His address is: Department of Computer Science, University College Dublin, Dublin 4, Ireland.

Manuela M. Veloso is Finmeccanica assistant professor of computer science at Carnegie Mellon University. She received her Ph.D. degree in computer science from Carnegie Mellon University. Her Ph.D. dissertation research was on learning by analogical reasoning in general problem solving. Her current research interests include planning and learning and the integration of machine vision and machine learning. In 1995 she cochaired the First International Conference on Case-Based Reasoning in Sesimbra, Portugal. Her address is: School of Computer Science, Carnegie Mellon University, Pittsburgh, PA 15213.

Linda M. Wills is a research scientist in the School of Electrical and Computer Engineering at the Georgia Institute of Technology. She received her Ph.D. degree from the Massachusetts Institute of Technology. Her research interests are in engineering problem solving and artificial intelligence, particularly automated software understanding, design recovery, reengineering, and reuse. She is Chair of the IEEE Committee on Reverse Engineering and is program cochair of the Second and Third Working Conferences on Reverse Engineering. Her address is: School of Electrical and Computer Engineering, Georgia Institute of Technology, Atlanta, GA 30332-0280.

David Wilson is currently a Ph.D. candidate at Indiana University. He received his B.A. with high honors in computer science and mathematics from Rockford College and his M.S. in computer science from Indiana University. His research interests include case-based reasoning, memory, knowledge representation, and cognitive science. His address is: Computer Science Department, Indiana University, Bloomington, IN 47405.

Preface

Case-based reasoning (CBR) is now a mature subfield of artificial intelligence. The fundamental principles of case-based reasoning have been established, and numerous applications have demonstrated its role as a useful technology. Recent progress has also revealed new opportunities and challenges for the field. This book presents experiences in CBR that illustrate the state of the art, the lessons learned from those experiences, and directions for the future.

True to the spirit of CBR, this book examines the field in a primarily case-based way. Its chapters provide concrete examples of how key issues—including indexing and retrieval, case adaptation, evaluation, and application of CBR methods—are being addressed in the context of a range of tasks and domains. These issue-oriented case studies of experiences with particular projects provide a view of the principles of CBR, what CBR can do, how to attack problems using case-based reasoning, and how new challenges are being addressed. The case studies are supplemented with commentaries from leaders in the field providing individual perspectives on the state of CBR and its future impact.

This book provides experienced CBR practitioners with a reference to recent progress in case-based reasoning research and applications. It also provides an introduction to CBR methods and the state of the art for students, AI researchers in other areas, and developers starting to build case-based reasoning systems. It presents experts and nonexperts alike with visions of the most promising directions for new progress and for the next generation of CBR systems.

Case-Based Reasoning

Experiences, Lessons,
& Future Directions

1   CBR in Context: The Present and Future

David B. Leake

A father taking his two-year-old son on a walk reaches an intersection and asks where they should turn. The child picks a direction, the direction they turned at that intersection the day before to go to the supermarket. The child explains: "I have a memory: Buy donut."

Another Vietnam?

Recently, [this question has] been asked in discussions over a deeper U.S. involvement around the world — in Bosnia, in Somalia, in Haiti.

— Ed Timms, Dallas *Morning News*

Windows 95: Microsoft's Vietnam?

— Headline on the *IN Jersey* Web page

Reasoning is often modeled as a process that draws conclusions by chaining together generalized rules, starting from scratch. Case-based reasoning (CBR) takes a very different view. In CBR, the primary knowledge source is not generalized rules but a memory of stored *cases* recording specific prior episodes. In CBR, new solutions are generated not by chaining, but by retrieving the most relevant cases from memory and adapting them to fit the new situations. Thus in CBR, reasoning is based on remembering. As the passages starting this section illustrate, remindings facilitate human reasoning in many contexts and for many tasks, ranging from children's simple reasoning to expert decision-making. Much of the original inspiration for the CBR approach came from the role of remindings in human reasoning (Schank 1982).

The CBR approach is based on two tenets about the nature of the world. The first tenet is that the world is regular: similar problems have similar solutions. Consequently, solutions for similar prior problems are a useful starting point for new problem-solving. The second tenet is that the types of problems an agent encounters tend to recur. Consequently, future problems are likely to be similar to current problems. When the two tenets hold, it is worthwhile to remember and reuse prior reasoning: case-based reasoning is an effective reasoning strategy.

CBR can also be beneficial, however, when a reasoner must solve problems that are quite different from prior experiences. As a case-based reasoner applies cases to increasingly novel problems, the CBR process changes from simple reuse to more creative problem-solving. The child in the example starting this chapter performs very straightforward CBR; he remembers a previous path when confronted with an identical decision point—a previously-visited intersection—and suggests repeating a prior plan. The commentators who apply lessons of Vietnam to Bosnia, however, must do more subtle reasoning to determine whether and how Vietnam applies to the new situation. The wag who sees Vietnam in Windows 95® is adapting a reminding to a very new context, and reasoning in a creative way.

Regardless of whether a case-based reasoner solves a routine or novel problem, and of whether the problem-solving outcome is success or failure, the case-based reasoner learns from its experience. Complementary with the principle of *reasoning by remembering* is the principle that *reasoning is remembered*—that reasoning and learning are intimately connected. The knowledge of a case-based reasoner is constantly changing as new experiences give rise to new cases which are stored for future use. A case-based reasoner learns from experience to exploit prior successes and avoid repeating prior failures.

This chapter provides context for the remainder of this book, introducing key principles of CBR, its basic algorithm and relationship to other approaches, and discussing the state of the field, new trends, and key challenges. Chapter 2 provides a tutorial introduction to the field and to the principles for developing CBR systems. Later chapters provide case studies of key issues, in the context of specific projects. They are followed by perspectives that examine lessons learned and provide visions of the future of case-based reasoning.

Why CBR?

The study of CBR is driven by two primary motivations. The first, from cognitive science, is the desire to model human reasoning and learning. The second, from artificial intelligence, is the pragmatic desire to develop technology to make AI systems more effective.

Interest in CBR as a cognitive model is supported by studies of human reasoning which demonstrate reasoning from cases in a wide range of task contexts. For example, studies support the importance of remindings of prior examples in learning to use a computer text editor (Ross 1984), learning programming (Pirolli and Anderson 1985), mathematical problem solving (Faries and Schlossberg 1994, Ross 1984), diagnosis by automobile mechanics (Lancaster and Kolodner 1987) and physicians (Schmidt, Norman, and Boshuizen 1990), explanation of anomalous events (Read and Cesa 1991), and decision-making under time pressure (Klein and Calderwood 1988, 1989). Understanding these processes requires developing and testing models of how humans store, retrieve, and apply prior cases (Kolodner 1994b, Leake 1996).

Observations that people use case-based reasoning have also spurred interest in CBR as an AI technology. Humans are robust problem-solvers; they routinely solve hard problems despite limited and uncertain knowledge, and their performance improves with experience. All of these qualities are desirable for real-world AI systems. Consequently, it is natural to ask how CBR can advance AI technology. Discussions of this question have identified five main problems that can be ameliorated by case-based reasoning.

1. **Knowledge Acquisition.** A classic problem in traditional knowledge-based systems is how to provide the rules on which the systems depend. The rule acquisition process can be laborious and unreliable: it may be difficult to elicit rules, and there is no assurance that those rules will actually be sufficient to characterize expert performance.[1] In some domains, rules may be difficult to formalize or the number of rules required may be unmanageably large.

   Because case-based reasoners reason from complete specific episodes, CBR makes it unnecessary to decompose experiences and generalize their parts into rules. Some task domains are especially natural for CBR, with cases that are suitable for CBR already collected as part of standard problem-solving procedures. In those domains, the cost of knowledge acquisition for CBR is very low. Mark, Simoudis, and Hinkle (Chapter 14) describe their experience in one such domain, autoclave loading. Other reports corroborate comparatively rapid development times for other CBR applications (e.g., Simoudis and Miller 1991).

   Of course, not all domains are natural CBR domains; cases may be unavailable, or may be available but in a hard-to-use form (e.g., cases described with natural language text). In these situations, applying CBR may depend on a significant "case engineering" effort to delimit the information that cases must contain, to define the representation for that information and to extract that information from available data. Likewise, applying CBR requires developing criteria for indexing and reapplying prior cases. (See, e.g., Kitano and Shimazu, Chapter 15; Mark et al., Chapter 14; Voss 1994). However, even if this initial process requires considerable effort, CBR can still provide overall benefits for knowledge acquisition. First, experts who are resistant to attempts to distill a set of domain rules are often eager to tell their "war stories"—the cases they have encountered. This facilitates gathering the needed data for CBR. Second, as discussed in the following point, after the initial case engineering effort it is often simple to augment and maintain the knowledge a CBR system needs.

2. **Knowledge Maintenance.** Defining an initial knowledge base is generally only the first step towards a successful AI application. Initial understanding of the problem is often imperfect, requiring system knowledge to be refined. Likewise, changes in task requirements and circumstances may render existing knowledge obsolete. Although refinement of case representations and indexing schemes may be required as a task becomes better understood, CBR offers a significant benefit for knowledge maintenance: a user may be able to add missing cases to the case library without expert intervention.

   Also, because CBR systems do incremental learning, they can be deployed with only a limited set of "seed cases," to be augmented with new cases if (and only if) the initial case library turns out to be insufficient in practice. A CBR system needs only to handle the types of problems that actually occur in practice, while generative systems must account for all problems that are possible in principle.

3. **Increasing Problem-solving Efficiency.** People achieve satisfactory problem-solving performance despite the fact that commonplace problems in everyday reasoning, such as explanation and planning, are NP-hard (Bylander et al. 1991, Chapman 1987). Reuse of prior solutions helps increase problem-solving efficiency by building on prior reasoning rather than repeating prior effort. In addition, because CBR saves failed solutions as well as successes, it can warn of potential problems to avoid.

4. **Increasing Quality of Solutions.** When the principles of a domain are not well understood, rules will be imperfect. In that situation, the solutions suggested by cases may be more accurate than those suggested by chains of rules, because cases reflect what really happens (or fails to happen) in a given set of circumstances. In medical reasoning, for example, anecdotes about specific cases go beyond codified knowledge, serving as "the as-yet-unorganized evidence at the forefront of clinical medicine" (Hunter 1986).

5. **User Acceptance.** A key problem in deploying successful AI systems is user acceptance: no system is useful unless its users accept its results. To trust the system's conclusions, a user may need to be convinced that they are derived in a reasonable way. This is a problem for other approaches: neural network systems cannot provide explanations of their decisions, and rule-based systems must explain their decisions by reference to their rules, which the user may not fully understand or accept (Riesbeck 1988). On the other hand, the results of CBR systems are based on actual prior cases that can be presented to the user to provide compelling support for the system's conclusions.

Successful use of CBR depends on addressing issues in how to acquire, represent, index, and adapt existing cases. The next section highlights how these issues fit into the CBR process and how they are being addressed in current systems. The following section highlights how these methods relate to other approaches.

A Sketch of the CBR Process

Case-based reasoning tasks are often divided into two classes, *interpretation* and *problem-solving* (e.g., Kolodner 1993; Rissland, Kolodner, and Waltz 1989). Interpretive CBR uses prior cases as reference points for classifying or characterizing new situations; problem-solving CBR uses prior cases to suggest solutions that might apply to new circumstances.

Case-based Interpretation

In interpretive CBR, the reasoner's goal is to form a judgment about or classification of a new situation, by comparing and contrasting it with cases that have already been classified (e.g., Ashley and Rissland 1987a). For example, interpretive CBR plays a fundamental role in interpreting legal concepts and applying laws in the American legal system (e.g., Ashley 1990, Bain 1989, Branting 1991b, Cuthill 1992, Sanders 1994). A tax lawyer arguing that his or her client should receive a home-office deduction does so by using precedents: by showing that the deduction was granted in similar previous cases and showing that those cases are more relevant than cases in which the deduction was not granted. Interpretive CBR is also important for tasks such as diagnosis; a problem can be diagnosed by comparing and contrasting the current symptoms to those in previous cases to determine the best diagnosis (e.g., Bareiss 1989a).

In its simplest form, interpretive CBR involves four steps. First, the reasoner must perform *situation assessment* (Kolodner 1993, Owens 1991), to determine which features of the current situation are really relevant. Second, based on the results of situation assessment, the reasoner retrieves a relevant prior case or prior cases. Third, the reasoner then compares those cases to the new situation, to determine which interpretation applies. Finally, the current situation and the interpretation are then saved as a new case on which to base future reasoning.

Case-based Problem-Solving

The goal of problem-solving CBR is to apply a prior solution to generate the solution to a new problem. For example, case-based design, planning, and explanation systems all retrieve and adapt solutions of similar prior problems.

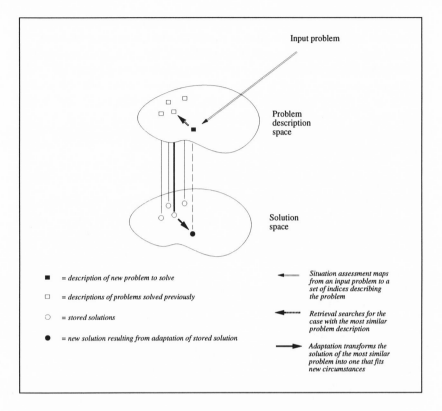

Figure 1. How basic case-based problem-solving generates a new solution.

Like interpretive CBR, problem-solving CBR involves situation assessment, case retrieval, and similarity assessment/evaluation. In addition, the similarities and differences between new and prior cases are used to determine how the solution of the previous case can be adapted to fit the new situation. For example, a basic case-based planning system generates a new plan by retrieving a prior plan for a similar goal, determining the differences between the old and new goals, and adapting the plan to take the new goals into account.

Case-based problem-solving can be seen as exploiting the relationship between two different types of similarity. These types of similarity apply to two different spaces, the space of problem descriptions and the space of problem solutions. We illustrate their role with the basic solution generation process in figure 1. When presented with a new problem, the CBR system does situation assessment to generate a problem description, and then searches for a prior problem with a relevant problem description. The solution of the most relevant problem is used as the starting point for generating a solution to the new problem, With the right way of describing a problem, similar problems have solutions that are usefully similar—i.e., easy to adapt to the new situation.

The figure also suggests another benefit of CBR: that multiple types of knowledge can be used to encode equivalent information (Richter 1995). Information is contained not only in the case representation/indexing scheme and case base, but also in the similarity metric and adaptation knowledge, and the information contained by these knowledge sources overlaps. Consequently, the system developer has the flexibility to choose the best alternative for representing the needed knowledge.

Learning from Successes and Failures

After a solution has been generated, the final step is to apply the solution, to repair it if problems arise, and to learn from the experience. Learning in CBR systems is driven by both successes and failures, and encompasses both speedup learning and acquisition of new knowledge.

Success-driven Learning. When the CBR process is successful, the resulting solution is stored for future reuse, avoiding the need to rederive it from scratch. When CBR is combined with generative problem-solving, it can provide speedup learning (Veloso discusses an experimental demonstration of this speedup in Chapter 8). If the generative system has an imperfect domain theory, the benefit goes beyond speedup. In that situation, stored cases provide information beyond the information contained in the original domain theory: they provide the information that a particular solution did or did not work in a specific real situation. In this way, case acquisition refines initial domain knowledge and allows the system to favor solutions that are likely to be successful, based on its experience. In addition, if solutions are provided by an external source, storing cases with those solutions may increase the range of problems that the system can solve.

Failure-driven Learning. CBR is committed to the value of learning from failures as well as successes. First, failures reveal that learning is needed. Second, failures help focus decisions about what to learn: the needed learning must help avoid future failures. CBR systems learn both from task failures, in which their solutions are unsuccessful, and expectation failures (Schank 1982), in which observed outcomes differ—for better or for worse—from predictions. For example, when a planner generates a plan that is expected to work and doesn't, there are two failures. The task failure prompts the system to try to learn a successful plan; the expectation failure prompts the system to learn how to anticipate similar problems in the future, in order to avoid them (e.g., Hammond 1989c). When a planner generates a plan that is successful even beyond expectations, there is no task failure, but there is still an expectation failure, prompting learning about how to anticipate and perhaps harness the unexpected good effects.

In CBR systems, failures can trigger multiple types of learning. When a failed solution is repaired, the new solution is stored; this is simply learning from a new successful solution. In addition, however, information about the failure itself can be stored as data for future analysis when new information becomes available (Riesbeck 1981; Schank 1982, 1986) or to provide a warning about possible future failures that should be avoided (e.g., Bareiss 1989a, Hammond 1989c, Kolodner and Simpson 1989). Failures can also prompt revision of indexing criteria, to retrieve better cases in the future (e.g., Bhatta and Goel 1993; Fox and Leake 1995b, 1995c; Hammond 1989c; Ram 1993; Redmond 1992; Sycara and Navinchandra 1989).

A Closer Look

The previous section's description blurs many differences in CBR methods. This section illustrates a sampling of important variations in how fundamental issues are being addressed. Chapter 2 describes a number of them in more detail.

What Cases Contain. The previous section assumes that problem-solving systems will store and adapt prior solutions. An alternative approach is for them to store and reuse traces of how those solutions were derived, instead of the actual solutions. By capturing and replaying the reasoning trace involved in selecting problem-solving operators, rather than the problem solving steps themselves, the *derivational analogy approach* facilitates application of stored traces of processing to a wider class of problems (Carbonell 1986; Veloso 1994, Chapter 8). This approach has attracted interest not only for domain problem-solving tasks, but also in a number of systems that store and reuse reasoning traces for introspective reasoning and learning (e.g., Kennedy 1995; Leake, Kinley, and Wilson, Chapter 11; Oehlmann 1995; Ram and Cox 1994).

How to Retrieve. The previous sketch used purely top-down retrieval: A problem description was formed and used to select a relevant case. However, the indices needed are inextricably tied to the contents of the case library (which may change). Consequently, CBR research is also investigating the role of bottom-up influences to guide retrieval, favoring features that are useful to discriminate between the cases in memory (e.g., Cunningham, Bonzano, and Smyth 1995; Owens 1991). Although many CBR systems base retrieval on carefully constructed indexing vocabularies and problem descriptions in order for retrieval to "zero in" on a small subset of the case library, other approaches include search (Rissland et al., Chapter 6), marker passing (Martin 1993), and spreading activation (e.g., Ram and Francis, Chapter 10; Wolverton and Hayes-Roth 1994). Some also exploit parallel hardware to maintain quick retrieval while considering large sets of cases (Kettler et al. 1994, Kolodner 1988b, Owens 1991, Stanfill and Waltz 1986). Retrieval based on nontraditional types of input information, such as bitmap images and CAD plans, is also being investigated (Voss 1994). As is discussed in the subsection "Case Adaptation," later methods are also being developed to make retrieval focus on cases that are likely to be easy to adapt.

Adaptation. Developing case adaptation criteria is a central open challenge for CBR (e.g., Allemang 1993, Kolodner 1991, Leake 1994a). The case adaptation process in CBR systems is usually done by rule-based systems. Consequently, correct case adaptation requires that those rules capture both a theory of case adaptation, and the needed aspects of the domain theory to carry out changes. However, as has already been described, an important motivation for using CBR is often the lack of a reliable domain theory. As a result, developers defining adaptation rules must re-confront the knowledge acquisition problem for rule-based systems. Additional problems may arise because available cases can lack the internal structure needed for effective adaptation. For example, in case-based educational systems whose cases are video clips, the case content is simply not accessible.

Difficulties with case adaptation have led many CBR systems to simply dispense with adaptation, replacing the retrieve-evaluate-adapt cycle with *retrieve and propose* systems (e.g., Kolodner 1991). Such systems exploit the memory processes developed in CBR research, while relying on a human user to adapt and evaluate solutions. This framework is the basis for many successful CBR applications, some examples of which are described in this volume (Kitano and Shimazu, Chapter 13 and Mark et al., Chapter 14).

New approaches are now being developed to overcome the adaptation problem. Because this is a central problem for the future of CBR, we devote the subsection "Case Adaptation" that follows to the promising new methods for addressing problems of automatic adaptation.

Similarity Assessment. One issue in similarity assessment is how to determine the right features to compare. Decisions about which features are important are often based on explanations of feature relevance, but those explanations may be imperfect, leading to a need for robust similarity metrics that take the difficulties in specifying important features into account (e.g., Bento 1994, Veloso 1994). Another problem is that for some tasks, input problem descriptions are not sufficient to determine the similarity of old and new situations. For example, for the task of case-based explanation of anomalous events during understanding, the need to explain arises precisely because the input case is imperfectly understood. Thus situation assessment and similarity assessment may need to be combined. One method for the combination is *constructive similarity assessment*, which builds up a description of the input situation based on prior cases, and judges similarity by whether the retrieved case is adaptable to the new situation, rather than according to any static criteria (Leake 1992a, 1995b).

There is also growing recognition that the role of similarity judgments is to determine which cases are most *usefully* similar, given the desired results of the CBR process. A single set of static similarity criteria may not capture the right distinctions. Different cases may be most appropriate to consider depending on the relative importance of different dimensions for judging the success of the CBR process. For example, for case-based planning, some of the criteria might be reliability of the resulting plan, execution time for that plan, the time required to generate the solution, or even, if a creative solution is desired, the novelty of the result. The desire for similarity criteria to more strongly reflect intended use is reflected in approaches which replace traditional similarity judgments with judgments based instead on adaptability (Böerner 1994; Leake 1992a, 1995b). For those approaches, similarity is aimed at facilitating solution generation.

Case Evaluation. Like case adaptation, evaluation of the goodness of retrieved cases may be problematic for CBR systems, because evaluating candidate solutions may require considerable domain knowledge and reasoning effort. Although schemes have been developed to do rapid evaluation of some types of cases (e.g., Leake 1992b), providing the right evaluation knowledge is difficult. An alternative approach is to base evaluation on the cases in the case library itself. Once a case is adapted to produce a new solution, similar cases can be retrieved and used as a dynamic benchmark for judging the quality of the adaptation: If similar solutions were unsuccessful, the cases provide a warning (Mark et al., Chapter 14).

Storage. Early CBR systems simply stored each case they generated. New work examines the effects of design decisions about the maximum size of the case library (Santamaría and Ram, Chapter 12) and the utility of learning (Doorenbos and Veloso 1993; Francis and Ram 1993, 1995), as well as how to decide which cases must be stored in order to provide sufficient coverage (e.g., Smyth and Keane 1995b). Some systems also reason about which cases to try to acquire (Hunter 1989, Ram 1991).

Relationship to Other Approaches

Questions often arise about how case-based reasoning relates to areas such as memory-based reasoning, analogical reasoning, and other learning methods. This section highlights some relevant relationships and differences.

Memory-based Reasoning

Memory-based reasoning (MBR) is often considered a subtype of CBR; MBR solves problems by retrieving stored precedents as a starting point for new problem-solving (e.g., Stanfill and Waltz 1986, Waltz 1989). However, its primary focus is on the retrieval process, and in particular on the use of parallel retrieval schemes to enable retrieval without conventional index selection.

Parallel models can lead to very fast retrieval, but also raise new questions to address about the criteria for knowledge access (Kolodner, Chapter 16).

Analogical Reasoning

Case-based reasoning can be viewed as fundamentally analogical: CBR solves new problems and interprets new situations by applying analogous prior episodes. As Burstein (1989) points out, cognitive models of analogy and CBR examine the same cognitive process; there is no clear line between research "on analogy" and "on CBR." Nevertheless, research on analogy was originally more concerned with abstract knowledge and structural similarity, while research on CBR is more concerned with forming correspondences between specific episodes based on pragmatic considerations about the usefulness of the result.

In addition, there have traditionally been differences in the scope of the process studied. Research on analogy has focused largely on analogical mapping; CBR in addition studies related processes that occur both before and after mapping. For example, how to retrieve a source case is a fundamental part of CBR, while models of analogy may assume that the source concept is provided as input (e.g., Mitchell 1993). Also, after a mapping between old and new situations suggests an analogous solution, CBR adapts that solution to fit the new situation, and stores it for future use.

If "analogy" is taken to refer only to analogical mapping, a possible description of the relationship between analogy and CBR is:

Case-based reasoning = retrieval + analogy + adaptation + learning

However, two caveats are necessary. First, some research on analogy takes a more extensive view, focusing not only on mapping but also seriously addressing related issues such as retrieval (e.g., Gentner and Forbus 1991). Second, despite the breakdown of steps in this description of CBR, the steps of the CBR process are not independent. Considering them together provides an advantage over studying them individually, because their relationships can be exploited to facilitate and constrain processing in each one. For example, Leake (1995b) discusses how analogical mapping for explanations is facilitated by linking retrieval and mapping criteria, and the subsection "Case Adaptation" discusses the value of integrating other parts of the CBR process with case adaptation.

Databases and Information Retrieval Systems

Given that storage and retrieval are central aspects of CBR, a natural question is the relationship between CBR systems and databases or information retrieval systems (IR). Although an obvious difference is that full CBR systems adapt the cases they retrieve, the question is more subtle for case-based "retrieve-and-propose" systems or case-based educational systems that present cases but do not perform adaptation.

The retrieval process in CBR differs from that of information retrieval systems and standard databases by being more active. Database systems and IR systems leave the problem of how to formulate the right query largely to the user. In CBR systems, the system itself is often designed to start from an input description using features that are quite different from those included in the cases in memory, and to determine appropriate retrieval cues (e.g., Burke and Kass, Chapter 5; Rissland et al., Chapter 6; Wills and Kolodner, Chapter 4). The input description may also be incomplete (Cunningham, Bonzano, and Smyth 1995; Leake 1992a, 1995b; Owens 1991). Thus a crucial difference between IR and CBR is the importance of situation assessment and problem description processes in CBR.

Database systems are designed to do exact matching between queries and stored information, while the goal of CBR is to retrieve a "most similar" case or set of most similar cases. The most similar cases may include conflicts with some of the attributes that were specified in the retrieval query. In CBR, whether a particular case should be retrieved depends not only on the case itself, but whether there are better competitors. Despite these differences, databases can provide useful foundations for case memories and CBR can have useful synergies with information retrieval (e.g., Anick and Simoudis 1993). For example, Kitano and Shimazu (Chapter 13) advocate the use of relational database management systems, combined with supplementary mechanisms to allow flexible query specification and partial matching during retrieval, to manage the case libraries for large-scale corporate CBR applications.

Likewise, techniques from CBR can be used to facilitate information retrieval, and the information available in information retrieval systems can be used to augment traditional case libraries. For example, Rissland and Daniels (1995) describe a retrieval approach in which CBR methods are used to retrieve a set of relevant cases from a richly-represented CBR case base, and the retrieved cases are in turn used as "seed" documents for the relevance feedback mechanism of a full-text information retrieval system. The IR system then retrieves additional cases from a large IR corpus of shallowly represented cases. The aim is twofold: to enable access to many more cases than normally available to CBR systems, and to improve recall and precision of retrieval from the IR corpus compared to standard IR techniques.

Learning Methods

The learning done by CBR systems has interesting relationships with both inductive and explanation-based learning methods.

Inductive Learning. When case-based classification systems save exemplars of a concept, their learning can be viewed as a form of inductive concept learning. However, unlike traditional symbolic and neural network approaches to inductive learning, which define concepts by generalizations and discard the exemplars on which the generalizations are based, CBR systems define concepts entirely by the specific cases saved.

Retaining specific cases has important advantages. First, it makes decisions more explainable by enabling a system to point to concrete cases supporting its decisions. Second, it makes the decisions more verifiable because the user (whether a human or another system) can examine the cases directly to assess their applicability. Third, it is useful for resolving conflicts. For example, if the two most similar previous cases provide contradictory advice, it might be useful to know that they are contradictory and to explicitly compare and contrast them, balancing them against each other in light of the current situation, in order to decide which to follow. In systems that combine conflicting advice to offer only a single answer (e.g., neural networks), the specific conflict is hidden.

Another benefit of case learning in CBR is that it is incremental. No matter how few cases are contained in the case library, performance on those cases will be correct; as soon as a case has been stored by a CBR system, that case is available for use. As mentioned previously, this is an important advantage for applications, because it enables prototype CBR systems to function with a small set of "seed cases" and to add coverage by storing new cases incrementally if they prove to be needed (e.g., Mark et al., Chapter 14).

The CBR approach also contrasts with knowledge-poor inductive learning methods because it emphasizes the semantics of a domain, through similarity and retrieval criteria and case adaptation knowledge.

Instance-based learning (IBL), also called *case-based learning,* is an inductive learning method closely related to CBR. Rather than forming generalizations, IBL algorithms (Aha, Kibler, and Albert 1991) store previously-categorized episodes and use them to classify new inputs by assigning the same classification that was assigned to the most similar previous case (or cases). IBL systems forgo complex indexing, use feature-value representations, and do not address case adaptation, but they nevertheless appear very promising for certain applications (see Riesbeck, Chapter 17). They have also attracted attention as a form of CBR that is amenable to formal analysis (e.g., Jantke 1992).

Explanation-based Generalization. Explanation-based generalization (EBG) uses rules about a domain to explain why a training example has particular properties, and uses the explanation to guide generalization. The generalization is then stored for future use (DeJong and Mooney 1986; Mitchell, Keller, and Kedar-Cabelli 1986). Chunking (Laird, Rosenbloom, and Newell 1986), which collects traces of problem-solving steps and packages them for reuse, is a similar approach. Unlike inductive generalization, explanation-based generalization can do reliable learning from single examples.

CBR is similar to EBG in allowing single-example learning. However, CBR does not generalize cases at storage time. Instead, CBR adapts cases when adaptation is needed to solve a new problem. Thus CBR can be viewed as a form of *lazy learning* (e.g., Aha 1996). (Because CBR does generalize *indices* (Hammond 1989c), ungeneralized cases can still be retrieved to deal with novel problems.)

Waiting to adapt cases avoids expending effort unless it is certain that the effort will help solve an actual problem. For example, the SWALE system, which uses a case-based method to build explanations for story understanding, stores its explanations without generalization, and generalizes them only if generalization is needed to subsume future situations. Even then, generalization is only done to the extent needed to subsume them (e.g., Kass, Leake, and Owens 1986).

Another important difference between CBR and EBG is that adaptation is often much more flexible than explanation-based generalization. Adaptation can include operations other than generalization, such as specialization and substitution, and may involve modifications that are not guaranteed to be correct. For example, SWALE's adaptation process may use heuristics that include hypothesizing new causal rules. The flexibility of case adaptation precludes applying the "eager" approach of EBG generalization to case adaptation—it would be possible to generate an overwhelming number of variants for any candidate solution, many of them unreliable and most of them unlikely to be reused. However, because case adaptation in CBR is only done in response to the need to solve a specific new problem, and because adaptations are only done to the extent required by the new situation, the process is constrained, and the reasonableness of results can be verified in context (Leake 1995a).

Progress and Directions

To take stock of the state of CBR, this section looks at progress on general CBR issues, at some particularly noteworthy current task areas, and at work on the area of CBR that is least understood, and consequently the greatest research challenge: case adaptation.

Progress on General Issues in Applying CBR

Kolodner's (1993) CBR textbook concludes with a list of general challenges and opportunities for CBR, including knowledge engineering issues such as scaleup, evaluation, and developing CBR tools. Since that time, important progress has been made in each of those areas.

Scaling Up. A vital question for applying ideas developed in testbed systems is whether they will "scale up" to large problems. The scale-up of CBR algorithms is now being tested in both CBR research and applications. For example, Veloso (Chapter 8) describes tests confirming successful scaleup of PRODIGY/ANALOGY with a library of 1000 cases; Kitano and Shimazu (Chapter 13) describe the development and deployment of SQUAD, a software quality control advisory system with a case library of over 25,000 cases; Cassiopée, a case-based diagnostic aid for jet engines, uses 16,000 cases for its diagnosis process (Goodall 1995); and ALFA, a case-based system for power plant load forecasting, is in operation with a case library of 87,000 cases (Jabbour et al. 1988). These and other examples support that current technology is sufficient for CBR to be viable with large case bases. However, as Kolodner points out in Chapter 16, it is important to note that large case bases are not necessarily required by CBR. The size of the required case base depends strongly on the task being addressed. For some tasks, suitable performance may require only a few cases; for others, many thousands may be required.

Evaluation. Initial CBR research focused primarily on identifying key issues and methods for attacking them; progress was measured by qualitative advances in the types of problems that could be solved and by the insights they provided about human reasoning and reminding. As the field has matured, increased attention has been given to more quantitative evaluations of CBR systems and methods. Many case studies of evaluation of CBR systems and discussions of how to perform that evaluation are available in the proceedings of the 1994 AAAI Workshop on Case-Based Reasoning (Aha 1994). The chapters in this volume substantiate approaches with a mixture of qualitative and quantitative evaluations.

One difficulty in using quantitative evaluation to guide system construction is that CBR systems are complicated artifacts whose performance depends on many subtle interactions between components, as well as on the characteristics of the domain. Santamaría and Ram (Chapter 12) describe a methodology that addresses this problem by developing models of system performance, doing experimentation to validate those models, and using the models to guide design decisions.

From the perspective of applied CBR in a production setting, all evaluation criteria are subsumed in a single criterion: the effect on the bottom line. In order to be useful, CBR systems must be cost-effective. Many fielded applications attest to the cost-effectiveness of CBR applications and also suggest when and how CBR should be applied (e.g., Kitano and Shimazu, Chapter 13, and Mark et al., Chapter 14).

Tools. Because one of the motivations for CBR is to decrease the burden of developing intelligent systems, the ease of developing CBR systems is a crucial concern. The need for tools to enable an expert to participate directly in the case acquisition and case engineering process has been recognized from the early days of CBR (e.g., Riesbeck 1988). An important part of current work on large-scale CBR projects is developing tools that manage basic parts of the CBR process (e.g., Kitano and Shimazu, Chapter 13, and Mark et al., Chapter 14). The FABEL project, for example, has developed a suite of both general and domain-specific tools to support case management, retrieval, assessment and adaptation of architectural designs (e.g., FABEL Consortium 1993; Voss 1994).

Some projects have also developed tools to ease the construction of particular classes of case-based systems. Examples include Design-MUSE (Domeshek et al. 1994), which eases construction of case-based design aids, REPRO (Mark et al., Chapter 14), which is a tool kit to help in the development of case-based advisory systems, and the ASK tool, for building browsable corporate memories (Ferguson et al. 1991). Tools have also been developed to help to build case-based teaching systems to facilitate students' case acquisition in new domains. For example, the GuSS tool facilitates building learning-by-doing systems that allow a student to do active learning in a low-risk, simulated social environment (Burke and Kass, Chapter 5).

Commercial CBR shells are available as well. CBR shells provide mechanisms to support case retrieval, such as nearest-neighbor retrieval or automatically generated decision trees, and may allow users to interactively provide additional information as needed during retrieval. They may also provide sophisticated interfaces to facilitate creating and editing the case base, as well as facilities for importing information in existing databases. Watson (1995a) provides a comparative sketch of a number of tools including ART*Enterprise, Case-1, Casepower, the Inference CBR2 family, Eclipse, ESTEEM, KATE, ReCall, ReMind, and CBR Works. Althoff et al. (1995) provide a detailed comparative evaluation of five CBR shells: CBR Express, ESTEEM, KATE, ReMind, and CBR Works.[2] Mark et al. (Chapter 14) discuss some experiences with commercial shells and the strategy of building components that add needed functionality "on top of" the functionality provided by a commercial CBR shell.

As Riesbeck (Chapter 17) points out, additional tools are needed to aid human indexing (see Goldstein, Kedar, and Bareiss 1993, and Osgood and Bareiss 1993, for examples of this type of tool), and another need is "catalogs" of the types of indices appropriate for particular tasks and domains (e.g., Domeshek 1992, Leake 1992b, Schank and Osgood 1990). Likewise, tools are needed to facilitate acquisition of adaptation knowledge (one method under development is sketched in Leake, Kinley, and Wilson, Chapter 11).

Methodologies. Full acceptance of CBR by industry depends on establishing software development methodologies for CBR, to define how to organize and develop CBR projects. Lessons from CBR applications form a foundation for defining such methodologies. As Kitano and Shimazu describe, those lessons have already been used to define a methodology for building and maintaining large scale experience-sharing CBR systems at NEC.

One fundamental principle revealed by many experiences is the value of an iterative development process. Because CBR systems can provide useful results even with a partial case library, systems can be fielded with a set of seed cases that is augmented as gaps are revealed during use. Additional study is needed on issues in initial case engineering and case-base maintenance throughout the life-cycle of CBR applications.

Some Noteworthy Uses of CBR

CBR has been applied to a full spectrum of AI tasks, such as classification, interpretation, scheduling, planning, design, diagnosis, explanation, parsing, dispute mediation, argumentation, projection of effects, and execution monitoring. Many of these areas will be discussed in the following chapter. This subsection will discuss a few others that reveal noteworthy aspects of the CBR process and its relevance to important areas.

Creative Reasoning. A common misconception about case-based reasoning is that it only applies if new problems are very similar to those solved in the past. Although CBR is a simple and effective method for that type of reuse, it is also an interesting framework for creative reasoning. Creativity can enter into the CBR process in flexible retrieval processes that result in novel starting points for solving new problems, in mapping processes that form novel correspondences, and in flexible case adaptation to generate novel solutions. These processes have been used as a basis for case-based models of creative explanation (e.g., Kass 1990, 1992; Schank 1986; Schank and Leake 1986; Schank and Leake 1989), design and problem-solving (e.g., Bhatta, Goel, and Prabhakar 1994; Kolodner and Penberthy 1990; Kolodner 1994a; Wills and Kolodner, Chapter 4), story generation (Turner 1994), and understanding (Moorman and Ram 1994a, 1994b).

Case-based Aiding Systems. Case-based aiding systems use automated case memories to support human reasoners. The case memories provide the experiences that human reasoners may lack, suggesting successful prior solutions and warning of prior failures. The human reasoners maintain final control, performing adaptation and evaluation of solutions. Not only does this interaction provide practical advantages, by avoiding the need for automatic case adaptation and evaluation, but humans readily accept and appreciate the availability of advice. A classic example is Lockheed's Clavier (Mark et al., Chapter 14), an aiding system which uses its case library both to suggest autoclave layouts and to provide feedback on user solutions. Another is the SQUAD system at NEC (Kitano and Shimazu, Chapter 13).

A task area with particularly active research is interactive decision-aiding for design (e.g., FABEL consortium 1993; Griffith and Domeshek, Chapter 3; Gómez de Silva Garza and Maher 1996; Hua and Faltings 1993; Smith, Lottaz, and Faltings 1995; Sinha 1994; Sycara et al. 1991). Case-based design-aiding systems often support the design process not only with suggestions, but through mechanisms to facilitate case combination and adaptation by the user. There is also considerable interest in case-based decision-aiding for medical applications such as design of radiation treatments (e.g., Berger 1995a, Kahn and Anderson 1994, Macura and Macura 1995).

A particularly active area in fielded applications is case-based help desk systems. Such systems provide a resource for human help desk employees, who can call upon an automated case library to present similar prior questions and answers. Case-based help desk systems can provide significant performance improvements with rapid development time. Compaq's SMART system (Acorn and Walden 1992), a case-based call tracking and problem resolution system that aids customer service representatives at a central help line, was built in six months and improved productivity sufficiently to pay for itself within a year. CBR aiding systems are also being used to provide direct support, bypassing the need for customer service representatives. Compaq's QuickSource, a CBR application for printer diagnosis (Nguyen, Czerwinski, and Lee 1993), was not only used as part of SMART but also shipped directly to customers with printers to allow them to perform their own diagnosis. Some issues in developing case-based help desks are discussed by Kriegsman and Barletta (1993) and Mark et al. (Chapter 14).

Corporate Memories. Case bases are an appealing way to capture and share experiences of multiple agents. The case libraries accumulated by case-based help desk systems are one example of corporate memories, and are an interesting example of the use of cases for knowledge sharing. Case bases for particular help desk domains are now available as commercial products (Inference Corporation 1995), providing a form of "instant experience" that can be augmented by adding cases if novel problems arise. In this volume, Kitano and Shimazu (Chapter 13) describe the use of CBR as the basis of a large-scale corporate *experience sharing architecture.*

Case-based Education. Large-scale efforts are also under way to apply lessons from the cognitive model of case-based reasoning to training and teaching. Although case studies already play a useful role in legal and medical education, students using them generally do not confront the complexity of real episodes and do not have the opportunity to act to execute, evaluate, and revise their solutions (Williams 1992). In Chapter 15, Schank examines the ramifications of CBR for education and argues for a new educational curriculum designed to support case acquisition through learning by doing. He proposes that learning be done in *goal-based scenarios* (Schank et al. 1993/1994), rich learning environments in which students learn skills and conceptual knowledge through activities in pursuit of compelling goals. Such learning environments can use CBR methods to facilitate students' own case acquisition, by presenting students with information about others' experiences, in the form of relevant cases, when they are likely to be useful. Burke and Kass

(Chapter 5) describe a case-based teaching system reflecting this philosophy. More generally, the computational models developed by CBR can contribute to education by providing concrete suggestions about what makes a good problem, the range of problems that students should solve, and the kinds of resources that should be made available to student learners (Kolodner, Hmelo, and Narayanan 1996).

Knowledge Navigation. The knowledge access issues that are crucial to CBR will also play a central role in developing "digital libraries" of on-line information. Consequently, a promising new area for applying the results of CBR is "knowledge navigation" to search and browse on-line repositories of information. For example, lessons learned about indexing and retrieval in CBR can be used to help in characterizing information and guiding information search.

The capability of CBR systems to describe and refine information needs by examples also promises to play an important role in making digital libraries easier to access. As Hammond (Chapter 7) points out, it is often natural to request information by reference to specific examples (e.g., when being shown a car by a car salesman, to ask for "something like that, but a little sportier"). CBR methods to support that type of query have the potential to significantly facilitate interaction with on-line repositories of information.

Opportunities for Combining CBR with other Methods

In many different task areas, attention is also being devoted to the combination of CBR with other methods. That combination can involve CBR systems using other methods for support, CBR systems integrated with other methods, or CBR systems in a purely support role.

Supporting CBR with Other Methods. The strong CBR stance towards cognitive modeling is that CBR is the central human reasoning process. Although other sources of knowledge and other reasoning processes may be used, their role is to support the CBR process (Kolodner, Chapter 16). An example of a combined system that uses other methods to support CBR is the case-based design system JULIA (Hinrichs 1992), which uses supporting systems such as a constraint poster (Stefik 1981) and a reason maintenance system (Doyle 1979) to support a fundamentally case-based design process. Other CBR systems fall back on rule-based reasoning as a backup to CBR, using rules when no relevant cases are available (e.g., Goel, et al. 1994; Koton 1988a, 1988b).

Integrated Systems. More balanced combinations of CBR with other reasoning methods are also being investigated. For example, the INRECA project focuses on combining CBR and inductive learning techniques to perform diagnosis (Auriol et al. 1995). Likewise, case-based and rule-based reasoning may be combined in many ways. Cases may guide interpretation of rules; cases may be used to focus rule-based reasoning; or the CBR system may be one component among equals in a multistrategy reasoning system (Althoff and Wess 1991, Auriol 1995, Bartsch-Spoerl 1995, Branting and Porter 1991, Koton 1988b, Goel 1989, Golding and Rosenbloom 1991, Portinale and Torasso 1995, Skalak and Rissland 1991). Metareasoning about system performance, based on a self-model, can be used to guide learning to refine the CBR process itself (e.g., Arcos and Plaza 1994; Birnbaum et al. 1991; Fox 1995; Fox and Leake 1995a, 1995b, 1995c; Leake, Kinley, and Wilson, Chapter 11; Ram and Cox 1994). CBR may be also be applied in a fully integrated framework that performs strategic reasoning about each processing step (e.g., Aamodt 1994, Armengol and Plaza 1994). Veloso (Chapter 8) describes the use of CBR within an integrated architecture.

Hybrid approaches have proven useful for applications as well. Mark et al. (Chapter 14) argue that CBR should be viewed as part of a technology mix, and Hammond (1993) has described the usefulness of a class of CBR systems—that he calls "CBR-lite™" systems—which exploit the most applicable parts of a number of technologies, including CBR, to maximize performance.

CBR to Support Other Systems. Riesbeck (Chapter 17) proposes that a key future role of CBR will be for building "intelligent components" to improve the performance of a surrounding system with minimal development cost. Because CBR systems retrieve complete solutions, they offer an "anytime" ability to produce a first-pass solution rapidly, and then to refine it if the time constraints of the surrounding system allow additional processing to be done (Dean and Boddy 1988). Learning from actual processing episodes also automatically tailors the output of the intelligent component towards precisely what the surrounding system needs.

Case Adaptation

A final research challenge and opportunity centers on one of the basic steps of CBR: case adaptation. Adaptation plays a fundamental role in the flexibility of problem-solving CBR systems; their ability to solve novel problems depends on their ability to adapt retrieved cases to fit new circumstances and on their ability to repair solutions that fail.

The difficulty arises in how to perform the adaptation. There are many ways to adapt a case; effective adaptation depends on having both knowledge of possible adaptations and ways to select those that will be appropriate and effective in a particular situation. The problem is illustrated by a joke concerning Michael Jordan, a basketball superstar. In 1993 he shocked his fans by announcing that he had decided to leave basketball for baseball. In 1995, he was frustrated by a baseball strike that resulted in the baseball team owners locking out their teams and hiring replacement players, and rumors suggested that he would soon return to basketball. A joke framed the decision as Jordan selecting an adaptation to repair the situation:

Recent speculation is that Michael Jordan is switching back to basketball. We think there is a simpler explanation: He's trying to settle the baseball strike by using replacement owners.[3]

Central questions for adaptation are which aspects of a situation to adapt, which changes are reasonable for adapting them, and how to control the adaptation process. Answering those questions may require considerable domain knowledge, which in turn raises the question of how to acquire that knowledge. Many CBR systems depend on that knowledge being encoded a priori into rule-based production systems. Unfortunately, this approach raises the same types of knowledge acquisition issues that CBR was aimed at avoiding. It has proven a serious impediment to automatic adaptation.

Recognizing that practical retrieval technologies are available, but that the general adaptation problem remains extremely difficult for CBR systems, experts in both CBR research (e.g., Kolodner 1991) and applications (e.g., Barletta 1994; Mark et al., Chapter 14) agree that the best use of CBR for today's applied systems is as advisory systems that rely on the user to perform evaluation and adaptation.

However, understanding case adaptation remains important both from a cognitive modeling perspective—for understanding human case-based reasoning—and from a practical one—for developing fully autonomous CBR systems. Recent calls have been made for renewed attention to case adaptation (Leake 1994b, Aha and Ram 1995), and some promising approaches are emerging. These new approaches fall into two categories. The first category focuses on the knowledge and methods used during the adaptation process itself. The second addresses the problem indirectly, by trying to decrease the need for adaptation. For example, the adaptation problem can be alleviated by retrieving cases that require less adaptation to fit the current task, or by revising the task to decrease the need for adaptation.

Improving Adaptation Capabilities

Most research on case adaptation has assumed that adaptation must be done in a completely autonomous way by rule-based systems. This results in a knowledge acquisition problem for adaptation rules. Two alternatives are to decrease the need for domain-specific adaptation rules, by making adaptation rules more flexible, or to avoid the need for adaptation rules by applying a case-based approach to the adaptation process itself:

Using Flexible Adaptation Rules. One of the problems in developing adaptation rules is how to balance the operationality and generality of adaptation rules. Abstract case adaptation rules have good generality, with a small set characterizing a wide range of possible adaptations (e.g., Carbonell 1983, Koton 1988b, Hammond 1989c, Hinrichs 1992), but they may be hard to apply without additional specific domain knowledge. Specific rules, on the other hand, may be more operational, but cannot easily be applied to new tasks, forcing new rules to be coded for each new task and domain.

For example, the adaptation rule *add a step to remove harmful side-effect* has been proposed to repair plans with bad side-effects in case-based planning (Hammond 1989c). This rule is widely applicable—it applies to any plan—but it gives no guidance about how to find the right step to add in order to mitigate a given side-effect. For example, if the case-based planning system is attempting to build a plan for X-ray treatment, and the X-ray dose needed to destroy a tumor will result in an excessive radiation dose to healthy tissue, finding the right step to add to mitigate the bad effect may require considerable domain knowledge. An alternative is a very specific version of the rule, such as *add the step "rotate radiation sources" to remove harmful side-effect "excess radiation"* (Berger and Hammond 1991). Such rules can be applied effectively, but hand building such rules in advance requires intimate knowledge of a domain. In addition, an enormous number of rules may be needed, especially in systems that reason about multiple tasks and domains.

One approach to the operationality/generality tradeoff is to replace traditional adaptation rules with adaptation strategies that operationalize abstract rules by packaging them with memory search information (Kass 1990, 1994b). They strike a balance between domain-independent and domain-specific rules by providing domain-independent information about how to find the domain-specific information needed to solve a particular adaptation problem.

Derivational Analogy. Another alternative is to change the nature of the case that is stored. Rather than storing and directly reusing a solution itself, the CBR system can store a trace of how that solution was generated and replay it in the new situation. When the solution is replayed to solve future problems, the replay process can directly take into account differences between the old and new situations (e.g., Carbonell 1986; Veloso, Chapter 8).

Using Adaptation Cases. Because CBR has been shown to decrease the knowledge acquisition burden for domain knowledge in general, another appealing direction is case-based adaptation (e.g., Berger 1995b, Leake 1994b, Sycara 1988). Problems remain, however, in how to acquire these adaptation cases, and how to apply adaptation cases to novel situations. Normally the reuse of adaptation knowledge is restricted to situations in which prior adaptations apply very directly.

Supporting Adaptation with Introspective Reasoning. Introspective reasoning about the adaptation process can be used to guide adaptation decisions and carry out adaptations and the search for needed information in a more flexible way (Leake 1993b, 1995d; Leake, Kinley and Wilson, Chapter 11; Oehlmann et al. 1993; Oehlmann 1995).

Combining Rules and Cases for Adaptation Learning. A new direction based on introspective reasoning is to combine rule-based and case-based adaptation, using reasoning from general heuristics when necessary, but whenever possible reusing more specific information from stored introspective reasoning traces for prior adaptations. This method allows flexible solution of new problems while relying on specific experiences when possible (Leake, Kinley, and Wilson, Chapter 11).

Hierarchical Approaches and Reuse of Subcases. Another way to facilitate adaptation is by representing cases hierarchically (e.g., Aha and Branting 1995; Goel et al. 1994; Marir 1995; Redmond 1992; Smyth and Keane, Chapter 9). Hierarchical representations allow cases to be reused at the most specific level of abstraction that can be easily applied to the new situation. In addition, when individual subparts of a retrieved solution must be adapted, they can be adapted in context of the abstract outline of the entire solution. Ram and Francis (Chapter 10) describe a model of reuse of subcases in which an asynchronous memory mechanism retrieves relevant pieces of multiple prior cases to be spliced in as adaptation progresses.

Decreasing the Need for Adaptation

Case adaptation takes place within a larger context, including both the interaction with other components of the CBR system and with the user of the entire system. This context provides a range of possibilities for decreasing the need for adaptation.

Alleviating the Adaptation Burden by Refining Other Components. One way to alleviate the problem is to tie other components of the CBR system more closely into the adaptation process. These methods aim at more perspicacious case retrieval and similarity assessment, as well as at stored cases that are easier to adapt:

- *Refining indices to favor more adaptable cases.* Because the difficulty of case adaptation depends crucially on the cases that are retrieved, improvements in retrieval can significantly ameliorate the adaptation task. Fox and Leake (1994, 1995b, 1995c) apply introspective reasoning after problem-solving to evaluate whether the best case was retrieved, and, if not, to adjust retrieval criteria to focus future retrievals on more adaptable cases.

- *Basing retrieval directly on adaptability.* Given that indexing and similarity criteria are simply proxies for adaptability, another promising direction is to integrate retrieval and similarity judgments with adaptation. Adaptation-guided retrieval, described by Smyth and Keane in Chapter 9, retrieves directly on the basis of evidence of likely adaptability.

- *Basing similarity judgments on adaptability.* Many CBR systems use a two-step retrieval process, first retrieving a set of promising candidate cases, and then doing a finer-grained evaluation of the similarity of the retrieved cases and the new situation. Because the goal of their similarity judgment is to determine which cases can be applied to the new situations, it can be beneficial to integrate the similarity decision with the adaptation process, to favor cases not by the match between their features but instead by how easily their features can be adapted to match (Boerner 1994; Leake 1992a, 1995b).

- *Preparing for adaptation at storage time.* CBR practitioners have long recognized the need for case representations to provide the information needed to facilitate future adaptation (e.g., Kass and Leake 1988). This basic tenet for designing representations can be taken further, however, to guide preprocessing of specific cases at storage time in order to facilitate future adaptation. For example, Redmond's (1992) snippets facilitate reuse by making subparts of an episode individually accessible; Garland and Alterman (1995) propose that before plans are stored, they should be summarized and refined to remove superfluous information and inefficient steps, and then segmented into units expected to be useful.

- *Learning from user adaptation.* When the user manually adapts a case in an interactive CBR system, a trace of the user's adaptation process can be recorded for future use. That trace can then be replayed when needed for similar adaptation problems (Leake, Kinley, and Wilson, Chapter 11). This approach to adaptation learning can be viewed as a form of derivational analogy for reuse of case adaptations.

Supporting User Adaptation. Applied CBR systems often forgo adaptation entirely. They function solely as memories, retrieving cases and presenting them to the user, who adapts them on his or her own. However, some recent projects have begun to take a middle approach. The idea is for the CBR system to support and facilitate user adaptation while still leaving the process primarily under user control. For example, the user may make high-level adaptation decisions, with the system using model-based information to suggest possible adaptation points and inform the user of relevant constraints or track important interactions (e.g., Bell, Kedar, and Bareiss 1994; Smith, Lottaz, and Faltings 1995; Sinha 1994). After a case has been adapted to provide a new solution, the CBR system can also help evaluation of the result by presenting the user with similar prior solutions and their outcomes (Mark et al., Chapter 14).

Adapting the Context, not the Case. The goal of a CBR system is to generate a useful solution. Normally, this is accomplished by adapting a prior solution to apply to a new problem. An alternative method is to adapt the problem situation itself, so that the retrieved case can apply to the new problem without adaptation. For example, in CBR systems that retrieve and display video clips for educational purposes, no adaptation of the video clips is possible. However, for the purposes of such systems it is equally effective to adapt the context, by explaining why the retrieved video clip is relevant. "Bridging" generates a description of why a case is relevant, showing how the case applies. Burke and Kass (Chapter 5) describe a system which presents students with video clips and explanations of their significance. The "bridge" provided by that explanation makes the retrieved case useful.

The Contents of this Book

This book presents a selection of recent progress, issues, and directions for the future of case-based reasoning. It includes chapters addressing fundamental issues and approaches in indexing and retrieval, situation assessment and similarity assessment, and in case adaptation. These chapters provide a "case-based" view of key problems and solutions in context of the tasks for which they were developed. It then presents lessons learned about how to design CBR systems and how to apply them to real-world problems. It closes with perspectives on the state of the field and the most important directions for future impact.

The case studies presented involve a broad sampling of tasks, such as design (Chapters 3, 4, and 9), education (Chapters 5 and 15), legal reasoning (Chapter 6), planning (Chapters 10, 11, 12), decision support (Chapters 3, 13 and 14), problem-solving (Chapters 4, 8 and 14), and knowledge navigation (Chapter 7). In addition, they experimentally examine one of the fundamental tenets of CBR, that storing and reusing experiences improves performance (Chapters 8 and 12). The chapters also address other issues that, while not restricted to CBR per se, have been vigorously investigated by the CBR community. These include creative problem-solving (Chapter 4), strategic memory search (Chapters 6 and 11), and opportunistic retrieval (Chapters 4, 5, and 10).

The discussion of research issues and results is complemented with experiences and lessons from building CBR applications. Case-based reasoning is a fielded technology with burgeoning activity, and this book illustrates its use for purposes such as experience sharing (Chapter 13), autoclave loading, diagnosis, help desk support (Chapter 14), and education (Chapters 5 and 17). These identify crucial issues and approaches for developing and deploying applied systems. They also suggest new avenues for research.

This book closes with perspectives on the state of case-based reasoning and its future impact. In Chapter 14, Mark et al. discuss insights about applying CBR, based on their experiences with a number of CBR applications. In Chapter 15, Schank examines the role of case acquisition in human learning and argues that case-based reasoning has profound implications for transforming education. In Chapter 16, Kolodner first identifies and dispels misconceptions that distort perceptions of CBR and then underlines key problems to attack in order to advance the field. In Chapter 17, Riesbeck presents a vision for the future of AI, the role CBR will play in that future, and the resulting challenges for the next generation of case-based reasoning systems. Thus this volume provides a view of the present and future of case-based reasoning research and applications.

Some CBR Resources

The tutorial in chapter 2 of this volume presents a more thorough discussion of key CBR principles and issues and how to develop CBR systems. Kolodner's (1993) textbook *Case-Based Reasoning* presents an extensive examination of CBR issues and survey of American CBR research. Riesbeck and Schank's (1989) *Inside Case-Based Reasoning,* and Schank, Riesbeck, and Kass's (1994) *Inside Case-Based Explanation,* present distillations of a number of influential dissertations on case-based reasoning research, in addition to "micro" versions of CBR programs developed to facilitate experimentation. Aamodt and Plaza's (1994) overview article includes an introduction to the field with highlights of American and international CBR research.

The most complete picture of the field is provided by the proceedings of the many case-based reasoning workshops. Proceedings are available for the larger workshops in the United States (Kolodner 1988a, Hammond 1989b, Bareiss 1991, Leake 1993a, Aha 1994) and in Europe (Wess, Althoff, and Richter 1994; Haton, Keane, and Manago 1995; Watson 1995b), as well as for the First International Conference on Case-Based Reasoning (Veloso and Aamodt 1995).

There are also numerous electronic CBR resources, including discussion lists and archives of many CBR sources. The following list is a sampling of those available at the time this chapter was written.

Mailing Lists/Newsletters

AI-CBR. A mailing list including announcements, questions, and discussion about CBR, managed by Ian Watson and Farhi Marir at Salford University. To join, send an electronic mail message to mailbase@mailbase.ac.uk with "join ai-cbr *your name*" as the body of the message.

CBR-MED. A mailing list for those interested in CBR for medical domains, including members of the CBR and medical communities. It is managed by Kurt Fenstermacher of the University of Chicago and Charles Kahn of Medical College of Wisconsin. To join, send a message to listproc@cs.uchicago.edu with "subscribe CBR-MED *your name*" as the body of the message.

CBR Newsletter. A quarterly electronic newsletter that originated as a publication of the Special Interest Group on Case-Based Reasoning (AK-CBR) in the German Society for Computer Science. It is managed by Dietmar Janetzko of the University of Freiburg and Stefan Wess of Inference Corporation. The home page for the newsletter is http://wwwagr.informatik.uni-kl.de/~lsa/CBR/cbrNewsletter.html.

Sites on the World Wide Web

The following sites include many references and links to other electronic CBR resources:

- David Aha at the Naval Research Laboratory maintains a site with URL http://www.aic.nrl.navy.mil/~aha/research/case-based-reasoning.html.
- Ralph Bergmann and Wolfgang Wilke at the University of Kaiserslautern maintains a site with URL http://wwwagr.informatik.uni-kl.de/~lsa/CBR/CBR-Homepage.html.
- Ian Watson at the University of Salford maintains a site with URL http://www.salford.ac.uk/docs/depts/survey/staff/IWatson/cbr01.htm.
- A current list including all these resources is maintained by the American Association for Artificial Intelligence at the url: http://www.aaai.org/Resources/CB-Reasoning/cbr-resources.html

Conclusion

This chapter has placed case-based reasoning in context, delineated some of its tenets, and pointed to new directions to be addressed by the case studies in the remainder of the book. The heart of CBR is the importance of experiences and lessons—of remembering and reusing specific experiences and the lessons that they provide. This volume applies that principle of CBR to examining CBR itself, by presenting experiences and lessons in using CBR.

Experiences with the current generation of CBR systems suggest central challenges for future research, such as the case adaptation problem; they also show how to apply CBR technology. Finally, they show where CBR may have the most impact. The chapters that follow present individual perspectives that illuminate important experiences, lessons, and future directions for applying and advancing case-based reasoning.

Acknowledgments

The initial idea for this book came out of The AAAI-93 Workshop for Case-Based Reasoning (Leake 1993a), sponsored by the American Association for

Artificial Intelligence. I would like to thank all the chapter authors for their contributions, and also to thank Ray Bareiss, Robin Burke, Eric Domeshek, Anthony Francis, Janet Kolodner, Ashwin Ram, Chris Riesbeck, Raja Sooria-murthi, and David Wilson, for their generous assistance as the book was being prepared. I am grateful to Ken Ford, Editor-in-Chief of the AAAI Press, for his enthusiastic support for this volume and his instrumental role in its coming into being, and to Mike Hamilton of AAAI Press, who helpfully guided arrangements and the production process. The author's work is supported by the National Science Foundation under Grant No. IRI-9409348.

Notes

1. See Forsythe and Buchanan (1989) for a discussion of some of the problems in knowledge elicitation.

2. CBR Works was previously named S³-Case, and is referred to by that name in both the references.

3. Tom Comeau, March, 1995.

2 A Tutorial Introduction to Case-Based Reasoning

Janet L. Kolodner and David B. Leake

ase-based reasoning means reasoning based on previous cases or experiences. A case-based reasoner uses remembered cases to suggest a means of solving a new problem, to suggest how to adapt a solution that doesn't quite work, to warn of possible failures, to interpret a new situation, to critique a solution in progress, or to focus attention on some part of a situation or problem. An example will illustrate.

A host is planning a meal for a set of people who include, among others, several people who eat no meat or poultry, one of whom is also allergic to milk products, several meat-and-potatoes men, and her friend Anne. Since it is tomato season, she wants to use tomatoes as a major ingredient in the meal. As she is planning the meal, she remembers:

"I once served tomato tart (made from mozzarella cheese, tomatoes, dijon mustard, basil, and pepper, all in a pie crust) as the main dish during the summer when I had vegetarians come for dinner. It was delicious and easy to make. But I can't serve that to Elana (the one allergic to milk). I have adapted recipes for Elana before by substituting tofu products for cheese. I could do that, but I don't know how good the tomato tart will taste that way."

She decides not to serve tomato tart and continues planning. Since it is summer, she decides that grilled fish would be a good main course. But now she remembers something else:

"Last time I tried to serve Anne grilled fish, she wouldn't eat it. I had to put hotdogs on the grill at the last minute."

This suggests to her that she should not serve fish, but she wants to anyway. She considers whether there is a way to serve fish that Anne will eat.

"I remember seeing Anne eat mahi-mahi in a restaurant. I wonder what kind of fish she will eat. The fish I served her was whole trout with the head on. The fish in the restaurant was a fillet and more like steak than fish. I guess I need to serve a fish that is more like meat than fish. Perhaps swordfish will work. I wonder if

Anne will eat swordfish. Swordfish is like chicken, and I know she eats chicken."

This hypothetical host uses remembered cases to suggest a means of solving the new problem (e.g., to suggest a main dish), to suggest how to adapt a solution that doesn't quite fit (e.g., substitute a tofu product for cheese), to warn of possible failures (e.g., Anne won't eat fish), and to interpret a situation (e.g., why didn't Anne eat my fish, will she eat swordfish?).

If we watch the way people solve problems, we are likely to observe case-based reasoning all around us. Attorneys are taught to use cases as precedents for constructing and justifying arguments in new cases. Mediators and arbitrators are taught to do the same. Other professionals are not taught to use case-based reasoning, but often find that it provides a way to solve problems efficiently. Consider, for example, a doctor faced with a patient who has an unusual combination of symptoms. If the doctor has seen a patient with similar symptoms previously, he or she is likely to remember the old case and propose the old diagnosis as a solution to the new problem. If formulating the diagnosis was time-consuming previously, this results in a big savings of time. Of course, the doctor can't assume the old answer is correct. He or she must still validate it for the new case in a way that doesn't prohibit considering other likely diagnoses. Nevertheless, remembering the old case makes it easy to generate a plausible answer. Similarly, a car mechanic faced with an unusual mechanical problem is likely to remember other similar problems and to consider whether their explanations apply to the new one.

Doctors evaluating the appropriateness of a therapeutic procedure or judging which of several options are appropriate are also likely to remember instances of using each procedure and to make their judgments of which to use based on previous experiences. Remembering instances of problems that arose when using a procedure can be particularly helpful here; they tell the doctor what could go wrong, and, when they include an explanation of why the old problem occurred, they focus the doctor in finding out the information needed to make sure the problem won't show up again.

We hear cases being cited time and again by our political leaders in explaining why some action was taken or should be taken. Many management decisions are made based on previous experience. In addition, the "case method" of teaching is used extensively in law, business, and medicine. Cases provide context for discussing more abstract issues and they provide illustrations of those abstract guidelines that students remember and apply in later reasoning.

Case-based reasoning is also used extensively in day-to-day common-sense reasoning. When we order a meal in a restaurant, we often base decisions about what might be good on our other experiences in that restaurant and those like it. As we plan our household activities, we remember what worked and didn't work previously and use that to create our new plans.

In general, when people solve problems, the second time solving the problem is easier than the first because they remember and repeat the previous solution. We are more competent the second time because we remember our mistakes and go out of our way to avoid them. One of the hallmarks of a case-based reasoner is its ability to learn from its experiences, as a doctor might do by committing to memory a hard-to-solve problem in order to solve it easily another time, or by remembering being mislead by a confusing set of symptoms, in order to avoid being mislead in the future.

Case-based reasoning provides a wide range of advantages:

- Case-based reasoning allows the reasoner to propose solutions to problems quickly, avoiding the time necessary to derive those answers from scratch.
- Case-based reasoning allows a reasoner to propose solutions in domains that aren't completely understood.
- Case-based reasoning gives a reasoner a means of evaluating solutions when no algorithmic method is available for evaluation.
- Cases make it possible to interpret open-ended and ill-defined concepts.
- Cases help a reasoner to focus its reasoning on important parts of a problem by pointing out what features of a problem are the crucial ones.
- Cases can warn of the potential for problems that have occurred in the past, alerting a reasoner to take actions to avoid repeating past mistakes.

In summary, reference to old cases is advantageous in dealing with situations that recur. Reference to previous similar situations is often necessary to deal with the complexities of novel situations. Thus, remembering a previous case to use in later problem solving (and integrating that case with what is already known) is a necessary learning process. Case-based reasoning suggests a model of reasoning that incorporates problem solving, understanding, and learning, and integrates all with memory processes.

Case-Based Reasoning Systems

Case-based reasoning, as a paradigm for building intelligent computer systems, is based on the previous observations. Cases serve three sorts of purposes in case-based reasoning systems.

- Cases provide context for understanding or assessing a new situation.
- Cases provide suggestions of solutions to problems.
- Cases provide context for evaluating or criticizing suggested solutions.

As suggestion-providers, cases provide ballpark solutions that are adapted to fit a new situation or merged with each other to provide a novel solution. The reasoner in the initial example used cases in this way to suggest several main dishes and to suggest means of adapting one of them for someone allergic to milk.

As context-providers, cases provide concrete evidence for or against some interpretation of a situation. They also provide means of projecting the results of a suggested solution—one recalls cases with similar solutions and assesses whether their results are relevant to the new situation. In the initial example, the case of Anne eating mahi-mahi in a restaurant provides concrete evidence that Anne does indeed eat some fish, helping the reasoner to decide why Anne didn't eat the trout she was served and whether she might eat some other fish.

Case-based systems have been developed for problem solving tasks, such as design, planning, and diagnosis, and for interpretive tasks, such as legal reasoning and assessment of proposed solutions. Some case-based reasoning systems are autonomous; some work along with a human user to solve problems; and some are embedded in larger autonomous and interactive systems, often for educational purposes.

Requirements for Successful Case-Based Reasoning Systems

The most important component of a case-based reasoning system is its library of cases—the experiences it refers to as it makes its inferences. This library may be collected by interviewing human experts and collecting their experiences or by collecting the experiences of automated computer systems. As the system processes new problems, its case library grows as new cases from its own experiences are stored.

However, although a less experienced system has fewer experiences to work with than a more experienced reasoner, the answers given by the less experienced system won't necessarily be worse than those given by the experienced one. First, if the novice reasoner has, by chance, had an experience particularly relevant to a novel situation, its answers can be equal to those of an expert. It is important, then, that a case-based reasoner start with a representative set of cases. Second, a less experienced reasoner may do just as well if it is creative in understanding the new situation and adapting solutions it does have available.

The quality of a case-based reasoning system's reasoning depends on five things:

- The experiences it has had or been given
- Its ability to understand the relevance of old experiences to new situations
- Its adeptness at adapting prior solutions to fit new situations
- Its adeptness at evaluation of new solutions and repair of flawed solutions
- Its ability to integrate new experiences into its memory appropriately.

The Process of Case-Based Reasoning

Case-based reasoning is a process of "remember and adapt" or "remember and compare." While some composition is necessary to solve large problems, composition of rules, knowledge, or cases is not the primary process. And, rather than remembering abstract operators, concrete instances are recalled.

Cases are used to help in understanding and assessing situations and to help in solving problems. In the general course of everyday reasoning, these processes tend to be interleaved. We can't solve a problem when we don't understand the situation it is embedded in; we often need to solve problems in order to understand the implications of a situation well. We evaluate our solutions by projecting their results using assessment methods; and we may need to solve new problems in the course of evaluation. For simplicity, however, it makes some sense to refer to two different styles of case-based reasoning. *Problem solving* situations call primarily for the use of cases to propose solutions; *interpretive* situations call primarily for using cases for criticism and justification.

This discussion suggests the primary processes required for case-based reasoning, illustrated in figure 1. First and foremost, partially-matching cases must be retrieved to facilitate reasoning. Thus, *case retrieval* is a primary process, as is its adjunct process, *case storage* (also called *memory update*). The retrieval process depends on choosing appropriate indexes to guide search for relevant cases in memory. In order to make sure that poor solutions are not repeated along with the good ones, both styles of case-based reasoning *criticize* candidate solutions to identify potential problems. In order to become more proficient, a reasoner must be able to *evaluate* its performance, based on external feedback. In case-based reasoning, after feedback is analyzed, cases are updated and their outcomes recorded, and cases that were used to solve the problem are re-indexed based on analysis of their usefulness.

The two styles of case-based reasoning, however, each require that different reasoning be done once cases are retrieved. In problem solving CBR, a ballpark solution to the new problem is *proposed* by extracting the solution from some retrieved case. This is followed by *adaptation*, the process of revising an old solution to fit a new situation. *Criticism* of the candidate solution often triggers further adaptation before the solution is applied.

In interpretive CBR, a ballpark interpretation or desired result is *proposed*, sometimes based on retrieved cases, sometimes imposed from the outside (as when a lawyer's client requires a certain result). This is followed by *justification*, the process of creating an argument for the proposed solution, done by comparing and contrasting the new situation to prior cases, looking for similarities between the new situation and others that justify the desired result and differences that imply that other factors must be taken into account. Sometimes justification is followed by a *criticism* step in which hypothetical situations are generated and the proposed solution applied to them in order to test the solution, before the argument is actually evaluated (e.g., by using it in court and observing the outcome).

These steps and styles are in some sense recursive. The criticize and adapt steps, for example, often require new cases to be retrieved. There are also sev-

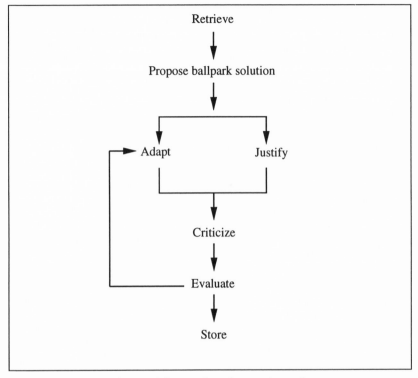

Figure 1. The case-based reasoning cycle.

eral loops in the process. As reflected in figure 1, for example, evaluation of a potential solution may lead to additional adaptation to repair problems. And when reasoning is not progressing well using one case, the whole process may need to be restarted, beginning by choosing a new case to start from.

Representing and Indexing Cases

In this section, we will define the "case," discuss the two major functional parts to a case, and examine indexing.

What is a Case?

Definition: A case is a contextualized piece of knowledge representing an experience that teaches a lesson fundamental to achieving the goals of the reasoner.

Cases come in many shapes and sizes. They may cover a situation that evolves over time (as in designing a building or following a patient through several illnesses), they may represent a snapshot (as in choosing a particular type of window for a building or recording a judge's ruling), or they may cover any size time slice in between those extremes. They may represent a problem solving episode (as do medical and architectural cases), associate a situation description with an outcome (as in legal cases), or some combination.

What is common to all cases is that they represent an experienced situation. That situation, when remembered later, forms a context in which the knowledge embedded in the case is presumed applicable. When a similar situation arises, those decisions and the knowledge that went into making them provide a starting point for interpreting the new situation or solving the problem it poses.

But not every situation that occurs is a useful case. Memorable cases—the ones that it is useful to remember—are different in some way from what is expected—expected by other cases or expected by general knowledge. This changes as normative expectations change.

Not every difference is important, however. There is another criterion for deciding if some experience or situation should usefully be recorded as a case: *Does the case teach a useful lesson?* This criterion requires us to define what a useful lesson is. Perhaps the best guideline we can give on this is that cases recorded in a case library should contribute to achieving the goals of the reasoner. As people, we have a wide variety of goals, and any small difference from a norm might teach a lesson relevant to one of our goals. Thus, from the point of view of human cognition, it is difficult to predict exactly which cases people record when and for what intentions.

For a machine, however, it is somewhat easier. AI systems normally have a limited number of goals. Some are goals for action (move the block), others are goals for reasoning (identify the patient's disorder, evaluate the design of the building, design a heat pump, compare two instances and show the differences). A case has an important lesson to teach if it records a new way of achieving some goal, if it records the results of considerable effort to find ways to achieve a goal, if an unexpected failure occurred when trying to achieve a goal, or if the effect of some situation causes a new goal to arise. There are thus many different kinds of lessons a case can teach:

- how to achieve a goal,
- how to achieve several goals in conjunction,
- the circumstances in which a set of steps for achieving a goal can be carried out successfully,
- how to bring about the state required for achieving some important goal,
- the kinds of problems that might arise in achieving a goal (what might go wrong),
- the effects of an action.

> - A case represents specific knowledge tied to a context. It records knowledge at an operational level.
> - Cases can come in many different shapes and sizes, covering large or small time slices, associating solutions with problems, outcomes with situations, or both.
> - A case records experiences that teach a useful lesson: that have the potential to help a reasoner achieve a goal or set of goals more easily in the future, that warn about the possibility of a failure, or point out an unforeseen problem.

Table 1: The nature of cases.

In general, a case teaches a useful lesson when it exemplifies some new way of doing something or some new effect that is likely to be useful in later reasoning. Table 1 summarizes these points, but the bottom line here is this: *If what is different in a new situation teaches something that could not have easily been inferred from the cases already recorded, then it is useful to record it as a new case.*[1]

The Role of General Knowledge. There are several implications of our definition of cases. First, it implies that cases are not the only type of knowledge our intelligent systems need in order to function. If we were building a full cognitive model, we would want to include in it both cases and generalizations of those cases. Generalizations might be the vehicle to use to record what is normal. Second, it implies that the organization of abstractions and cases in a memory changes dynamically over time and with experience. What might start as a new experience, different from the norm, and teaching a new lesson, may eventually become the norm. In a full cognitive model, memory's organizational and representational structures need to change to reflect these changes.

In case-based reasoning systems, general knowledge tends to be recorded in adaptation strategies and in the *models* (Hayes 1985, Forbus 1988, deKleer and Brown 1984) that some adaptation and matching procedures use. General knowledge, when available, can guide the choice of indices (as in KRITIK [Goel 1989]), the determination of how well a new situation matches a stored case (as in CASEY [Koton 1988b]), and the choice of adaptation strategies (as in KRITIK and CASEY).

The Content of Cases

Our discussion also suggests that there are two major functional parts to a case:
- the lesson(s) it teaches—its content
- the context in which it can teach its lesson(s), described by its indexes;

designating the circumstances in which it would be appropriately retrieved

We cover case content here, indexes in the next subsection.

There are three major parts to the content of any case (though for any particular case, they may not all be filled in):

1. *Problem/situation description:* the state of the world when the episode recorded in the case occurred, and if appropriate, what problem needed solving at that time.

2. *Solution:* the stated or derived solution to the problem specified in the problem description.

3. *Outcome:* the resulting state of the world when the solution was carried out.

The first component, the *description of the problem* that was being solved or the *description of the situation* being understood, describes relevant previous circumstances. A description includes the goals of the reasoner when the episode recorded in the case was happening, the task the reasoner was engaged in, and any features of the environment that had a bearing on the solution chosen or the outcome that resulted.

The second component, the *case solution,* tells the reasoner how a problem was solved in a particular instance. This component may simply record the solution itself, or it may also include a trace of the way the solution was derived (e.g., Carbonell 1986; Veloso, Chapter 8) and/or the rationale associated with each subpart of the solution. With these two case components, new problems can be solved in a case-based way by first finding a relevant case and then adapting the solution for that problem to fit the new situation.

Any reasoner whose cases have just these two components can be used to shortcut reasoning. For example, CASEY (Koton 1988b), a program for diagnosing cardiac problems, uses cases with only these two components. When it has a similar prior case to reason from, it is several orders of magnitude more efficient than the model-based program it is based on.

In situations with many unknowns, however, severe inaccuracies can result from reasoning using cases that record only problems and solutions. In particular, taking only the unevaluated solutions to old cases into account in proposing new solutions, it is just as easy to suggest poor solutions as good ones. CASEY avoids this problem by storing only correct solutions and because its domain model, which guides adaptation, is very accurate. But in many situations, accurate models of the world are not available. In such situations, systems are bound to make mistakes. A system that mindlessly uses the knowledge it has to solve problems and stores every new problem and solution becomes more efficient over time, but it also repeats its mistakes as often as its good solutions.

The purpose of the third component, *outcome,* is to allow a reasoner to record feedback from the environment and analysis of that feedback. Outcome records what happened as a result of applying a solution, whether the result was a success or failure, in what ways it succeeded or failed, and when available, an explanation of why. With outcome included in cases, a reasoner can suggest solutions that worked and use cases with failed solutions to warn of potential failures. It can also evaluate whether repeating an old solution will result in the outcome it wants in the new situation. When much is unknown or unpredictable, previous cases that record their outcomes provide clues about the intricacies of a problem situation and can be used to predict the effects of a proposed solution.

Indexing

The indexes of a case act like indexes to books in a library. A case's indexes are combinations of its important descriptors, the ones that distinguish it from other cases. Just as we use the card catalog in a library to direct us toward books that are likely to fulfill our reading needs, retrieval algorithms use a case's indexes to select cases likely to fulfill the needs of the reasoner. When we add a new case to the case library, we assign indexes to it, just as we assign indexes to a book that gets added to the library.

At retrieval time, retrieval algorithms are given information about the new situation the reasoner is in and the goals and tasks of the reasoner in that situation (e.g., in the situation described at the beginning of this chapter, that the reasoner is trying to come up with a main dish to serve). The new situation is used as a retrieval key. Its important components are used to guide searching and matching functions as they attempt to find and identify the cases that can best address the reasoner's goal.

The *indexing problem* is the problem of making sure that a case is accessed whenever appropriate. This means the case should be indexed so as to be accessible whenever appropriate, and also that retrieval algorithms be able to use those indexes to get the right cases out at the right times.

Assigning Indexes to Cases. The indexing problem has several parts. First is the problem of assigning labels to cases at the time that they are entered into the case library to ensure that they can be retrieved at appropriate times. A case is appropriately retrieved if it has the potential to help the reasoner fulfill its goals. *Indexes predict a case's usefulness.* In general, these labels designate circumstances under which the case might have a lesson to teach, and therefore when it is likely to be useful.

Indexes might represent surface features or more abstract derived features. More important than whether they are surface or derived, specific or abstract, shallow or deep, is that they be those descriptors that are naturally articulated in the process of reasoning or doing some task. Thus, the indexes that are useful in supporting one task might be different than those that are useful for another. This functional and pragmatic approach to indexing suggests a task-related method for choosing a case's indexes:

> Look at the tasks a case might be used for (e.g., suggesting a solution, anticipating a failure) and choose as indexes those sets of its features that describe when it can be useful for each task. A case may have multiple indexes.

This is a fundamentally different approach to indexing than has been taken traditionally in information retrieval and database work. In those conceptions of indexing, features chosen as indexes are the ones that divide a set into partitions of approximately equal size. The ideal is to keep the organizational structures balanced, so a feature is a good discriminator if it helps balance the organizational structure. In the CBR conception of the problem, on the other hand, we require indexes to distinguish cases from each other for some purpose. We are not concerned with balancing the organizational structure. Rather, we are concerned with cutting the case library into conceptually useful pieces.

In addition to needing to be relevant to a task, good indexes for case-based reasoning satisfy two other properties:

- Indexes should be abstract enough to retrieve a relevant case in a variety of future situations.
- Indexes should be concrete enough to be easily recognizable in future situations.

An example will illustrate the process of choosing indexes for a case and what these abstract principles mean. Consider the following case.

> **Problem:** Twenty people were coming to dinner, it was summer and tomatoes were in season, we wanted a vegetarian meal, and one person was allergic to milk products.

> **Solution:** We served tomato tart (a cheese and tomato pie). To accommodate the person allergic to milk, we used tofu cheese substitute instead of cheese in one of the tarts.

A step by step process allows us to choose indexes based on the principles above:

Step 1: Determine what the case could be useful for by designating its points of relevance to the set of tasks the reasoner is being asked to carry out.

Step 2: Determine under what circumstances it would be useful for each of these tasks.

Step 3: Translate the circumstances into the vocabulary of the reasoner, making them recognizable.

Step 4: Massage the descriptions of the circumstances to make them as generally applicable as possible.

The first two steps designate the lessons the case teaches, or the points it makes, and for each, the circumstances in which those lessons can usefully be taught. In Step 3, identified circumstances are put into the right form and represented appropriately. In Step 4, they are generalized appropriately. We will demonstrate this process for our sample case.

Step 1: There are two uses for this case, or two lessons it teaches:

1. It provides conditions for success when choosing a vegetarian main dish with tomatoes: *Choose tomato tart to feed vegetarians in the summer.*

2. It provides conditions for success when trying to accommodate a person allergic to milk when a main dish with cheese is being served: *When trying to adapt a dish with cheese in it for someone who eats no milk products, use tofu cheese substitute.*

Determining how a case could be useful in future reasoning is an introspective process on the part of the indexer. People generally find it easy to look at a case and recognize some of the lessons it teaches, but the goal is to determine the full range of lessons a case teaches and to index it for all of those. One way to get at the full range of lessons a case can teach is to consider how cases are used by the system. Do they suggest solutions? Do they point out the potential for failure? Do they help in projecting results? For any particular system, the useful lessons a case can teach are those that are of a type the system knows how to use. The indexer thus asks of each case, "For which tasks that case-based reasoning supports in this system can this case provide guidelines?" In our example, the case provides guidelines for the tasks of constructing a solution and choosing an adaptation method.

Step 2: The next step in choosing indexes is to determine under what circumstances this case would be useful for each of the possible uses designated in Step 1. Sometimes this question will have been answered by the time Step 1 is done. Sometimes, additional reasoning is needed. In the first use for our example—constructing a solution—there are two circumstances when the case would be helpful, and in the second use—adapting a solution—there is one.

1. When the case is useful for constructing a solution:

   When the goal is to choose a main dish, dish is to be vegetarian, dish is to include tomatoes.

   When the goal is to chose a main dish, dish is vegetarian, time is summer.

2. When the case is useful for adapting a solution:

   When main dish has cheese as an ingredient, one or a few guests are allergic to milk products, goal is to accommodate those guests.

Note that different people will have different ways of specifying these circumstances. For example, one person may see the circumstances as pertaining to a main dish with cheese, others to a dish with cheese. The next two steps normalize the specification.

Step 3: Descriptions are translated into the vocabulary of the reasoner, making them *recognizable* to the reasoner. The indexer needs to consider how indexes are structured and the set of legal values for each role. We address the choice of indexing vocabulary (dimensions recorded in indices, and their possible values) in the next subsection. For now, let us suppose a simple set of dimensions (slots) for representation of possible indices: *guests, host, cuisine, ingredients, preparation method, dishes (subdivided into salad, main dish, sides, beverage, dessert, and dessert-beverage), reasoning goal, constraints, season,* and *results.* Let us further suppose that some of these slots have further substructure. Each dish, for example, has several optional descriptors: cuisine, taste, texture, ingredients, preparation method, constraints. We represent an index by filling in the slots for relevant features of the case. The process results in the following three indexes for this case, one corresponding to each situation in which the case is expected to be useful:

1. reasoning goal: choose main dish
   main dish:
         constraints: vegetarian
         ingredients: tomatoes
2. reasoning goal: choose main dish
   main dish:
         constraints: vegetarian
         season: summer
3. reasoning goal: adapt dish
   main dish:
         constraints: no milk
         ingredients: cheese

Step 4: We massage the designated indexes to make them as *generally applicable* as possible, either by generalizing a vocabulary item that fills a slot (e.g., *tomato* is a kind of *salad vegetable,* so it will be useful to retrieve the case whenever the goal is to choose a vegetarian main dish including salad vegetables), or by generalizing a slot itself (e.g., *main dish* is an element of the more general set of *dishes,* and it may be useful to retrieve the case when attempting to find any dish involving tomatoes). One can use the suggestions made by this case not only when choosing a main dish, but also when designing a meal with vegetarian dishes and tomatoes or for vegetarians in the summer. This is designated by generalizing *choose main dish* to *design meal,* and then moving the constraint designations to their appropriate place with respect to the new goal (e.g., *main dish* is one of the set of *dishes* in a meal).

The new indexes cover the whole meal rather than only selection of a main dish, suggesting that tomato tart be served. The third index is made more generally applicable by generalizing *main dish* to *dish:* the adaptation the case teaches is useful not only for adapting main dishes, but also for adapting any dish with cheese in it for the needs of someone who can't eat milk products. These three more general indexes can be designated as follows:

1. reasoning goal: design meal
   dishes:
         constraints: vegetarian
         ingredients: tomatoes
2. reasoning goal: design meal
   dishes:
         constraints: vegetarian
   season: summer
3. reasoning goal: adapt dish
   dishes:
         constraints: no milk
         ingredients: cheese

Properties of a Good Indexing Vocabulary. The previous example assumes that we start from a given indexing vocabulary. Some efforts have been made to establish general indexing vocabularies for particular classes of reasoning tasks (e.g., Domeshek 1992b, Leake 1992b, Schank and Osgood 1990), but the developer of a case-based reasoning system must usually derive an indexing vocabulary. While indexes are chosen for particular cases, indexing vocabulary needs to cover the domain or set of domains to be handled by the CBR system.

In general, vocabularies have two parts: a set of *descriptive dimensions* and a set of *values* along each dimension. The bottom line in choosing an indexing vocabulary is this:

> The indexing vocabulary must capture those dimensions of the domain that need to be captured for useful reminding. The level of detail required in the symbols used for representation depends on how specifically-similar cases must be to provide credible advice.

Because retrieval cues must be based on the representational structures built in the normal course of processing, it is also important that the indexing vocabulary match the vocabulary of the reasoner:

- Indexing should be by concepts that are normally used by the reasoner to describe the items being indexed.
- Indexing vocabulary should anticipate the vocabulary a retriever might use.
- Indexing should anticipate the circumstances in which a retriever is likely to want to retrieve something (i.e., the task context in which it will be retrieved) and the descriptors the retriever is likely to have available to describe the item it wants to retrieve.

This pragmatic advice follows from the qualities of indexes presented above: Indexes should allow useful remindings. If we can determine, for any domain and task, the dimensions that are useful for judging similarity, then we know what dimensions the vocabulary must cover. When we determine how detailed and how specifically-applicable advice from cases needs to be to adequately cover the assigned tasks, we can determine the level of detail that must be captured in the symbols representing values for each dimension.

A warning is in order, however. Coming up with a complete and correct set of dimensions and vocabulary terms that is efficient in terms of matching, covers everything, and is adequately expressive is a monstrous—if not impossible—task. Just when a domain has been analyzed almost in its entirety, a counter-example might be discovered that shows a fault in the vocabulary. There is no way to insure against that and no way to prove that the vocabulary is right. Nevertheless, there is a need in any system for a vocabulary that works. The spirit of vocabulary-definition must be to propose a vocabulary that works *most* of the time. It should make intuitive sense, provide reasonable coverage, be reasonably expressive, and support a large number of remindings.

Defining an Indexing Vocabulary. Two approaches can be helpful for gathering the information needed to set up an indexing vocabulary for a domain or set of domains:

- *The functional approach:* Examine a corpus of available cases and the tasks that must be supported, looking at what each case can be used for and the ways it needs to be described to make it available.

- *The reminding approach:* Examine the kinds of remindings that are natural among human experts who do the designated task, looking for relevant similarities between new situations the experts are put in and the cases they are reminded of to find out which kinds of descriptors are the important ones for judging similarity and in what circumstances.

The results of these analyses tell us important dimensions to focus on, the range of values each can take on, and the level of detail that is advantageous in a representation. This analysis is done keeping three things in mind.

- *The range of tasks the case-based reasoner is responsible for.* This allows us to constrain the vocabulary to only what is needed for the designated tasks.

- *The range of cases available to support those tasks.* This acts to both constrain and broaden. If only cases from a particular domain are available, it tells us to constrain the vocabulary to cover only the domain. If cases that are available span domains, it tells us that dimensions and vocabulary must be chosen to be more generally applicable.

- *The degree and directions in which the system will be expanded in the future.* This warns us that if we make the choice of index vocabulary too narrow to begin with then we may not be able to easily expand the system later.

More generally, the process of choosing an indexing vocabulary is as follows:

1. Collect a representative set of cases. Overall, cases should be representative of the problems that arise in the domain, the contexts in which problems arise, solutions, and solution outcomes.
2. Identify the points each case can make, or the lessons it can teach.
3. Characterize the situations in which each case can appropriately make each of its points.
4. For each, describe indexes that would allow the case to be recalled in each designated situation, making sure that descriptions of indexes are both abstract enough to be generally-applicable and concrete enough to be recognizable.
5. Design the vocabulary to cover these needs, extracting dimensions first, values along each dimension second.

Reasoning with Cases

In this section, we will discuss retrieval issues, adaptation, and justification.

Retrieval and Memory Update

There are several retrieval issues that need to be addressed. First, the CBR system must have some means of identifying the cases that have the potential to be most useful. This is done by *matching* and *ranking procedures*. The pattern matching community and many in the analogical reasoning community find it natural to talk about identifying items that are most similar to a new item. They define mapping and matching algorithms that know how to compare two items to each other and score their degree of match. Indeed, degree of match is an important component of determining usefulness of a case. But determining the degree of usefulness of a case also requires consideration of what purpose the case will be put to after retrieval and what aspects of cases were relevant to outcomes in the past. These considerations allow matching procedures to determine which dimensions of a case are important to focus on in judging similarity.

Since the indexes of a case mark the important dimensions to focus on in judging similarity, matching algorithms can use indexes as a guide in determining which features to focus on for similarity judgments. But since any case might be indexed in multiple ways, matching algorithms must be able to distinguish which indexed features to focus on at any time.

For this reason, input to retrieval algorithms includes both a description of the new situation and also an indication of what the reasoner will use the case for. Usually this description is in terms of reasoning tasks to be accomplished or reasoning goals to be achieved. Matching and ranking procedures use this description to determine which features of a case are the most important to focus on in judging similarity.

Second, retrieval depends on the *retrieval algorithms* themselves. These are the processes that know how to search the case library to find cases with the potential to match the new situation well. Matching procedures are applied to those cases identified by retrieval algorithms as potentially useful.

As we know from studies of data structures and algorithms, one cannot discuss algorithms for retrieval without also discussing the structures those algorithms must search. A list is searched differently, for example, than a complex tree structure. It is the same in discussing retrieval of cases. Different organizations of cases give rise to different algorithms for retrieving them. A list of cases requires different kinds of retrieval algorithms, for example, than does a complex tree or graph structure. Each has its advantages and disadvantages. One can be sure, for example, in a flat memory (a list) that the best case will be retrieved, but if the memory is large, it may take too much time. Complex tree structures, on the other hand, require less computation to get to a useful case, but they do not guarantee that the best-matching case will be retrieved.

The CBR community has identified a number of strategies and algorithms for organizing and retrieving cases—some are serial, some parallel; some use flat or shallowly-indexed organizing structures, others use hierarchical, more deeply-indexed structures. Some use indexes to build structures that discriminate cases from each other at a very fine grain-size; other structures discriminate more coarsely; others hardly discriminate at all (Kolodner 1993). The most widely-used method is similar to inverted indexes—a shallowly-indexed structure that can be searched serially or in parallel. Such methods have been efficient even for very large case libraries (25,000 or more records; see Kitano and Shimazu, Chapter 13).

Retrieval algorithms and matching functions are, indeed, the major pieces of case retrieval. There is, however, one additional piece to the process. That piece is called situation assessment. Situation assessment is the process of analyzing a situation and elaborating it such that its description is in the same vocabulary as cases already in the case library. For example, consider a judge's task of determining sentences for crimes, which was modeled by the CBR system JUDGE (Bain 1989). The law gives judges considerable latitude in determining sentences, but appropriate sentences can be determined by retrieving cases of similar previous crimes and adjusting their sentences depending on the degree to which the new crime is more or less severe. Unfortunately, the descriptions of a crime that are established in court may not be directly useful for retrieving cases of similar crimes, requiring analyzing the situation to determine relevant features. For example, a description of the facts of a fight, as processed by JUDGE, might be:

John punched Joe in the nose. Joe punched John back, knocking him down.

John got back up again, this time with a knife in his hand. He tried to stab Joe. Joe pulled out his gun and shot John, killing him.

This description gives the sequence of events in the fight, but there is much unstated. We can see, for example, that the violence escalated, starting with punching, moving on to stabbing, and finally to shooting. We can see that Joe was acting, at least partially, in self-defense, i.e., that his motive was saving himself from John, who had started the fight. We can guess that Joe was scared and that John was angry. We might wonder what Joe did to provoke John, if anything. While none of these descriptors are in the sequence of events itself, they can all be descriptors of the case. And some are descriptors that, if known, help a reasoner to draw conclusions about the situation.

Noticing that the violence escalated, that it was initiated by John, that Joe had to defend himself, and perhaps even that Joe was scared are all important to determining the sentence. They are also the features that are useful in comparing this situation to others to make sure that the proposed sentence is consistent with other similar crimes. It is these descriptors, rather than those in the raw description of the case, that are useful as indexes to cases. It makes little sense to index by who the fighters were or what weapons they used—neither of those is predictive of how to sentence the crime, and neither is generally-applicable enough to be worth indexing on. It makes more sense to index cases by whether the killer was defending himself, whether the fight was initiated by the killer or the person who was killed, and so on. If cases are indexed in the case library by those dimensions, then retrieval of useful cases can happen only after those dimensions are inferred for a new situation.

Situation assessment is tricky, however. There are always innumerable features of new situations that could be elaborated, some of which are quite expensive to infer. And often, old cases need to be retrieved to help with elaborating a new situation. Thus, while situation assessment is an important component of retrieval, it must be controlled.

Putting all these aspects of retrieval together, the (idealized) retrieval process is as illustrated on the left side of figure 2. The reasoner asks the retriever for cases by describing the new situation and its current reasoning goal. The new situation is analyzed. Its description is elaborated by situation assessment procedures, which determine where similar cases are likely to be in memory, i.e., what the indexes for the new situation would be if it were stored in the case library. Retrieval algorithms use the case and the computed indexes to search the case library. As they search, they call on matching procedures, either to assess the degree of match between the new situation and cases that are encountered, or to assess the degree of match along individual dimensions. Retrieval algorithms return a list of partially-matching cases, each of which has at least some potential to be useful. Ranking procedures analyze

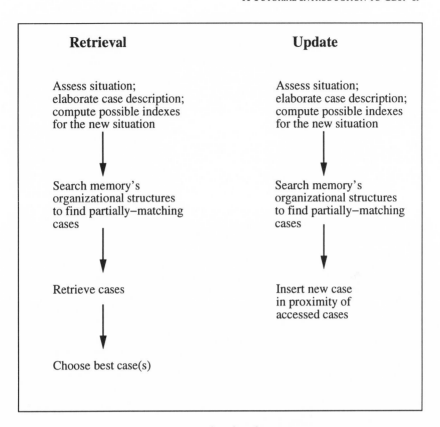

Figure 2. Retrieval and update processes.

the set of cases to determine which have the most potential to be useful, and those are returned to the reasoner.

An analogous process is carried out when cases are inserted into the case library (the right side of figure 2). Index-selection procedures determine the way the case should be indexed. Insertion algorithms use those indexes to insert the case appropriately into the case library's organizational structures. In general, they do the same sort of search done by retrieval algorithms. They look for a place to insert the case rather than for a place to retrieve a similar case from, but the two searches are exactly the same. One would expect to find a similar case in the place where the new case would be inserted. At this point, the two processes diverge. Where retrieval algorithms rank the usefulness of retrieved cases at this point, insertion algorithms invoke insertion procedures to insert the case in the case library and reorganize its organizational structures as necessary.

Adaptation

Because no old situation is ever exactly the same as a new one, a problem-solving CBR system must usually adapt old solutions to apply them to new situations. In adaptation, one takes a problem description and a solution that isn't quite right and manipulates the solution to make it better fit the problem description.

Adaptation might be as simple as substituting one component of a solution for another or as complex as modifying the overall structure of a solution. Substituting vegetarian lasagna for a more traditional lasagna in a meal is a simple substitution. Adding a new step to a plan modifies the overall structure of a solution.

Adaptation can happen during solution formulation or after a problem has been pointed out by feedback (either from projecting the results of applying a solution, or actually applying the solution in the world). Adaptation can take several forms: something new might be inserted into the old solution, something might be deleted from it, some item might be substituted for another, or some part of the old solution might be transformed.

Kolodner's (1993) case-based reasoning textbook describes ten methods by which adaptation can be done:

- Substitution methods
  - Reinstantiation
  - Parameter Adjustment
  - Local Search
  - Query Memory
  - Specialized Search
  - Case-based substitution
- Transformation methods
  - Common-Sense Transformation
  - Model-Guided Repair
- Special-purpose adaptation and repair
- Derivational Replay

The six substitution methods substitute values appropriate for the new situation for values in the old solution. *Reinstantiation* is used to instantiate an old solution with new objects. For example, consider CHEF (Hammond 1989c), a case-based reasoning system that generates new recipes by retrieving and adapting recipes for similar previous dishes. CHEF uses reinstantiation to create a chicken and snow peas recipe from a recipe for beef and broccoli. Chicken is substituted for beef everywhere in the recipe, and snow peas are substituted for broccoli.

Parameter adjustment is a heuristic for adjusting numerical parameters of an old solution. It relies on specialized heuristics that relate differences in input specifications to differences in output. JUDGE, for example, uses parameter adjustment to sentence a criminal to a shorter sentence than another criminal because the crime was less violent.

Local search provides a way of searching an auxiliary knowledge structure for a replacement for some old value or structure that is inappropriate for the new situation. If in an old menu, one served oranges for dessert but they are not currently available, local search allows the reasoner to search the semantic network of foods to find a close relative of oranges (say apples, another winter fruit) that can serve as a substitute.

Query memory means asking either auxiliary knowledge structures or the case memory to return something with a given description. In *specialized search,* both auxiliary knowledge structures and case memory are also queried, but specialized search heuristics are used to guide memory search.

Case-based substitution uses other cases to suggest substitutions. For example, a meal planner that has determined that the lasagna he or she is planning for the main dish is inappropriate may choose a substitute by recalling other Italian meals with pasta as a main dish.

Transformation methods are used to transform an old solution into one that will work in a new situation. In *common-sense transformation,* common-sense heuristics are used to replace, delete, or add components to a solution. A common-sense heuristic called "delete secondary component", for example, can be used to transform lasagna into vegetarian lasagna by deleting the meat. *Model-guided repair* is transformation guided by a causal model. Reasoning about devices, whether for diagnosis or design, can often be guided by a model.

Special-purpose adaptation and repair heuristics are used to carry out domain-specific and structure-modifying adaptations not covered by the other methods. These heuristics are indexed by the situations in which they are applicable. CHEF, for example, uses a specialized adaptation heuristic to insert a "defatting" step into any recipe that includes duck. The meal planner JULIA (Kolodner 1987, Hinrichs 1992) uses specialized adaptation heuristics to modify the structure of its solutions. One such heuristic knows how to remove redundancies from a structure, for example, while another recognizes when two functionally similar components must both be included in a solution. Such heuristics can also implement strategies for repairing solutions after they have been carried out and failed. CHEF uses specialized repair heuristics for this purpose. Each is a rather abstract strategy for repairing a faulty solution, indexed by the type of failure it repairs (e.g., the problem caused when a side effect of one plan step disables a precondition for another plan step).

Special-purpose adaptation heuristics are often implemented as critics and controlled through use of a rule-based production system. Critic application also provides a way of implementing parameter adjustment, common-sense transformation, and model-guided repair. CASEY's model-guided repair heuristics are implemented as critics.

Derivational replay reuses the method for deriving an old solution or solution piece to derive a solution in a new situation. For example, a menu planner that knows that it previously chose oranges for dessert by a process of choosing a fruit appropriate to the season (winter) can adapt its old menu for a summer meal by using the same process to find a fruit appropriate to the summer season. Like case-based substitution, derivational replay provides a case-based means of doing adaptation.

Justification

The task of an interpretive CBR system is to decide whether a concept fits some open-ended or fuzzy-bordered classification, to demonstrate the rightness of an argument or position, or to predict outcomes, in context of previous examples. This evaluation in context is something we do every day. Members of university admissions committees evaluate the potential of applicants to succeed at their school by comparing and contrasting them to other similar students who have and have not done well. Doctors distinguish between patients having one illness and another similar one by comparing and contrasting the current case to previous examples. Parents use comparisons to prior examples to answer questions like "My daughter wants to see a scary movie. Is this one appropriate for her or will she cry and run out like the last time?" and "My son says he has a sore throat. Should I keep him home from school or send him and see what develops?" In the example at the beginning of this chapter, the process is used to answer the question "Is swordfish a fish Anne will eat or isn't it?"

For these tasks there are often no hard-and-fast rules that can be applied, or knowledge to apply them; a case-based reasoner makes up for these lacks by assuming that the world is consistent. Justifying a classification by prior cases depends on comparing the new situation and prior cases, asking questions such as "how similar are swordfish and mahi-mahi?", "Is my son's complaint like other ones he's made when he's just tired, or is it more like those he makes when he is really sick?" or "In what ways is this new applicant similar to those who have done well in graduate school? In what ways is he similar to those who have done less well?"

In addition to looking at similarities, justification looks at what differentiates the new situation from old similar ones to ascertain whether or not the old interpretation is likely to hold. Perhaps an applicant is similar in some respects to students who have not done well (e.g., his grades and GRE scores are low like theirs), but he has extensive experience, maturity, and drive that most of those students didn't have. Maybe that means we shouldn't pay attention to the similarities. Perhaps the movie the daughter wants to see is like others in which she walked out scared and crying, but she has changed since then (e.g, has become more mature), rendering the interpretation based on the old situations unsuitable. To determine if she will get scared and cry at this one, the parent has to consider how this situation is like others the daughter has been in, in what ways it is different, and whether those differences are enough to justify the prediction that she won't be too scared this time. This requires considering similarities and differences between this movie and others she's seen and also considering similarities and differences between her when she saw those movies and now, since those are the two major factors determining whether she will get scared or not. The subsection CBR for Design that follows sketches how some particular interpretive CBR systems perform justification.

Learning

A case-based reasoner gets more efficient over time as a result of collecting more experiences and indexing them properly. It can get more effective over time if, in addition, it analyzes the effects of its solutions and keeps track of what worked and didn't work and why. There are few special processes needed to make learning happen in a case-based system. Effective learning can happen as a byproduct of the reasoning and memory update.

A case-based reasoner's performance becomes *more efficient* by remembering old solutions and adapting them rather than having to derive answers from scratch each time. If a case was adapted in a novel way, if it was solved using some novel method, or if it was solved by combining the solutions to several cases, then when it is recalled during later reasoning, the steps required to solve it won't need to be repeated for the new problem.

Case-based reasoners also become *more competent* over time, deriving better answers than they could with less experience. One of case-based reasoning's fortes is in helping a reasoner to anticipate and thus avoid mistakes it has made in the past. This is possible because it caches problem situations, indexing them by features that predict its old mistakes. Remembering such cases during later reasoning provides a warning to the reasoner of problems that might come up, enabling the reasoner to work to avoid them.

Within AI, when one talks of learning, it usually means the learning of generalizations, either through inductive or explanation-based means. While the memory of a case-based reasoner notices similarities between cases and can therefore notice when generalizations should be formed, inductive formation of generalizations is responsible for only some of the learning in a case-based reasoner. Case-based reasoning achieves most of its learning in two other ways:

- through the accumulation of new cases, and
- through the assignment and unassignment of indexes.

New cases give the reasoner additional familiar contexts for solving problems or evaluating situations. A reasoner whose cases cover more of the domain will be a better reasoner than one whose cases cover less of the domain. One whose cases cover failure as well as successful instances will be better than one whose cases cover only successful situations. New indexes allow a reasoner to fine tune its recall apparatus so that it remembers cases at more appropriate times.

That is not to say that generalization is not important. Indeed, the cases a case-based reasoner encounters give it direction in the creation of appropriate generalizations, i.e., those that can be useful to its task. How can that work? When several cases are indexed the same way and all predict the same solution or all can be classified the same way, the reasoner knows that a useful generalization can be formed. In addition, the combination of indexes and a predicted solution or classification also give the reasoner guidance in choosing the level of abstraction of its generalizations. Some case-based reasoners use only cases, others use a combination of cases and generalized cases. Even when a case-based reasoner does not use generalizations to reason, they are useful in helping the reasoner organize its cases.

Case-based reasoning is not the first method that combines reasoning and learning, but it is unique in making learning little more than a byproduct of reasoning. A case-based reasoner that remembers its experiences learns as it reasons. Feedback from early experiences gives it insight for solving later problems. Reports of fielded case-based reasoners bear this out. Clavier, for example, configures composite parts for loading in an autoclave (Barletta and Hennessy 1989; Hennessy and Hinkle 1992; Mark et al., Chapter 14). In over a year of use at Lockheed, its case library grew from 20 to over 150 cases, it became a more efficient problem solver, and its solutions became more accurate. At the same time, it served as a corporate memory for those who work on the shop floor. It accumulated the experiences of all those workers in its memory, learning not only what one of them had been able to learn but rather learning the things all of them had learned.

In addition to the learning that happens as a natural consequence of reasoning, one can think about enhancing a case-based system with learning capabilities designed to make its components work more efficiently. For example, one could put controls on which cases are added to a case library so that retrieval can be kept as efficient as possible. One could have a reasoner learn which solutions are costly to carry out and which are inexpensive (to enhance its selection of cases), which elaborations are costly to carry out and which are inexpensive (to make situation assessment more efficient), and so on. One can also use cases to enhance general knowledge.

Some Uses of CBR

Case-based reasoning has been applied to problem-solving tasks, interpretive tasks, and as a retrieval tool to augment people's memories, aid in decision-making, and teaching. In the following subsections, we will explore some of these uses for CBR.

Problem Solving CBR

Case-based reasoning has been applied to a wide variety of problem solving tasks, including planning, diagnosis, and design. In each of these tasks, cases are useful in both suggesting solutions and in warning of possible problems that might arise. There are additional specific advantages for each of these problem solving tasks.

CBR for Design. In design, problems are defined as a set of constraints, and the problem solver is required to provide a concrete artifact that solves the constraint problem. Usually the given constraints underspecify the problem (i.e., there are many possible solutions). Sometimes, however, the constraints overconstrain the problem (i.e, there is no solution if all constraints must be fulfilled). In addition, in design, the solutions of individual pieces of a design problem are tightly coupled to solutions of other pieces. While constraints can be used to maintain the connections between pieces, methodologies that require backtracking are too tedious for complex problems. Case-based reasoning addresses all of these issues.

- Cases suggest solutions to underconstrained problems. The solutions might not be exactly right, but because many different solutions might be appropriate, adaptation heuristics can generally create a satisfactory solution easily.

- When problems are over-constrained, cases suggest an alternative set of constraints that has worked in combination in the past. While some adaptation might still have to be done, the full application of constraint relaxation can be avoided.

- When problem subparts are tightly coupled, cases can provide the glue that holds a solution together. Rather than solving the subparts by decomposing, recomposing, and fixing discrepancies, as is done in solving nearly-decomposable problems, a case suggests an entire solution, and the pieces that don't fit the new situation are adapted in place.

Several problem solvers have been built to do case-based design. JULIA designs meals, and the meal planning examples shown above are all among those JULIA has solved. CYCLOPS (Navinchandra 1988) uses case-based reasoning for landscape design. KRITIK and KRITIK-2 (Goel 1989, Goel and Chandrasekaran 1989, Stroulia et al. 1992) combine case-based with model-based reasoning for design of small mechanical and electrical devices. They use case-based reasoning to propose solutions and use model-based causal knowledge to verify their proposed solutions, to point out where adaptation is needed, and to suggest adaptations. CADET (Sycara and Navinchandra 1989) also uses a combination of case-based and causal knowledge to do design.

An active current area focuses on case-based tools to aid human designers. As mentioned previously, Clavier is in production use at Lockheed to support design of autoclave layouts. ARCHIE and its successor ARCHIE-2 (Domeshek and Kolodner 1992; Griffith and Domeshek, Chapter 3) are retrieval-only systems built to help architects do conceptual design, MIDAS (Domeshek et al. 1994) helps aircraft designers with the conceptual design of aircraft subsystems; while AskJef (Barber et al. 1992) aids human-computer interface designers with their task. A tool for creating case-based advisory systems for design, Design-MUSE (Domeshek, Kolodner, and Zimring 1994) has been created based on these projects.

In almost all design problems, more than one case is necessary to solve the problem. Design problems tend to be large, and while one case can be used to solve some of it, it is usually not sufficient for solving the entire problem. In general, some case can provide a framework for a solution, while other cases can be used to fill in missing details. In this way, decomposition and recomposition are avoided, as are large constraint satisfaction and relaxation problems.

CBR for Planning. Planning involves a number of complexities (Charniak and McDermott 1987, provide an excellent overview). Good plans must be sequenced appropriately so that late steps in a plan don't undo the intended results of earlier steps, so that preconditions of late steps in a plan are not violated by the results of earlier ones, and so that preconditions of later plan steps are fulfilled before the steps are scheduled. As the number of plan steps increases, the computational complexity of projecting effects and comparing preconditions increases exponentially. In addition, a planner dealing with the real world must face the real world's complexity, including the fact that it is in many ways unpredictable and that time is not limitless. Streams of goals might need to be achieved almost simultaneously. Time used for planning can take away from the time available for execution. Because conditions in the world can change between coming up with a plan and carrying it out, a plan might fail at execution time and require replanning, recovery, or repair. A planner with little time might miss opportunities during planning, and opportunities may need to be noticed and taken advantage of during execution (Marks, Hammond, and Converse 1989).

Case-based reasoning can address many of these planning issues:

- Cases provide already-worked-out plans in which sequencing, protection maintenance, and scheduling of preconditions have already been worked out. Rather than reasoning from scratch, the planner is required only to make fixes in old plans.

- If cases are indexed by the conjunctions of goals they achieve, they can be used to suggest ways of achieving several goals simultaneously or in conjunction with each other.
- Warnings provided by cases can help a planner anticipate and avoid problems, decreasing the likelihood of failure at execution time.
- Suggestions made by cases can shortcut the planning process, providing relatively more time for execution.
- Suggestions made by cases allow the reasoner to notice some opportunities (e.g., to achieve goals simultaneously) easily during planning.
- Adaptation strategies used to adapt old plans to new situations can also be used for execution-time recovery and repair, and to update plans during execution to take advantage of opportunities.

CBR planning research addresses many of these issues. PLEXUS (Alterman 1986, 1988), a program that adapts knowledge about riding a subway to other tasks, is able to do execution-time repairs by adapting and substituting semantically-similar steps for those that have failed.

CHEF addresses the problem of anticipating difficulties before execution time by learning from its problematic experiences. When problems happen at execution time, CHEF attempts to explain them and then to figure out how they could be repaired. It stores the repair in memory, and indexes the case by features that are likely to predict that the problem will recur. Before it begins to derive future plans, it looks for potential failure situations, anticipates the problems they point out, and uses the previous repair to suggest a plan that will avoid the problem it has anticipated.

Other case-based planners address others of these problems. TRUCKER (Marks, Hammond, and Converse 1989) is an errand running program that keeps track of its pending goals and is able to take advantage of opportunities that arise that allow it to achieve goals earlier than expected. MEDIC (Turner 1994) is a diagnosis program that is able to reuse previous plans for diagnosis but is flexible enough in its reuse to be able to follow up on unexpected turns of events. EXPEDITOR (Robinson and Kolodner 1991), plans the events in the life of a single parent who must deal with children and work. It caches its experiences at achieving multiple goals by interleaving them. While it is slow in its initial planning, it gains competence over time as it is able to reuse its plans.

CBR for Diagnosis. In diagnosis, a problem solver is given a set of symptoms and asked to explain them. A case-based diagnostician can use cases to suggest explanations for symptoms and to warn of explanations that were found to be inappropriate in the past.

Of course, one cannot expect a previous diagnosis to apply intact to the new case. Just as in planning and design, it is often necessary to adapt an old case to fit a new situation. CASEY diagnoses heart problems by adapting the diagnoses of previous heart patients to new patients. CASEY's adaptations are based on a valid causal model, so its diagnoses are as accurate as those made from scratch using the same causal model.

Cases are also useful in diagnosis for pointing the way out of previously-experienced reasoning quagmires. PROTOS (Bareiss 1989a), which diagnoses hearing disorders, is designed to ensure that this happens in an efficient way.[2]

In PROTOS' domain, many of the diagnoses manifest themselves in similar ways, and only subtle differences differentiate them. A novice is not aware of the subtle differences; experts are. PROTOS begins as a novice, and when it makes mistakes, a "teacher" explains its mistakes to it. As a result, PROTOS learns these subtle differences. As it does, it leaves difference pointers in its memory that allow it to move easily from the obvious candidate diagnosis to the correct one.

Generating a diagnosis from scratch is a time-consuming task. In almost all diagnostic domains, however, there is sufficient regularity for a case-based approach to diagnosis generation to provide efficiency. Of course, no person or program can assume that a case-based suggestion is correct. The case-based suggestion must be validated. Often, however, validation is much easier than generation. In those kinds of domains, case-based reasoning can provide big wins.

Interpretive CBR

Interpretive case-based reasoning is used for tasks such as classifying a new situation in context, showing cause or demonstration of rightness of an argument, position, or solution, or predicting the effects of a solution.

Classification. One way a case-based classifier works is to ask whether the new concept is enough like another one known to have a given classification. PROTOS provides an example. Rather than classifying new hearing disorders using necessary and sufficient conditions, PROTOS does classification by trying to find the closest matching case in its case base.

Its first step is to guess what category the new problem fits into by looking at how the important features of the new case overlap with important features of categories of hearing disorders it knows about. This guess is PROTOS's first hypothesis about what category the new case fits into. PROTOS verifies its hypothesis by comparing the new case to exemplars in the hypothesized category to see if it can find a good match. If it finds a match, it chooses that category for the new case. However, PROTOS is also aware of the kinds of classification mistakes that are commonly made in its domain. In particular, it knows instances of examples that have been misclassified because of strong similarity to cases in the wrong category. If it finds that the new case matches one of these failure cases, it makes a new hypothesis—that the new case is an instance of the category this failure case was an instance of. It repeats the matching process in that category, continuing until it finds a good match.

The case-based classification procedure PROTOS implements models the largely unconscious automatic processing we do as we recognize objects in the world around us. PROTOS has no strategies for weighing evidence for and against a series of conclusions. However, weighing competing evidence is an essential part of another interpretive task, adversarial reasoning.

Adversarial Reasoning. Adversarial reasoning means making persuasive arguments to convince others that our positions are right. A persuasive argument states a position and supports it, sometimes with hard facts and sometimes with valid inferences. But often the only way to justify a position is by citing relevant previous experiences or cases. Law thus provides a good domain for the study of adversarial reasoning and case-based justification, and much research in this area uses the legal domain (Ashley and Rissland 1987a, Ashley 1990, Bain 1989, Branting 1989, Rissland 1983). In general, cases are useful in constructing arguments and justifying positions when there are no concrete principles or only a few of them, if principles are inconsistent, or if their meanings are not well-specified.

A program called HYPO (Ashley and Rissland 1987a, Ashley 1990) models the argumentation lawyers do. HYPO not only determines which cases are most similar to its new situation, but it also uses its cases to create cogent and coherent arguments in support of some position or other. HYPO's method for creating an argument and justifying a solution or position has several steps. The new situation is first analyzed for relevant factors. Based on these factors, similar cases are retrieved. They are positioned with respect to the new situation. Some support the new position and some are against it. The most on-point cases of both sets are selected. The most on-point case supporting the new situation is used to create an argument for the proposed solution. Those in the non-support set are used to pose counter-arguments. Cases in the support set are then used to counter the counter-arguments. The result of this is a set of three-ply arguments in support of the solution, each of which is justified with cases. An important side effect of creating such arguments is that potential problem areas get highlighted.

Argumentation procedures can provide the basis for critiquing solutions before using them in the world. Strategic planners do such critiquing as they create plans. Teachers do this sort of critiquing as they create lesson plans. Generals do this sort of critiquing as they create battle plans. All problem solvers that plan for contingencies must do at least some critiquing to ascertain which contingencies are the ones to plan for. Comparing and contrasting with previous cases provides a means of dealing with the complexities inherent in dealing with situations in which much is unknown.

When no case matches well enough, it is sometimes necessary to consider hypothetical situations. HYPO uses hypotheticals for a variety of tasks necessary for good interpretation: to redefine old situations in terms of new dimensions, to create new standard cases when a necessary one doesn't exist, to explore and test the limits of reasonableness of a concept, to refocus a case by excluding some issues, to tease out hidden assumptions, and to organize or cluster cases. HYPO creates hypotheticals by making "copies" of a current situation that are stronger or weaker than the real situation for one side or the other. This work is guided by a set of modification heuristics that propose useful directions for hypothetical case creation based on current reasoning needs. HYPO's strategies for argumentation guide selection of modification heuristics.

When a concept is being created on the fly, interpretation requires an additional step: derivation of a set of relevant features for a category. For example, to decide if Anne will eat swordfish, one must first attempt to characterize what makes a fish that Anne will eat acceptable to her. Otherwise, there is no basis for comparing swordfish to fish that she will eat. Mahi-mahi, a fish she has eaten, is meat-like. Trout, which she won't eat, looks like fish. These are the dimensions we need to use in determining if swordfish is in the category of fish she will eat. It is easy for us (as people) to determine what those dimensions are, but getting a computer to do it automatically is a challenge equivalent to the credit assignment problem.

Projecting Effects. Projection, the process of predicting the effects of a decision or plan, is an important part of the evaluative component of any planning or decision making scheme. When everything about a situation is known, projection is merely a process of running known inferences forward from a solution to see where they lead. More often, however, in real-world problems, not everything is known and effects cannot be predicted with accuracy based on any simple set of inference rules.

Cases provide a way of projecting effects based on what has been true in the past. Cases with similar plans that were failures can point to potential plan problems. Cases with similar plans that were successes give credence to the current plan.

Automated use of cases for projection has not been a focus of case-based reasoning research, but aid to a person doing projection is being addressed. CSI's Battle Planner (Goodman 1989) is a case-retrieval system whose interface is set up to allow a person to use cases to project effects. A student commander can propose a solution plan to the system. The Battle Planner retrieves the best-matching cases that use a similar plan and divides them into success and failure situations. The person can examine the cases, use them to fix his plan, and then attempt a similar evaluation of the repaired plan. Or, the person can use the system to do a sensitivity analysis. By manipulating the details of his situation and looking at the changes in numbers of wins and losses (in effect, asking a series of "what-if" questions), he can determine which factors of the current situation are the crucial ones to repair. SCIED (Chandler 1994, Chandler and Kolodner 1993) uses similar methods to help teachers make science activities work for their classrooms.

Case-Based Decision Aiding and Teaching

Psychologists have found that people are comfortable using cases to make decisions (Ross 1989a, 1989b, Klein and Calderwood 1988, Read and Cesa 1991) but don't always remember the right ones (Holyoak 1985, Gentner 1987). To alleviate this problem, the computer can be used as a retrieval tool to augment people's memories. Several systems mentioned earlier are designed with this in mind: Archie-2, Scied, the CSI Battle Planner, and AskJef.

We can also create teaching strategies and build teaching tools that teach based on good examples. If people are comfortable using examples to solve problems and know how to do it well, then one of our responsibilities as teachers might be to teach them the right examples and effective ways to index them (see Burke and Kass, Chapter 5, and Schank, Chapter 15). Indeed, the teaching methodology called problem-based learning holds much in common with CBR and is based on this notion (Kolodner, Hmelo, and Narayanan 1996). Third, if we understand which parts of this natural process are difficult to do well, we can teach people how to do better case-based reasoning. One criticism of using cases to make decisions, for example, is that it puts unsound bias into the reasoning system, because people tend to assume an answer from a previous case is right without justifying it in the new case. This tells us that we should be teaching people how to justify case-based suggestions and that justification or evaluation is crucial to good decision making. If we can isolate other problems people have in solving problems in a case-based way, then we can similarly teach people to do those things better.

Building Case-Based Reasoners

Applying CBR depends on selecting the most useful type of process for a given task and how to gather the needed cases. The above discussion suggests three types of case-based systems, all three of which have been implemented:

Autonomous systems solve problems by themselves. They carry out retrieval, adaptation, and evaluation steps by themselves, as the typical expert system does, but using case-based methods. Chef, Julia, Plexus, Casey, Protos, and Hypo are examples of autonomous CBR systems.

Human-machine systems work along with people to solve problems or interpret situations. The system and person together comprise the case-based reasoning system. The system does what tends to be difficult for people—retrieving and presenting cases. People do what tends to be more difficult for machines—adapting cases to fit new situations and comparing and contrasting cases to interpret new situations. The simplest of these systems are retrieval-only systems, but a system might also help a person with adaptation or evaluation. Help with adaptation generally involves carrying out adaptations when asked. Help with evaluation generally means showing the user the factors that should be considered during evaluation and clustering cases to make comparison easy. The CSI Battle Planner, ARCHIE-2, Clavier, and SCIED are all examples of retrieval-only human-machine CBR systems.

Embedded systems are those in which a retrieval-only or autonomous case-based system is embedded as a component in a system with a larger purpose than problem solving or situation interpretation (see Riesbeck, Chapter 17). For example, several interactive learning environments and training systems have the larger purpose of helping users to learn some task or domain. A case library associated with each system holds stories that help the system to illustrate its points to students (e.g., Burke and Kass, Chapter 5).

Determining which type of system to build requires analyzing the task that needs to be carried out, which requires answering questions such as:

- How much creativity is required to derive solutions?
- How much complexity is involved in evaluating solutions and effecting repairs?
- Are esthetic judgments or value judgments necessary?
- Where does a person working on this task have trouble? Which parts are easy?

Straightforward parts of the task can be done by the machine. Those requiring esthetic or value judgments might be done by the machine, with approval given by the user, or might be done by the user with retrieval and/or adaptation help provided by the system. When much creativity is involved in deriving solutions, or when there is much complexity involved in evaluating solutions and effecting repairs, a human-machine system is best.

What is required for the simplest of systems is a library of cases that coarsely cover the set of problems that come up in a domain. Both success stories and failures must be included. And, the cases must be appropriately indexed. This library, along with a friendly and useful interface, provides augmentation for human memory; automated processes can be built on top of it incrementally.

Several case-based reasoning shells are available on the market (see Chapter 1). When using CBR shells, system builders are responsible for collecting cases for the case library. In some shells the system builders assign their indexes; other shells guide retrieval with decision trees or use keyword retrieval. Some shells require system builders to know knowledge engineering (e.g., Cognitive Systems' ReMind). Others are designed to require only expertise in a domain (e.g., Design-MUSE is aimed toward design professionals).

Case Collection

Case collection has two phases—initial collection of cases, or *seeding* of the case library, and testing of the case library to make sure it provides the coverage and reliability that are required. The result of testing and subsequently refining the case library is that the library is trained for the tasks it will support. Training, itself, is a life-long process—one that, in general, needs to continue throughout the life cycle of a system.

Three general principles guide case collection.

- Cases should cover the range of reasoning tasks the system will be responsible for doing or supporting.

- Over this range of reasoning tasks, cases should cover the range of well-known solutions and well-known mistakes.

- Collecting cases is an incremental process—we do the best we can to provide coverage initially, and then we find out what's missing by trying to use the cases that have already been collected.

In general, cases need to be collected according to the needs of the reasoner, that is, based on the reasoning tasks and goals it will do or support. Cases in the case library should provide as much coverage as possible about both achieving reasoning goals and the obstacles that are likely to be encountered in achieving them. But a case-based system, like an expert, needs to be given time to grow. No matter how careful we are at initially seeding the case library, there will be some problems that are beyond its capabilities. As those are encountered and the limits of the case library are found, new cases need to be added to fill the gaps. Interestingly enough, the very cases that the system can't solve, when added to the case library (with the help of an expert), can generally play that role.

While the first pass at building a case library is unlikely to provide full coverage, an organized approach to determining the kinds of cases that need to be collected can result in good initial coverage. Subsequent training using those cases will expose three kinds of problems:

- Gaps in the library's coverage
- Inadequacies of the indexing scheme
- Inadequacies in the contents of cases in the case library

Maintenance of a case library after the system is fielded is also an issue. It will generally be necessary to add cases and refine indexes in the case library as the system is used. Kitano and Shimazu (Chapter 13) present a case study of a long-term case acquisition and refinement process.

Summary

Case-based reasoning can mean adapting old solutions to meet new demands, using old cases to explain new situations, using old cases to critique new solutions, or reasoning from precedents to interpret a new situation or create an equitable solution to a new problem. A case-based reasoner learns as a byproduct of its reasoning activity. It becomes more efficient and more competent as a result of storing its experiences and referring to them in later reasoning.

In a departure from traditional methods of reasoning investigated by AI researchers and psychologists, case-based reasoning views reasoning as a process of remembering one or a small set of concrete instances or cases and basing decisions on comparisons between the new situation and the old one. Decomposition and recomposition are, as a result, de-emphasized, as is the use of general knowledge. Instead, emphasis is on the manipulation of knowledge in the form of concrete specific instances. Large chunks of composed knowledge are seen as the starting point for reasoning.

A case, however, is more than a large chunk of composed knowledge. It is a contextualized piece of knowledge representing an experience, and any case worth recording in a case library (whether human or machine) teaches a lesson fundamental to achieving the goals of the reasoner who will use it. Cases are indexed by combinations of their descriptors that predict the situations in which they will be useful. Cases represent knowledge at an operational level. They come in many different shapes and sizes, covering large or small time slices, associating solutions with problems, outcomes with situations, or both.

Because case-based reasoning integrates reasoning and learning, it is not enough for a case-based reasoner to stop reasoning after it derives a solution. Rather, it must continue by collecting feedback about its solution and evaluating that feedback. Without evaluation processes based on feedback, learning could not happen reliably, and case-based reasoning itself would be too unreliable to depend on.

The quality of a case-based reasoner's reasoning depends on the experiences it has had, its ability to understand new situations in terms of those old experiences, its adeptness at adaptation, and its adeptness at evaluation and repair. The major processes employed by a case-based reasoner are case storage and retrieval, adaptation, and criticism.

Case-based reasoning is applicable to a wide range of real world situations, ranging from knowledge-rich situations in which construction of solutions is complex to knowledge-poor situations in which cases provide the only available knowledge. It has many advantages, allowing a reasoner to propose solutions to problems quickly, to reason in domains that are not well understood, to evaluate solutions when algorithmic methods are not available, to avoid previous problems, and to focus on important parts of a situation. Its major disadvantages are linked to using cases poorly, for example, relying too heavily on their proposals without evaluating them. Yet case-based reasoning is a natural way of reasoning for people and one that shows considerable promise for machines.

There are several kinds of case-based systems that can be built. Automated systems solve problems from start to finish. If we take case-based reasoning seriously as a cognitive model, however, we can think about building systems that can interact with people in a natural way to solve problems. The simplest of these uses the machine's case library to augment the memory of a person, leaving the human user to reason based on retrieved cases. More sophisticated systems embed case-based reasoners or case retrievers in more broad-purpose systems, e.g., interactive learning environments, to provide more active assistance.

Acknowledgments

This chapter is adapted, with the permission of the publisher, from Kolodner, Janet L., 1993, *Case-Based Reasoning*, Morgan Kaufmann Publishers, Inc., San Mateo, CA. More detail about each of the issues discussed in this article can be found in that book. The work reported in this article was partially funded by DARPA under contract no. N00014-91-J-4092, monitored by ONR; by ONR under contract no. N00014-92-J-1234; by National Science Foundation under contract no. IRI-8921256; and by ARI under contract no. MDA903-90-K-0112.

Notes

1. Of course, now we must consider what easily inferred means. This is something a system builder must determine for his/her domain and task.

2. PROTOS's task includes aspects of both problem-solving and interpretive CBR. The next section discusses how PROTOS uses cases to interpret open-ended classifications.

3 Indexing Evaluations of Buildings to Aid Conceptual Design

Anna L. Griffith and Eric A. Domeshek

It is the norm for expert performance in cognitively challenging tasks to depend on extensive experience. Researchers in the AI paradigm of case-based reasoning (CBR) have been building computational models that account for this fact, and have aimed to produce systems that perform effectively by relying on records of past experiences (Hammond 1989c, Hinrichs 1992, Koton 1988b, Mark 1989).

More recently, insights gleaned from a decade of CBR research have been turned towards the problem of building systems that aid humans in performance of real-world tasks (Schank et al. 1991, Ferguson et al. 1991). At Georgia Tech, we focused on design tasks such as architecture, engineering, and lesson planning (Domeshek and Kolodner 1991, Domeshek and Kolodner 1992, Chandler and Kolodner 1993). We were building what we called *case-based design aids* (CBDAs)—systems that help human designers by making available to them a broad range of critiqued designs that can serve to highlight important design issues, to explicate abstract design guidelines, and to provide suggestions or warnings about possible design solutions.

Any system that bases its performance on the selective use of items from a large memory must find some way to organize that memory so that the right items can be found at the right time. In CBR, this problem of how to ensure effective selective retrieval goes by the name of the indexing problem, and has long been recognized as one of the key issues in the field (Schank 1982, Hammond 1989c, Domeshek 1992). Research has provided some insight into how this challenge must be addressed, and has produced a sampling of exemplary indexing systems for particular domains and tasks.

This chapter reports on the development of an indexing system for one of our CBDAs—ARCHIE-II, an aid for conceptual design in architecture. The story we have to tell of the evolution of this indexing system is interesting for several reasons. First of all, there has been relatively little work in the

CBR community on indexing systems for physical artifact design tasks. Secondly, because we have been designing indexes for an aiding system we have had the burden and the opportunity to grapple with cases of far greater complexity than is possible when working on autonomous reasoners; the domains in which it is practical to build autonomous systems are necessarily much less complex than those in which humans routinely engage (and in which humans are likely to need aid). Finally, it is an interesting question to what extent the demands of indexing for autonomous and aiding systems may differ; the information available in situation descriptions (which is thus information easily available for indexing to past experiences), may be different when a system is engaged in problem solving than when it is responding to a user's queries.[1]

In the context of an aiding system, the indexing problem shades into an HCI or interface problem, and in the face of a usefully complex domain such as conceptual design of buildings, the usability problem is exacerbated. What is required to succeed here is an understanding of the processes used by our users: how do architects think about their task during the early stages of design?

Indexes to Design Lessons

The first thing to note when considering how to index design cases for architects is that buildings are probably not the right units of storage and retrieval. Buildings are too big and complex to be designed as one piece; instead there are many small decisions that go into a building design, and what would best serve an architect are lessons about which issues are important, how to address these important problems, and what outcomes are likely. Thus, the primary unit of memory in ARCHIE-II is the lesson-bearing story. As an example, consider the following story (Building Diagnostics, 1988):

> The location of the main lobby information desk in the Bristol County Courthouse is inconvenient and makes it difficult for people to find their way. The desk is located in the telephone office, which is off to the left of the main lobby entry. There is a small sign on the telephone office indicating that it is also the information desk, but on first entering the courthouse there is no immediate indication where to go for information.[2]

Since the items being indexed are stories that teach lessons about design issues, it is appropriate that indexes to these stories center on design issues. But issues vary from one part of a building to another, and even pervasive issues, such as efficient circulation, may vary significantly in their implications throughout the building. Accordingly, our stories tend to focus on how an issue plays out in some part of a building, and thus our indexes must also specify the relevant parts. Issues also tend to arise at different times during the life of a building: some are important during construction, others during use or renovation. Likewise, not all issues affect all of the stakeholders in a building: some are of most importance to the owners, others to long-term residents, and still others to occasional visitors.

With one final distinction, this analysis of features that differentiate issues provides an outline for our indexes. We recognize two different ways of slicing a building into parts: spatially and functionally. Spaces are physically localized building chunks such as floors, wings, or offices. Functional systems such as the electrical and plumbing systems may be distributed throughout a building and are defined in terms of their purpose. So we recognize five primary dimensions as relevant to describing the point of a story with a simple lesson:

- *Issue:* Goal to be achieved by the artifact's design
- *Space:* Part of designed artifact defined spatially
- *System:* Part of designed artifact defined functionally
- *Stakeholder:* Role with respect to artifact defining a point of view on the issue
- *Life Cycle:* Part of artifact's history when the issue matters

A combination of some subset of these descriptors is sufficient to identify a single point that might characterize the lesson of one of our stories (thus serving as a memory *label*), or might express a user's browsing interests (thus serving as a retrieval *probe*). But often, a story is interesting because of what it says about the *interaction* between issues. In one courthouse, the prisoner holding area was located far from the courtrooms, which led to a desirable lack of noise in the court, but also contributed to security problems when the prisoners were being transferred through the building. Stories that address the interaction between issues are best indexed by a pair of the five-featured structures above.

The index outline just sketched, whether used singly or in pairs, does not say much about what sorts of issues, spaces, systems and so forth we will have to represent. It is essentially a road map to the work required for a fully specified indexing system. To give a sense for how such a system is developed, this chapter will concentrate on just one of these dimensions: *spaces*.

Designing an Indexing Vocabulary

Designing an indexing vocabulary is an exercise in exploring the possible descriptions of objects, concepts,and relationships in the domain, and settling on a system that meets several criteria (Kolodner 1993):

Relevance

Index vocabulary must capture those aspects of situations that indicate when one is relevant to another (with respect to a task or tasks). This is just a baseline, common sense guide to help decide what sorts of features ought to be included in an indexing vocabulary.

Extent

Index vocabulary must be sufficiently extensive to describe an existing or expected corpus of memory items for the range of intended uses. We want to cover a large corpus of design stories, and eventually would like to allow users to enter their own stories.

Specificity

Index vocabulary must get specific enough to make all useful discriminations among items in memory. We want to retrieve only those stories that are most relevant to a designer's situation.

Generality

Index vocabulary must also contain components general enough to capture relevant similarities among the items in memory. We want to be able to retrieve stories whose indexes are inexact matches to a designer's situation, if that is the best there is in memory.

Usability

In an aiding system, it is helpful if the indexing vocabulary corresponds closely to practitioners' conceptions of their domain and task. We want designers to feel comfortable using the system and we want to minimize the amount of inference required of the system at retrieval time.

Actually, extent, specificity, and generality are all closely related. What it means to cover a corpus (to have sufficient extent) is just to be able to note the similarities and differences between the items in the corpus. Any (relevant) feature introduced into an indexing vocabulary is likely to improve the system's extent, and may serve both specificity and generality; the feature will appear in some indexes but not in others, and thus will discriminate; but for all indexes in which the feature appears, it will be capturing a similarity.

An architectural design aiding system presents serious challenges in balancing the criteria. To be useful, we must build a large corpus, we must index it using terms an architect might naturally employ, and we must build in sufficient flexibility to satisfy the often idiosyncratic approaches of many different architects. All this must be accomplished while not burdening the user (or the indexer) with too many choices.

Satisfying all the criteria in any interesting domain is actually a hard design problem. Arriving at an acceptable solution generally requires an iterative process of analyzing the domain and task, proposing index components, and evaluating those components with respect to the criteria (which may involve actually building partial memories based on those proposals). We have been following this process for ARCHIE-II's indexes, and are currently on the third major loop through the cycle for the space components. The next section describes the history of that design process with particular attention to the rationale for our current solution.

Spaces as Index Components

The possible spaces in a building are many and various. There are also many possible ways of describing those spaces. Here we summarize three approaches considered for the ARCHIE-II system.

Spaces: A First Pass

The first attempt at an indexing vocabulary for spaces was developed, in part, to suggest the way such attempts might proceed in general. Based on a corpus of stories we then had in hand, a list of quite specific space types was created; since our cases were drawn from courthouses, this list included such items as parking-lot, entry, lobby, information-desk, vestibule, and courtroom. Just as we characterized our initial index proposal in terms of a set of five dimensions, we proceeded to pick out dimensions (in this case four of them) that together began to characterize the spaces in our list.

The four dimensions selected to describe spaces were ownership, purpose, size, and position. *Ownership* encoded common patterns in who used the space. *Purpose* was intended to indicate what the space was used for. *Size* was specified in terms of square footage. Finally, *position* encoded the space's location within the building.

For each dimension we then proceeded to specify a set of possible fillers. In principle, this system was not limited to the original list of named spaces any combination of the defined fillers for any subset of the dimensions could be used to describe a space. In practice, these dimensions and the fillers provided for them were not even sufficient to do a good job of describing the spaces in our original list. For instance, we could not distinguish criminal from civil courtrooms.

Still, this initial proposal had some positive features. Because it allowed use of a set of everyday names for spaces, it was relatively easy for an architect to use. The interface problem created by a potentially lengthy list of names to choose from was somewhat mitigated by the ability to enter a partial description of a space (by choosing fillers for any of the dimensions); given such a partial description, the system would then prompt the user with a limited menu, including only those spaces that satisfied the specified conditions. Of course, here the limited expressivity of the space description language became a problem, as did the fact that choosing fillers for the dimensions was not as intuitive as the straightforward choice of space names.

Limiting the characterization of spaces to the four dimensions and their fillers not only affected usability, but also failed the tests of extent, specificity and generality. The following example illustrates a failure of specificity. Imagine an architect is designing an office suite for a large accounting department and is concerned with appropriate use of natural lighting. Currently, ARCHIE-II only stores courthouse stories, so while it has stories about lighting in several office spaces, the names associated with the spaces include "probation office," "judge's lobby," and "magistrate's office," but not "accounting department." Now, by choosing from among available values for the purpose and ownership dimensions the user could tell the system that the space she is concerned with is a work area generally off limits to the public. On that basis, the system might retrieve stories associated with any of the courthouse office spaces mentioned earlier. But consider that of all those spaces, there is one that is clearly most similar to an accounting department; the probation office is an office suite that includes a large private office for the manager, a group of smaller offices for staff, and a place for a receptionist. Other courthouse office spaces do not house the same number of people, nor break up the space with the same sorts of dividers. When the system retrieves lighting stories from all the courthouse offices, the user is forced to sift through a large collection of stories, most of which are unlikely to be relevant to her lighting problem.

Spaces: A Second Pass

In our second attempt at a vocabulary for spaces our primary concerns were to increase the expressivity of the language and to take a better account of the features that mattered during conceptual design (and thus that would determine the relevance of a story's lesson). Among the constraints architects face when designing spaces, some of the most powerful stem from who will use the space, what they will use it for, and what kinds of support are required for such use. For example, a room where the primary activity is discussion must be set up differently than a room where the primary activity is lecturing; a room for discussions by groups of 20 must be designed differently than a room for discussions by 3 or 4; a typical manager's office must function not only as a small group discussion room, but also as a place for private desk-work.

In a sense, answering these questions would force us to expand on the original dimensions of ownership and purpose. A separate effort was anticipated to capture more of the physical attributes of spaces (in effect, expanding beyond the original pair of dimensions, size and position); note that this second extension would more likely address the shortcomings identified in the office lighting example of the last section. The focus on issues critical to conceptual design also led us to introduce in this second pass an important set of features that had not been considered at all the first time around. Often a space's design is strongly influenced by its interactions with other spaces. So while focusing on uses of spaces, we also began to look at the *relationships* between uses of separate spaces.

As a way of encoding descriptions of the people, activities, and props associated with a space we adopted the script formalism (Schank and Abelson 1977). Under this proposal, the space dimension of our five-part index outline was to be filled with a set of scripts and references to related spaces. Similarities among the specific activities, role-fillers, props, and spaces would help determine the system's judgments of similarity between story indexes and user queries. Figure 1 is an example of a script-based space description for a court clinic (a court clinic is where a psychologist or social worker counsels young probationers).

The kinds of information included in this space description are, in fact, important to architects; our second pass at index design improves on the original scheme by significantly broadening its extent. Unfortunately, this approach swings too far in the direction of detail. Users will not put up with having to constantly be explicit about much that is normally left as tacit knowledge about a design problem, so usability has actually deteriorated. What makes this more than just an interface problem is that there still remain important similarities and differences among spaces that cannot be described in terms of scripts and related spaces (or in terms of some improved vocabulary for physical description).

Consider the constraints on a juvenile courtroom. A description of what goes on in a juvenile trial will not really be able to capture the important notion of confidentiality, and a design for a juvenile courtroom will not succeed without taking confidentiality into account. The fact that court proceedings are supposed to remain confidential is actually a matter of what does not happen: someone not associated with the trial does not get to observe it. Scripts do not normally include such negative statements, and even if they did, requiring a user to express such a basic concept in such particularly terms would be awkward.

Finally, we note that in addition to excluding some important features, the script approach to describing spaces may include many features that do not contribute much to discriminating stories in our corpus. For example, while the need for props such as a desk, file storage, chairs, and tables in a space for

---

Court Clinic:

Role:
        Psychologist/social worker
        Juvenile probationer

Props:
        Desk
        Toys/toy storage

Activities:
        Psychologist talks to probationer
        Probationer talks to psychologist
        Psychologist works at desk
        Probationer plays with toys

Related Spaces:
        Waiting room
        Juvenile probation office
        Conference room

Figure 1. Example of a script-based space description for a court clinic.

office-work places some constraint on the space design, when dealing with a building like a courthouse, where many of the spaces share that feature, we are not getting much return for our descriptive effort.

Spaces: A Third Pass

The first attempt at an indexing vocabulary for spaces captured only a small number of the relevant features, and the second attempt, while capturing more, still neglected many important abstractions and required too much attention to detail. Our strategy for arriving at a system with the right amount and level of detail was to go back and pay more attention to the way architects do the work we aim to support.

Accordingly, we have been devoting more effort to studying architects' processes of conceptual design. We need answers to the pair of questions: What kinds of decisions do architects make during conceptual design, and what features of the design problem and its evolving solution do they use to make those decisions? So far, we have a preliminary answer to the first question that breaks down conceptual design issues into two major categories: the *organization* of spaces and the *features* of individual spaces. The features of the spaces break down, in turn into three categories: the people and things that play important roles in the space, features of the exterior, and features of the interior. So in all, we have four clusters of features to consider.

There are four components to space *organization:*

O1 Relationships between spaces

O2 The strength of inter-space relationships

O3 Distances between spaces

O4 The orientation of spaces to the site

Roles fit into three categories. *Primary* and *secondary roles* indicate who is using a space, differentiating between those who use the space frequently and those using it less frequently. *Props* are inanimate objects associated with particular spaces. These then are the three role components:

R1 Primary roles

R2 Secondary roles

R3 Props

The *exterior* can be described along four dimensions:

E1 Openings (such as doorways and windows)

E2 Materials

E3 Three-dimensional shape or form

E4 Space flow (paths between spaces, and the 3-D shape of those paths)

Finally, *interiors* can be described using three dimensions:

I1 Function

I2 Materials

I3 Space characteristics (such as size, lighting, and thermal comfort)

This outline of conceptual design issues serves as the bias for space descriptions in our indexing vocabulary. Most of these features apply to a space; some apply to *relationships* between a space and some other space. When describing any particular space (considered the focal space) we characterize it using both sets of features. The features that characterize the space's relationships to other spaces implicate two other sets of spaces: *included* spaces cover parts of the focal space (differentiated based on function); *related* spaces are other disjoint spaces with interesting relationships to the focal space. The included and related spaces can in turn be described using these kinds of features. Applying these features to a focal space and its relationships to other spaces results in the following form for space descriptions (figure 2).

Most features apply directly to a particular space, and are shown in figure 2

Focal Space

    O4 - Orientation to site

    R1 - Primary Roles

    R2 - Secondary Roles

    R3 - Props

    E1 - Exterior openings

    E2 - Exterior materials

    E3 - Form

    I1 - Function

    I2 - Interior material

    I3 - Space characteristics

    Included Spaces [Pointers to other spaces]

    Related Spaces [Pointers to other spaces]

        O1 - Relationship type

        O2 - Relationship strength

        O3 - Distance

        E4 - Spaceflow

Figure 2. Form for space descriptions.

associated with the focal space. Note that included and related spaces are themselves spaces that can, potentially, be described by the same features. A smaller set of features (O1-O3 and E4) bear directly on relationships between spaces, and these are shown here nested beneath the related spaces.

At any given point in the design process, the architect is most directly concerned with some particular level of analysis that defines what counts as focal spaces and what counts as included spaces. For example, during conceptual design of an entire courthouse, a likely unit of analysis is the judges' lobby, consisting of judges' offices plus associated support areas such as clerks' offices and private rest rooms. At the point where the judges' lobby is a focal space, we expect most of the relationships of interest to be expressed as relationships between the lobby and other areas, such as the courtroom. This contrasts with another, finer level of analysis, at which relationships might be noted between included spaces such as a judge's office and the judge's bench in the courtroom.

Focal Space	Jury Room
R1 Primary Roles	Jurors
I1 Function	Isolate primary role
I3 Space characteristics	
Acoustics	Isolation
Included Space	Meeting Area
Included Space	Private Rest room
Related Space	Jury Pool Room
O1 Relationship Type	Same primary role
O2 Relationship Strength	5
Related Space	Courtroom
O1 Relationship Type	Same primary role
O2 Relationship Strength	5

*Figure 3. Description a jury room as part of a query about juror
circulation patterns to and from the room.*

We illustrate this new approach by describing a jury room as part of a
query about juror circulation patterns to and from the room. The architect
knows that jurors play a primary role not just in their jury deliberation room,
but also in courtrooms and in the jury pool room (where jurors are selected
for trials). If the architect is concerned about how to arrange circulation to
and from a jury room, the following description of that room (figure 3) can
serve as a useful piece of a query for relevant stories.[3]

In figure 3, the jury deliberation room is the focal space with respect to
which the architect is concerned about circulation. The architect specifies
only a few aspects of this room: its primary residents will be jurors, and its
primary function is to keep jury deliberations confidential (which is to be
accomplished by physically isolating the jurors from other building users
and by making sure that the room is acoustically isolated from other spaces).
The two included spaces describe a logical guess by the architect: there
should be room to allow the jurors to discuss the case, and there should be a
private rest room. In this context, the architect specifies no further details of
the included spaces (which could, potentially, have been treated as fully
specified spaces in their own rights). The two related spaces are mentioned
because the architect sees their overlapping primary roles as important; her
purpose is to explore the implications of these relationships. The relationships' types are characterized in terms of the shared role fillers, and their

strengths are rated very high—they are pegged at 5 on a scale from 1 to 5.

The space description in figure 3 would be accompanied by other index components to indicate the architect's interest in stories about the implications of jurors' circulation to and from the Jury Room during normal use of the building for trials. Given this description, the system could have a basis for choosing the following warning story describing circulation patterns for jurors moving between the related spaces that fail to ensure desired isolation:

> On the second floor, the superior court and municipal court jury assembly rooms are placed around a service core that serves both of them. This core contains direct access to the stairs and elevator use by the staff. This can give jurors an opportunity to take the elevator to other floors and make contact with people in the staff areas, which are supposedly segregated from the public.

This system, based on modeling the indexes after the actual decision made during conceptual design, does better at satisfying our criteria than did the previous attempts. Extent, specificity and generality are all improved by attending to a wider range of features that are attended to by architects. This scheme is not as susceptible to the sort of failing we saw with our first proposal, when the system could not notice how an "accounting department" was more like a "probation office" than a "judges' lobby" or "magistrate's office." Despite including descriptors such as the role filler "juror" this scheme also need not be unduly bound to the idiosyncrasies of the courthouse domain; we have preliminary breakdowns of such categories in terms of underlying attributes that capture their relationship to the building and its spaces. We take it as a constraint on the vocabulary items we posit that they not only contribute to distinguishing among our courthouse cases, but that they also contribute to identifying distinctions likely to matter in other architectural (and even other design) domains.

Bubble Diagrams and a Bubble Editor

Hewing to architects' own distinctions and vocabulary as done in the third pass, should improve expressiveness. Unfortunately, the complexity of this query format is likely to raise serious problems with usability. We are therefore trying to provide a reasonably intuitive way for architects to designate spaces of interest. Architects love graphic representations, and are adept at visualizing spaces. It would be nice, if we could allow our users to pose queries simply by pointing at representations of spaces on the screen. The problem is that there is no canonical graphic representation for all the features of spaces relevant during conceptual design (and, it would premature to draw detailed CAD diagrams at such an early stage of design).

It turns out that architects have, however, developed graphic forms appropriate to conceptual design: many architects develop their early ideas using bubble diagrams. In a bubble diagram, a bubble (a blob that does not necessarily represent shape but does represent size) is drawn to represent each space. Lines are drawn between bubbles to indicate relationships: dark, thick lines represent strong relationships while light, thin lines represent weaker relationships.

We intend to provide users of ARCHIE-II with a bubble diagram editor for creating and viewing these schematic design aids. Ideally this tool will comfortably support their normal conventions but will also make it easier to capture the features we need for query processing. When a bubble is drawn in the editor a template will pop up on the screen asking the user to fill in the blanks for the various features of the space. When a line is drawn between bubbles another template will pop up asking the user to describe the relationship between the two spaces.

The bubble editor will assist the architect with conceptual design in three ways. The first way is simply to improve on a representational technique they are already using by automating editing and preserving an on-line record of their work. The second way is by helping the architect describe features of the spaces. The third way is by helping to form queries to the case-based design aiding system.

Conclusions and Future Work

This chapter has focused on two issues. The first was explaining and illustrating the iterative process of designing an indexing system. The second was arguing for the appropriateness of the current system for indexing stories that teach lessons about conceptual design in architecture. By describing stories using features that architects consider during conceptual design, the indexing system should naturally provide users with an easy way to specify probes to the case-based system.

It is interesting to study both the evolution of our indexing system and its current state. Everything seemed to fall into place once we focused on basing the index vocabulary on the decisions made during conceptual design. This made the vocabulary familiar to the architect and opened up opportunities for graphical representations. It seems like common sense to base the vocabulary on the decisions made, but it is sometimes useful to have the obvious stated. Although we have not made the attempt yet, we believe that this approach is transferable to conceptual design in other fields.

Further studies with architects, including interviews and observation, are planned to help us refine this approach still further. We hope to learn more about what space characteristics are important to architects during conceptual design. We also hope to learn more about how architects use bubble diagrams, since they appear to be a strategically impoverished representation that force focus on those central issues that matter early in design.

Acknowledgements

Many people have worked on the development and conception of the system described in this chapter. Janet Kolodner and Craig Zimring have shaped this project from the start. Richard Billington, our research programmer, has been a constant collaborator throughout. The ARCHIE-II team also includes Kadayam Vijaya, Ali Malkawi, Ellen Do, and David Brogan. Interviews with architects have been invaluable; the architects included Lane Duncan, Rufus Hughes, Michael Lincolt, and Von Rivers. This work has been supported in part by the Defense Advance Research Projects Agency, monitored by ONR under contract N00014-91-J-4092. All views expressed are those of the authors.

Notes

1. An aiding system looking over a user's shoulder, and trying to explain aspects of the user's problem solving process, likely results in still different sorts of information being easily available for indexing.

2. Note that ARCHIE-II's stories are always shown with a presentation (usually graphic) of the artifact being discussed, and are generally accompanied by an illustration that amplifies the point being made in the text.

3. Note that many attributes are left blank because the architect is not yet committed to their values, and retrieved stories may offer advice on how to flesh them out.

4 Towards More Creative Case-Based Design Systems

Linda M. Wills and Janet L. Kolodner

Creativity in design derives from enumerating several solution alternatives, redescribing and elaborating problem specifications, and evaluating proposed solutions, based on criteria and constraints that go beyond the stated constraints on a solution. It arises out of a confluence of processes (including problem redescription, remembering, assimilation, and evaluation), which interact with each other in complex ways. Often creativity arises from interesting strategic control of these processes, which in themselves may be quite mundane (Boden 1990; Chandrasekaran 1990; Gero and Maher 1993; Navinchandra 1992).

These processes rely heavily on previous design experiences and knowledge of designed artifacts (Goel and Chandrasekaran 1992; Hinrichs 1992; Kolodner and Penberthy 1990; Kolodner and Wills 1993). An expert designer knows of many design experiences, accumulated from personally designing artifacts, being given case studies of designs in school, and observing artifacts designed by others. The designer draws on these experiences to perform such activities as generating design alternatives, reformulating and elaborating the problem specification or proposed solutions, and predicting the outcome of making certain design decisions. The experiences that are most valuable are often those that are highly contextualized pieces of knowledge about artifacts, such as how a device behaves in some context of use, circumstances in which it can fail, and knowledge about situations that might come up not only in use, but in all phases of its life cycle.

Given the nature of these experiences, we believe case-based representations and reasoning techniques lend themselves to supporting creative design. Research in case-based reasoning (CBR) has provided extensive knowledge of how to reuse solutions to old problems in new situations, how to build and search case libraries (for exploration of design alternatives), and how to merge and adapt cases. It has developed powerful techniques for partial matching and the formation of analogical maps between seemingly disparate situations (Kolodner 1993).

However, most existing CBR systems are not living up to their potential. They tend to adapt and reuse old solutions in routine ways, producing robust but uninspired results. They do not attempt to extend their exploration by deriving constraints and preferences that improve or go beyond those stated in the original problem. (See (Kolodner 1993, appendix) for a recent survey.)

Some of this potential is buried in processes that have been downplayed or even missing in most standard CBR systems. In particular, little research effort has been directed towards the kinds of situation assessment, evaluation, and assimilation processes that facilitate the exploration of ideas and the elaboration and redefinition of problems that are crucial to creative design. Also, to facilitate the kinds of opportunism inherent in creative reasoning, CBR systems need to break out of their typically rigid control structure to allow flexible interleaving and communication among processes. In addition, more research attention must be payed to the strategic control mechanisms that guide a creative designer in deciding what to do next.

In this chapter, we describe the types of behavior we would like case-based design systems to support, based on an exploratory study of designers working on a mechanical engineering problem. We show how the standard CBR framework should be extended and we describe an architecture we are developing to experiment with these ideas. We end with a set of open issues.

What Do Creative Designers Do?

To gain insights into the knowledge and reasoning involved in creative design, we observed a four-person team engaged in a seven-week undergraduate mechanical engineering (ME) design project. The task was to design and build a device to quickly and safely transport several eggs from one location to another. The device could be constructed from any material, but its size, weight, and cost were restricted.

After exploring several schemes for launching, moving, stopping, and protecting the eggs, the team decided to use a cylindrical egg carrier (of radius 7 cm., length 22.5 cm.), with the eggs wrapped in pipe insulation to protect them inside the carrier. The carrier was dropped down (0.8 m.) from a starting platform and would roll into a target zone (within a 5 m. radius of the starting platform). The team had two possible launch mechanisms up until the final design demonstration day: a spring mechanism and a simple ramp (the spring launch base could be inverted to become a ramp, which was the final choice). In both cases, a string, with one end attached to the launch base, was wrapped around the device, so that as the cylinder dropped, it spun down the string, hit the ground, and rolled into the target zone. The wrapped string gave the carrier momentum and it also prevented it from rolling beyond the target zone.

One of us participated as a member of the team, allowing us to become immersed in the issues and to observe the design process in a natural setting, in both informal and "official" team meetings. We recorded the group's conversations on audiotapes and collected copies of all their design documents and drawings.

We are particularly intrigued by a set of three processes we observed underlying many creative design activities: 1) generation of multiple descriptions or views of a problem, 2) gradual emergence of evaluative issues, constraints and preferences, and 3) serendipitous recognition of solutions to pending problems, sometimes seeing new functions and purposes for common design pieces in the process. We are not claiming that this is a complete set. (For example, our design study has revealed a variety of influences on creativity from collaborative activity.) Rather, we are interested in these processes because they are key processes in design that current case-based systems neglect.

Problem Redescription

The initial problem statement given to our designers was ambiguous, incomplete, contradictory, and underconstrained. They spent a great deal of effort to turn it into something with more detail, more concrete specifications, and more clearly defined and consistent constraints. An important part of this process involved attempting to understand the problem, view it from multiple perspectives, and redescribe it in terms familiar to the designers. They had to refine and operationalize several vague or abstract constraints, while sometimes having to generalize constraints that were too specific.

For example, many of the ideas of one designer, who had a keen interest in automobiles, came from recalling devices and concepts from the car domain, such as shock absorbers, unit-body vs. single-frame construction, and airbags. Being able to recall these required viewing the problem of protecting the eggs as one of absorbing shock or transferring energy and as a problem of protecting passengers in general, not just eggs.

Our designers also explored the given constraints, deliberately stretching or strengthening them to see what ideas became possible. For example, the initial problem statement was ambiguous about whether or not the device could land (i.e., touch down) short of the target zone and then move into it. The designers considered the extreme possibility of landing as far short of this zone as possible, in which case the device would not fly at all, but would be pushed off or lowered to the ground, where it would then move itself into the safety zone. Visualizing this possibility reminded them of devices, such as elevators and yo-yo's, that could implement parts of this behavior.

This continual elaboration and redescription of the problem helped the designers derive connections between the current problem and similar problems in other domains, facilitating cross-contextual transfer of design ideas. It also primed them to serendipitously recognize relevant objects in the environment that might be reused for a new purpose.

Evaluation

One of the key forces driving evolution of the problem specification is the evaluation of proposed design alternatives. Evaluative issues emerge in the course of evaluating. Designers do not merely depend on constraints that have already been specified. Rather, they bring up additional constraints and criteria as proposals are examined. Proposed solutions often remind them of issues to consider. The problem and solution "co-evolve" (Fischer 1993).

One interesting criteria that emerged in the course of the ME design project was *versatility*—the ability of the device to apply in more than one situation. This criteria was not mentioned or required in the original statement of the problem. It arose in response to ambiguity in the initial problem statement, which described three similar problems but did not specify which one would be assigned. Each problem differed only in the device's starting position (from either the center of a child's wading pool or from a platform of one of two heights) and in its target destination distance. (This is similar in the real world to situations in which the engineers are designing for multiple potential customers with different needs). To deal with the uncertainty and reduce the complexity this variability introduced, the designers began searching for solutions that could be used to solve all three problems or could be easily adapted to apply to each. That is, they began to evaluate proposals on the basis of versatility in addition to the other criteria already in the problem specification. Being able to do this is central to creative design.

Assimilation

Problem redescription provides not only a means for recalling relevant solution alternatives, but also a vocabulary for describing and, in many cases, reinterpreting objects in the designer's environment. This often leads to a new way of viewing the function of some object and facilitates the recognition of potential solutions to pending problems in the external environment.

For example, our designers went to a home improvement store for materials for a spring launch mechanism. While comparing the strengths of several springs by compressing them, they noticed that the springs tended to bend. One designer wrapped a hand around the spring to hold it straight as it was compressed and said the springs would each need to be enclosed in a tube to keep them from bending. Another added that the tube would need to be collapsible (to compress with the spring). The designers could not think of an existing collapsible tube and did not want to build one due to time pressure. They gave up on the springs and started thinking about egg protection. During their search for protection material, they walked through the bathroom section of the store, where they saw a display of toilet-paper holders. They immediately recognized them as collapsible tubes which could be used to support the springs.

By playing with the springs, noticing problems and suggesting fixes, the designers formed a specific, concrete, and operationalized description of what a solution would look like to the bending-springs problem. However, the toilet-paper holder was not recalled on the basis of this description. Instead, the description was used to reinterpret the toilet-paper holder when it was encountered in the external environment and to recognize its additional function of preventing springs from bending upon compression. The designers were able to interpret objects seen in the environment, or recalled from memory, from a new viewpoint. This viewpoint was based on descriptions and feature dimensions that had been revealed to be important in attempts to solve recent and pending problems.

We refer to this process as *assimilating* the objects into a problem context. It not only involves reinterpreting solution alternatives under consideration, but also comparing and contrasting alternatives with one another, along the dimensions relevant to the problem context. This helps reveal those that are not really new ideas, so that they can be ignored. It can also cause new evaluative issues to emerge as new dimensions or criteria are generated to distinguish seemingly identical ideas.

Strategic Control

The designers we observed did not follow a rigid, methodical plan detailing what to do next. Rather, they moved fluidly between various problem pieces and design processes (e.g., idea generation, adaptation, critiquing, problem refinement, elaboration, and redefinition) in a flexible and highly opportunistic manner.

Our designers employed a variety of strategic control heuristics, some of which are opportunistic. For example, when an alternative was proposed that satisfied some desired criteria extremely well compared to the other alternatives, they directed their efforts toward elaborating that alternative, optimistically suspending criticism or discounting the importance of criteria or constraints that were not satisfied as well. Sometimes this led to reformulation of the problem as constraints were relaxed or placed at a lower priority.

Being able to take advantage of such opportunities requires being able to judge whether progress was being made along a certain line of attack and to choose which ideas are more promising or more likely to lead to something unusual and novel.

Some strategic control heuristics are more deliberate, based on reflection. For example, one heuristic our designers used was to try quick, easy adaptations of a proposed solution first before stepping back and reformulating the problem or relaxing constraints. Other deliberate heuristics attempted to make non-standard substitutions, apply adaptation strategies in circumstances other than the ones they were meant for, and merge pieces of separate solutions with each other in nonobvious ways.

In many cases, the processes that are composed together leading to a novel idea are not in themselves novel and may be quite mundane. The trick is knowing when to do them.

How CBR Systems Can Do Better

Most current CBR systems tend to stick to well-known interpretations of problems and routine ways of adapting old solutions, neglecting exploration of alternatives if something good enough has been found. We believe the CBR paradigm can be extended to support more creative problem solving.

Problem Redescription

Problem redescription corresponds closely to the process of situation assessment—redescribing a problem in the vocabulary of the indexing system. In most CBR systems, situation assessment is skipped; the assumption is made that the initial representation of the problem is sufficient for solving the problem. But, as our observations show, investigating a problem in depth makes available a large set of relevant cues for retrieval. Generating multiple ways of describing a problem provides several different contexts for specifying what would be relevant, if remembered.

Research on indexing has found that it is the combination of setting up a context for retrieval and having already interpreted something in memory in a similar way that allows retrieval. When some case or piece of knowledge is entered into memory, it is not always possible to anticipate how it might be used. Situation assessment processes aim to bridge that gap by helping to redescribe a new problem in a way that is similar to something seen before.

Research into situation assessment and problem reformulation (e.g., in CASEY (Koton 1988b), CYRUS (Kolodner 1983a), MINSTREL (Turner 1994), BRAINSTORMER (Jones 1992), and STRATA (Lowry 1987)), show different ways it can be done. However, these techniques have not yet made it into widespread use in practical CBR systems. They should certainly be included in any system aimed at reuse of experience across domains.

Evaluation

CBR systems currently evaluate solutions by checking a set of constraints that have been given to the system. Evaluative procedures are typically buried within case manipulation to predict or test whether a modified case satisfies the specified constraints. Observations of our designers suggests that evaluation should play a more prominent role in case-based design systems, allowing evaluative issues to emerge in the course of evaluating. Navinchandra (1991) calls this criteria emergence and shows an example of how it can arise from case-based projection. In addition to criteria, constraints in general (Prabhakar and Goel 1992) and relative priorities among them also gradually emerge. This type of evaluation is a key driving force within creative design, feeding back to situation assessment and guiding case manipulation.

Assimilation

A key idea underlying dynamic memory (Schank 1982), one of the principle foundations of case-based reasoning, is that remembering, understanding, and learning are all inextricably intertwined. The ability to determine where something fits in with what we already know (understanding) is a key part of being able to assimilate objects in our environment into our problem solving. This environment includes not only external objects, but also cases that have been retrieved, elaborated and adapted. Understanding how these fit into a problem context may involve a useful reinterpretation of something already in memory, suggesting in a new way of indexing it.

Strategic Control

Our exploratory study suggests that a linear, sequential composition of CBR processes is much too simple. In reality, these processes are highly intertwined and interact in interesting ways. For example, problem elaboration and redescription tactics specify contexts for search that retrieval processes use, while evaluation of recalled or adapted alternatives feeds information back to these situation assessment tactics, resulting in even better contexts for search. In some cases, what suggests a particular problem refinement or redescription results from trying to confirm the legality of a proposed solution during evaluation and finding a loophole or ambiguity in the current problem specification. In addition, comparing and contrasting a proposed solution with other proposals during assimilation can bring new evaluative issues into focus.

CBR systems need to break out of their typically rigid control structure and allow more interaction and opportunism among processes. This requires making strategic control mechanisms explicit, so they can be easily modified, reasoned about, extended, and learned. More research needs to be directed at identifying and capturing the types of strategic control heuristics designers use.

Proposed Architecture

We are developing an experimental case-based system that emphasizes the processes of situation assessment, evaluation, and assimilation, integrating them with the usual CBR processes of retrieval, elaboration (case manipulation, adaptation, merging, prediction), and learning. It has a flexible, opportunistic control structure which allows us to keep control tactics separate, explicit, and modifiable.

The processes within our system are not applied in a strictly linear succession. Rather, the system has a blackboard-style architecture. The processes are centered around and act upon data structures that represent the evolving problem specification and the set of design alternatives under consideration.

Situation assessment procedures act on the problem specification to evolve it along multiple directions. Evaluation examines design alternatives, checking them against the current specification, to reveal inconsistencies, ambiguities, and incompletenesses in the specification that suggest new redescriptions. Evaluation also brings up new criteria, and constraints which are incorporated into the problem specification.

Elaboration procedures transform alternatives under consideration into new alternatives by applying a variety of adaptation and merging strategies. These strategies are typically suggested by the critique formed by an evaluation of some alternative. Elaboration procedures also augment alternatives with information derived about their consequences and expected behavior. These "data collection" elaborations are currently accomplished by manual augmentations of alternatives with experimental data, but in general can be achieved by case-based projection, simulation, actual experimentation, or visualization.

The evolving problem description is also used by both the retrieval and the assimilation processes. Retrieval interfaces with a library of cases which models, in part, long-term memory. The problem description is used as a probe into memory to pull relevant design cases into consideration (for evaluation, elaboration, etc.). The assimilation process is the dual of retrieval. It accumulates design alternatives proposed (i.e., those retrieved, elaborated, or viewed directly in the external environment) into the pool of design alternatives under consideration, organizing the alternatives with respect to each other.

The data structure holding the set of design alternatives forms an extension of the long-term memory. We call this extension the "problem context." The evolving problem description determines the focal vocabulary of the current problem context. As the specification evolves, the focus changes on the relevant vocabulary to be used for organizing alternatives in the memory (e.g., shape, construction cost, personal safety). In a sense, the problem context is providing a point of view with respect to which objects in the environment and cases recalled can be interpreted and organized by the assimilation process.

The coordination of the various processes is controlled by explicit strategic control mechanisms. There are a set of monitoring procedures, associated with each of the processes, which watch for opportunities for some task to be performed. The opportunities noticed are placed on an "opportunity agenda." Opportunities are chosen and pulled from the agenda by strategic control heuristics. For example, a monitor associated with the assimilation process watches for an alternative to be added that is much better than any other alternative proposed so far, with respect to some desired criterion. This yields an opportunity to change the problem description by increasing the priority of that criterion and/or by relaxing constraints that are not met by that proposal. This simulates the behavior of changing the relative importance among criteria to accommodate an unexpectedly good solution that is stumbled upon. An example strategic control heuristic would be to pursue elaboration opportunities for alternatives that satisfy a desired criteria extremely well before pursuing evaluative processes that would negatively critique the alternatives. This simulates the behavior of optimistically pursuing an idea, suspending all but constructive criticism.

Status, Limitations and Open Issues

Our system currently has implemented procedures for evaluation, assimilation, and retrieval, as well as data structures representing the case library, pool of design alternatives, evolving problem specification, and the opportunity agenda data structure. We have standard agenda management routines. However, these routines currently do not model the ephemeral nature of opportunities (which can either expire or be forgotten). Several monitors surrounding the assimilation process have been implemented, but we still need to define and capture those relevant to the other processes.

Much more work is needed to identify and define strategic control heuristics, situation assessment procedures, and elaboration techniques. Also, not all strategic control mechanisms are triggered by noticing an opportunity. Some may become applicable due to some complex condition that must be inferred through reflection. (For example, realizing that you are reasoning in circles might cause you to make an effort to try a brand new technique.) More research needs to focus on how to represent and infer these kinds of conditions and also how the application of these more reflective strategic control mechanisms can be interleaved with the triggering of opportunistic ones.

We are starting to understand how criteria, constraints, preferences, etc., emerge during evaluation, but more effort is needed in modeling this emergence.

There are a number of interesting open issues concerning how assimilation is managed when the design problem is complex, having several interacting subproblems, each of which have different sets of alternatives and requirements. Assimilation must find the appropriate problem context for interpreting and evaluating a given design alternative. The ability to do this facilitates the serendipitous recognition of solutions to pending problems, as we saw in the bending-springs problem. (See also Seifert et al. 1994.)

Another open issue is that the designers we studied were not expert mechanical engineers. An interesting empirical question is: would experts, having knowledge of "design principles," behave differently?

It may not be the expert versus novice distinction, but how open-ended the problem is, that is important. After all, the students were familiar with and experienced in solving everyday mechanical problems using objects in their world. We believe that for open-ended, nonroutine problems, expert designers are likely to display the same sorts of behaviors as do our students.

Finally, there are some aspects of creative design that we have not yet explored. In particular, we would like to analyze more carefully the influences collaboration had on creativity in the design project. Our agenda-based model of opportunity management lends itself to simulating the exploration of several opportunities in parallel, and employing multiple control strategies at once. This will allow us to simulate these aspects of collaborative activity and use computational experiments to explore hypotheses about the role of collaboration in creative design.

Conclusion

Our intention in building our system is not to automate design, but to test our hypotheses about the cognition of creative design. We are trying to understand creative processes better, using a case-based cognitive model. As we increase our understanding (and in the process, push CBR technology), we will be able to answer the question how best to assist human designers.

This may include 1) aiding the formalization, reformulation, and refinement of specifications (Reubenstein and Waters 1991; Johnson, Benner, and Harris 1993), 2) bringing up evaluative issues (Domeshek and Kolodner 1993), 3) retrieving pending problem contexts to help recognize the applicability of solutions, or 4) proposing new control strategies.

We are taking a case-based approach to understanding creative design for two reasons. One is that many creative design activities are highly memory-intensive and rely on past design experiences, so case-based reasoning has much to offer in this study. The other is that we hope to make case-based systems themselves more creative. By using the paradigmatic tools CBR provides, we are starting to find computational models of the behaviors and processes we observed in our exploratory study. At the same time, our modeling attempts have deepened our understanding of case-based processes and memory issues and have suggested extensions that will yield more creative design systems in the future.

Acknowledgements

We appreciate the insightful discussions we have had with Terry Chandler, Eric Domeshek, Lucy Gibson, Todd Griffith, Kenneth Moorman, Nancy Nersessian, Ashwin Ram, and Mimi Recker. We would like to thank Otto Baskin, Jon Howard, and Malisa Sarntinoranont, for their invaluable cooperation. We also appreciate the insights and helpful comments of our anonymous reviewers.

This research was funded in part by National Science Foundation Grant No. IRI-8921256 and ONR Grant No. N00014-92-J-1234.

5 Retrieving Stories for Case-Based Teaching

Robin Burke and Alex Kass

Is case retrieval a quick, associative process or is it a strategic, inferential one? Case retrieval can be viewed as a simple process that gathers raw material for the rest of the case-based reasoning process to use (Waltz 1989). However, there are many uses for cases that require domain-specific retrieval reasoning driven by strategic considerations. We have been investigating strategic case retrieval for educational purposes by building a program, story producer for interactive learning (SPIEL), to approximate what an instructor does in recalling a pedagogically-appropriate story to tell to a student.

Tutorial storytelling involves using stories in a variety of educational roles. They can project possible results of students' actions, provide counter-examples, and give suggestions, to name just a few possibilities. This chapter describes in detail three of the retrieval strategies that are used to produce SPIEL's storytelling behavior. Each involves a comparison between a story and the situation in which it might be told, a comparison that differs according to the needs of the educational context. SPIEL's retrieval strategies select different subsets of features from a story's index and use a variety of measurements of fitness including similarity, dissimilarity and other kinds of relations.

What SPIEL Does

SPIEL is designed to assist students who are learning social skills. It is embedded in an intelligent learning-by-doing architecture called guided social simulation (GuSS). GuSS provides a social simulation in which students can safely practice social skills, such as those required by diplomacy or business. This architecture was used to develop an application, YELLO, for teaching account executives the fine points of selling yellow pages advertising. The goal in YELLO, and other GuSS applications, is to accomplish for the social environment what the flight simulator accomplishes for the physical environment of the cockpit, letting the student learn by doing. For more about GuSS and its precursor ESS, see Blevis and Kass (1991), Kass and Blevis (1991), and Kass et al. (1993).

Within GuSS, SPIEL is like an experienced instructor watching over the student's shoulder. It monitors the simulation and presents stories from its library when they are relevant to the student's situation. Telling stories in the context of simulation is a particularly useful way to connect the student with an expert's experience. Stories help bring the simulation to life, and the student's activity in the simulation helps make the stories comprehensible. SPIEL's stories are video clips of practitioners telling anecdotes about their own on-the-job experiences. SPIEL's knowledge of its stories comes from manually-constructed indices entered into the system to describe each story. The system currently has about 180 such stories gathered from interviews with account executives experienced in yellow pages sales.

IR, CBR, and Case-Based Teaching

SPIEL's task is a kind of information retrieval (IR) task, but it is not one that fits comfortably within the classical model of information retrieval (Salton and McGill, 1983) because in the classical model the computer system is too passive. In the standard model of IR, the computer responds to well-formulated retrieval requests issued by a user. This model is appropriate only when intended users can be expected understand their information needs well enough to initiate requests at appropriate times and to formulate those requests correctly. Experts may sometimes understand their information needs well enough to fit this model, but nonexperts learning a new, complex task rarely do. Systems intended to teach students to perform a complex task must, therefore, be more than passive data retrievers. They must be able to initiate retrieval and formulate retrieval requests automatically.

Active retrieval, including automatic formation of retrieval cues, has been investigated extensively in the context of case-based reasoning (CBR) research (Kolodner 1993). For instance, a case-based planner, such as CHEF (Hammond 1989c) attempts to solve new problems by retrieving and adapting stored plans, and must be able to extract features of new problems and use those features to retrieve a suitable plan from its library.

GuSS is an implementation of the *case-based teaching architecture* (Schank 1990a, Edelson 1993, Burke 1993). This architecture is a framework for building computer-based learning environments that present cases (such as experts' stories) to a student who is engaged in a complex task within a computer environment. Case-based teachers are not really case-based reasoners in the full sense, because they do not need to manipulate the internal content of their cases; they just need to retrieve and present them at appropriate times. However, case-based teachers and case-based reasoners have in common the need to initiate the retrieval process and form retrieval cues. Case-based teachers are a good platform from which to study the retrieval problem because they isolate retrieval from the other hard CBR problems, such as evaluation and adaptation.

The need for precision in educational case retrieval demands a system that understands the uses to which retrieved material will be put. In other words, just as an effective plan retriever must be based on a theory of goals and planning, an effective retriever of tutorial cases must be based on a theory of the educational purposes that the retrieved cases can serve. Three types of theories are needed; our discussion of how SPIEL works will touch on each.

1. *A theory of indexing vocabulary:* Storing a story appropriately requires a representation language that can be used to form labels for each story. To be effective, indices must encode the educationally-significant features of stories.

2. *A theory of educational relevance:* Knowing when to tell a story requires a taxonomy of the different kinds of points that stories can be used to make. This taxonomy has implications for a theory of the features of stories that are important for making these kinds of points, and the features of a student's situation that are appropriateness conditions for making points.

3. *A theory of opportunity recognition:* Recognizing storytelling opportunities requires that the tutor infer high-level descriptions of the student's actions from a stream of low-level event descriptions. It must draw reasonable conclusions about what the student is trying to accomplish, and relate its observations to the contents of the story base.

A Case-Presentation Example

The following example illustrates the kind of interaction that SPIEL has with students using the YELLO program.

Student:	So, we're going to go ahead with the 1/4 page ad with color?
Customer:	OK.
Student:	Just sign right here.
Customer:	[signs]
Student:	I think the color is really going to attract people to your ad.
Customer:	I sure like the way it looks.
Student:	Ask your customers what they think. I'll bet you'll find its an attention-getter.
Customer:	See you next year.
Student:	See you. [leaves]

This is a sales success, but SPIEL has a cautionary story to tell. Every moment the student remains after the close of the sale gives the customer an opportunity to retract his buying decision. Although that did not happen here, it is a possibility that the student should be aware of. SPIEL intervenes in the following way: First, it signals to the student that it has a story available by sounding

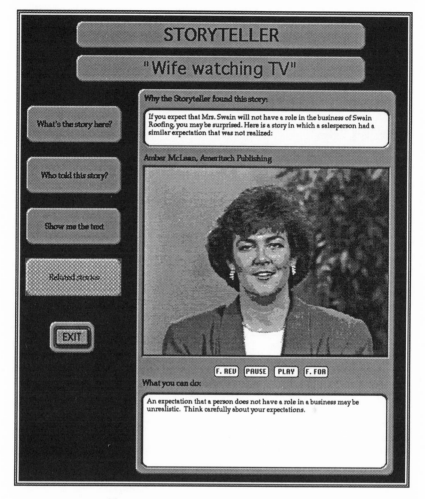

Figure 1. Presenting a story to the student.

a beep and presenting a one-line announcement, which we call the *headline*. Then, if the student expresses an interest in hearing the story (through a button press), the system presents some *bridge* text, which explains how the story is relevant to the student's current situation in the simulation. Next, the tutor shows a video in which an experienced salesperson relates a personal experience. Finally, the storyteller sums up the story in a *coda*, a brief block of text connecting connecting back to the simulation. Figure 1 shows what the GuSS screen looks like when the bridge, video, and coda are visible.

In this example, the intervention works as follows:

Headline: A story showing the risks of your approach.

Bridge: You kept talking to the client after the sale was closed. Nothing bad happened but here's a story in which doing that led to problems:

Transcript of video:

I was in the South Bend/Mishawaka area. This was my first or second year. I was calling on a swimming pool contractor. He had quarter page in South Bend. I was proposing a quarter page in another directory. It was sitting at his kitchen table. And the guy was hesitating; he didn't know... So, after a few more attempts, he says to me "OK, I'll go with the other quarter page." He bought it. I pushed the order form in front of him. He signed it. It's done.

As I'm putting my stuff together, I made this comment that cost me the quarter page. I said, as I'm packing up, "I'm sure that you're going to get a lot of phone calls from that new ad." He looked at me and he said, "You know, I don't need any more phone calls. I'll tell you what, let's not do that this year, maybe next." I talked myself out of a quarter page. I've never done it since. I walked out. There was nothing I could say. I had it and I lost it. All I had to say was "Thank you very much Joe. See you next year." But I didn't. I had to tell him about the calls, which I'd already done twenty times.[1]

Coda: Nothing bad happened to you because you kept talking to the client after the sale was closed, but sometimes the client changes his mind.

In this example, the storyteller augments the student's simulated experience in an important way. Without the "Talked Myself Out of a Sale" story, the student, who was successful, might never realize the risks inherent in remaining after the sale. The story arrives just at the time when it is most relevant, after the risk is past and the student thinks all went well, and it is exactly on point as a counterexample: it shows a situation in which the same tactic had an opposite outcome.

Story Retrieval Versus Case Retrieval

Educational tasks emphasize different requirements for case retrieval than most problem-solving tasks. Table 1 summarizes some of the most important differences in emphasis.

Cue Composition. One of the major differences between SPIEL and the standard problem-solving CBR model (Kolodner and Jona 1992) is the way retrieval cues are put together. CBR systems create a retrieval cue by analyzing a statement of the problem to be solved. SPIEL retrieves its stories based on a continuous stream of actions by the student and the GuSS simulation. Any event in the history of the interaction could be relevant to the retrieval of a

	Standard problem-solving	Story retrieval in SPIEL
Cue composition	Before retrieval	Incremental
Retrieval criteria	Solves a similar problem	Makes an educational point
Case structure	Represents problem solution	Video clip
Mandatory retrieval	Yes	No
Case evaluation	Yes	No
Between-case competition	Yes	No

Table 1. Differences between case retrieval in problem-solving CBR and story retrieval in SPIEL.

tutorial story. So, SPIEL has to build its retrieval cues incrementally throughout this on-going process.

Mandatory Retrieval. Any time a problem is posed, a case-based problem solver must retrieve something, otherwise there will be no basis for building a solution. If what is retrieved is not a directly-applicable solution, it can be adapted. However, in teaching, there are many student states for which there will be no appropriate story to tell. Because it cannot adapt its stories, SPIEL has to retrieve only closely-relevant ones. A story that is far afield from the student's immediate concerns will be confusing. If SPIEL cannot find a very good story, it is better off waiting for the student to do something else. Usually, there is an appropriate story about once every 10–20 student actions.

Case Evaluation. In the standard CBR model, the retrieval step uses indices to retrieve a set of candidate cases. The candidate cases themselves are then examined and evaluated, and the best case is chosen as the basis for a problem solution. The evaluation step enables the system to reject inappropriately retrieved cases. SPIEL has no language capacity with which to understand or evaluate the video clips it retrieves. It must retrieve conservatively, because whatever is retrieved will be presented to the student.

Between-Case Competition. Educational stories are not in competition to be the single right answer, as in many retrieval models, such as Thagard et al. (1990). If there are stories from experts with opposing viewpoints on the student's situation, SPIEL needs to show the student the whole range of opinion by making all retrieved stories available. These differences have consequences throughout the design of SPIEL, making the system quite different from case-based problem-solving systems and information retrieval systems. The most important consequences are in the areas of indexing, retrieval strategies, and retrieval implementation.

Indexing. Because SPIEL does not have access to the content of what it is retrieving, the index has to contain everything that the system will need to decide to tell the story. It needs indices that are more detailed and complex than those typically used in case retrieval.

Retrieval Strategies. There is an implicit theory of problem solving in the standard similarity metrics found in problem-solving CBR: the more similar the input problem is to the problem solved by the case, the more likely it is that the solutions will also be similar. SPIEL's retrieval strategies also embody a theory of good cases for the educational context. They involve different kinds of judgments from those found in similarity metrics.

Implementation: In SPIEL, a tutorial opportunity is defined as a situation for which there is a relevant story to tell. It does a storyteller no good to recognize a good time to tell a story it doesn't have. A similar insight was behind the design of ANON (Owens 1990), which used its case base to determine what features to search for in the input problem. SPIEL uses its story base in a similar way to guide the search of the events in the simulation.

The remainder of this chapter focuses primarily on retrieval strategies, but we touch briefly on the indexing and implementation issues to put the strategies in context.

Implementing Storytelling Strategies

One way to think about the problem an educational storyteller faces is to think of each story as a possible lesson and each strategy as a way to teach it. Storytelling strategies indicate the conditions under which the goal of telling a story can be achieved. Since a storyteller has many stories, any one of which could be relevant at any time, it is useful to think of it as an opportunistic system whose task is to recognize storytelling opportunities. However, educational storytelling is not as open-ended as the general case of opportunism whose complexities were laid out in Birnbaum (1986). SPIEL's storytelling strategies compare stories about an activity to specific contexts of student action. They seek coherence and relevance, not distant analogies. It is possible to describe concretely what an opportunity to tell a story using a particular strategy would look like.

SPIEL also has a strong advantage over the problem of opportunism in that it is embedded in a simulation. No truly novel actions can occur in GuSS since the student is constrained by the program's interface and the simulation operates in known ways. SPIEL knows with certainty what actions can and cannot happen in its world. SPIEL's problem of opportunism is therefore much simpler than the general one. The simulated world provides a limited space in which events can occur; storytelling strategies single out precise areas of the space that constitute opportunities. These properties enable SPIEL to use what Birnbaum calls the "elaborate and index" model of opportunism:

> ...spend some effort, when a goal is formed, to determine a number of situations in which it might be easily satisfied...and then index the goal in terms of all the features that might arise in such situations. (pg. 146)

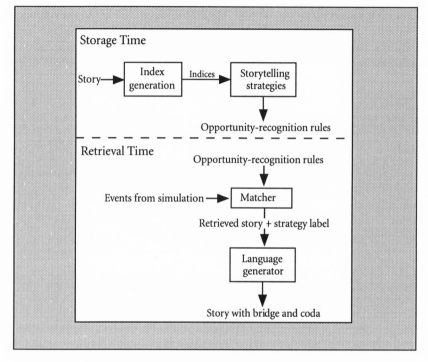

Figure 2. SPIEL's processing.

SPIEL works from its database of stories to determine what is an opportunity for intervention. Its processing can be divided into two phases: storage time, when new stories are put into the system and the system considers how it might tell them; and retrieval time, when a student interacts with the GuSS system and SPIEL watches for opportunities to give tutorial feedback. Figure 2 shows these phases.

At storage time:

1. Indices are attached manually to each story in the database.

2. SPIEL's storytelling strategies are applied to each index. If the strategy is applicable to the index, a set of rules is generated that will recognize an opportunity to tell that story using the storytelling strategy.

At retrieval time:

1. Opportunity-recognition rules are matched against the state of the simulation.

2. When the rules for a particular combination of story and strategy match successfully, the story is retrieved.

3. After retrieval, natural language bridge and coda are generated to integrate the story into the student's current context.

Indices for Educational Stories

SPIEL's indices are created manually. Since the stories are in video form, automatic processing would entail speech (and possibly gesture) recognition as well as natural language understanding. SPIEL's design therefore calls for a human indexer to watch each story being told and use an indexing tool to compose indices that capture interpretations of the story's meaning. Although the indices are complex, the development of interactive tools made it possible to reduce indexing time to under 2 minutes per story, not including the time required to watch each video (Burke 1993, Kedar, Burke and Kass 1994).

These interpretations have the general form, "x believed y, but actually z," which is a form of *anomaly*. An anomaly is a failure of expectation that requires explanation (Schank 1982) . Typically, anomalous occurrences are what make stories interesting and useful, and they are a natural way to summarize what a story is about. Anomalies are especially important in stories about social activity since students are learning what expectations they should have and how to address expectation failures.

The anomaly forms the core of SPIEL's indexing representation. Consider the story transcribed here whose index is shown in figure 3.

> I went to this auto glass place one time where I had the biggest surprise. I walked in; it was a big, burly man; he talked about auto glass. So we were working on a display ad for him.

> It was kind of a rinky-dink shop and there was a TV playing and a lady there watching the TV. It was a soap opera in the afternoon. I talked to the man a lot but yet the woman seemed to be listening, she was asking a couple of questions. She talked about the soap opera a little bit and about the weather.

> It turns out that after he and I worked on the ad, he gave it to her to approve. It turns out that after I brought it back to approve, she approved the actual dollar amount. He was there to tell me about the business, but his wife was there to hand over the check.

> So if I had ignored her or had not given her the time of day or the respect that she was deserved, I wouldn't have made that sale. It's important when you walk in, to really listen to everyone and to really pay attention to whatever is going on that you see.

The index contains (1) the anomaly in the story, which can be phrased as "the salesperson assumed the wife would have the role of housewife, but actually she was a business partner;" (2) the setting, the story's position within the overall social task, including a representation of the social relationships between the actors in the story, and (3) intentional chains surrounding and explaining the anomalous occurrences.

SPIEL's indices are considerably more complex than those typically found in case-based reasoning systems. The fact that SPIEL's cases are video clips is part

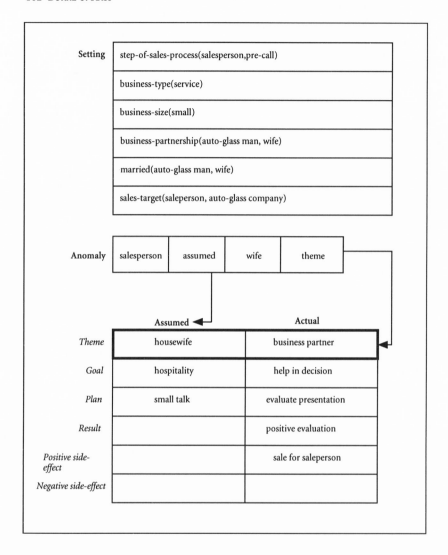

Figure 3. Index for "Wife watching TV" story.

of the reason. Its indices have to say everything that SPIEL needs to know about its stories since the stories themselves cannot be evaluated. Another reason that SPIEL's indices show complexity is the task of educational storytelling itself. SPIEL has a variety of reasons for telling stories, each of which requires a slightly different perspective on the index. SPIEL needs complex indices to meet the demands of a variety of strategies. The three strategies we describe next show some of these uses. The others can be found in Burke (1993).

The "Warn About Plan" Storytelling Strategy

A storytelling strategy is a way of using a story to teach. Consider the following situation, which shows the *warn about plan* strategy in action:

- The student doesn't gather very much information at the pre-call stage.
- Back at the office, the student prepares a very large ad campaign.
- When the student presents this to the client, the client says "You know, I really have to talk to Ed about this..." and is inwardly very doubtful of the value of such a large expenditure.

The student could lose a lot of time in a futile effort to make this sale. At this point, the storyteller intervenes with a story about an analogous situation where, instead of stalling, the customer rejected the ad program and rebuked the salesperson.

Headline:	A story about a failure in a situation similar to yours...
Bridge:	You made a recommendation that was much larger than Dave's expectations. Here is a story in which doing that led to problems:
Transcript of video:	
	I remember my first year 1970. I was on my first yellow page sales canvass. In those days, they didn't give you a lot of time to show ability and I wasn't doing very well. My manager told me that I had one week to start producing or they were going to let me go.
	I called on a graphic artist in Indianapolis. He had a 2HS, a one-inch ad. I walked in, asked two minor questions, and I laid down a quarter-page piece of spec in front of this man and told him he needed this ad. The man looked at me and he said, "Would you buy this ad?" He turned it right back to me. I didn't know what to say. It shocked me.
	Finally, I said, "No, I wouldn't." He didn't need a quarter page; a one-inch ad is what he needed. The gentleman proceeded to give it to me, up one side and down the other. He told me that I was there for my own greedy interests, trying to make commissions instead of taking care of his advertising and caring about him. He said, "If you're ever going to make it in this business, you'd better start paying attention to your customers."
	I walked out of that call a different salesman because I realized then that the only way to sell yellow pages is to sell what the customer needs, not what I need. Learning that lesson turned my sales career around. I started making sales, and by the end of the canvass, I was one of the top producers.
Coda:	You made a recommendation that is much larger than the client's expectations. That might not be a good idea.

Telling the story at this point is valuable because it helps the student identify the problem before going too far along in this direction. However, an accurate assessment of how far to let the student go would require a great deal of knowledge about the scenario the student is engaged in, more knowledge than is available to Spiel. GuSS's open-ended simulation design does not allow any quick read-out of what outcomes are likely and how far away the student is from obtaining them. Spiel would have to perform a complete envisionment of possible simulation outcomes to find out, more processing than can be accomplished in the midst of student interaction. Instead, Spiel uses prototypical knowledge about inconclusive outcomes. For Spiel to tell the "Would you buy this ad?" story in the example, it must know that overcoming the customer's stall in this kind of case is time-consuming and not particularly educational.

At storage time, each storytelling strategy selects stories that are compatible with its educational role. A story with a good outcome could not be sensibly used with *warn about plan,* for example. The second task of the storytelling strategy is to generate, for each compatible story, a *recognition condition description* (RCD), a representation that describes a situation in which the story could be told using the strategy, a tutorial opportunity provided by the story. Computing the RCD involves making inferences based on the story's index, essentially asking the question "What would have to happen for this story to be good to tell?" The answer to this question is different for every storytelling strategy. For *warn about plan,* the most important condition of relevance is that the student is pursuing a plan similar to the plan in the story. A second condition that makes it useful to tell a story to warn about a plan is when the feedback from the simulation itself that the plan is not working is subtle or delayed. If immediate feedback that a plan is likely to fail is available from the simulation, than telling a *warn about plan* story may be redundant, but if not, the story can make it much easier for the student to understand the risks of his or her actions. So the system looks for an inconclusive outcome which resulted from a plan similar to one in the story.

A description of the RCD that characterizes the tutorial opportunity in the example would therefore look something like this:

WHEN   the student is closing the sale and speaking to someone who is the
              decision maker,

LOOK FOR   the student to present a very large ad program,
              the client to have a negative belief about that program, and
              the client to defer the decision to another,
                 or the client to put the decision off to another time,

THEN TELL   "Would You Buy this Ad?"

AS   a "Warn about Plan" story.

This is the format of an RCD. It contains a trigger (the "when" part) that describes the conditions under which the opportunity becomes possible, usually a function of the stage of the sales process that the student is in, combined with characteristics of the other agents involved in that stage. If the triggering conditions are met, the system tries to gather evidence that similar intentions are at work in the simulation.

Warn about plan can also be used to show effects that would not appear within the scenario. For example, scare tactics may persuade a customer to buy once, but they hurt the client relationship and eventually result in lost business. This problem does not show up in YELLO since a scenario ends when the student makes one sale. A student who successfully uses this tactic in the simulation might think it is a good idea in general unless the storyteller can show an example to demonstrate otherwise.

Another use of the storytelling strategy is in the generation of the natural language texts that surround and explain the story. As shown above, there are three parts to the explanation: the headline, for the attention-getting initial statement; the bridge, the introductory paragraph explaining why the story has come up; and the coda, that closes the story presentation with a recommendation or evaluation. Each strategy has a set of natural language templates for these texts, which are filled in by generating appropriate phrases at retrieval time.

The "Demonstrate Risks" Storytelling Strategy

There is tremendous variability in the social world. Approaches that have always worked may fail in a new situation for no apparent reason; unlikely strategies may fortuitously succeed. Both in GuSS's simulator and in real life, the learner gets to see only one outcome at a time. One important role that real-world stories can play is to illustrate the range of real experience by presenting counterexamples that contrast with what is happening to the student. Studies of apprenticeship situations indicate that experts often use stories in exactly this way (Lave and Wenger 1991).

The *demonstrate risks* strategy shows that a successful result in the simulation is not always repeatable in the real world. Consider the situation described in the section "What SPIEL DOES," where the student closes a sale, but continues conversing with the customer. This is risky, since it gives the customer an opportunity to reconsider. To show the risk, SPIEL tells about a salesperson who lost a sale through a careless remark made after a sale was closed.

This strategy resembles *warn about plan* because it uses a story about a failure to warn the student. The difference is that the *warn about plan* strategy is used when the simulation is not likely to give immediate feedback about the student's actions. The *demonstrate risks* strategy looks for the simulation giving feedback, but of the wrong kind. It waits for the simulation to do something opposite from the outcome found in the story, and tells a story to show how the real world can be different from the simulation.

This approach to retrieving counterexamples differs from existing CBR systems that use contrasting examples, such as HYPO (Ashley and Rissland 1987a). HYPO retrieves cases based on similarity along certain dimensions and builds a structure, the claim lattice, of the retrieved cases, enabling it to identify contrasts along other dimensions. SPIEL uses its knowledge of contrasts in the retrieval process itself, so that it only retrieves those cases that make the needed educational point.

To arrive at the recognition condition description for such a tutorial opportunity, SPIEL must look for a result that would be opposite from what occurs in the story. The story described above showed a salesperson losing a sale during conversation after the close of a sale. SPIEL uses an opposite-finding inference mechanism to identify a outcome which is opposite from the one shown in the story. The story is a good counterexample if the student does a similar action, but does not lose anything.

The "Warn about Assumption" Strategy

Newcomers to a social domain may inappropriately transfer expectations from the rest of their social lives. A new salesperson may think, for example, that a friendly, talkative customer is more likely to buy than a "get down to business" type, when in many cases, the opposite is true. Since the indices used for stories incorporate the difference between a person's view of the world and how the world actually turned out to be, SPIEL is well poised to help students by pointing out their unrealistic expectations.

If the program has evidence that the student has a particular assumption, the *warn about assumption* strategy calls for it to tell a story about a time when a similar assumption was wrong. Suppose the student has an opportunity to gather information about a client's business from the client's spouse, but does not take that opportunity. It is reasonable to infer that the student assumes that the spouse does not have an important role in the business. SPIEL can tell the "Wife Watching TV" story at this point, showing a case where a similar assumption proved wrong.

We call this type of strategy a *perspective-oriented* strategy, because what is important is the contrasting perspective found in the story. Recognizing stories that are relevant in this way is more difficult than recognizing stories that contain similar actions. Perspective-oriented strategies need knowledge about how certain actions are characteristic indicators of the student's mental state. Students do not always act in ways that clearly indicate their beliefs, but if they do, the system should be prepared to respond.

In this story, the salesperson assumes, in an information-gathering context, that the client's spouse will not have a business role. If the system had to identify the student's preconceptions first, and then find lessons that address them, using perspective-oriented strategies would essentially amount to plan recognition, a difficult unsolved problem. However, the case-based teaching architecture involves a different approach. It already has the case, which tells it that this mistake about a customer's spouse is one that someone else has made before. It can look specifically for this faulty assumption because it knows it has a story to tell about it. This is consistent with a case-based view of letting prior experience guide the interpretation of new situations.

SPIEL works backwards from stories to the situations in which they might be relevant; it reasons from the source of interest (the possibly-faulty assumption) to determine what evidence would be needed in order to reasonably believe that the student will have that interest. The primary mechanism for this reasoning is what are called *manifestation rules,* rules that SPIEL uses to reason about the mental states it is trying to recognize. Manifestation rules let the system infer observable correlates of mental states that are likely to appear as the student acts in the simulated world. In this example, we are looking for an assumption that the spouse of the client will not have the role of business partner, which is a role critical for the formation of sales strategy, but instead to have the role of housewife, which is not important in sales strategy. How can this assumption be recognized? One possibility is that the student will specifically articulate an expected role for a person in the simulation. The student (if particularly sexist) might say something like: "Why don't we go into the next room, so your wife can continue fixing dinner?" This would be a pretty good indication that the student does not believe she has a role that is critical to the sales process. Another possibility is that the student fails to ask such questions of someone when given the opportunity, this is a good indication of an assumption on the student's part that there is no information to gather.

Here are three of the manifestation rules by which SPIEL reasons about the "Wife Watching TV" story:

IF   the expectation is that someone has role that is not critical to a particular stage of the sales call, a POSSIBLE MANIFESTATION is an exclusion of that person from the main activity of that stage.

IF   looking for an exclusion of a person from an activity, a POSSIBLE MANIFESTATION is a statement of the desire to exclude that person from the activity.

IF   looking for an exclusion of a person from an activity and that activity is the main activity for the context, a POSSIBLE MANIFESTATION is a failure to engage in the activity.

Storytelling strategy	Summary	Story is about:	Tutorial opportunity
Warn about plan	Tell a story about an unsuccessful plan when the student has begun executing a similar plan.	The negative outcome of a plan.	Look for similar setting, similar goal and similar plan. Look for a negative, but inconclusive outcome.
Demonstrate risks	Tell a story about a negative result of a particular plan when the student has just executed a similar plan but had success.	The negative outcome of a plan.	Look for similar setting, similar goal and similar plan. Look for an opposite outcome.
Warn about assumption	Tell a story about an erroneous assumption that someone made when the student appears to have made the same assumption.	An assumption that didn't hold.	Look for similar setting. Look for actions that are indicative of the assumption.

Table 2. Summary of the three storytelling strategies.

Conclusion

The three storytelling strategies described in this chapter and summarized in Table 2 show some of the demands that the task of educational storytelling places on a case retrieval system. The retriever must not only respond to crucial similarities between a story and the situation in which it is told, but also differences, such as opposite outcomes as called for by the *demonstrate risks* strategy, and evidential relations, used by *warn about assumption* and other perspective-oriented strategies that look for actions that indicate beliefs.

The design of SPIEL is a response to these demands. It uses structured, strategic comparisons between stories and the situations in which they are told. These retrieval strategies are an explicit counterpart to what is implicit in the similarity metrics used in standard problem-solving case retrieval: a theory of what cases are useful for the task. Extensions of the standard problem-solving paradigm (Kolodner 1989) and new applications for case-based reasoning technology, such as education, entail new notions of utility, and with them, new metrics that combine similarity judgments and other measures of fitness.

Putting such strategies to work need not render case retrieval prohibitively inefficient. Since strategies are implemented as procedures that operate at storage time, SPIEL performs a minimum of inference at retrieval time, yet still remains sensitive to the strategic considerations involved in recognizing tutorial opportunities.

Acknowledgments

GuSS is the product of many minds and efforts. The project prospered under the guidance of Roger Schank. Eli Blevis also provided leadership to a team that included Mark Ashba, Greg Downey, Debra Jenkins, Smadar Kedar, Jarret Knyal, Maria Leone, Charles Lewis, John Miller, Thomas Murray, Michelle Saunders, Jeannemarie Sierant, and Mary Williamson. The sales and sales training organizations of Ameritech Publishing have also contributed to this research in many ways.

This work is supported in part by the Defense Advanced Research Projects Agency, monitored by the Air Force Office of Scientific Research under contract F49620-88-C-0058 and the Office of Naval Research under contract N00014-90-J-4117, by ONR under contract N00014-J-1987, and by the AFOSR under contract AFOSR-89-0493.

Note

1. SPIEL's stories are videos taken from videotaped interviews with experienced yellow pages account executives. All transcriptions are by the authors.

6 Using Heuristic Search to Retrieve Cases that Support Arguments

Edwina L. Rissland, David B. Skalak, & M. Timur Friedman

Case-based reasoning (CBR) is often used in service of a task such as teaching, planning, design or argumentation. Part of the challenge in building CBR systems is to create a bridge between the superficial level at which cases can be input and the constraints of the ultimate task. A variety of useful techniques have been used to good advantage to provide case indexes that support the task at hand, including, among others, influence graphs (Sycara and Navinchandra 1991), explanation-based generalization (Barletta and Mark 1988), thematic abstractions (Owens 1988), and the declarative reification of task constraints (Ashley and Aleven 1991). We focus on the task of creating legal arguments, where the vocabulary of the constraints on an emerging argument is different from the indexing vocabulary immediately available for case retrieval. We propose best-first heuristic search of a case base as one tool for case retrieval in support of an application task such as legal argument.

To take an extreme (but real) example of vocabulary mis-match between a task and the immediately available cases and indices, suppose that the cases are full-text legal opinions and Boolean combinations of keywords are the only indices available. Further suppose the requirement of the argument is to supply a case that uses the opponent's best theory, so that one can distinguish the case from the current problem and thereby discredit application of the opponent's theory. The constraints of this task cannot be readily expressed in terms of the available indices: there is a mis-match between the indexing and the task vocabularies.[1] Barring revision of the indexing vocabulary or a reconceptualization of the domain, some search of the information resources may improve case retrieval.

Indexing and search present two extremes for retrieval. At one extreme, indices may function as database retrieval keys, and no search of the case memory need be done, only whatever minimal search is required to match the database key. Cases are pre-indexed to permit immediate retrievals. At the other extreme, search is relied on entirely. Through an evaluation function, spreading activation, planning, blind rummaging, or some other technique, the case space is searched for the desired cases. Search may be useful even in an apparently well-indexed case base, for example, if the domain is changing rapidly, or if cases need to be retrieved in ways not anticipated or enabled by the original indexing.

The approach in this chapter is to narrow the gap between an available indexing scheme and the requirements of argument through the use of best-first search guided by evaluation functions defined at various levels of abstraction. At the lowest level—the domain level—the evaluation function uses only information readily available from the indexing immediately provided by domain resource materials. At the highest level—the overall argument level—the evaluation uses information addressing the overall substance and quality of the argument. At an intermediate level—the argument piece level—the evaluation function uses information computable from the domain level but geared to the needs of the argument level.

In summary, our program BankXX incorporates a hybrid search-indexing approach that couples indexing with exploration of cases and other domain knowledge through best-first search in order to (1) address shortcomings in the indices inherent in superficial domain knowledge, and (2) increase the leverage obtainable from these existing indices.

In the next section we present a capsule summary of the approach to case-base search in BankXX. The following section describes knowledge representation in the BankXX system, including the structure of the case-domain graph, a graph of cases and other domain knowledge. Next, the search mechanisms used to retrieve cases are discussed. We then turn to experiments performed with each evaluation technique. A discussion of related research and a summary close the chapter.

Overview of the Search Model used by BankXX

BankXX creates an argument as a by-product of its best-first heuristic search of the case-domain graph informed by one of three evaluation functions. The argument is built incrementally as nodes are examined and mined for their contributions, which are collected, fit into argument components, and amalgamated into an argument. The critical aspects of the search model used by the system are summarized in figure 1 and described later in detail.

In general, state-space search is defined by a triple: *(initial state, set of operators on states, set of goal states)*. In best-first search, an evaluation function is also used to guide the exploration of the state space (Barr et al., 1981). The

Search States:	Set of nodes in a case-domain graph representing either a case at some level of abstraction or a legal theory.
Initial State:	(1) Problem situation or (2) user-specified node in the case-domain graph.
Operators on States:	Set of functions that trace a single link or a sequence of links in the case-domain graph. Here called *neighbor methods*.
Goal States:	None.
Termination Criteria:	(1) Empty open list, or (2) user-specified time bounds exceeded, or (3) user-specified space bounds exceeded.
Heuristic Evaluation:	Three linear evaluation functions at different levels of abstraction.

Figure 1. Critical aspects of the search model used by BankXX.

search performed by BankXX differs from the usual applications in two ways: the complexity of node expansions through the neighbor methods and the absence of well-defined goal states. Neighbor methods are described in the following section. We do not include goal states in our model because of the difficulties inherent in defining an "argument goal" in a way that is consistent with our informal understanding of how humans develop and evaluate legal arguments. In short, it is hard in general to say that an argument does or does not meet some plausible persuasive or rhetorical goal, or even that one has completed the supporting research.

Knowledge Representation in BankXX

BankXX's legal domain is an area of federal bankruptcy law dealing with the issue of "good faith" in proposing Chapter 13 bankruptcy plans. Chapter 13 provides that an individual debtor with regular income may present a plan to pay off debts over time. This plan is usually the focus of a Chapter 13 proceeding, which specifies, among other things, what debts are to be paid to what creditors, and to what extent partial payment will be accepted as full satisfaction of a financial obligation. When presented with a problem situation that describes a proposed plan, the debts at issue, and other features of the bankruptcy problem, BankXX provides argument support for or against approval of the plan.

However, this approach is applicable to complex, weak-theory domains that contain a highly interconnected base of cases and other knowledge. Part of our motivation for using search to build arguments is to find a general method applicable to weak-theory domains.

Case-Domain Graph

The primary knowledge representation structure of BankXX is the case-domain graph. Its nodes represent legal cases or legal theories, and the links represent connections between them. The case base is a subgraph of the case-domain graph.

Several paths to each case in BankXX's case memory may be traversed, because cases are embedded in a graph, rather than a discrimination tree (see, for example, Kolodner 1983b, and Turner 1988). Multiple paths to cases, found through the sequential application of distinct types of indices, provide several computational advantages: they (1) can be coupled with distinct representations of cases at different levels of granularity, (2) can help resolve typical retrieval problems, such as too few or too many cases retrieved, as described in detail in Rissland, Skalak, and Friedman (1993b), and (3) can increase the robustness of case retrieval in "real world" domains in which cases can be indexed incorrectly, since mis-indexing a case by one index does not make it inaccessible where other indices still provide a path.

Multiple Case Representations

Case nodes represent cases from each of four different points of view or levels of abstraction:

1. *Case as collection of facts*—a set of hierarchical frames capturing entry-level factual information.
2. *Case as vector of computed domain factor values*—a vector of values of factors (implemented as dimensions) computed on the facts of representation (1).
3. *Case as recurring prototypical story*—a script representing a general fact pattern or story.
4. *Case as a bundle of legal citations*—a typed list of citations.

The implementation currently contains 186 case nodes.

Theory nodes represent legal theories as a list of factors that are necessary for determining how a particular theory applies to a case. Not yet implemented, a legal theory node also specifies a way to combine the factors—for instance, a weighting scheme—to apply the theory. Legal theory nodes are linked by pointers that describe the relationships between legal theories, such as "overlaps with," "rejects," "is derived from," and "conflicts with." (See figure 2.) Legal theories have been culled from legal opinions

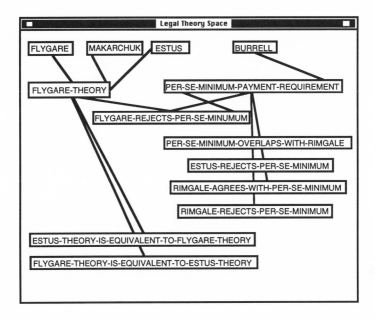

Figure 2. A small subgraph of the case-domain graph, showing inter-theory links and links from theories to cases.

by ourselves. The system contains 17 legal theories.

Nodes of like type are partitioned into subspaces of the case-domain graph, each of which uses a designated set of link types. For instance, in Citation-space, cases represented as citation-bundles are connected by citation links representing the stylized connections between a case and the cases that it cites or that cite it in various ways. The links in Citation-space are based on citation signals such as "see," "but see," and "compare," used in legal writing (Ashley and Rissland 1987b), and link types, such as "affirmed," "overturned," "distinguished," used in legal databases. See Rissland, Skalak, and Friedman (1993b) for a detailed description of the subspaces of the case-domain graph, including the legal theory space and the case spaces in which cases are represented as fact situations, domain factor vectors, prototypes, and citation-bundles.

Neighbor Methods

Neighbor methods use links in the case-domain graph to generate a list of potential nodes to examine in the search of the graph. Some neighbor methods follow pointers in a straightforward way. Others are similar to macro-operators that trace a sequence of actual links to reflect a new, virtual link.[2] For example, one simple method *(case-theory-neighbors)* gathers all the cases that have applied a theory. Neighbor methods used by BankXX include: *theory-cases-theory, theory-prototype, cited-by, case-theory, cites-case-theory, theory-theory, cites,* and *case-theory-theory-case.* These names can be interpreted as composite functions of graph nodes. For instance, the first can be thought of as the composite function *theory(case(legal-theory-node)):* find the theories applied by any of the cases that use the theory of the current node. (Cases may apply more than one theory.) BankXX has 12 neighbor methods. Some neighbor methods depend on the problem context, so that different nodes in the case-domain graph will be opened (discovered) for different problems.

Argument Data Structures

The Building Blocks of Argument: Argument Pieces. We have chosen a simple representation of an "argument" for this implementation. In this application, an argument is a collection of argument pieces, which represent fragments of arguments or pieces of legal knowledge that an advocate would ideally like to have to support his or her position. The argument pieces represent building blocks of argument. We recognize that this idealization of argument does not reflect the logical and rhetorical connections between the various pieces of an argument, or the complexity of argument in general (Rissland 1990). Our immediate goal is to gather the information necessary to support a complete argument. The 12 argument pieces currently used in BankXX are:

- cases decided for the current viewpoint
- best cases[3]
- leading cases
- cases sharing a large proportion of domain factors
- contrary cases decided for the opposing side
- contrary best cases for the opposing viewpoint
- family-resemblance
- prototypes[4]
- supporting citations
- applicable legal theories
- nearly applicable supporting legal theories
- the factual prototype story category of the case
- factor analysis of the current problem

Each argument piece contains a functional predicate that determines if a node can supply that useful piece of an argument. Argument pieces also contain an object slot to store entities that satisfy its predicate. BankXX builds up their content incrementally as its search proceeds, and the collection of argu-

SUPPORTING-CASES: (<MYERS> <SOTTER> <MEMPHIS>...)

SUPPORTING-BEST-CASES: (<SOTTER>)

LEADING-CASES: (<DEANS>)

DOMAIN-FACTOR-OVERLAP:
  (<AKIN-FACTOR-ANALYSIS-CGN-DOMAIN-FACTOR>)

CONTRARY-CASES: (<BAEZ> <ASHTON><CRUZ>
  <OKOREEH-BAAH> <DEANS> <ALI>)

CONTRARY-BEST-CASES: (<ALI>)

SUPPORTING-CITATIONS:
  (<SCHAITZ-CITES-RASMUSSEN-CGN-CITATION>
  <SCHAITZ-CITES-CALDWELL-CGN-CITATIONS>
  <SCHAITZ-CITES-RIMGALE-CGN-CITATIONS> ...)

APPLICABLE-SUPPORTING-THEORIES:
  (<KITCHENS-KULL-THEORY-CGN-LEGAL-THEORY>
  <OLD-BANKRUPTCY-ACT-GOOD-FAITH-DEFINITION>
  <MEMPHIS-THEORY-CGN-LEGAL-THEORY>)

NEARLY-APPLICABLE-SUPPORTING-THEORIES: NIL

FACTUAL-PROTOTYPE-STORY: NIL

DIMENSIONAL-ANALYSIS-CURRENT-PROBLEM:
  <CHURA-FACTOR-ANALYSIS>

FAMILY-RESEMBLANCE-PROTOTYPE: NIL

*Figure 3. Example of partially instantiated argument pieces produced by
BankXX for In re Chura, 33 B.R. 558 (Bkrtcy. 1983).
"CGN" means Case-domain Graph Node.*

ment pieces is output at the conclusion of BankXX's processing (figure 3). There is no argument text generation facility within BankXX, however.

Evaluating Arguments: Argument Dimensions. Just as cases may be indexed and compared on the basis of domain factors or HYPO-style "dimensions" (Rissland, Valcarce and Ashley 1984, Ashley 1990), so arguments may be evaluated on the basis of argument factors that capture dimensions along which arguments may be compared and contrasted. In particular, the third type of evaluation function is based on these factors. They are also used to evaluate the "final" argument. BankXX currently uses 5 implemented argument dimensions:

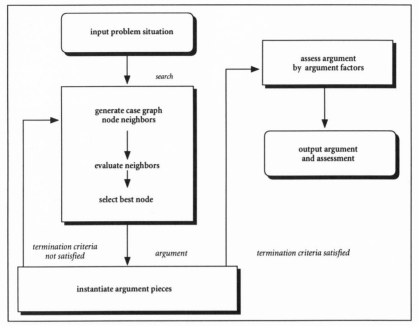

Figure 4. BankXX control flow diagram.

1. strength-of-best-case-analogies,
2. win-record-of-theory-for-factual-prototypes,
3. win-record-of-theory,
4. centrality-of-theory,
5. centrality-of-best-cases.

Space limitations prevent a complete description of these factors, but, for example, *strength-of-best-case-analogies* is based on the average number of legal factors common to the current problem and the best cases cited in the argument.

Indexing and Search in BankXX

In this section we discuss the operation of BankXX, and discuss in detail the three types of evaluation functions it uses to search the case base.

Control and Search Mechanisms

The control flow in BankXX is grounded in best-first search of the case-domain graph. The user specifies or the system selects a start node to begin the search. The system iterates through a loop: using the neighbor methods, compute the set of all nodes to which it is possible to move, evaluate each one of these opened nodes, select the open node with the highest evaluation function, and attempt to use that best node in all the relevant argument pieces. This loop continues until a specified time limit is exceeded, a user-specified number of nodes have been opened or until the open list is empty. At the conclusion of the run, the argument pieces are collected into an argument that is assessed with respect to the argument factors. The instantiated argument pieces and the evaluation by argument dimensions are output. See figure 3.

Best-first Search of Case Knowledge for Argument Generation

We have experimented with three types of evaluation functions that differ in the level of abstraction each uses to evaluate nodes in the case-domain graph. All the evaluation functions are simple linear functions of the form $\sum w_i f_i(c, *)$ where w_i are scalar weights and the f_i are scalar-valued functions of the current node c. The asterisk (*) denotes that the f_i may take additional functional arguments, described below. Since our focus is on the degree of abstraction of the terms of the evaluation function, the weights are arbitrary integers in [0, 10], except that higher weights are associated with terms involving legal theories.

The three evaluation functions applied can be analogized to those used in game-playing. By analogy, the first uses empirical game board features, such as the location of each type of piece. The second uses intermediate-level features, such as the "center-control" or "piece advantage" found in Samuel (1967). The third assesses the overall quality of a completed game.

Approach 1: Evaluation at the Domain Level

In approach 1, search is guided by an evaluation function that evaluates case-domain graph nodes according to their general potential for providing information of a type known to be useful in argument. For instance, a citation-bundle node can contribute case citations, a legal theory node contributes a legal theory. This *node-type evaluation function* looks only to the type of a node—cases as facts, cases as computed domain factors, cases as citation-bundles, cases as factual prototypes, and legal theories—that is being evaluated.

The form of the node-type evaluation function is:

$$w_1 \ type\text{-}pred_1(c) + w_2 \ type\text{-}pred_2(c) + \ldots + w_n \ type\text{-}pred_n(c)$$

In the evaluation function of approach 1, each *type-pred$_i$* is a function computed on features of the current case-domain graph node c. These functions are currently implemented as characteristic functions that return 1 if the domain node is of a certain class, such as a citation-bundle graph node, and 0 otherwise. Since there are five types of case-domain nodes there are five terms in this evaluation function. For the work reported in this chapter, they

Argument Piece	Node-Type Evaluation Function	Argument Piece Evaluation Function	Argument Factor Evaluation Function
Supporting cases	5.3	3.0	9.2
Best cases	1.3	2.9	1.4
Leading cases	4.6	4.5	4.8
Overlapping factor cases	1.7	3.6	0
Contrary cases	5.4	3.0	8.3
Contrary best cases	1.2	2.1	1.4
Supporting citations	3.1	4.2	0.2
Applicable theories	1.9	1.9	0.3
Nearly applicable theories	0	0	0
Factual prototype story	0.6	0	0.2

Table 1. Average numbers of nodes that fill 10 argument pieces.

are weighted slightly to emphasize nodes representing legal theories.

The question asked of a node with this evaluation function is: "How well will this node contribute information of a *type* known to be useful to argument?" This evaluation does not check the current state of the argument—only whether a node has the potential to contribute information known to be useful to arguments in general. It can cause the system to ignore information valuable to an evolving argument, such as the prototypical story type of the problem if one has not been found, or to pursue information less valuable overall, such as additional on-point cases when there is already a surfeit of them.

Approach 2: Evaluation at the Argument Piece Level

In approach 2, search is guided by an evaluation function that evaluates nodes according to their contributions to the system's library of argument pieces. The question asked of a node with this *argument-piece evaluation function* is: "How well will this node contribute directly to instantiating the list of argument pieces?" This approach attends to progress on a wish list of argument desiderata represented by the argument pieces.

The form of the argument-piece evaluation function is:

$$w_1 \ arg\text{-}piece\text{-}pred_1(c,a) + w_2 \ arg\text{-}piece\text{-}pred_2(c,a) + \ldots + w_n \ arg\text{-}piece\text{-}pred_n(c,a)$$

Each *arg-piece-pred$_i$* is a two-place argument-piece predicate computed from features of the current node c and the current state of the argument a: if the *ith* argument piece can be instantiated by the current node and is not already filled, the predicate returns 1, and 0 otherwise. This intermediate-level evaluation function discourages BankXX from wasting computing resources through unnecessary bolstering of parts of the argument that are already established. It is more informed than approach 1 and attends to the overall evolving argument. BankXX currently uses 12 argument pieces, and thus

Argument Dimension	Node-Type Evaluation Function	Argument Piece Evaluation Function	Argument Factor Evaluation Function
Strength of best case analogies	0.2	0.3	0.2
Theory win record for prototype	0.1	0.1	0.03
Win record of theory	0.4	0.4	0.1
Centrality of theory	4.8	4.8	0.8
Centrality of best cases	0.1	0.1	0.2

Table 2.
Average values along each argument dimension for the arguments
created using each of the three evaluation functions,
computed over the 54 cases in the case base.

there are 12 terms in the evaluation function.

Approach 3: Evaluation at the Argument Dimension Level

Approach 3 carries this attention to the overall argument one step further by evaluating its quality. Overall quality is assessed with the use of argument dimensions: factors that address desirable aspects of an argument, such as centrality of the cases cited or the coverage of cases by a legal theory. The question asked of a node by the *argument-factor evaluation function* is: "How well will this node contribute to the overall quality of the argument?"

The form of the argument-factor evaluation function is:

$$w_1 \; arg\text{-}dim\text{-}fcn_1(c,a,a^*) + w_2 \; arg\text{-}dim\text{-}fcn_2(c,a,a^*) + \ldots + w_n \; arg\text{-}dim\text{-}fcn_n(c,a,a^*)$$

Each *arg-dim-fcn$_i$* is an argument dimension function that takes three arguments (c,a,a^*), where a^* is the argument that would result from incorporating the knowledge in node c into the current argument a. The argument dimension function *arg-dim-fcn$_i$* returns 1 if the current node c can improve the argument along argument dimension i, and 0 otherwise. BankXX currently employs five argument dimensions and thus there are five terms in this evaluation function. Currently, the weights emphasize legal theories in this function as well.

The search moves to a node only if the node has the potential to make a favorable argument dimension applicable or to improve the value of an already applicable argument dimension. In approach 3, the search may be thought of as being conducted in "argument space" in that the system evaluates states representing snapshots of a partially evolved argument as constituted by the partially instantiated argument pieces and argument dimensions.

BankXX Performance Using Various Evaluation Functions

In this section, we describe the system's performance under the three evaluation functions described in the previous section: node-type, argument-piece, and argument-factor functions. Our purpose is to compare the quality of the arguments generated using the three evaluation functions, measured in terms of both the argument pieces and the argument dimensions. The data given were collected by running each of the 54 cases in the case base as a new problem with a space resource limit of 30 visited nodes. In order to treat each case as presenting a new problem, all its links and any theories it promulgated were excised from the case-domain graph. The starting node was always the *Estus* case, the leading case in this area of the law.

Quantitative Comparison of Several Evaluation Functions

In Table 1, for each of 10 argument pieces, we give the average number of nodes BankXX found by the completion of its run.[5]

These preliminary data suggest that the argument-piece evaluation function engenders a somewhat more balanced argument than the other two, as expected. For instance, it caused retrieved cases to be spread more evenly over a variety of types, whereas the other two over-concentrate cases in supporting cases and contrary cases. For instance, the evaluation function based on argument dimensions retrieved cases at the expense of completing other argument pieces, such as applicable theories and supporting citations.[6]

Comparison of Arguments along Argument Dimensions

Arguments may be assessed for quality in a number of ways. For this experiment, we have used the argument dimensions to assess the quality of the argument ultimately generated for each case. For each of the three evaluation functions, Table 2 gives the average argument dimension values for the arguments created using that function. Thus the argument dimensions play two roles: they drive the search in the argument dimensions evaluation function, but are used to assess the final quality of the argument for each of the evaluation functions used.

It may be surprising that the evaluation function based on argument dimensions performed somewhat less well overall than the other two functions. We speculate that the argument dimensions may be too abstract to be used alone to drive the search. Intuitively, they may "flatten" the search space and fail to grade adequately the potential utility of a node for argument. The node-type and argument-piece evaluation functions performed comparably according to the argument dimensions. In future research we plan to extend the set of argument dimensions to capture more and subtler aspects of argument quality.

That no one level of evaluation stands out as best is consistent with the complexity of argument generation, which, we argue, requires that control decisions take various levels of constraints into account simultaneously (Skalak and Rissland 1992). While these statistics represent average results, a comparison of an argument created by BankXX with an actual judicial opinion is given in Rissland, Skalak, and Friedman (1993a).

Related Research

Other retrieval systems have organized case memory as a graph and permit multiple paths to a case. Kolodner's CYRUS (1983b) is perhaps the best classical example of a multiply-indexed case memory. Turner's MEDIC program (1988) incorporates several different types of knowledge structures in a case memory of linked discrimination nets, which allow multiple paths to diagnostic schemata. The PROTOS program (Bareiss 1989a) uses a fixed strategy for classification that takes advantage of three kinds of indexing knowledge: reminding, prototypicality and feature differences. The measure of prototypicality of an exemplar is incrementally learned by PROTOS on the basis of expert user feedback. Rose and Belew (1991) have created a hybrid symbolic and sub-symbolic system, SCALIR, that uses a variety of inter-case links that are known a priori (including Shepard's citation links) and applies West's key number taxonomy as citation links in a network. However, SCALIR applies a spreading numerical activation algorithm to search the network, rather than heuristic best-first search. Direct memory access parsing (DMAP, Martin, 1993) is a case-based architecture that uses a semantic network of case frames that is searched via a marker-passing algorithm to instantiate frames that are expected in the problem context. However, none of these systems uses the constraints of argument formation—incorporated into a classical heuristic evaluation function—to drive the search of the case base.

Search has been applied in at least two systems to create arguments or to perform parts of the argument generation task (Bhatnagar 1989 and Branting 1991a). Bhatnagar's algorithm involves search of a hypergraph using A* search, but depends on the determination of probability of the truth of a proposition in a potential model. Branting's GREBE uses A* search to do case matching preparatory to making an argument in the area of worker's compensation law.

The problem orientation of research into "case-based search"—how previous solution paths prune a search space (Bradtke and Lehnert 1988, Ruby and Kibler 1988)—is to be contrasted with this project's research orientation. These reported experiments with case-based search used case retrieval to guide search for a prototypical search problem, the 8-puzzle. This project investigates the "complementary" task: how to use search to guide case retrieval in a general case-based problem setting.

Other systems have made use of "utility" or "cost" functions in case search and retrieval. Sycara's PERSUADER (1987) is a CBR system that created arguments in the domain of labor negotiation by searching a belief structure, which is a graph of the "persuadee's" goals and subgoals and their utilities. Veloso and Carbonell (1991) have studied how to balance the relative costs of search and case retrieval in a hybrid architecture combining a search-based planner with an analogical reasoner.

Summary

In this chapter we have discussed how case retrieval may be performed using heuristic search of a knowledge base that uses a variety of indices and interconnections. Preliminary experiments with our BankXX system show that the paradigm of best-first heuristic search can be profitably employed in a case-based argument generation system, and that evaluation functions can help bridge the gap between simple low-level domain indices and complex higher level argument considerations. We are continuing to study the level of abstraction appropriate for the heuristic evaluation of case and domain information as well as the problem of argument evaluation.

Acknowledgments

This work was supported in part by the National Science Foundation, under grant IRI-890841, and the Air Force Office of Scientific Research under contract 90-0359.

Notes

1. An analogous vocabulary gap between instances and their generalizations has been noted by Porter, Bareiss, and Holte (1990).

2. Thus the branching factor of the search space is actually greater than the branching factor of the static case-domain graph consisting of the case nodes, legal theory nodes, and link edges.

3. Based on the definition of best case used in HYPO (Ashley 1990).

4. The cases decided with the desired viewpoint that have the greatest family resemblance to the given case.

5. We do not provide data for two argument pieces: the *factor-analysis-of-the-current-problem* piece was computed for each case, thus making its value uniformly 1, and the *family-resemblance-prototype* piece is being revised.

6. It also retrieved no cases with significant domain factor overlap simply because no implemented argument dimension addresses cases that are somewhat similar to the current problem but that are not "best" cases.

7 A Case-Based Approach to Knowledge Navigation

Kristian J. Hammond, Robin Burke, & Kathryn Schmitt

The Artificial Intelligence Laboratory at the University of Chicago has begun development of a new set of software agents designed to manage the flood of data colloquially called the "information superhighway." Our approach takes its lead from case-based technology (Hammond, 1989c; Hammond Seifert, 1993) in that we are building systems that emphasize the use of examples over explicit queries or questions for communicating with the user.

We propose to develop three sorts of systems: browsing systems (called FIND-ME systems), preference-based task organizers (called BUTLERS), and internet news group agents (called CORRESPONDENTS). All three types of agents are designed to help a user navigate through an information space and either find or construct responses to fit the user's needs.

Two features distinguish these systems. The first is that they are derived from the case-based ideas of using retrieve and adapt as the core problem solving model. The second is that they use existing archives and data-bases as resources to be "mined" on demand rather than as fodder for batch processors that learn new concepts or construct new knowledge bases independently of a user. This too draws from the case-based philosophy of waiting until a problem arises to solve it.

Our proposed efforts will investigate all three sorts of software agents. The focus of this proposal, however, will be on the FIND-ME systems and CORRESPONDENTS, the most developed of our projects.

Find-me Agents

The FIND-ME systems are designed to allow a user to navigate through a set of possible solutions or products that fit their needs. The class of problems addressed by the FIND-ME systems is best explained through an example:

You want to rent a video. In particular, you'd like something like *Back to the Future* which you've seen and liked. How do you go about finding something?

Do you want to see *Back to the Future II?* Do you want to see another Michael J. Fox movie? Do you want to see *Crocodile Dundee,* another movie about a person dropped into an unfamiliar setting? *Time After Time,* another time travel film? *Who Framed Roger Rabbit?,* another movie by the same director?

The goal of the FIND-ME project is to develop systems that deal with this sort of search problem. These problems relate to domains with the following features:

- There are many choices. (Approximately 20,000 in the video domain.)
- New elements cannot be generated by the system or the user. (The system cannot recommend a movie that doesn't yet exist.)
- The space is defined by a vocabulary of features that may not be accessible to the user. (How many people would know to describe *Back to the Future* as an instance of a "stranger in a strange land" theme?)
- The user discovers new examples in the course of his or her search. (New movies that the user hasn't seen are presented.)
- The user discovers the features that define the domain in the course of his or her search. (Figuring out that "buddy" films exist.)
- While they may not be able to articulate their own absolute constraints, users are able to comment on examples. (You may not know exactly how funny you want a movie to be, but you know that *To Kill a Mockingbird* doesn't match your preferences.)
- Person-to-person interaction within the domain takes the form of trading examples. (e.g., "If you liked *Back to the Future,* you're sure to like *Crocodile Dundee.*")

Many complex selection problems have these characteristics, such as, for example, personnel selection. It is difficult to specify completely what kind of person is right for a job, but it is easier to look at a person's resume and come up with a response such as "Give me someone like this, but with more leadership experience."

In order to cope with these task features, we take the approach in FIND-ME of always presenting examples and allowing the user to suggest changes, which then are used to retrieve further examples. The user never has to articulate exactly what he or she wants, but only has to comment on what is right (or wrong) with an example that they are looking at. Users move through the space by looking at examples and communicating their likes and dislikes to the system. The system responds by adjusting its search strategy. By working from examples we avoid the need for the user to have extensive prior knowledge about the domain in order to find what he or she wants in a database.

The Central Ideas

The FIND-ME projects are driven by three main concerns: *interface metaphors, reasoning through examples,* and the support of *non-hierarchical search.*

One of the core ideas of the FIND-ME systems is to develop user interfaces that are metaphorically linked to known artifacts. Just as the Macintosh® environment makes use of the desk-top metaphor, we have constructed interfaces that are analogs to existing artifacts that aid search within a domain. This allows users to have strong predictions about the effects of their own actions, reducing the explanatory burden on the systems. The overall goal is to provide users with a sense of where they are in the domain space and how they got there.

The aim is to protect the user from the fact that he or she is searching through an multi-dimensional feature space. Instead we present the user with a familiar artifact, such as a magazine or video store aisle, that has the added feature of being dynamic. This means that users can browse through an environment that stays stable with respect to what they have already seen, but is dynamic in that the next items are always those suggestions that the system believes the user wants.

The second major insight that we bring to knowledge navigation is that we can use the differences between a presented example and a user's target to formulate a description of the target itself, which is then used to access a knowledge base of further examples—an iterative process of exploring the space of examples. Rather than using the absolute features that define the space, we are far more concerned with giving users the ability to say, in essence, "Yes, but..." and change a feature with respect to an example.

Finally, we have designed the overall FIND-ME notion with an eye to avoiding hierarchical search of a space. We don't see the selection process as one of narrowing. Instead we see it as moving through a space of possibilities where any feature can be changed at any time. The danger in a truly open-ended search in a large, multi-dimensional space is that the user can easily become lost. To assist the user's search, FIND-ME systems have active clerks that constantly view a user's current preferences and suggest alternative tracks through the space that reflect the clerk's unique goal organization and retrieval strategies. For example, in our CAR NAVIGATOR, each class of cars has its own clerk that attempts to change the user's focus when a match within its class exceeds a fitness threshold. This allows users to break away from any tunnel vision that they might have because of either ignoring a feature in the space or simply not knowing how that feature has been constraining the search.

The Car Navigator

The most mature of our systems is the CAR NAVIGATOR, a FIND-ME system that allows users to explore the domain of new cars. The interface to the CAR NAV-

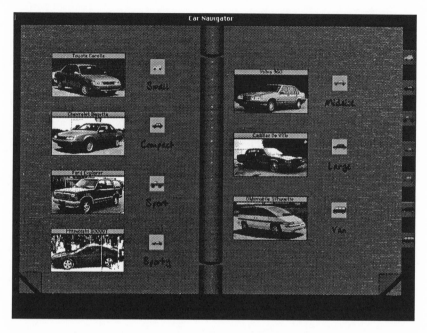

Figure 1: The first page of the "Car Navigator Magazine."

IGATOR is designed to resemble a car magazine. The initial page (See figure 1) is a table of contents, showing pictures of seven cars, each labeled by class (e.g., small, compact, midsize, large). There is an icon representing each of these classes next to the picture, and the same icons are used along the edges of the virtual magazine as tabs into the various sections of the magazine. The user can examine cars in any car class by clicking the tab with the icon of that class.

To start, the user selects a car class by clicking the picture of the car representing the desired car class. The page turns and the 5 most typical examples of that car class are displayed on the left page (See figure 2). On the right page the picture of the top-most car from the left side is repeated and underneath it is a collection of icons and controls. Each icon represents an attribute of a car, such as horsepower, price, or gas mileage.

A list of desired attributes representing the system's current understanding of the user's preferences is displayed to the right of the control. The user gets a feel for how well the displayed car matches his current preferences according to the color background of each feature. This color pattern is echoed in the color tabs on the cars remaining on the left page. The user can adjust his preferences at will and the resulting changes in degree of match are immediately reflected in the color fields.

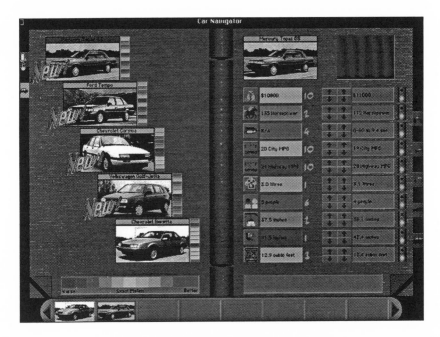

Figure 2: Browsing within the Car Navigator.

Often a user requests an attribute value that cannot be attained without altering one or more of the desired values for other attributes. This results in a "yellow light" coming on in the features linked to the one that has been changed, followed by a Quicktime movie containing an explanation. For example, if a user requests good gas mileage and then requests high horsepower the yellow light will come on next to the gas mileage and horsepower features. When this happens, a car salesman explains (via a Quicktime movie) that there is a trade-off between horsepower and gas mileage. The user will have to decrease either the desired level of fuel economy or the amount of horsepower he is requesting.

When users have set the preferences to their liking, they request the retrieval of a new set of cars by clicking the folded corner at the bottom of the right hand page, "turning the page" to reveal a new set of 5 cars, those that best fit the new preferences. Users' preferences may change enough to move them into a different car class. If a better match is found in a car class other than the current one, Car Navigator signals this fact with a yellow exclamation mark displayed over the tab with the icon representing the car class with the better match. Users can turn to this section to see the proposed alternative.

The ability to make small changes in the search criteria and see corresponding examples is useful in exploring local areas of the information space, but it does not work as well for making large jumps. If the user wants a car that is "sportier" than the one he is currently examining, this implies a number of changes to the feature set: larger engine, quicker acceleration, and a willingness to pay more, for example. For the most common such search strategies, CAR NAVIGATOR supplies four big buttons, located on the left-hand page: sportier, roomier, cheaper, and classier. Each button modifies the entire set of search criteria in one step, pushing the search in the direction that the user has indicated.

CAR NAVIGATOR uses a weighted-sum similarity metric for comparing cars. The values along each feature are grouped into qualitative classes: very quick acceleration, quick acceleration, etc. which are related in a semantic network. For each feature of each car, the distance between the user's desired feature and the corresponding one for the vehicle is computed, multiplied by the weight given to that feature in the search criteria, and summed. Preference is given to cars in the same class as the current example but the individual clerks light up class markers when a match is found in a different class.

While simple, the CAR NAVIGATOR approach would be useful for searching any space of examples defined by technical criteria, for example, in procurement. The user need only have general knowledge about the set of items and only an informal knowledge of his or her needs; he or she can rely on the system to know about the tradeoffs (yellow lights), category boundaries (red lights), and useful search strategies (big buttons).

Video Navigator

We have used our experience in building the CAR NAVIGATOR to begin work on a VIDEO NAVIGATOR that draws from a database on the order of 20,000 movies. In this domain, it is not possible for the system to have an internal representation of the entire database for manipulation. The VIDEO NAVIGATOR, therefore, is an intermediary between the user and a large movie database. Like the CAR NAVIGATOR, the VIDEO NAVIGATOR starts from a core of examples and the user communicates by noting differences. However, the features of movies are not as simple as the largely-numeric values manipulated in the CAR NAVIGATOR.

In the VIDEO NAVIGATOR we are continuing to develop the idea of clerks (see figure 3). The clerks in VIDEO NAVIGATOR each have specialized knowledge about different aspects of movies and specialized retrieval strategies for finding appropriate movies. For example, the clerk that specializes in knowledge of actors has a taxonomy of actor types and several strategies for finding similar actors, such as comparing actor types or looking for actors who have been in similar kinds of movies.

The user can browse in the film database by looking for standard search terms: actors, directors, movie titles. However, the clerks are continually

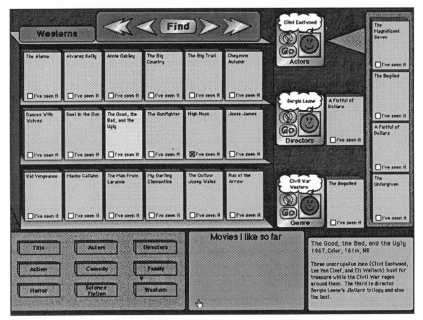

Figure 3: The Video Navigator and its various clerks.

monitoring the user's actions and making suggestions. For example, in figure 3, the actor clerk has observed the user's search for movies containing the actor Arnold Schwarzenegger and suggested another action hero: Bruce Willis. The user can take this suggestion (by clicking on the "Good idea!" button) or can ignore it. The clerk's suggestions help the user avoid a narrow search path; they bring in examples of movies that are relevant to the user's search, but that the user would not necessarily encounter if left unassisted.

The development of FIND-Me technology exemplified by VIDEO NAVIGATOR applies to a class of problems where selection must be made among examples whose specifications are complex and not fully specified. It would be difficult for a computer to look at a person's resume and decide if they have sufficient leadership experience for a particular task, any more than the computer can guess about what movie will be sufficiently funny, but the person doing the browsing can easily make such decisions. It is the job of various clerks to use their knowledge of the domain to take the user's feedback and search for suitable examples.

Browsing and Case-based Reasoning

We feel that browsing is an important application of case-based reasoning. People prefer to move about in information spaces in ways that are consonant with their own understanding of the domain (Ferguson et al. 1992). Standard database-style interfaces to large libraries are only acceptable when users are sufficiently knowledgeable to know the literal information recorded in the database: exact names, titles or numbers.

Most people's understanding of cars and movies (and other complex domains) is not so literal. We believe therefore that a browsing system should always make available a "reasonable next place to go," given where the user is now. In the CAR NAVIGATOR, the next place to go is provided by the ability to turn the page of magazine, and get a new collection of cars organized around one's current preferences. In the VIDEO NAVIGATOR, because the features of movies are complex and difficult to make explicit, we provide a host of clerks, each of which tries to find a reasonable next step for the user, based on its specialized knowledge.

Further, there is an interesting relationship between the "tweaking" in browsing and the notion of adaptation in standard CBR. In case-based planning systems that do adaptation, the modifications are done by the system in response to a failure or a gap between the goals of the user and the goals satisfied by some plan that the program has retrieved. The result is the creation of a new plan that was not previously in memory. In the sort of browsing systems that we are developing, the same sort of adaptation takes place, but the final product is not a new plan (or new movie, car, etc) but is instead a new prototype that the system can now use to construct indices into memory for an existing plan (or movie, car, etc.). The basic flow of retrieve and adapt is still in place, but their role is altered by the presence of the user and the fixed nature of the knowledge base.

Butlers

The second type of agent, BUTLERS, is designed to be expert at specific tasks that can be done using on-line information, such as figuring out where to get your muffler repaired, or what hotel to stay in, or where to have a business dinner. The idea is to build specific agents for each task and have them do the work of looking things up in on-line databases. BUTLERS are information intermediaries that are even more active than FIND-ME systems; they actively accumulate information relevant to their tasks from multiple sources.

For example, we propose to develop a restaurant BUTLER that uses knowledge of your personal tastes, where you last ate, who you are eating with, and what sort of dinner it is to search for a place that fits your desires, schedule, and budget. The BUTLER will use information from on-line guides such as the ZAGAT restaurant guide, its own city maps, and your personal schedule to figure out the time and place that suits your needs. In the end, we intend for the Butler to hand feedback back to the restaurant and even broadcast favorable or negative reviews to other BUTLERS, with the idea that this information can then be used by them to make better choices.

Our first step in developing this system will be to create a restaurant Butler that is accessed through a personal digital assistant (such as Apple's NEWTON®). The hand-held device will communicate with a central server, which in turn searches on-line information sources. Like the FIND-ME systems, much of the selection process will be based on the idea of the differences between current examples and the user's wants, a gentle way of coaxing out a user's preferences rather than forcing the user to compile an explicit query for every search.

Correspondents

In the early days of the Internet, news groups were simply public areas into which users could post messages. They have matured with the addition of moderators, archives, moderated databases, and frequently-asked-questions files. Our goal in building CORRESPONDENTS is to continue this development by adding intelligent agents that draw from this accumulated experience recorded by users.

At the core of correspondents are case-based retrieval systems that are like fully-automated FIND-ME systems. Correspondents read posted requests or problem descriptions, construct queries with which to search a case-library of possible answers or solutions, and post the answers they find.

FAQFinder

The first correspondent we propose to develop is FAQFINDER, an automated question-answering system that uses the files of "frequently-asked questions" (FAQs) associated with many USENET newsgroups. These files are compendiums of the accumulated wisdom of the newsgroup on topics that are of frequent interest. FAQFINDER will take a user's query on any topic, attempts to find the FAQ file most likely to yield an answer, searches within that file for similar questions, and returns the given answers.

The technology we intend to use to develop FAQFINDER is fairly simple (see figure 4) Given a user's question, the system selects the appropriate FAQ file, using a statistical IR package (Buckley 1985) applied to both the FAQ files and the compiled word listings from the new postings themselves.

Once an appropriate FAQ file has been identified, the matching of the user's question against the file is done using a parser that compares question templates and canonical semantic elements. The goal here is not to parse into an unambiguous meaning, but instead to parse into a rough representation that can be used to support matching. If a match is found, the matching question/answer pair is presented to the user. At every stage of this process, the user is given some control over disambiguation and selection of the final

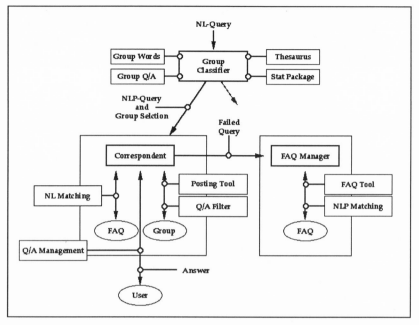

Figure 4. The Organization of FAQFINDER.

"answer." If no answer is found, the question is handed to a FAQ manager that posts the question to the newsgroup and incorporates the resulting answer(s) into the FAQ file.

While the FAQFinder program is in some sense a browser, our actual goal is to free users from doing any browsing at all. Rather than forcing users to traverse the knowledge space, we are providing active agents that will do this for them. A similar approach can be applied to the querying of other large textual information sources, such as procedure and documentation manuals.

The FAQFinder project is also interesting in that we intend to use not just the existing archives on the internet, but also the existing sociology. One of the more powerful aspects of the newsgroups is the desire on the collective part of the users to "get it right." This drive has already resulted in the FAQ files themselves, and we plan to extend this concept to the development of augmented FAQ files that extend beyond the range of the "most" frequently asked questions.

Cyber Chef

We also propose to develop a system called CYBER CHEF that is designed to read requests posted to the rec.food.recipes news group and respond with

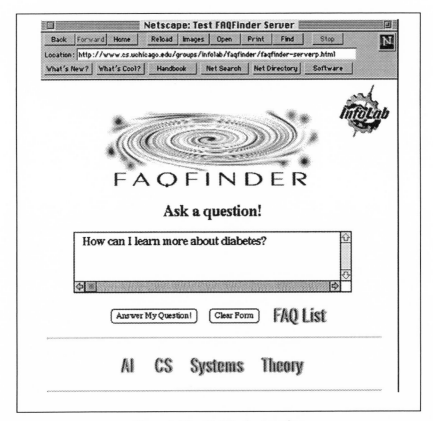

Figure 5: The FAQFinder interface.

recipes based on the newsgroup's own archive. CYBER CHEF is an extension of Hammond's original work on CHEF (Hammond 1986a), a case-based program which retrieved and modified recipes from a small case library to satisfy requests for particular dishes. CYBER CHEF will perform these same functions, but with a greatly expanded case library taken from various on-line recipe archives, and with input requests in natural language taken from the Usenet newsgroup rec.food.recipes.

The use of the case library in CYBER CHEF will differ somewhat from the original CHEF. The old CHEF's library was analogous to a real chef's personal memory of recipes that are known by heart; CYBER CHEF's case library is analogous to a shelf filled with cookbooks, which the chef is familiar with and knows how to find things in, but does not have completely memorized. Thus, in CHEF, recipes were stored in program-interpretable memory structures representing the ingredients and steps of the recipe, whereas CYBER CHEF's recipes are stored as raw text, annotated with program-interpretable indices. The text of the recipe will be interpreted and represented bit-by-bit when the recipe needs to be modified (as if the chef, having found the appropriate cookbook, were looking over the recipe to see what needed to be changed).

Ultimately, CYBER CHEF is intended to pull recipe requests from the newsgroup, retrieve and possibly modify recipes from the case library to satisfy the requests, and post the results back to the newsgroup. We intend the program to make use of email sent by newsgroup readers in response to the recipes—both as feedback to replace the original CHEF program's simulator feedback, and as additions to some of indices under which the recipe is stored.

Our current implementation deals with a scaled-down recipe library containing only recipes for sauces. It is capable of retrieving, but not modifying, recipes from this library, in response to natural-language requests. The program does not yet read or post to the newsgroup, although the input requests currently used for testing consist of the text of request postings from rec.food.recipes.

Like all of these systems, CYBER CHEF is making use of the core ideas of case-based reasoning in communication, case selection, and plan modification. The insight here is that examples serve to make problems concrete and give the user and the system a common context to refer to.

Conclusion

Our work to date with CAR NAVIGATOR and preliminary implementations of VIDEO NAVIGATOR leads us to believe that this approach is a natural way to help users search in complex and poorly-structured domains. It works best when users can easily evaluate examples, but have difficulty articulating the features they are interested in.

We propose to move from small, self-contained databases (as in CAR NAVIGATOR), to large unstructured collections, such as the submissions to USENET newsgroups. This scaling-up process involves some significant new challenges, such as the matching of natural language questions in FAQFINDER and the adaptation of only-partly understood recipes in CYBER CHEF.

8 Flexible Strategy Learning: Analogical Replay of Problem Solving Episodes

Manuela M. Veloso

The machine learning approaches to acquiring strategic knowledge typically start with a general problem solving engine and accumulate experience by analyzing its search episodes. The strategic or control knowledge acquired can take many forms, including macro-operators (Fikes and Nilsson 1971, Korf 1985), refined operational operators (DeJong and Mooney 1986, Mitchell, Keller, and Kedar-Cabelli 1986), generalized chunks of all decisions taken by the problem solver (Laird, Rosenbloom, and Newell 1986), explicit control rules that guide the selection of domain-level subgoals and operators (Minton 1988), annotated or validated final solutions (Hammond 1986, Mostow 1989, Kambhampati and Hendler 1992), or justified derivational traces of the decision making process during search, as presented in this chapter.

This chapter describes the integration of analogical reasoning into general problem solving as a method of learning at the strategy level to solve problems more effectively. The learned knowledge is acquired and used flexibly. Its construction results from a direct and simple explanation of the episodic situation, and it is proposed to be used also in situations where there is a partial match for the relevant parts of its applicability conditions.

The method is based on derivational analogy (Carbonell 1986) and it has been fully implemented within the PRODIGY planning and learning architecture, in PRODIGY/ANALOGY. It casts the strategy-level learning process as the automation of the complete cycle of constructing, storing, retrieving, and reusing problem solving experience (Veloso 1992).

In this chapter, I focus on presenting the learning techniques for the acquisition and reuse of problem solving episodes by analogical reasoning. The method is illustrated with examples, and empirical results are provided, showing that PRODIGY/ ANALOGY is amenable to scaling up both in terms of domain and problem complexity.

The contributions of this work include the demonstration of learning by analogy as a method for successfully transferring problem solving experience in partially matched new situations; and a flexible replay mechanism to merge (if needed) multiple similar episodes that jointly provide guidance for new problems. The method enables the learner to solve complex problems after being trained in solving simple problems.

Generation of Problem Solving Episodes

The purpose of solving problems by analogy is to reuse past experience to guide generation of solutions for new problems avoiding a completely new search effort. Transformational analogy and most CBR systems reuse past solutions by modifying *(tweaking)* the retrieved final solution as a function of the differences found between the source and the target problems. Derivational analogy instead is a *reconstructive* method by which *lines of reasoning* are transferred and adapted to a new problem (Carbonell 1986) as opposed to only the final solutions.

Automatic generation of the derivational episodes to be learned occurs by extending the base-level problem solver with the ability to examine its internal decision cycle, recording the justifications for each decision during its search process. I used NOLIMIT (Veloso 1989), the first nonlinear and complete problem solver of the PRODIGY planning and learning system, as the base-level problem solver.[1] Throughout this chapter, NOLIMIT refers to the base-level planner and PRODIGY/ANALOGY refers to the complete analogical reasoner with the capabilities to generate, store, retrieve, and replay problem solving episodes.

NOLIMIT's planning reasoning cycle involves several decisions, namely: the *goal* to select from the set of pending goals; the *operator* to choose to achieve a particular goal; the *bindings* to choose in order to instantiate the chosen operator; *applying* an operator whose preconditions are satisfied or continuing *subgoaling* on a still unachieved goal. PRODIGY/ ANALOGY extends NOLIMIT with the capability of recording the context in which the decisions are made. Figure 1 shows the skeleton of the decision nodes. We created a language for the slot values to capture the reasons that support the choices (Veloso and Carbonell 1993a).

There are mainly three different kinds of justifications: links among choices capturing the subgoaling structure (slots *precond-of* and *relevant-to*), records of explored failed alternatives (the *sibling-* slots), and pointers to any applied guidance (the *why-* slots). A stored problem solving episode consists of the successful solution trace augmented with these annotations, i.e., the derivational trace.

Goal Node	Chosen Op Node	Applied Op Node
:step	:step	:step
:sibling-goals	:sibling-ops	:sibling-goals
:sibling-appl-ops	:why-this-op	:sibling-appl-ops
:why-subgoal	:relevant-to	:why-apply
:why-this-goal		:why-this-op
:precond-of		:chosen-at

Figure 1. Justification record structure.
Nodes are instantiated at decision points during problem solving.
Each learned episode is a sequence of such justified nodes.

Example

I use examples from a logistics transportation domain introduced in (Veloso 1992). In this domain, packages are to be moved among different cities. Packages are carried within the same city in trucks and between cities in airplanes. At each city there are several locations, e.g., post offices and airports. The problems used in the examples are simple for the sake of a clear illustration of the learning process. Later in the chapter, I will comment briefly on the complexity of this domain and show empirical results where PRODIGY/ANALOGY was tested with complex problems.

Consider the problem illustrated in figure 2. In this problem there are two objects, *ob*4 and *ob*7, one truck *tr*9, and one airplane *p*11. There is one city *c*3 with a post office *p*3 and an airport *a*3. In the initial state, *ob*4 is at *p*3 and the goal is to have *ob*4 inside of *tr*9.

The solution to this problem is to drive the truck from the airport to the post office and then load the object.

There are two operators that are relevant for solving this problem. The operator *LOAD-TRUCK* specifies that an object can be loaded into a truck if the object and the truck are at the same location, and the operator *DRIVE-TRUCK* states that a truck can move freely between locations within the same city.

Figure 3 (a) shows the decision tree during the search for the solution. Nodes are numbered in the order in which the search space is expanded. The search is a sequence of goal choices followed by operator choices followed occasionally by applying operators to the planner's internal state when their preconditions are true in that state and the decision for immediate application is made.

This trace illustrates NoLimit handling multiple choices of how to instantiate operators. There are two instantiations of the operator *load-truck* that are

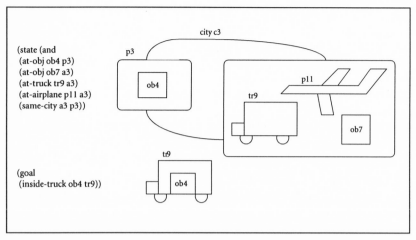

Figure 2: Example. The goal is to load one object into the truck. Initially the truck is not at the object's location.

relevant to the given goal, i.e., the instantiations *(load-truck ob4 tr9 p3)* and *(load-truck ob4 tr9 a3)* add the goal *(inside-truck ob4 tr9)*. An object can be loaded into a truck at both post office and airport locations. Node *n2* shows that the alternative of loading the truck at the airport *a3* is explored first. This leads to two failed paths. The solution is found after backtracking to the alternative child of node *n1*. Nodes *n8* through *n12* show the final sequence of successful decisions. Node *n8* shows the correct choice of loading the truck at the post office, where *ob4* is located. The solution corresponds to the two steps applied at nodes *n11* and *n12*: the truck *tr9* is driven from *a3* to *p3*, as chosen at node *n8* and then it is loaded with *ob4*.[2]

Figure 3 (b) shows the case generated from the problem solving episode shown in figure 3 (a). The entire search tree is not stored in the case, but only the decision nodes of the final successful path. The subgoaling structure and the record of the failures are annotated at these nodes. Each goal is a precondition of some operator and each operator is chosen and applied because it is relevant to some goal that needs to be achieved. The failed alternatives are stored with an attached reason of failure.

As an example, node *cn2* corresponds to the search tree node *n8*. This search node has a sibling alternative *n2* which was explored and failed. The failed subtree rooted at *n2* has two failure leaves, namely at *n6* and *n7*. These failure reasons are annotated at the case node *cn2*. At replay time these justifications are tested and may lead to an early pruning of alternatives and constrain possible instantiations.

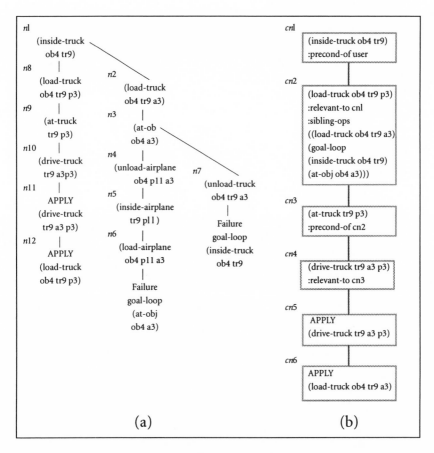

Figure 3. (a) The search tree to solve the problem in figure 2. The numbering of the nodes shows the search order.

(b) The corresponding learned problem solving episode to be stored (only a subset of the justifications is shown).

Flexible Replay of Multiple Guiding Cases

When a new problem is proposed, PRODIGY/ANALOGY retrieves from the case library one or more problem solving episodes that may partially cover the new problem solving situation. The system uses a similarity metric that weighs goal-relevant features (Veloso and Carbonell 1993c). In a nutshell, it selects a set of past cases that solved subsets of the new goal statement. The initial state is partially matched in the features that were relevant to solving these goals in the past. Each retrieved case provides guidance to a set of interacting goals from the new goal statement. At replay time, a guiding case is always consid-

1. Terminate if the goal is satisfied in the state.
2. Choose a step from the set of guiding cases or decide if there is need for additional problem solving work. If a failure is encountered, then backtrack and continue following the guiding cases at the appropriate steps.
3. If a goal from a past case is chosen, then
   3.1 Validate the goal justifications. If not validated, go to step 2.
   3.2 Create a new goal node; link it to the case node. Advance the case to its next decision step.
   3.3 Select the operator chosen in the case.
   3.4 Validate the operator and bindings choices. If not validated, base-level plan for the goal. Use justifications and record of failures to make a more informed new selection. Go to step 2.
   3.5 Link the new operator node to the case node. Advance the case to its next decision step.
   3.6 Go to step 2.
4. If an applicable operator from a past case is chosen, then
   4.1 Check if it can be applied also in the current state. If it cannot, go to step 2.
   4.2 Link the new applied operator node to the case node. Advance the case to its next decision step.
   4.3 Apply the operator.
   4.4 Go to step 1.

Table 1. The main flow of control of the replay procedure.

ered as a source of guidance, until all the goals it covers are achieved.

The general replay mechanism involves a complete interpretation of the justification structures annotated in the past cases in the context of the new problem to be solved. Equivalent choices are made when the transformed justifications hold. When that is not the situation, PRODIGY/ANALOGY plans for the new goals using its domain operators adding new steps to the solution or skipping unnecessary steps from the past cases. Table 1 shows the main flow of control of the replay algorithm.

The replay functionality transforms the planner, from a module that expensively generates possible operators to achieve the goals and searches through the space of alternatives generated, into a module that tests the validity of the choices proposed by past experience and follows equivalent search directions. The replay procedure provides the following benefits to the problem solving procedure as shown in the procedure of Table 1.

- Proposal and validation of choices versus generation and search of alternatives (steps 2, 3.1, 3.3, 3.4, and 4.1).

Past Cases	New Problem
(*goal* (inside airplane ob3 p15 (*relevant-state* (at-ob ob3 < ap3>) (at-airplane p15 a12))	(*goal* (inside-airplane ob3 p15 (inside-truck ob8 tr2)) (*initial-state* (inside-truck ob3 tr2) (at-truck tr2 p4) (at-airplane p15 a12) (at-obj ob8 p4))
(*goal* (inside-truck ob8 tr2)) (*relevant-state* (at-obj ob8 p4) (at-truck tr2 <ap7>))	

Figure 4. Instantiated past cases cover the new goal and partially match the new initial state. Some of the case variables are not bound by the match of the goals and state.

- Reduction of the branching factor—past failed alternatives are pruned by validating the failures recorded in the past cases (step 3.4); if backtracking is needed PRODIGY/ANALOGY backtracks also in the guiding cases through the links established at steps 3.2, 3.5 and 4.2 and uses information on failure to make more informed backtracking decisions.

- Subgoaling links identify the subparts of the case to replay—the steps that are not part of the active goals are skipped. The procedure to advance the cases, as called in steps 3.2, 3.5 and 4.2, ignores the goals that are not needed and their corresponding planning steps.

PRODIGY/ANALOGY constructs a new solution from a set of guiding cases if needed, and is not restricted to a single past case. Complex problems may be solved by resolving minor interactions among simpler past cases. However, following several cases poses an additional decision making step of choosing which case to pursue. We explored several strategies to merge the guidance from the set of similar cases. In the experiments from which we drew the empirical results presented in the next section, we used an exploratory merging strategy. Choices are made arbitrarily when there is no other guidance available. This strategy allows an innovative exploration of the space of possible solutions leading to opportunities to learn from new goal interactions or operator choices.

Example

Figure 4 shows a new problem and two past cases selected for replay. The cases are partially instantiated to match the new situation. Further instantiations occur while replaying.

Figure 5 shows the replay episode to generate a solution to the new problem. The new situation is shown at the right side of the figure and the two past guiding cases at the left.

The transfer occurs by interleaving the two guiding cases, performing any additional work needed to accomplish remaining subgoals, and skipping past work that does not need to be done. In particular, the case nodes $cn3'$ through $cn5'$ are not reused, as there is a truck already at the post office in the new problem. The nodes $n9$-14 correspond to unguided additional planning done in the new episode.³ At node $n7$, PRODIGY/ANALOGY prunes out an alternative operator, namely to load the truck at any airport, because of the recorded past failure at the guiding node $cn2'$. The recorded reason for that failure, namely a goal loop with the ($inside$-$truck\ ob8\ tr2$), is validated in the new situation, as that goal is in the current set of open goals, at node $n6$. Note that the two cases are merged using a bias to postpone additional planning needed. Different merges are possible.

Empirical Results

I ran and accumulated in the case library a set of 1,000 problems in the logistics transportation domain. In the experiments the problems are randomly generated with up to 20 goals and more than 100 literals in the initial state. The case library is accumulated incrementally while the system solves problems with an increasing number of goals.

The logistics transportation is a complex domain. In particular, there are multiple operator and bindings choices for each particular problem, and those choices increase considerably with the size or complexity of the problem. For example, for the goal of moving an object to an airport, the problem solver does not have direct information from the domain operators on whether it should move the object inside of a truck or an airplane. Objects can be unloaded at an airport from both of these carriers, but trucks move within the same city and airplanes across cities. So if the object must go to an airport within the same city where it is, it should be moved in a truck, otherwise it should be moved in an airplane. The specification of these constraints is embedded in the domain knowledge and not directly available. The city at which the object is located is not immediately known, as when the object is inside of a carrier or a building, its city location is specified indirectly. PRODIGY/ANALOGY provides guidance at these choices of operators and bindings through the successful and failed choices annotated in past similar problem solving episodes.

PRODIGY/ANALOGY increases the solvability horizon of the problem solving task: Many problems that NOLIMIT cannot solve within a reasonable time limit are solved by PRODIGY/ANALOGY within that limit. Figure 6 (a) plots the

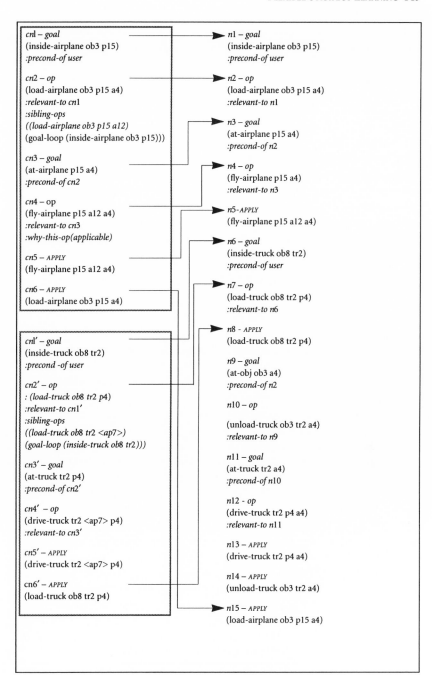

Figure 5. Derivational replay of multiple cases.

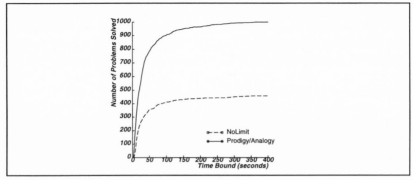

Figure 6. (a) Number of problems solved from a set of 1,000 problems
versus different running time bounds.
With a time limit of 350s NoLimit solves only 458 problems, while
Prodigy/Analogy solves the complete set of 1,000 problems.

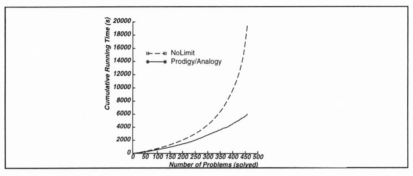

Figure 6. (b) Cumulative running times for the 458 problems
solved by both configurations.

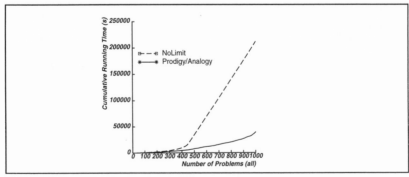

Figure 6. (c) Cumulative running times for all 1,000 problems. The problems
unsolved by NoLimit count as the maximum time limit given (350s).

number of problems solved by NOLIMIT and PRODIGY/ANALOGY for different CPU time bounds. NOLIMIT solves only 458 problems out of the 1,000 problems even when the search time limit is increased up to 350s.

Figure 6 shows a significant improvement achieved by solving problems by analogy with previously solved problems. Although not shown in the figure, the percentage of problems solved without analogy decreases rapidly with the complexity of the problems. The gradient of the increase in the performance of PRODIGY/ANALOGY over the base level NOLIMIT shows its large advantage when increasing the complexity of the problems to be solved.

In other previous work, comparisons between the performance of a problem solver before and after learning control knowledge were done by graphing the cumulative running times of the two systems over a set of problems. Figure 6 (b) shows the cumulative running time for the set of problems (458) that were both solved by both configurations. The graph shows a final factor of 3.6 cumulative speed up of PRODIGY/ANALOGY over the base NOLIMIT. (The maximum individual speed up was of a factor of approximately 40.) In figure 6 (c) this comparison is extended to account also for the unsolved problems (similarly to what was done in previous comparisons [Minton 1988]). For each unsolved problem, the running time bound is added.

I also compiled results on the length of the solutions generated by PRODIGY/ANALOGY and on the impact of the size of the case library in the retrieval time (Veloso 1992). I concluded that PRODIGY/ANALOGY produces solutions of equal or shorter length in 92 percent of the problems. PRODIGY/ANALOGY includes an indexing mechanism for the case library of learned problem solving episodes (Veloso and Carbonell 1993c). I verified that with this memory organization, the potential utility problem was reduced (or avoided) (Doorenbos and Veloso 1993): The retrieval time suffers no significant increase with the size of the case library.

Discussion and Related Work

PRODIGY's problem solving method is a combination of means-ends analysis, backward chaining, and state-space search. PRODIGY commits to particular choices of operators, bindings, and step orderings as its search process makes use of a uniquely specified state while planning (Fink and Veloso 1994). PRODIGY's learning opportunities are therefore directly related to the choices found by the problem solver in its state-space search. It is beyond the scope of this chapter to discuss what are the potential advantages or disadvantages of our problem solving search method in particular compared with other planners that search a plan space. Any system that treats planning and problem solving as a search process will make a series of commitments during search. The pattern of commitments made will produce greater efficiency in some kinds of domains and less in others (Stone, Veloso, and Blythe 1994).

The goal of strategy learning is precisely to automate the process of acquiring operational knowledge to improve the performance of a particular base-level problem solving reasoning strategy. Each particular problem solver may find different learning opportunities depending on its reasoning and searching strategies. However, the following aspects of this work may apply to other problem solvers: learning a chain of justified problem solving decisions as opposed to individual ones or final solutions; and flexibly replaying multiple complementary learned knowledge in similar situations as opposed to identical ones.

This work is related to other plan reuse work in the plan-space search paradigm, in particular Kambhampati and Hendler (1992). In that framework, it proved beneficial to reuse the final plans annotated with a validation structure that links the goals to the operators that achieve each goal. In PRODIGY/ANALOGY we learn and replay the planner's decision making process directly. The justification structures in the derivational traces also encompass the record of past failures in addition to the subgoaling links as in Mostow (1989), Blumenthal (1990), Kambhampati and Hendler (1992), and Bhansali and Harandi (1993). The derivational traces provide guidance for the choices that the problem solver faces while constructing solutions to similar problems. Adapted decisions can be interleaved and backtracked upon within the replay procedure.

Learning by analogy can also be related to other strategies to learn control knowledge. In particular analogical reasoning in PRODIGY can be seen as relaxing the restrictions to explanation-based approaches as developed in PRODIGY (Minton 1988, Etzioni 1993). Instead of requiring complete axiomatic domain knowledge to derive general rules of behavior for individual decisions, PRODIGY/ANALOGY compiles annotated traces of solved problems with little post processing. The learning effort is done incrementally on an "if-needed" basis at storage, retrieval, and adaptation time. The complete problem solving episode is interpreted as a global decision-making experience and independent subparts can be reused as a whole. PRODIGY/ANALOGY can replay partially matched learned experience increasing therefore the transfer of potentially over-specific learned knowledge.

Chunking in SOAR (Laird, Rosenbloom, and Newell 1986) also accumulates episodic global knowledge. However, the selection of applicable chunks is based on choosing the ones whose conditions match totally the active context. The chunking algorithm in SOAR can learn interactions among different problem spaces.

Analogical reasoning in PRODIGY/ANALOGY learns complete sequences of decisions as opposed to individual rules. Under this perspective analogical reasoning shares characteristics with learning macro-operators (Yang and Fisher 1992). Intermediate decisions corresponding to choices internal to each case can be bypassed or adapted when their justifications do not longer hold. Furthermore cases cover complete problem solving episodes and are not proposed at local decisions as search alternatives to one-step operators.

Conclusion

Reasoning by analogy in PRODIGY/ANALOGY consists of the flexible reuse of derivational traces of previously solved problems to guide the search for solutions to similar new problems The issues addressed in this chapter include the generation of problem solving cases for reuse, and the flexible replay of possibly multiple learned episodes in situations that partially match new ones. This chapter shows results that empirically validate the method and demonstrate that PRODIGY/ANALOGY is amenable to scaling up both in terms of domain and problem complexity.

Acknowledgements

Special thanks to Jaime Carbonell for his guidance, suggestions, and discussions on this work. Thanks also to Alicia Perez and the anonymous reviewers for their helpful comments on this chapter.

This research is sponsored by the Wright Laboratory, Aeronautical Systems Center, Air Force Materiel Command, USAF, and the Advanced Research Projects Agency (ARPA) under grant number F33615-93-1-1330. The views and conclusions contained in this chapter are those of the authors and should not be interpreted as necessarily representing the official policies or endorsements, either expressed or implied, of Wright Laboratory or the U.S. Government.

Notes

1. NoLIMIT was succeeded by the current planner, PRODIGY4.0 (Carbonell et al. 1992, Fink and Veloso 1994).

2. Note that domain-independent methods to try to reduce the search effort (Stone, Veloso, and Blythe 1994) in general do not capture domain specific control knowledge, which must be then acquired by learning.

3. Note that extra steps may be inserted at any point, interrupting and interleaving the past cases, and not just at the end of the cases.

9 Design à la Déjà Vu
Reducing the Adaptation Overhead

Barry Smyth and Mark T. Keane

In design and planning tasks, case-based reasoning systems typically replace a first-principles problem-solver with cases and knowledge-weak adaptation rules to modify these cases. The ultimate success of these systems rests on their ability to find a suitable case (or cases) to solve subsequent target problems. We believe that this success can be assured by using two novel techniques: hierarchical case-based reasoning with multiple case reuse in the context of an adaptation-guided retrieval method (see Smyth and Cunningham, 1992; Smyth and Keane, 1994, 1995a). In this chapter, we review these two techniques in the context of the Déjà Vu system for software design. The next section introduces the software plant-control domain used by the system. Later on we provide some empirical evidence to support our claims for these methods.

The Plant-Control Domain

The primary application domain of Déjà Vu is plant-control software design. Plant-control programs regulate the action of autonomous vehicles within real industrial environments. The examples in this chapter are taken from a steel-mill environment where a system of track-bound vehicles (called coil-cars) load and unload spools and coils of steel. Figure 1(a) illustrates a sample plant layout. Figure 1(b) depicts a schematic of a basic Load/Unload task involving a coil-car, a mill (tension-reel), a loading bay (skid), and a spool or coil of steel. In Load/Unload tasks coil-cars are used to load or unload spools or coils of steel to and from tension-reels and skids. Very briefly, these tasks involve complex sequences of actions whereby coil-cars are aligned with skids and tension-reels to pickup and release spools or coils.

Fortunately, Déjà Vu's software domain involves a high-level, target programming language in which operations are represented as nodes on a solution graph (see figure 2 for an example). This graph can be compiled by a

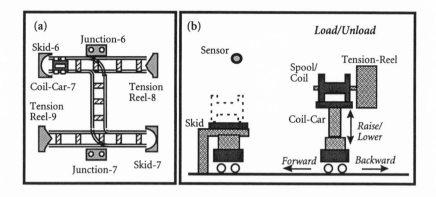

Figure 1. (a) Track layout; (b) Load/unload task schematic.

code generation system to produce machine executable code (Ono et al. 1988, Sakuri et al., 1990). The rectangular nodes correspond to primitive plant-control actions. The oval nodes correspond to sensor checks. The cross marks mean that program control cannot pass until both inputs have been complete (a logical AND). For example, the first cross mark of figure 2 indicates that the coil-car will not be slowed down until it has first been moving at its fast speed and it has reached a point 200 mm before the skid.

Hierarchical Case-Based Reasoning

A successful CBR system must be able to find suitable cases for presented target problems. Typically, this means that the system's case-base and adaptation rules should cover the target problems likely to arise (see Smyth and Keane 1995b). In complex tasks, like design, successful systems appear to have to use multiple cases (see Hanney et al 1995); perhaps because a system using single cases would require too large a case-base or very extensive adaptation knowledge. But, solving a problem by combining parts from multiple cases is non-trivial. Previous research suggests some directions. Redmond (1990) uses a case-base that is structured as a collection of *snippets* that map directly onto goal structures in target problems (see Veloso 1992) for a related idea for interacting goal structures). Déjà Vu achieves multiple case reuse by representing cases at multiple levels of abstraction. At the top of this hierarchy of cases, abstract cases are retrieved and adapted to provide high-level, skeletal, solutions to target problems. These solutions are further refined by retrieving and adapting more detailed cases. So, this *hierarchical CBR technique* (HCBR), composes a solution from different parts of multiple cases at various levels of

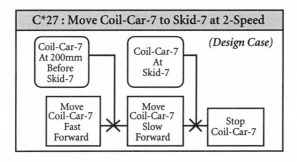

Figure 2. Example case solution

abstraction; see also Branting and Aha (1995) for a similar technique dealing with route-planning tasks.

Case Hierarchies

Déjà Vu's cases can be divided into two basic types, *design cases* and *decomposition cases*. Design cases correspond to what one would normally expect to find in the case-base of a software design system; they store actual software design solutions. In contrast, the solutions found in decomposition cases are abstract representations of a final software design. They are composed of abstract operators called *link descriptors*, instead of primitive plant-control software commands (see figure 3).

Collections of these cases are organized as abstraction hierarchies that, as a unit, correspond to complete, complex software designs. The solution of the root case of a hierarchy corresponds to the most abstract view of the problem represented by the cases in this hierarchy. The actual software design encoded by the hierarchy can be reconstructed from the individual solutions of each of the design cases located at the leaf (or terminal) nodes. Intermediate level cases store solutions at intermediate levels of design abstraction. The hierarchical linkages that join cases are not explicit. They emerge because the link descriptors found in abstract solutions can be viewed as case specifications as well as abstract solution operators. Thus a decomposition case can be viewed as a collection of sub-problems. The cases that are linked to a decomposition case are those that satisfy the requirements laid out in its link descriptors. By "satisfied," we mean a case that can be retrieved and adapted to meet the link descriptor requirements. Thus, exact matches between decomposition cases and more detailed cases are not strictly necessary. This enables hierarchies to share cases thereby reducing redundancy within the case-base.

Figure 3 sketches part of one particular case hierarchy. The hierarchy solves

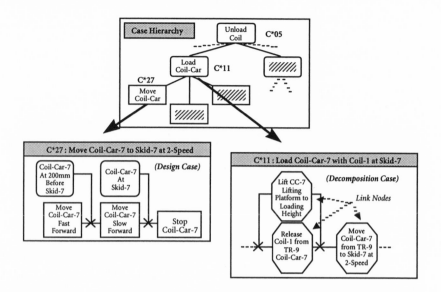

Figure 3. A portion of a sample case hierarchy.

an unload task; a coil-car must unload a coil of steel from the milling press (tension-reel) and deposit it on a skid. The complete solution is quite complex and is built up from many separate design cases. The inserts show the details of two of the cases (C*11 and C*27) in the hierarchy. The lower insert shows a design case (C*27) and the top insert shows a second level decomposition case (C*11). To accommodate abstract solutions the plant-control software language has been extended to allow for a new node type to represent link descriptors; these nodes are octagonal in the diagram. The C*11 insert shows three link descriptors, one of which (the "move" link) points to C*27; this means that if this "move" link descriptor is used as a specification then C*27 will be retrieved and adapted.

The Hierarchical CBR Procedure

The two critical stages in the hierarchical CBR algorithm are *decompose* and *integrate* (see figure 4; retrieve and adapt are described in the Adaptation-Guided Retrieval section of this chapter). Problem decomposition occurs as a natural consequence of retrieving and adapting abstract decomposition-cases. Decompose takes a newly adapted abstract solution and isolates each link descriptor as a separate sub-problem specification. Each of these is then added to the specification queue to be used later to retrieve and adapt a more detailed case. During *integration,* newly adapted solutions (whether abstract

```
Input:      TargetSpecification  -   Target Specification
            CB                   -   The Case-Base
            AKN                  -   The Adaptation Knowledge


Output:     TargetSolution       -   The Target Solution


HCBR(TargetSpecification,CB,AKN)
  SpecificationQueue := TargetSpecification
  Until Empty?(SpecificationQueue) Do
     CurrentSpecification:=First(SpecificationQueue)
     CurrentBase:=RETRIEVE(CurrentSpecification,CB,AKN)
     CurrentSolution:=ADAPT(CurrentSpecification,CurrentBase,AKN)
     If Abstract?(CurrentBase) then
       SpecificationQueue:=SpecificationQueue+DECOMPOSE(CurrentSolution)
     EndIf
     TargetSolution:=INTEGRATE(CurrentSpec.,CurrentSolution,TargetSolution)
  EndUntil
  Return(TargetSolution)
```

Figure 4. The hierarchical case-based reasoning procedure.

or concrete) are added to the target solution structure. In this way the target solution evolves hierarchically, from an initial abstract solution (the integration of the initial abstract case) to a collection of PC software solutions (as design cases are added).

Since decomposition cases can be adapted, it is possible to solve a target problem by reusing cases from a number of different case hierarchies. Déjà Vu is not restricted to using only those cases from one hierarchy, because the adapted link descriptors constitute altered sub-specifications that may cause the retrieval of cases from other hierarchies. This is entirely desirable and helps to significantly reduce the adaptation work that needs to be done during problem solving.

Returning to the previous example, we may retrieve C*11 (loading a coil onto a skid) when we want to load a coil onto a tension-reel. This means that the solution of C*11 will be adapted, so that for example the move link descriptor will specify the target tension-reel as the move destination instead of the base skid. It may then turn out that C*27 is no longer the best available case to solve the move sub-problem. A different case that is easier to adapt may be retrieved, saving on adaptation cost.

Adaptation-Guided Retrieval

As we said before, a successful CBR system must be able to find suitable cases for presented target problems. This places a large onus on the system's retrieval method to deliver the *correct* case from the case-base. Most CBR systems retrieve cases using semantic-similarity metrics, based on the assumption that similar cases will be the most useful and easiest to adapt to a target problem. However, this assumption can be unwarranted; the most similar case may not be the easiest to adapt and may even be impossible to adapt. Our solution to the putative inaccuracy of similarity-based retrieval is to integrate adaptation knowledge into the retrieval process. This novel technique, called *adaptation-guided retrieval* (AGR) assesses the adaptation requirements of cases during retrieval. AGR makes direct use of specially-formulated adaptation knowledge to determine simple surface-changes, structural transformations, and complex interactions (Smyth and Keane 1994). Furthermore, AGR works without incurring the full cost of adaptation during retrieval (in the next section we will show that it can even be more efficient than conventional methods).

The idea that retrieval should be sensitive to adaptation requirements has been mooted before (see Birnbaum et al. 1991, Fox and Leake 1995c, Goel 1989, Keane 1993, Kolodner 1989, Leake 1992a). Kolodner (1989) argues that some classes of matches, "easily-adapted" matches, should be preferred over "hard-to-adapt" matches during retrieval. Similarly, Goel's KRITIK system (Goel 1989) prefers candidate design-cases that satisfy the functional specifications of the target design and hence have easily-adaptable matches. Birnbaum, et al. (1991) proposed a system that learns to index cases on the basis of their adaptability, overriding semantic similarity where appropriate and Fox and Leake (1995c) have implemented just such a system. The difference between these techniques and adaptation-guided retrieval is that they all involve an across-the-board promotion (or demotion) of certain matches based on their likely rather than their actual ease-of-adaptation. They make an educated guess as to the adaptability of cases rather than a detailed assessment of their adaptation requirements. Adaptation-guided retrieval makes direct use of the system's adaptation knowledge during retrieval.

Déjà Vu's Adaptation Knowledge

Déjà Vu's adaptation component adapts candidate cases using two forms of knowledge: *adaptation specialists* to perform specific, local modifications to cases, and *adaptation strategies* to solve problematic interactions within cases.

Adaptation specialists correspond to packages of design transformation knowledge each concerned with a specific adaptation task. Each specialist can make specific, local modifications to a retrieved case. For instance, in the plant-control domain, retrieved "move" cases often differ from a target prob-

```
SPEED-SPECIALIST*1

Capability
    (:TASKS      Move)
    (:MAPPINGS   ((vehicle constraint-speed target-speed?)
                 (vehicle constraint-speed base-speed?)))
    (:TESTS      (= target-speed? 2-speed) (= base-speed? 1-speed))
Action
    (Insert-Command
        (def-command Move <vehicle> Fast <direction>)
    :BEFORE
        (def-command Move <vehicle> Slow <direction>))
    (Insert-Command
        (def-command Distance-Check
                     <vehicle> <slowing-distance>
                     <orientation> <destination>)
    :BEFORE
        (def-command Move <vehicle> Slow <direction>))
```

Figure 5. A speed specialist.

lem in the speed of the coil-car (one- or two-speed). So, Déjà Vu has a dedi-
cated speed specialist to modify the coil-car speed in retrieved cases to meet
the appropriate target specifications (see figure 5). Specialists contain two
parts: *capability*—information describing the nature of the adaptation task
(e.g., the specialist in figure 5 is designed to alter the speed constraint of a
movement task from 1-speed to 2-speed); and *action*—the procedural know-
how needed to perform a particular kind of adaptation (e.g., to upgrade the
speed of a case a number of additional solution nodes must be added to the
one-speed solution chart). In short, the capability information describes what
must be adapted and the action information describes how this adaptation
can be carried out. As we shall see, it is the capability information that allows
specialists to be used during retrieval. During adaptation many specialists
may act on the retrieved case to transform it into the desired target design.
Thus, through specialist activity, the differences between the retrieved case
and the target are reduced in a piecemeal fashion.

Adaptation strategies deal with interactions that arise during the adaptation of a case by the specialists. Specialists are local and therefore ignorant of
global interactions between case elements that may lead to problem-solving
failures; interactions cause problems in many planning and automated design
systems. Déjà Vu's adaptation strategies detect and repair different classes of
interactions that arise. The strategies are organized in terms of the interactions they resolve and each is indexed by a description of the type of failure it
can repair. Each strategy also has a set of repair methods for fixing a particular interaction.

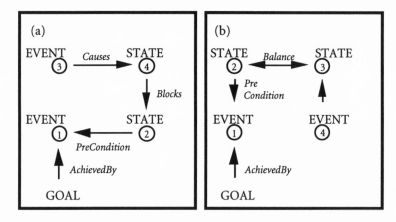

Figure 6. (a) Blocked-precondition; (b) Balance-interaction.

For example, one common interaction involves the effect of one event preventing the occurrence of a later event. Figure 6(a) depicts this situation; a
goal event (1) is prevented by the disablement of one of its preconditions (2),
the precondition having been blocked by some earlier event (3) causing a
conflicting state (4). This *blocked-precondition interaction* could occur when
the speed of a coil-car is increased (during adaptation), causing a power
availability problem that results in the coil-car running out of power (power
being a precondition of the movement goal). This interaction can be repaired
by adding an event before the blocking event (3) that prevents its blocking effect; for example recharging the coil-car before initiating the move. The
blocked pre-condition adaptation strategy contains a description of this situation along with appropriate repair methods.

Another type of interaction, a balance-interaction, can occur when the
value of one state is proportionally dependent on another (see figure 6(b)).
Here, some necessary goal-achieving event (1) has a precondition state (2)
that depends on another state (3) that has resulted from some other event
(4). For example, before moving a coil-car across the factory floor the height
of the carrying platform must be adjusted to accommodate the load being
transported; there is a balance condition between the height of the lifting
platform and the diameter of the coil of steel being carried. If this balance is
not properly maintained then a failure may occur (the coil-car may collide
with an overhead obstacle).

The system currently uses 4 strategies to deal with all the interaction problems that arise in the plant-control domain. Our investigations suggest that
many of these strategies are applicable to other domains, although other new
ones may also be required. For example, Hammond (1989d) uses similar strat-
egy-types in CHEF in the domain of Chinese cookery and recipe planning.

```
Input:      TargetSpecification    -    Target Specification
            CB                     -         The Case-Base
            AKN                    -    The Adaptation Knowledge
Output:     BaseCase               -    The most "adaptable" case
            AKN'                   -    Relevant Adaptation Knowledge


RETRIEVE(TargetSpecification,CB,AKN)

   Candidate Selection
     Eliminate cases that do not share any active specialists with the target


   Local Adaptability
     Align target features with case features (candidate mappings)


     Establish a mapping only if it is adaptable, i.e. if there is
     specialist connecting this target and case feature.
     Remove uncovered cases—where target features remain unmapped.
     Compute local adaptability of remaining cases (total specialist cost)

   Global Adaptability
     Collect active specialists over remaining cases.
     Compute case global adaptability (total strategy cost)
   Produce a final ordering of cases using local and global adaptability scores.
   Return the best case
```

Figure 7. The adaptation-guided retrieval procedure

The Adaptation-Guided Retrieval Procedure

Adaptation-guided retrieval involves three distinct processing steps (see figure 7): candidate selection, local adaptability assessment and global adaptability assessment.

Candidate selection is a base-filtering stage that quickly eliminates irrelevant cases from further consideration. Basically, it removes any cases which exhibit differences that cannot be dealt with by any specialists. This stage treats all adaptable features as equally relevant and simply locates cases that are potentially adaptable to the target situation.

Local adaptability assessment maps the target's features with those of the candidate cases. A feature mapping is only established if it is deemed adaptable, that is if there is a specialist to support the mapping. Briefly, a case is said to cover the target if some feature of the case can map on to each relevant feature of the target and if all of these mappings are adaptable. A local adaptability metric is applied to the remaining cases to estimate their ease of adaptation in terms of their applicable adaptation specialists.

Finally, during *global adaptability assessment,* the strategies that are applicable to each of the remaining candidates are determined and a second metric is used to grade these cases according to the different repair methods that are suggested by each strategy. Different strategies are differentially weighted according to the amount of change their repair methods incur. Some repair methods will significantly reorder a proposed solution whereas others may just require a deletion of an existing goal structure. Overall, the candidates are ordered according to both their local and global adaptability and the case that minimizes both measures is chosen.

The output of the retrieval stage is an ordered set of candidate cases, their feature mappings, and the adaptation specialists and strategies applicable to each candidate. So, AGR is unlike conventional retrieval methods which simply return the chosen case, the feature mappings, and a similarity measure, with no support for adaptation and repair.

An AGR Example

The following example works through a sample retrieval session taken from the plant-model of figure 1(a). The target problem is to move coil-car-7 from tension-reel-9 to skid-7 using 2-speed motion carrying coil-1, a coil of steel, and the case memory contains just a single case for moving a coil-car from tension-reel-8 to skid-6 using 1-speed motion, and carrying no load. The adaptation knowledge consists of a number of specialists designed to cater for transformations involving speed, direction, start and end locations, and the contents of vehicles in movement tasks. The two relevant strategies are the blocked-precondition strategy and the balance-interaction strategy mentioned above.

Figure 8 is a representation of the types of structures built during retrieval. Since the target and base differ in terms of speed, direction, locations, and vehicle content, a variety of relevant specialists are activated and shown. A number of points are worth noticing here. First, only relevant features (i.e., features that are adaptable) partake in the mapping process. This contrasts with many knowledge-weak retrieval methods that *have* to consider the mapping of all specified problem features. As a result adaptation-guided retrieval computes significantly fewer mappings than other methods. One could of course build in some notion of relevance or context to avoid this, and many existing systems do use such techniques to greatly improve retrieval performance. However it is our contention that rather than building separate models of relevance, adaptation knowledge should be used, since, after all, it is adaptability that we are trying to measure.

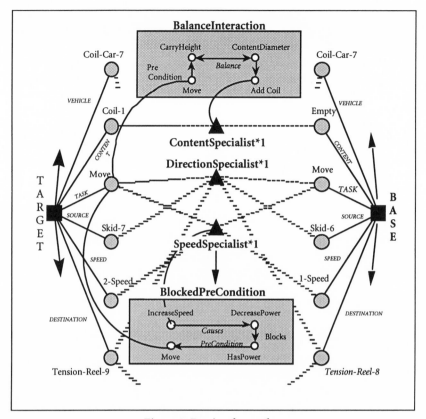

Figure 8. Retrieval snapshot.

Second, at this early stage non-adaptable cases can be identified and eliminated. For example, if a speed specialist did not exist then Déjà Vu would have no alternative but to find a different case, namely one that matched exactly on speed.

In this example, when the specialists are applied (during adaptation) further problems in the form of blocked-preconditions and balance-interactions arise (see figure 8). For instance, the content-specialist is set to change the base solution so that the target coil-car is carrying the target coil. However, there is a balance condition between the coil diameter and the carrying-height of the coil-car. This is detected at retrieval time because the content-specialist is known to affect a balance-state feature. Consequently, the balance-interaction strategy is stored with the applicable specialists. The speed specialist also results in a problematic interaction. A pre-condition of movement is that power be available to the coil-car. An effect of the speed-specialist is that the power consumption of the coil-car will increase and possibly lead to the lack of power, thereby blocking the movement pre-condition. Again this is spotted during retrieval and the blocked-precondition is also marked as applicable. In conclusion, the base case is judged to be adaptable. In a real retrieval session its precise adaptability would be computed in terms of the number of specialists and strategies needed and this measure would be used to discriminate among alternative adaptable cases.

Apart from the benefits of retrieving adaptable cases this method also offers more that just a case and a similarity measure to adaptation. It also offers a representation of the nature of the similarities and dissimilarities between the target and base in the form of the specialists and strategies that are deemed applicable. This additional knowledge is very useful during adaptation in pointing out precisely what needs to be adapted and how it may be adapted.

Experiments

The following three experiments demonstrate the accuracy and performance characteristics of adaptation-guided retrieval. Since all the experiments used Déjà Vu, they also test the effectiveness of hierarchical case-based reasoning (manipulations of HCBR were not done). Experiment 1 tests the retrieval accuracy of AGR versus a standard similarity model of retrieval. Experiment 2 examines the relationship between retrieval cost and the size of the case-base in AGR. Finally, Experiment 3 looks at the overall performance of AGR compared to a standard similarity model.

Experiment 1: Accuracy of Retrieval

Traditional approaches to retrieval select cases on the basis of semantic similarity in the hope that they will also be the most adaptable. Experiment 1 shows that this assumption can be unwarranted. The standard similarity model (SS) used was a classical, distance-based similarity metric that compares features on the basis of their separation distance in the knowledge-base; for example, identical matches obtain perfect similarity, objects that shared a common parent obtain less similarity, and objects that share a common grandparent obtain less again.

Trials were carried out with two different case-bases. Trial 1 used a case-base that contained 45 cases all from the same plant-model; that is, the same track layout and plant objects were used in each case. The same plant model was also used for the 45 target problems of the first trial. The most adaptable case in the case-base was computed for each target problem. The accuracy of the two retrieval methods was then measured for the 45 targets. The results showed that AGR selected the most adaptable case 100 percent of the time

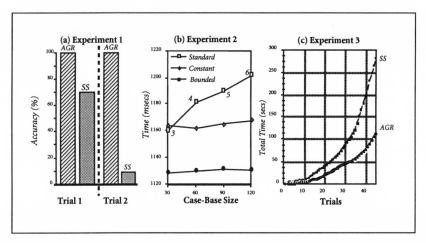

Figure 9. Experimental results: (a) Retrieval accuracy
(b) Retrieval performance (c) Overall system performance

whereas the SS method was only accurate 70 percent of the time; this difference was statistically significant (see Trial 1 in figure 9(a) ; $chi^2(1) = 14.295$, $p < .0001$).

In the second trial, we used a second case-base containing 120 cases involving 8 different plant-models. Various plant models were also used in the 45 target problems employed. The SS method fares even worse on this more realistic case-base; AGR was still 100 percent accurate, but SS decreased to 12 percent (see Trial 2 in figure 9(a); $chi^2(1) = 65.34$, $p = .0001$). The standard similarity method degrades because it tends to select cases from the same plant-model rather cross-model cases. It is mislead by exact entity matches between the target and cases involving the target's plant-model even though cases from different plant model are often easier to adapt.

Clearly, the standard similarity method could be improved with a more elaborate weighting scheme to closer approximate the concept of adaptability. However, such improvements would implicitly include the knowledge that is explicitly used in the AGR method. Furthermore, the tailoring of similarity metrics is a complex trial and error process that depends greatly on the current state of the system. Finally, as we shall see, it is not clear that such remedial adjustments actually result in any computational gain over AGR (see Experiment 3).

Experiment 2: Avoiding Swamping Problems

The AGR method is clearly more complicated than standard similarity methods. It is, therefore, important to ascertain whether it is particularly prone to a special case of the utility problem in CBR systems, known as the *swamping problem* (see Francis and Ram 1993; Smyth and Keane 1995b) Utility problems occur when the uncontrolled accumulation of knowledge results in a performance degradation because the cost of locating relevant knowledge is (on average) more than the saving obtained in using this knowledge. In many CBR systems the swamping problem arises because the cost of retrieval is directly proportional to the number of cases in the case-base; as a case-base expands overall problem solving performance may actually degrade.

One solution to this problem is to limit retrieval time; the best case found within a given time limit is selected (Veloso 1992). This solution invariably results in the retrieval of a sub-optimal case and, of course, such sub-optimal cases may be difficult or impossible to adapt. Adaptation-guided retrieval is less prone to the swamping problem, because the cost of retrieval does not depend on the size of the case-base as a whole but more so on the number of cases that are adaptable (relevant) to the target problem; the base-filtering stage of retrieval ensures that non-adaptable cases are not examined during retrieval. The avoidance of swamping in AGR is illustrated in Experiment 2.

In Experiment 2, we varied the size of the second case-base from 30 to 120 cases in units of 30. Twenty target problems were tested on each of these new case-bases. Figure 9(b) shows the mean retrieval times for the test problems under three different conditions. The *standard condition* shows the performance of the system on the test problems. Note that while there is a linear increase in retrieval time, it does not depend on the total size of the case-base. Rather it depends on the number of adaptable cases found (in this experiment roughly 10 percent or less of the total case-base). In figure 9(b) the numbers beside the boxes of the standard curve indicate the number of adaptable cases on each retrieval. The *constant condition* proves this point, by holding the number of adaptable cases in the case-base constant for each target (3 adaptable cases were used in each case-base). When the number of adaptable cases is fixed, the curve flattens relative to the standard condition.

Of course, it could be argued that the linear increase in the standard condition is still unacceptable. So, in the *bounded condition,* we examined performance by terminating retrieval when the first adaptable case is found (rather than the most adaptable case). This bounded retrieval method works well in that retrieval time remains more or less flat irrespective of the overall case-base size or the number of adaptable cases available. We should, however, remember that this version of the system does not retrieve the most adaptable case, so there may be more processing overhead in the adaptation stage.

These results show that the swamping problem is not a major issue for AGR. AGR's performance advantage is due to the fact that it only considers adaptable cases during retrieval and that these cases can be very quickly located by the indexing scheme offered by the adaptation knowledge. Many CBR approaches employ base-filtering methods to cut down the number of cases considered during retrieval but most of these approaches are either over general, and still select many more than just the relevant cases, or they are over specific and tend to ignore some easily adapted cases.

Experiment 3: Overall System Performance

In Experiments 1 and 2 we just considered retrieval. However, AGR should also have benefits for overall system performance (i.e., combining retrieval and adaptation). We have seen that AGR's retrieval accuracy is very respectable relative to a standard similarity model. AGR should be more accurate and faster in the adaptation stage because the retrieval stage identifies what adaptation knowledge should be used as well as retrieving an optimal case. In Experiment 3, we examined the effect of adaptation-guided retrieval on the overall problem-solving time. Two versions of Déjà Vu were used; one that used AGR (the AGR-system) and another that used semantic similarity-based retrieval and an adaptation component (the standard similarity-based, adaptation system or SS-system). Each system had the same case-base of 100 cases, the same adaptation knowledge, and was tested with the same 45 target problems.

Figure 9(c) shows the cumulative solution times for the two systems over the 45 problems (problems were roughly ordered in terms of their complexity). The AGR-system was considerably better than the SS-system taking only 120 seconds to solve the 45 problems compared to 280 seconds in the SS-system. The mean solution time for problems in the AGR-system ($M = 2.07$ seconds ; $SD = 2.07$) is about three times faster that in the SS-system ($M = 6.22$ seconds ; $SD = 5.66$ seconds)—a difference that is statistically reliable ($t(44) = 5.65, p < .0001$).

The performance of the AGR-system is much better than the SS-system because it retrieves the most adaptable case and locates the relevant adaptation knowledge for this case during retrieval. Furthermore, the benefits of AGR emerge most strongly when problems become more complex, because the sketchy nature of standard, similarity-based retrieval has a greater tendency to be mislead.

Conclusions

Déjà Vu is a case-based reasoning system for plant-control software design. This chapter has described its two main novelties, hierarchical case-based reasoning and adaptation-guided retrieval.

Hierarchical CBR integrates hierarchical problem solving with case-based reasoning. New target problems are solved by retrieving and adapting a number of cases at various levels of abstraction. To support this problem solutions are stored as hierarchies of cases, each case solving a different problem part at some level of abstraction. This hierarchical structuring of the case-base can reduce redundancy in the case-base because similar cases can be shared between hierarchies. Furthermore, cases from different hierarchies can be reused and combined to reduce the adaptation load.

Adaptation guided retrieval advocates the use of adaptation knowledge during retrieval to assess the adaptability of a case with respect to the target problem requirements. This means that certain guarantees can be made about retrieving cases which are adaptable and which are the easiest of those available to adapt. The same guarantees cannot be made by traditional retrieval approaches. A number of experiments were reported to demonstrate the potentials of AGR: AGR was shown to be a more accurate retrieval method than existing approaches (Experiment 1); the retrieval cost scaled well with increasing case-base size and could be kept near constant by bounding retrieval effort (Experiment 2); considerable overall performance improvements were also forthcoming because adaptation costs were greatly reduced (Experiment 3).

The major requirement for HCBR to work is for the domain in question to be decomposable. For AGR, adaptation knowledge must be represented in terms of specialists and strategies. Both of these requirements are satisfied in the plant-control design domain. The question is whether they are likely to be true of other domains. So far Déjà Vu has been used in one other domain, Motif graphical user interface design. And success in this very different software design task leads us to believe that these requirements are general enough to be satisfiable in a wide range of design domains.

10 Multi-plan Retrieval and Adaptation in an Experience-based Agent

Ashwin Ram & Anthony G. Francis, Jr.

The real world has many properties that present challenges for the design of intelligent agents. It is dynamic, unpredictable, and independent, poses poorly structured problems, and places bounds on the resources available to agents. Agents that operate in real worlds need a wide range of capabilities to deal with them: memory, situation analysis, situativity, resource-bounded cognition, and opportunism. In particular, agents need the ability to dynamically combine past experiences to cope with new situations, selecting and merging the relevant parts of remindings to take maximum advantage of their past experience.

To address these issues, we propose a theory of *experience-based agency* that specifies how an agent with the ability to richly represent and store its experiences could remember those experiences with a context-sensitive, asynchronous memory, incorporate the relevant portions of those experiences into its reasoning on demand with integration mechanisms, and direct memory and reasoning through the use of a utility-based control mechanism. We have implemented this theory in the NICOLE multistrategy reasoning system and are currently using it to explore the problem of merging multiple past planning experiences. NICOLE's control system allows memory and reasoning to proceed in parallel; the asynchronous and context-sensitive nature of that memory system allows NICOLE to return a "best guess" retrieval immediately and then to update that retrieval whenever new cues become available.

But solving the problem of merging planning experiences requires more than just memory and control. We need mechanisms to integrate new retrieved plans into the planner's current reasoning context whenever they are found. To ensure that those new retrieved plans are useful, we need ways to use the planner's current context to generate new cues that can help guide the memory system's search. To solve these subproblems, we have developed the multi-plan adaptor (MPA) algorithm, a novel method for merging partial-order plans in the context of case- based least-commitment planning. MPA allows the merging of arbitrary numbers of plans at any point during the adaptation process. It achieves this by dynamically extracting relevant case subparts and splicing those subparts into partially completed plans. MPA can also help guide retrieval by extracting intermediate goal statements from partial plans.

In this chapter, we briefly review the properties of the real world that present challenges for the design of intelligent agents, examining in particular the need to combine past planning experiences. We then review our theory of experience-based agency and its implementation in the NICOLE system. We present the MPA algorithm, illustrate how it supports the merging of plans at any point during the adaptation process, and describe its foundations in least- commitment case-based planning. We then discuss how MPA can be integrated into various control regimes, including systematic, pure case-based, and interleaved regimes, and describe our implementation of interleaved MPA in NICOLE. We conclude the chapter by reviewing other case-based planning work and then outlining our contributions.

Exploiting the Past

In this section, we will investigate the many real-world challenges faced by an intelligent agent, and explore the need to combine experiences.

The Challenges of the Real World

The real world presents many challenges to an agent—challenges that arise in both artificial domains and in the real-world problems humans face (Bratman 1987, Hammond 1989a, Orasanu and Connolly 1993, Pollock 1995, Sternberg 1985, 1986, Wooldridge and Jennings 1995). The real world is dynamic, changing independently from the actions of an agent, and it is unpredictable, changing in a way too complex for an agent to completely predict. To make things worse, the world and its changes are relevant to the agent's goals (so that they cannot be ignored), sensitive to the agent's actions (so that the agent cannot act with impunity) and place resource bounds on the agent's activity (so that the agent cannot just try everything until it works).

But the real world is also regular—patterns exist, encapsulating classes of objects and events and relationships of cause and effect. An agent's ability to effectively use its past experience with these patterns can be key to its successful performance and survival in real-world domains. In this chapter, we take as a given the traditional trappings of a sophisticated intelligent agent, which include *sensors* and *effectors* (Russel and Norvig 1995), *desires* (or values) and *goals* (Bratman 1987, Pollock 1995, Schank and Abelson 1977), *situation analysis* (Kolodner 1993, Pollock 1995), *context sensitivity* or *situativity* (Maes 1990), *efficient resource-bounded cognition* (Kolodner 1983, Pollock 1995), and *opportunism* (Hammond 1989a, Hayes-Roth and Hayes-Roth 1979, Simina and Kolodner 1995). In this context, we will focus on an agent's memory for past experiences and how relevant pieces of multiple past experiences can be effectively integrated during problem solving in order to synthesize solutions for new problems.

The Need to Combine Experiences

Taking advantage of past experiences is the foundation of case-based reasoning. When confronted with a problem, a case-based reasoner recalls a past experience and adapts it to provide the solution to the new problem. Unfortunately, in many real-world domains we cannot count on a single past experience to provide the outline of a solution to our problems. Consider the following examples:

> A graduate student asked to present his first paper at an overseas conference must draw on separate past experiences in preparing talks for conferences within his country and preparing his passport and flight arrangements for vacations outside of his country.

> A host planning his first large dinner party must recall both the outline of a menu as served at family gatherings and his separate experiences at preparing individual dishes for himself.

> A home hobbyist attempting his first large piece of furniture must recall both past examples of that type of furniture to provide a design and experiences with acquiring, assembling and finishing individual components.

All of these problems have something in common: every piece of the solution can be constructed entirely out of the agent's past experience (with suitable adaptation), but no single past experience suffices to solve the entire problem. For these types of problems, unless a case-based reasoning system has the ability to combine several past experiences, it will have to resort to expensive from-scratch reasoning in order to solve the problem.

Some CBR planning systems combine multiple cases during reasoning. However, they either gather all partial plans at retrieval prior to adaptation (e.g., PRODIGY/ANALOGY, Veloso, Chapter 8), break plans into snippets at storage time so they can be retrieved individually (e.g., CELIA, Redmond 1990 1992), or combine cases recursively, applying complete past cases to sub-problems within a larger problem (e.g., ROUTER, Goel et al. 1994, SBR, Turner 1989, PRODIGY/ANALOGY, Veloso, Chapter 8). None of these approaches is entirely satisfactory, for various reasons.

It is not entirely clear that all of the knowledge needed to solve a problem can be assembled at the beginning of problem solving. For example, in the furniture example, it is not entirely clear whether or not the agent needs to buy new sandpaper, and hence unclear whether the agent should recall past experiences of buying sandpaper at a hardware store. This uncertainty arises out of several concerns: the uncertainty of the world state (how much sandpaper does the agent have?), uncertainty in the effectiveness of agent actions (how much wood will a piece of sandpaper sand?) and the potential of exogenous events that can invalidate parts of the plan (if a friend drops and scars a piece of the furniture, will the agent have enough sandpaper to remove the scar, or will he need to buy more?). But it can also arise out of the plan itself: until the agent has decided on a design for the piece and how much wood will be involved, it is unclear precisely how much sandpaper is needed, and hence unclear whether or not a plan should be retrieved. If some amount of sandpaper is on hand, the goal of acquiring sandpaper may not even arise until late in the planning process, when it has become clear that the amount on hand is insufficient.

Precomputing case snippets also has drawbacks. While this allows us to extract subparts of a case to meet the needs of an open goal in a plan, these subparts need to be computed at storage time. Unfortunately, it is not clear that every useful breakdown of a case can be computed in advance. For example, in the foreign conference example, the two past experiences must be closely interleaved to produce a new plan. If the agent has not stored the passport experience as a separate snippet, the agent may not be able to extract that particular piece of a case if it is retrieved—if the agent was able to retrieve it at all.

Recursive case-based reasoning—using case-based reasoning to satisfy subgoals in a partial plan—is an effective way to combine multiple cases because information about the partially constructed solution can be used to help select additional cases to complete the solution. However, existing systems that use recursive case-based reasoning, such as ROUTER and PRODIGY/ANALOGY, can only retrieve whole cases and attempt to apply them to the subproblems at hand. These systems tend to fill in one "gap" at a time and neither search for nor attempt to use cases that might fill several gaps in the plan at once, even if such cases exist.

We advocate a more flexible approach: using more complete information about the *current* state of a partially adapted plan to guide the retrieval of cases that address as many deficiencies in the plan as possible, and dynamically selecting the relevant portions of those cases to integrate with our current reasoning process. We believe that the key to achieving this is not to attempt to solve this problem in isolation, but instead to look at how the design of a complete agent could provide us with the tools with which to solve the problem.

An Architecture for Real-World Domains

We now present our theory of experience-based agency, discuss its implications on memory, reasoning, and control, and explore how an experience-based agent can effectively exploit the past.

Experience-Based Agency

A growing community of AI researchers has come to believe that successfully meeting the challenges posed by the real world will require building comprehensive agent architectures, rather than by tackling individual problems separately and trying to combine the solutions after the fact (e.g., Anderson 1983, Hayes-Roth 1995, Newell 1990, Nilsson 1995, Pollock 1995). We subscribe to this view; in particular, we believe that the problem of deciding when and what cases to retrieve and how to integrate those cases into the system's current plans can only be solved in the context of the retrieval and reasoning needs of an entire agent functioning in a real- world domain.

To explore this problem, we have developed a theory of *experience-based agency,* which specifies a class of agent capable of not only integrating experiences on demand but also retrieving those experiences in a context-sensitive and asynchronous fashion. The theory has five primary components. The core components are a richly represented experience store and a global communications mechanism, which together lay the foundation for a context-sensitive asynchronous memory system. To cope with the potential retrieval of new information at any time, reasoning mechanisms are equipped with integration mechanisms; to coordinate reasoning and memory, the theory proposes a central metacontroller. Figure 1 illustrates our current implementation of these components in the NICOLE[1] multistrategy reasoning system.

Memory and Control in an Experience-Based Agent

An experience-based agent is designed to operate in a dynamic, unpredictable world with limited information, and as such naturally requires the ability to combine multiple experiences on demand, clip out their irrelevant subparts, and splice them together into a complete solution for the problem at hand. Driving this integration of experience is the asynchronous retrieval of relevant experiences by the independent memory system. In a dynamic world, we cannot guarantee that the cues and specifications that reasoning provides to memory will be sufficient to allow retrieval of the best experiences quickly enough to allow retrieval to continue uninterrupted; an experience-based agent avoids this problem by allowing memory to return a "best guess" initially while continuing to search memory in parallel with any reasoning, acting, or sensing operations being performed by the agent. Fig-

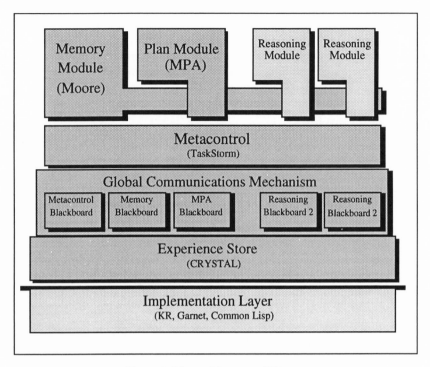

Figure 1. The architecture of NICOLE.

ure 2 illustrates the life history of a typical parallel memory search.[2]

The rich knowledge representation used in an experience-based agency system's experience store (implemented in NICOLE as a highly connected semantic network[3]) allows the memory to make connections between reasoning operations and past cases; the global communications mechanism (implemented in NICOLE as a set of task-specific blackboards) ensures that the content of reasoning operations is visible to the memory to make it context-sensitive. In contrast, where knowledge representation and the global communications mechanism aim to increase memory's ability to retrieve, the metacontroller limits it; it provides utility metrics that limit when memory (or other reasoning modules[4]) can execute. If no sufficiently suitable retrieval can be found, metacontrol ensures that the agent spends its time processing the information it already has, rather than allow the memory to return every partial match, no matter how slight.

Reasoning in an Experience-Based Agent

However, while these components are necessary to achieve the desired behavior, they are not sufficient; modification must be made within reasoning and

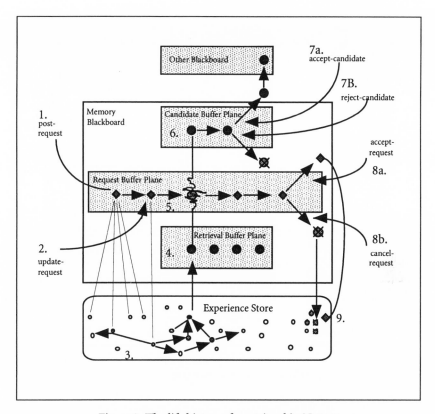

Figure 2. The life history of a retrieval in NICOLE.

1. A retrieval begins when a reasoning module calls *post-request,* which adds a new *request-node* (symbolized by a diamond) to the *request buffer* of the memory blackboard. 2. A request-node may be updated with a *update-request* call at any time. 3. Each time a request is posted or updated (or when activity occurs in other system blackboards) *activation* spreads to nodes in long term memory (the experience store). 4. On every retrieval cycle, a limited number of *active nodes* (symbolized by dark circles) are retrieved to the *retrieval buffer* for consideration. 5. Each pending request in the request buffer is matched against the candidates in the retrieval buffer. 6. Successful matches are posted to the *candidate buffer* to be copied to the requesting blackboard or process. 7. A retrieval candidate can be accepted or rejected by the *accept-candidate* and *reject-candidate* calls, which update the state of the request to allow it to more accurately select future matches. 8. The reasoning module may at any time decide to terminate processing of a request by accepting it through an *accept-request* call or rejecting it with a *cancel-request* call. 9. Terminated requests, both successful and unsuccessful, are stored in long term memory and used by the *storage module* (not shown) to adjust associative links in long term memory and retrieval parameters in the matching and candidate retrieval systems.

memory as well. Traditional reasoning algorithms have well-defined inputs and outputs, and it simply does not make any sense to say that "new information can be retrieved at any time" without some integration mechanism that can incorporate that information into reasoning. Similarly, traditional retrieval algorithms operate at the command of the reasoning system, performing each search of memory separately from every other and basing each search only on the cues and specifications provided at the particular moment the search was initiated. In order to take maximum advantage of an independent memory we must allow it to establish knowledge goals which are based on the needs of reasoning but which can be independently pursued, updated, and (eventually) satisfied.

Exploiting Past Plans in an Experience-Based Agent

In addition to the general need to combine past experiences into a coherent solution to its current problems, if an experience-based agent is called upon to perform planning tasks, it needs the specific capability to combine multiple plans on demand, clip out their irrelevant subparts, and splice them together into a complete plan. To solve this problem, we have configured NICOLE to implement an interactive multi-plan adaptation system (called NICOLE-MPA). NICOLE-MPA represents an advance over traditional case-based reasoning systems in two ways. First, NICOLE-MPA uses a novel algorithm called the multi-plan adaptor (MPA) to extend the concept of multi-plan adaptation to the least-commitment case-based planning framework. Within the context of the NICOLE system, the MPA algorithm also provides both an integration mechanism and a knowledge goal generation mechanism for least-commitment planners using partially ordered plans. Second, NICOLE-MPA provides a framework for the study of various heuristics for multi-plan adaptation.

To set the stage for NICOLE-MPA, we will discuss the least-commitment planning framework and its case-based implementation in systems like SPA, then detail the MPA algorithm itself and how it extends the traditional systems upon which it is founded. Then, we will discuss how NICOLE is configured to implement interactive multi-plan adaptation, and conclude by discussing the potential efficiency gains and hazards of NICOLE-MPA.

4. Interactive Multi-Plan Adaptation

In this section, we review case-based least-commitment planning, present MPA, our algorithm for multi-plan adaptation, and discuss how multi-plan adaptation can be controlled, made interactive, and benefit a system.

An Overview of Case-Based Least Commitment Planning

Least-commitment planning departs from traditional planning systems by delaying decisions about step orderings and bindings as much as possible to prevent backtracking (Weld 1994). Least-commitment planners solve problems by successive refinement of a partial plan derived from the initial and goal conditions of the problem. Plans are represented as sets of steps, causal links between steps, variable bindings and ordering constraints. Beginning with a skeletal partial plan based on the initial and goal conditions of the problem, a least-commitment planner attempts to refine the plan by adding steps, links and constraints that eliminate open conditions or resolve threats.

The *systematic plan adaptor* algorithm (Hanks and Weld 1995) is a least-commitment algorithm for case-based planning. SPA is based on four key ideas: treat adaptation as a refinement process (based on the generative least-commitment planner SNLP; McAllester and Rosenblitt 1991), annotate partial plans with *reasons* for decisions, add a *retraction mechanism* to remove decisions, and add a *fitting mechanism* to fit previous plans to current situations. Reasons support the fitting and retraction mechanisms by allowing SPA to determine the dependencies between steps. Once a plan has been retrieved, it may contain steps and constraints that are extraneous or inconsistent with the new situations; during fitting, reasons allow SPA to identify extraneous steps and remove them; during adaptation, reasons allow SPA to isolate steps which are candidates for retraction.

One limitation of SPA is that it is a single-plan adaptor; even if a new problem could be solved by merging several plans, SPA must choose only one and adapt it to fit. This limitation arises from SPA's attempt to maintain systematicity and completeness. A systematic planner never repeats its work by considering a partial plan more than once; a complete planner always finds a solution if it exists. SPA ensures these properties (in part) by choosing only one refinement at a time, by never retracting any refinement made during adaptation (to avoid reconsidering plans), and by adding all possible versions of any refinement it chooses (to avoid missing a solution). A full discussion of completeness and systematicity in SPA is beyond the scope of this chapter (but see Francis and Ram 1995; Hanks and Weld 1995).

Multi-Plan Adaptation

Because it adapts only one plan, SPA can resort to significant amounts of from-scratch planning even when the knowledge needed to complete the plan is present in the case library. To make the most effective use of the planner's past experience, we need the ability to recognize when a partial plan needs to be extended, select plans to that address the deficiency, and then extract and merge the relevant parts of the retrieved plan into the original plan. MPA resolves this problem in SPA by allowing the retrieval and merging of arbitrary numbers of cases at any point during the adaptation process. MPA also allows the dynamic extraction of relevant parts of past cases. To achieve this, we extended the SPA framework by adding three key mechanisms:

- a *goal deriver,* which extracts intermediate goal statements from partial plans
- a *plan clipper,* which prepares plans for merging using a modified plan fitting mechanism
- a *plan splicer,* which merges two plans together based on their causal structure

Intermediate goal statements are MPA's knowledge goals; they provide MPA with the ability to merge partial plans at any point of the adaptation process and contribute to its ability to dynamically extract the relevant subparts of retrieved cases. Intermediate goal statements are extracted by the inverse of a representational "trick" that SPA uses to construct a skeletal plan if it can't find a relevant case in its library. The trick is simple: build a skeletal plan by adding dummy initial and final steps whose post- and pre-conditions match the initial and goal conditions of the problem. This technique is also used in SPA's generative predecessor SNLP (McAllester and Rosenblitt 1991) as well as a host of other STRIPS-based planning systems. MPA inverts this trick by extracting new goals from the open conditions of a partial plan. As planning proceeds, open conditions in the goal statement are resolved, but new open conditions are posted as new steps are added. MPA constructs an intermediate goal statement by extracting these new open conditions and using them to form the new goal state, and by extracting the initial conditions of the partial plan can be extracted and using them to form the new initial conditions.[5]

Just like the original goal statement, the intermediate goal statement can be used to retrieve and fit a partial plan. However, the result of this process is not a complete fitted plan suitable for adaptation; it is a *plan clipping* that satisfies some or all of the open conditions of the partial plan from which the intermediate goal statement was derived. To take advantage of the plan clipping for adaptation, it must be *spliced* into the original partial plan. Together, plan clipping and splicing form MPA's integration mechanism for incorporating new plans into the current reasoning context (figure 3).

Our splicing mechanism uses the intermediate goal statement to produce a mapping between the partial plan and the plan clipping, pairing open conditions from the partial plan with satisfied goal conditions from the plan clipping. The plan splicer uses this mapping to perform a guided refinement of the original partial plan, selecting goal conditions from the clipping and using the links and steps that satisfied them as templates to instantiate similar steps and links in the original plan. As these steps are added, new mappings are established between open conditions in the new steps and satisfied preconditions in the clipping and are added to the queue of mappings that the splicer is processing. Hence, the plan splicer performs a backwards breadth-first search through the causal structure of the plan clipping, using links and steps in the clipping to guide the instantiation of links and steps in the original plan. Figure 4 briefly outlines the MPA algorithm.

Controlling Multi-Plan Adaptation

Merely having the ability to splice plans together does not allow us to take advantage of past experience. We need to decide what experiences to combine and when to combine them. Because the MPA algorithm can potentially be performed at any point during the adaptation process—using an initial skeletal plan derived from the initial and goal statement, using a fitted plan derived from retrieval, or using an adapted plan after some arbitrary amount of retraction and refinement—we have considerable flexibility in deciding what to retrieve, when to retrieve it and when to merge it.

We have considered three alternative control regimes, each of which makes different commitments about when to retrieve and when to adapt. On one end of the spectrum, *systematic MPA* preserves SPA's property of systematicity by splicing all retrieved cases before (generative) adaptation begins. On the other, *extreme MPA* never performs generative adaptation and instead uses a set of pivotal cases (Smyth and Keane 1995) to guarantee completeness.

Both systematic and extreme MPA make extreme commitments: either integrate all knowledge before generative adaptation begins, or never generatively adapt and rely solely on past experience. An alternative approach is to allow plan splicing at any point during adaptation. In the middle stands *interactive MPA*, a control regime that can potentially attempt a retrieval at any time, either with the initial skeletal plan or with partial plans produced as a result of adaptation. Since the results of splicing cause large jumps in the search space, this regime deliberately departs from the systematicity of SNLP and SPA in an attempt to solve the problem with less search.

However, allowing arbitrary plan retrieval and plan splicing is not without cost. Performing a full search of the system's case library at every step of the problem space could be computationally prohibitive. The costs of searching the case library at every step of the problem space could outweigh the benefits of reduced search, especially if the system enters a "slump"—an adaptation episode which begins and ends with the application of relevant clippings, but which goes through a series of intermediate plans for which the system cannot match any existing plans in its case library. Clearly, it is worthwhile to retrieve and apply clippings at the beginning and end of a slump, but a full search of the case library at each intermediate step could cost more than the benefits that the initial and final retrievals provide. This is the swamping utility problem—the benefits of case retrieval can be outweighed by the costs of that retrieval, leading to an overall degradation in performance as a result of

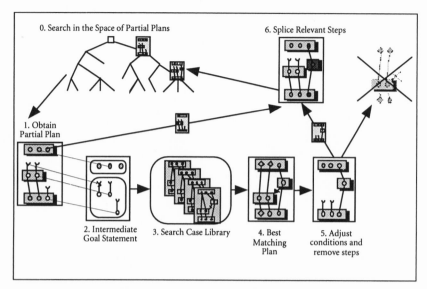

Figure 3. Overview of multi-plan adaptation

Multi-plan adaptation begins when (1) a partial plan is obtained, either directly from a goal statement, from an initial case fitting, or from ongoing adaptation processes. (2) An intermediate goal statement is extracted from the plan, consisting of the initial conditions known to be true in the world and the set of preconditions not yet satisfied in the plan. (3) The case library is searched for a matching plan in exactly the same way that it is searched for initial case fittings. (4) The best matching plan is retrieved and (5) is clipped to have the right set of initial and goal conditions and to remove extraneous plan steps. (6) The steps are recursively spliced into the plan, beginning with the links that match to the intermediate goal statement and then moving backwards through the plan along the paths of the causal links. (0) Finally, the successfully spliced plans are returned for further adaptation or splicing.

case learning (Francis and Ram 1995)

Interactive Multi-Plan Adaptation

Developing heuristics for deciding when and when not to retrieve is a challenging open problem. The experience-based agency theory suggests that plan adaptation should be driven by retrieval; to test this theory, we have implemented an Interactive MPA system within a specially configured version of NICOLE, called *NICOLE-MPA*.

NICOLE-MPA is an instantiation of NICOLE in which all of MPA's temporary data structures are implemented using NICOLE blackboards. Case adaptation,

```
Input:   A partial plan P, and a case library C.
Output:  A new partial plan P'.

procedure MPA (P, C):
1  P'← Copy-Plan(P)
2. igs ← GetIntermediateGoalStatement(P')
3. plan ← RetrieveBestPlan (C, igs)
4. {clipping, mapping} ← FitPlan (plan, igs)
5. for cgp in mapping do
6.       if Producer-Exists (oc-gl-pair, P')
7.             then    Splice-Link (oc-gl-pair, P', clipping)
8.             else    Splice-Step (oc-gl-pair, P', clipping)
9.          AddNewOpenCond-GoalPairs(mapping, P')
10. return P'
```

Figure 4. The MPA algorithm

intermediate goal statement generation, plan clipping, and plan splicing are all implemented as NICOLE task modules, which run in parallel with the memory module and other modules of the NICOLE system. Because of this parallelism, NICOLE-MPA can potentially attempt a retrieval at any time, either with the initial skeletal plan or with partial plans produced as a result of adaptation. To support this retrieval, goals, plans, and intermediate goal statements are augmented with plan tags, which allow the smooth integration of traditional least-commitment planning structures with the richly interconnected semantic network which makes up NICOLE-MPA's experience store. The plan tagging mechanism allows NICOLE-MPA to manipulate intermediate goal statements, plans and goals in a completely native fashion while providing the memory system with the cues necessary to continue to refine retrieval.

A typical problem-solving session in NICOLE-MPA begins with the presentation of a problem. From this problem, NICOLE-MPA generates a goal statement and uses the goal statement to post a retrieval request. If some partially matching case can be found, the system returns it as its current best guess; however, the retrieval request remains active. As the system adapts the plan (using a specially "wrapped" and modified version of the SPA algorithm incorporated into a NICOLE task module), it generates plan tags for each partial plan it generates, providing additional cues for the memory module to attempt further retrievals. When memory finds a new past case whose degree of match exceeds a certain threshold, NICOLE-MPA's metacontroller allows memory to return it as a new guess. If it is applicable, the metacontroller may schedule the plan splicing module, which will integrate it into the current partial plan.

The Benefits of Multi-Plan Adaptation

Both adapting a single partial plan and adapting merged partial plans can produce significant benefits over generative problem solving. The cost of generative planning is exponential in the size of the final plan produced, whereas fitting a plan is a linear operation in the size of the plan. Hence, the potential exists for substantial improvement through retrieval and adaptation if an appropriate past plan exists, especially for large plans. In certain domains, SPA has demonstrated significant improvements over generative planning. However, if large gaps exist in the retrieved partial plan, SPA must resort to adaptation, which, like generative problem solving, has an exponential cost in the number of steps that need to be added. While this amount of adaptation may be a significant improvement over complete from-scratch problem solving, the potential exists to reduce that even further by using MPA to clip and splice more partial plans. Fitting a clipping and splicing a clipping are linear operations in the size of the plan being spliced. Hence, the potential exists for substantial improvement through plan merging if an appropriate past plan exists, especially if the gaps in the existing plan are large. An initial implementation of MPA for a test domain indicated significant speedups (beginning at 30 percent) over SPA for even the smallest examples (solution size of the final plan = 5 steps).

Related Work

There are wide bodies of work on both least-commitment planning and case-based reasoning. The most relevant example of that work to this research is of course SPA, upon which MPA builds. Other similar plan reuse systems include PRIAR (Kambhampati and Hendler 1992) an SPA-like system based on NONLIN, and XII (Golden et al 1994), an SPA-like system that plans with incomplete information. Hanks and Weld (1995) discuss these and other plan reuse systems from the perspective of the SPA framework.

MPA's plan splicing mechanism is in many ways similar to DERSNLP (Ihrig and Kambhampati 1994), a derivational analogy system built on top of SNLP that uses eager replay to guide a partial order planner. While DERSNLP's eager replay mechanism is in some ways similar to a limiting case of Systematic MPA in which a single plan is retrieved and spliced into a skeletal plan derived from an initial problem statement, DERSNLP goes beyond SPA's reason mechanism and includes a full derivational trace of problem solving in its cases. While DERSNLP and its extension DERSNLP-EBL focus on when it is profitable to retrieve a partial plan, unlike NICOLE-MPA they do not provide the capability of interrupting adaptation as a result of an asynchronous memory retrieval, nor do they provide the ability to integrate the results of multiple plans.

Combining multiple plans in case-based reasoning is not a new idea. The PRODIGY/ANALOGY system (Veloso 1994, Chapter 8) can retrieve and merge the results of an arbitrary number of totally ordered plans during the derivational analogy process. However, because PRODIGY/ANALOGY manipulates and stores totally ordered plans, it runs into significant issues when deciding how to interleave steps (Veloso 1994, p. 124–127), an issue MPA avoids because of its least-commitment heritage. Furthermore, PRODIGY/ANALOGY deliberately limits its capability to retrieve and combine cases on the fly in an attempt to reduce retrieval costs.

The ROUTER path-planning system (Goel et al. 1994) has the ability to recursively call its case-based methods to fill in gaps in a planned route when no exactly matching case can be found. (PRODIGY/ANALOGY has a similar capability to call itself recursively, although the full implications of this ability have not yet been explored). Like NICOLE-MPA, ROUTER has the ability to combine multiple cases, although only in a synchronous fashion because its memory does not support spontaneous retrieval. However, each of these cases must be complete; ROUTER does not have the ability to clip out the relevant portion of a case at retrieval time. It does have the ability to break a case up into subcases at storage time, but the results show that computational costs of this storage computation outweigh the benefits in improved retrievals (Goel et al. 1994, p. 63).

The JULIA system (Hinrichs 1992) also has the ability to combine pieces of several past cases, but this is largely a domain-dependent algorithm for merging declarative structures, rather than a domain independent planning system. The CELIA system (Redmond 1990 1992) stores cases as separate snippets, case subcomponents organized around a single goal or set of conjunctive goals. Snippets provide CELIA with the ability to retrieve and identify relevant subparts of a past case based on the system's current goals. Note that while snippets are superficially similar to plan clippings, plan clippings are constructed dynamically during problem solving, whereas snippets need to be computed and stored in advance.

Clippings are similar to macro operators (Fikes et al. 1972) in that they use past experience to combine several problem solving steps into a single structure that can be applied as a unit, allowing the system to make large jumps in the problem space and avoid unnecessary search. However, macro operators differ from clippings in two important ways. First, macro operators are traditionally precomputed at storage time, whereas clippings are computed dynamically; second, macro operators are fixed sequences of operators, whereas clippings are partially ordered sets of operators that may be resolved in a wide variety of ways in the final plan.

Kambhampati and Chen (1993) built and compared several systems that retrieve partially ordered caselike "macro operators." They demonstrated that least-commitment planners could take greater advantage of past experience than totally-ordered planners because of their ability to efficiently interleave new steps into these "macro-operators" during planning. While this work focuses primarily on interleaving new steps into single past plans, the explanations the authors advance for the efficiency gains they detected could be extended to suggest that least-commitment planners would be superior to totally-ordered planners when interleaving multiple plans. The NICOLE-MPA system should provide us a testbed with which we can empirically evaluate this hypothesis.

Conclusion

We have presented the multi-plan adaptor, an algorithm that allows a case-based least- commitment planner to take advantage of the benefits of several past experiences. MPA provides the ability to retrieve and merge dynamically selected case components at any point during the adaptation process by extracting an intermediate goal statements from a partial plan, using the intermediate goal statement to retrieve and clip a past plan to the partial plan, and then splicing the clipping into the original partial plan.

Multi-plan adaptation has the potential for substantial speedup over single-plan adaptation, but in order for those benefits to be realized MPA must be embedded within a control regime that decides when the system attempts a retrieval, when the system merges, and when the system resorts to adaptation. We have used the NICOLE multistrategy reasoning system to implement an interactive control regime in which cases may be retrieved at any point during adaptation. To cope with the potentially swamping cost of retrieval at every adaptation step, NICOLE-MPA employs an asychronous, resource-bounded memory module that retrieves a "best guess" and then continues to monitor the progress of adaptation, returning a new or better retrieval as soon as it is found.

We believe that the ability to combine multiple plans and the ability to perform asynchronous retrievals form integral parts of any complete agent that functions in a complex domain. Moreover, actually implementing these capabilities in an efficient and sensible way can only be done by considering the architecture of a complete agent. Combined with a metacontroller sufficient to make them work together, multi-plan adaptation and asynchronous retrieval form the cornerstone of our theory of experience-based agency, a theory of how an agent could take maximum advantage of its past experiences to cope with the problems of the real world.

Notes

1. NICOLE is named after a sentient computer in a science fiction short story by one of the authors (Francis 1995).

2. Because of its ability to return a best guess, an experience-based agent has many similarities to the interactive "shoot-first" case-based reasoning systems advocated by Riesbeck (1993). Given a problem input by the user, a shoot-first system attempts to quickly retrieve an approximate set of cases and/or propose a sketchy solution, and then uses feedback from the user to redefine the problem, refine the search, or adapt the solution. Both experience-based agents and shoot-first systems require similar memory capabilities; however, the primary "user" of an experience-based agent's quick retrievals is the agent itself.

3. This semantic network is "highly connected" in two senses: both in the network structure (as in Kilmesch 1994) and in the semantics of the network, in which all nodes and links are reified concepts (as in Brachman 1985, Wilensky 1986b).

4. Reasoning modules are implemented in NICOLE as supertasks (Moorman and Ram 1994b) which combine characteristics of task-specific blackboard panes (Hayes-Roth and Hayes-Roth 1979) and extended reactive action packages (RAPs, Firby 1989).

5. Unfortunately, since ordering constraints and binding constraints may be posted to the plan at any time, only the initial conditions can be guaranteed to be valid conditions for the intermediate goal statement. Conditions established by other steps of the plan may be clobbered by the addition of new steps and new ordering constraints. However, it might be possible to develop heuristics that select additional initial conditions that are likely to hold, perhaps in conjunction with more complex retrieval, fitting and splicing algorithms. In general, deciding which parts of a plan can be extracted to form a sensible and effective intermediate goal statement is a difficult and unsolved problem.

11 Learning to Improve Case Adaptation by Introspective Reasoning and CBR

David B. Leake, Andrew Kinley, and David Wilson

Case-based reasoning (CBR) systems solve new problems by *retrieving* prior solutions of similar previous problems and performing *case adaptation* (also called *case modification*) to fit the retrieved cases to the new situation. Although much progress has been made in methods for case retrieval, both the American and European CBR communities have identified case adaptation as a particularly challenging open problem for the field (e.g., Allemang 1993 and Leake 1994a). The problem is so acute that the most effective current strategy for building CBR applications is to bypass adaptation entirely, building advisory systems that provide cases to human users who perform the adaptation themselves (e.g., Barletta 1994 and Kolodner 1991). However, despite the practical benefits of retrieval-only advisory systems, successful use of advisory systems may require considerable user expertise. Consequently, automatic case adaptation is important from a practical perspective, not only to enable CBR systems to perform autonomously but to enable them to aid naive users. Likewise, as we discuss in Leake (1995c), increased understanding of the case adaptation process and the knowledge required is also important from a cognitive modeling perspective, as a step towards understanding how humans adapt cases when they reason from prior episodes.

This chapter describes research based on characterizing case adaptation knowledge by decomposing it into two parts: (1) a small set of abstract structural transformations and (2) memory search strategies for finding the information needed to apply those transformations. This framework forms the basis of an approach to adaptation in which new adaptation problems are solved by first selecting a transformation indexed under the type of problem motivating adaptation, and then performing introspective reasoning about how to strategically search memory for the information needed to apply the transformation (Leake 1994b, 1995c). Not only does this approach provide increased flexibility in finding needed information, but it serves as a foundation for learning to improve adaptation performance from experience: A trace of this process can be stored as an *adaptation case* and used in future case-based reasoning about the adaptation process itself. Thus the approach is aimed at providing both the flexibility to deal with novel case adaptation problems and adaptation abilities that improve with experience.

We begin by discussing the significance of the case adaptation problem for CBR and the tenets of our approach. We then summarize an initial implementation that applies our approach to learning case adaptation for case-based planning (e.g., Hammond 1989) in the disaster response planning domain. We close by highlighting lessons learned and related research on case adaptation and memory search.

Acquiring Case Adaptation Knowledge

Coding effective adaptation rules can require extensive knowledge of the CBR system's task, its domain, and the contents of its memory. Unfortunately, this knowledge may not be available a priori. Thus in defining case adaptation rules, developers face the same problem of knowledge acquisition in imperfectly-understood domains that often impedes the development of rule-based systems in other contexts. In many of those contexts, the knowledge acquisition problem has been significantly ameliorated by the use of case-based reasoning. Consequently, it is natural to consider applying CBR to the case adaptation process itself, replacing pre-defined adaptation rules with adaptation cases that reflect prior adaptation experience (Berger 1995b, Leake 1994b, Sycara 1988).

An important question is the source of the needed library of adaptation cases. We propose a method that starts with a library of domain-independent adaptation rules, using them to solve novel adaptation problems. The results of applying those rules to specific adaptation problems are stored as adaptation cases to be re-used by case-based reasoning. The following sections first discuss the rule-based process and then the use of adaptation cases.

Adaptation = Transformations + Memory Search

Case adaptation knowledge is often characterized in either of two ways. The first is with abstract rules, such as the rule "add a step to remove harmful side-effect" for case-based planning (Hammond 1989). Such rules are applicable to a broad class of plan adaptation problems, but give no guidance about *how* to find the specific knowledge needed to apply them (e.g., to find the right step to add in order to mitigate a given side-effect). For example, if the planning task is to generate x-ray treatment plans, and the retrieved plan administers the minimum x-ray dose required to destroy a tumor, but also has the bad side-effect of exposing the spinal cord to excessive radiation, deciding which step to add in order to remove the bad side-effect may require considerable domain knowledge.

The second way to characterize adaptations is by relying on adaptation rules that include the required specific knowledge. For example, in the radiation treatment planning domain, the general rule "add a step to remove harmful side-effect" can be replaced by specific rules such as "add the step 'rotate radiation sources' to remove harmful side-effect 'excess radiation'" (Berger and Hammond 1991).

Both these approaches exhibit the classic operationality/generality tradeoff (e.g., Segre 1987). Abstract rules have generality: a small set of transformations appears sufficient to characterize a wide range of adaptations (Carbonell 1983, Hinrichs 1992, Kolodner 1993). However, abstract rules are difficult to apply. Specific rules, on the other hand, are easy to apply but have limited generality. In addition, defining such rules is difficult because of the specific knowledge that they require.

Kass (1990, 1994b) proposes one way to address the operationality / generality tradeoff. His approach uses hand-coded *adaptation strategies* that combine general transformations with domain-independent memory search strategies for finding the domain-specific information needed to apply the strategies. Our approach to adaptation builds on this idea in treating adaptation knowledge as a combination of knowledge about general transformations and about memory search. However, instead of relying on hand-coded memory search strategies, our model builds memory search strategies as needed. When presented with a novel adaptation problem, it performs a planning process that reasons introspectively to determine the information required to solve the particular adaptation problem and to decide which memory search strategies to use to find that information. This process guides the search for information needed to perform the adaptation.

From Rule-Based Adaptation to CBR

After an adaptation problem has been solved by reasoning from scratch, a natural question is how to learn from that reasoning. Initially, it appears that explanation-based generalization (EBG) (e.g., Mitchell, Keller, and Kedar-Cabelli 1986) would be the appropriate learning method, because it allows forming operational new generalizations: The memory search plan that found the needed information could be generalized and stored. However, one of the conclusions of our research is that using EBG to learn memory search rules is not practical (Leake 1994b). For EBG to apply successfully to memory search rules, those memory search rules must provide a complete and correct theory of the contents and organization of memory. Unfortunately, the contents and organization of a specific memory are highly idiosyncratic (Kolodner 1984, Schank 1982) and thus hard to characterize precisely. Consequently, a chain of memory search rules that finds desired information in one instance is not guaranteed to apply to other problems that appear to be within the scope of those same rules: explanation-based generalization may not yield reliable results.

In contrast, using case-based reasoning as the learning method for adaptation knowledge makes it possible for learned knowledge to reflect the idiosyncrasies of the memory's organization and its contents. Unlike abstract adaptation rules, cases that package particular adaptation episodes encapsulate the system's experience solving specific adaptation and memory search problems and reflect the system's specific task, domain, and memory organization. Consequently, we are applying CBR to learning adaptation cases. Our model acquires not only a library of problem-solving cases, through the standard CBR process, but also a library of cases representing episodes of case adaptation. The following section discusses our computer model of the entire adaptation process, including both case adaptation from scratch in response to novel adaptation problems and case-based adaptation to reuse the results of previous adaptation episodes.

DIAL

The task domain for our research is *disaster response planning* for natural and man-made disasters. Examples of such disasters include earthquakes, chemical spills, and "sick building syndrome," in which occupants of a building fall victim to problems caused by low air quality inside a building. Studies of human disaster response planning suggest that case-based reasoning plays an important role in response planning by human disaster planners (Rosenthal, Charles, and Hart 1989).

Our computer model, the case-based planner DIAL (disaster response with introspective adaptation learning), starts with a library of domain cases—disaster response plans from previous disasters—and general (domain-independent) rules about case adaptation and memory search. Like other case-based planners, it learns new plans by storing the results of its planning process. However, the central focus of our research is not on the case-based planning process per se, but on learning to improve case adaptation.

When DIAL successfully adapts a response plan to a new situation, it stores not only the problem solving episode, but also two types of adaptation knowledge for use in similar future adaptation problems: *memory search cases* encapsulating information about the steps in the memory search process, and *adaptation cases* encapsulating information about the adaptation problem as a whole, the memory search cases used to solve it, and the solution to the adaptation problem.

The entire DIAL system includes a schema-based story understander (that receives its input in a conceptual representation), a response plan retriever and instantiator, a simple evaluator for candidate response plans, and an adaptation component to adapt plans when problems are found. The case-based planning framework is based in a straightforward way on previous case-based planners (e.g., CHEF (Hammond 1989)). Consequently, this chapter will only discuss the adaptation component.

DIAL's adaptation component receives two inputs: an instantiated disaster response plan and a description of a problem in the response plan requiring adaptation. To illustrate, one of the examples processed by DIAL involves the following story:

> At Beaver Meadow Elementary School in Concord, New Hampshire, students have been complaining of symptoms like unusual fatigue, eye irritation, respiratory problems, and allergic reactions from being inside the building.

When DIAL processes this story, a straightforward schema-based understanding process identifies the problem as an air quality problem. DIAL then attempts to retrieve and apply a response plan for a similar disaster. The response plan retrieved is the plan for the following factory air quality problem:

> A & D Manufacturing in Bangor, Maine, has recently come under pressure from workers and union-representatives to correct perceived environmental problems in the building. Workers have been affected by severe respiratory problems, headaches, fatigue, and dizziness.

(These episodes are based on case studies from the *INvironment* newsletter for indoor air quality consultants.)

The response plan for A & D Manufacturing involves notifying the workers' union. DIAL's evaluator determines that the notification step does not apply to the current situation, because of a conflict with normative type restrictions on union members: elementary school students do not belong to unions. (The evaluation and problem characterization process is similar to that described in Leake 1992b). Consequently, the response plan must be adapted to apply to the students. DIAL's adaptation component receives two inputs describing this situation: the response plan for the A & D Manufacturing problem, applied to the new situation, and a description of the problem to repair by adaptation: that trying to notify the students' union is not reasonable, because students do not belong to unions. After a description of the general processing done in response to adaptation problems, we will discuss how it applies to this example.

Given inputs describing a candidate response plan and a problem to be adapted, the process performed by DIAL's adaptation component is as follows:

1. *Case-based Adaptation:* DIAL first attempts to retrieve an adaptation case that applied successfully to a similar previous problem. If retrieval is successful, that case is re-applied and processing continues with step 3.

2. *Rule-based Adaptation:* When no relevant prior case is retrieved, DIAL selects a transformation associated with the type of problem that is being adapted (e.g., role/filler mismatches, such as the mismatch between unions and students, are associated with substitution transformations: a mismatch can be repaired by replacing the role being filled or how the given role is filled). Given the transformation, the program generates a *knowledge goal* (Hunter 1989, Leake and Ram 1993, Ram 1987) for the information needed to apply the transformation. For example, for substitutions of role-fillers, the knowledge goal is to find an object that satisfies all the case's constraints on the object being replaced.

The knowledge goal is then passed to a planning component that uses introspective reasoning about alternative memory search strategies (Leake 1994b, 1995c) to find the information needed. This search process generates a memory search plan whose operators include both an initial set of memory search strategies and memory search cases stored after solving previous adaptation problems.

3. *Plan Evaluation:* The adapted response plan is evaluated by a simple evaluator that checks the compatibility of the current plan with explicit constraints from the response plan. A human user performs backup evaluation. If the new response plan is not acceptable, other adaptations are tried.

4. *Storage:* When adaptation is successful, the resulting response plan, adaptation case, and memory search plan are stored for future use.

The following subsections elaborate on the representation of knowledge goals, the memory search process, the adaptation case representation, and the examples currently processed.

Representing Knowledge Goals

In order to use our framework to guide rule-based case adaptation, a CBR system must be able to reason about how to find the information that it needs in order to apply a given transformation to a particular response plan. To do this reasoning, it must first have an explicit representation of the sought-after information. In DIAL, these needs are represented by explicit knowledge goals. Previous study of knowledge goals has developed a two-part representation combining a concept specification (Ram 1987) providing a template to match with candidate information and a description of how the information, once found, should be used.

To satisfy the requirements of memory search, however, we have found that the representation must include additional components (Leake 1995d). First, as is reflected implicitly in the retrieval mechanisms of many CBR systems, the goals of memory search must often be described in terms of the available alternatives in memory (e.g., searching for the matching problem whose solution appears easiest to adapt, compared to other alternatives), rather than described by simply matching a template. Consequently, DIAL's knowledge goal representation also includes a *comparative specification* describing how to choose between multiple alternatives that satisfy the concept specification. Also, DIAL's knowledge goal representation includes information on the amount of search effort allowed for satisfying the knowledge goal (measured in terms of the number of primitive memory operations that may be applied during memory search).

The Memory Search Process

During DIAL's initial rule-based adaptation process, it finds the information needed to apply adaptation transformations by an introspective reasoning process that implements memory search as a form of planning, using operators that describe actions within its internal, or "mental" world, rather than within the external world (Hunter 1990). Using a planning process facilitates flexible re-combination of memory search knowledge. By decoupling memory search knowledge from specific adaptation rules, memory search knowledge can be applied to any problem for which it appears relevant.

Two types of memory search knowledge are provided to the system. First, the system is provided with *knowledge goal transformation rules,* similar to Kolodner's (1984) query transformation rules, that reformulate the questions posed to memory. For example, one strategy for retrieving an instance of an event is to search for contexts in which it would have been likely to play a role. Second, the system is provided with a suite of domain-independent *memory search strategies* that depend on "weak methods" of memory search (e.g., ascending and descending abstraction hierarchies to find related nodes). DIAL currently includes six of these strategies. All strategies are defined in terms of a substrate of seven primitive memory access operations (e.g., to extract the "parent" of a node).

The results of the memory search process are filtered by constraints from the particular adaptation problem. The result is a relatively unguided initial search for information, but traces of this process are saved as *memory search cases* and made accessible for use during future memory search. These cases provide more precise guidance for memory search in similar future situations. In this model, cases are acquired solely by reasoning from scratch, which may require considerable processing effort. However, as will be discussed in a later section, we have also begun to investigate how this view of adaptation can be used to facilitate interactive acquisition of adaptation knowledge.

DIAL's memory search mechanism uses a reactive planning framework, inspired by the RAPS system (Firby 1989), to interleave planning with execution and respond to problems during memory search (e.g., that needed intermediate information cannot be found). In this process, DIAL's rule-based adapter accepts a knowledge goal and chooses a strategy or stored memory search case indexed by the knowledge goal. In the course of processing, a strategy may transform the current knowledge goal or may generate sub-knowledge-goals, also to be satisfied by the planning process. Throughout the memory search process, the adapter maintains a reasoning trace of the operators it applies. That trace is packaged with the search result, as a memory search case, and stored for future use.

Representing and Organizing Cases Learned from Adaptation Episodes

DIAL's memory search cases package the initial knowledge goal, a trace of knowledge-goal transformations and other memory search operations involved in the search process, a record of the search outcome (failure or success), the cost of the search in terms of primitive memory operations performed, and the information found. Memory search cases are indexed under the knowledge goals that they satisfy, and can suggest search operations to attempt in the future; they also have the potential to warn of previous search failures. Memory search cases are accessible to the knowledge planning process for memory search, augmenting the initial library of built-in operators. For future searches, successful search cases that match the largest subset of the current knowledge goals are re-used. When the result of the stored search case does not satisfy current constraints, the search is continued by local search.

DIAL also packages *adaptation cases,* which include both the transformation used for the adaptation and pointers to memory search cases used to search for information to apply the transformation. These provide more specific guidance about how to adapt cases to repair particular types of problems.

Examples Processed

DIAL's initial case library currently contains two disaster response plans, a response plan for the previously-described air quality disaster at A & D Manufacturing and a response plan for an industrial chemical spill. The system has been tested on four different stories exercising different parts of its adaptation mechanisms. The first concerns the indoor air quality problem at Beaver Meadow school, for which DIAL retrieves the A & D disaster response plan. (Like the stories processed, stored response plans are based on episodes from the *INvironment* newsletter.) The A & D disaster response plan includes many steps applicable to the new situation, providing the basis for a response to the school air quality problem. However, as previously described, one of the steps in the response plan for the air quality problem at A & D manufacturing does not apply: notifying the union of the victims. Because schoolchildren do not have unions, the notification step of the previous response plan must be adapted to apply to the schoolchildren. Many adaptations are possible, but a common suggestion from human readers is that the step involving notifying the union should be adapted into a step notifying the children's parents.

When DIAL is run on this example, no adaptations have yet been learned, so the program uses its rule-based adaptation process to perform the adaptation. It first selects a substitution transformation. (In DIAL, candidate transformations for repairing problems in retrieved cases are indexed directly under categories of problem types. For a description of possible problem types, see Leake 1992b.) In this case, the "role/filler mismatch" problem of the schoolchildren belonging to a union may be resolved by either of two substitutions: substituting a new filler (notifying someone else's union) or substituting a different concept in which the children play a similar role (notifying another group relevant to the children). To determine appropriate substitutions, the system must hypothesize the factors that were important in the relationship between workers and their union in the A & D manufacturing problem. Possible constraints can be obtained by examining alternative "views" of the relationship between the union and the workers in the original episode (Wilensky 1986a), based on the relationships represented in the system's memory. In DIAL's memory, one view of union membership involves *being represented*, suggesting searching for representatives of the children. This search yields "parents" as one possibility. (Other possibilities, like "student government," are also hypothesized but rejected during evaluation.) By storing the successful choices according to internal and external feedback, the system builds up information beyond the information in its initial world model about which adaptations to favor for particular adaptation problems.

A second example involves an air quality problem on a military base. The A & D manufacturing episode is the most similar in memory, but again the step of notifying the union fails to apply, this time because soldiers do not have unions. DIAL retrieves the previously-learned adaptation but finds that it too fails to apply: Notifying the soldier's parents is rejected by the user. Consequently, it applies a very simple adaptation to the adaptation case, discarding the final step in the memory search plan from the adaptation case and adding local search. In particular, it preserves that the representation relationship was important in the previous situation, and searches for representatives of soldiers. Using this guidance, it searches memory for representatives of soldiers and finds "commanding officers" as a possible group to notify.

Two additional examples involve another disaster at a school, to which the Beaver Meadow school response plan is reapplied in a straightforward way without adaptation, and the story of a chemical spill episode at a school. The chemical spill example illustrates the importance of learning new adaptations during CBR, instead of only learning new cases as traditionally done in CBR systems. For the chemical spill example, DIAL retrieves the previous chemical spill example as the most similar case, which is reasonable in light of the shared steps involved in cleaning up chemical

spills—the response plan learned from the Beaver Meadow air quality problem is not the most similar response plan. However, the adaptation learned
from processing the Beaver Meadow story is still useful: DIAL uses the adaptation learned from the Beaver Meadow school example to adapt the response to the previous chemical spill (which also involves notifying the
workers' union) by substituting the students' parents. This demonstrates
the value of decoupling case learning from adaptation learning: learning
both new adaptation cases and new problem-solving cases increases the effectiveness of a CBR system in responding to new problems.

Lessons Learned and Future Directions

The conclusions drawn from the project to date include a number of points
discussed in the previous sections: the usefulness of decomposing adaptation
knowledge into two parts, abstract transformations and memory search
knowledge; the appropriateness of CBR, rather than explanation-based learning, as the mechanism for learning the needed memory search information;
the need for a richer notion of knowledge goals than in previous research;
and the usefulness of a reactive model of memory search planning in order to
use incremental results of the search to guide further decisions.

Learning new strategies for adapting cases also has interesting
ramifications for similarity assessment. In current CBR systems, similarity assessment is generally based on fixed criteria. However, as a CBR system learns
how to adapt cases to deal with new types of problems, the similarity metric
should be adjusted to reflect the fact that (thanks to the adaptation learning),
those problems are no longer as great an impediment to applying the case.
Consequently, one area for further study is how best to make the similarity
assessment process reflect the changing state of system adaptation knowledge.
Methods that base similarity judgments directly on adaptability may be especially useful here (see Leake 1992a, 1995b; Smyth and Keane, Chapter 9).

We are now addressing a number of open questions. One of these is the
level of granularity to be used for memory search cases. At present, memory
search cases package entire memory search plans, but it is possible that making subparts of the search plans available, as in Redmond's (1992) *snippets,*
would be beneficial.

Another question being studied is the effectiveness of the planful memory
search process. To give an indication of the value of the knowledge planning
framework for memory search, the current examples have been processed
both using the planful process and using the simple *local search* strategy used
by a number of CBR systems to find substitutions (Kolodner 1993). In this
comparison, the knowledge planning method resulted in an order of magnitude savings in the number of primitive memory operations performed. This

improvement is encouraging, although at this point it cannot be taken too seriously because of the limited set of examples used. Likewise, not enough examples are yet implemented to have reliable data on the tradeoffs between memory search by knowledge planning and CBR. We are now extending the system with the aim of performing additional tests. In particular, an important tradeoff to investigate is the *utility problem* (Francis and Ram 1993, Minton 1988) as it applies to learned adaptation knowledge: the potential problem that processing overhead due to the proliferation of adaptation cases and memory search cases will counterbalance the benefits of the guidance that they provide. Addressing this issue may require refining the indexing scheme for memory search cases, or developing methods for selective case retention.

A final question involves the potential usefulness of this view of case adaptation for interactively acquiring adaptation knowledge. DIAL models the transition from adaptation by using unguided general rules to adaptation by using specific adaptation cases, by storing traces of successful rule-based adaptations. With this method, the initial rule-based adaptation phase may be quite expensive. An alternative method for acquiring adaptation cases is to use DIAL's model of adaptations—as transformations plus memory search—as the basis of an interface for direct acquisition of adaptation cases from a human user. Such an interface can enable a user to suggest transformations and search strategies and then store a trace of the user adaptation for future use. We have begun to investigate this approach, both for its own potential and as a way to more rapidly acquire adaptation cases to test and refine DIAL's case-based adaptation process.

The Manual Adapter: Capturing and Reusing User Adaptations

DIAL's manual adapter enables an expert to adapt a response plan while a trace of the adaptation process is recorded for future reuse. The manual adapter provides a menu-driven interface allowing a user to select types of transformations to apply and types of memory links to follow. The resulting adaptation traces implicitly reflect the user's knowledge of important features to consider when performing a particular type of adaptation.

The user of the manual adapter first classifies the problem being addressed by the adaptation, using a menu of problem types. The user then chooses a transformation to apply to repair the problem and guides search through DIAL's memory to find needed information. An adaptation case, with both the specific adaptation that was performed and a trace of how it was derived, is saved for future use. Because the adaptation case includes the derivational trace, DIAL can apply it to new adaptation problems in a flexible way.

Relationship to Other Approaches

In this section we discuss DIAL's relationship to other memory search and case adaptation approaches.

Memory Search

Although many sophisticated memory search schemes have been developed in CBR research, they are normally driven by opaque procedures, rather than being accessible to explicit reasoning and learning. Our research follows an alternative course, developing explicit models of the memory search process to increase the flexibility and effectiveness of memory search, in the spirit of Kolodner (1984), Rissland, Skalak, and Friedman (1994, chapter 6), and to make it accessible to learning, as in Cox (1994) and Kennedy (1995).

Case Adaptation

Some previous systems are able to learn knowledge useful for guiding adaptation. For example, although CHEF has a static library of domain-independent plan repair strategies, it augments that library with learned ingredient critics that suggest adaptations appropriate to particular ingredients. Likewise, PERSUADER (Sycara 1988) uses a combination of heuristics and case-based reasoning to guide adaptation, searching memory for similar prior adaptations to apply. In these systems, however, the adaptation information learned is quite domain and task specific, while DIAL's adaptation cases have more flexibility. The use of CBR for case adaptation has also been advocated by Berger (1995b), in the context of storing and reusing an expert's adaptations. An alternative approach to the case adaptation problem is to use derivational analogy, deriving a new solution by reapplying a prior solution process to new circumstances, rather than directly adapting the old solution itself (Carbonell 1986; Veloso 1994, Chapter 8). Our method for reusing adaptations can be seen as applying derivational analogy to the case adaptation process itself. Our use of introspective reasoning is also related to research on metacognitive adaptation (Oehlmann 1995, Oehlmann et al. 1993).

There is increasing interest in alleviating case adaptation problems by calling upon users to adapt cases manually and supporting user adaptation (e.g., Bell, Kedar, and Bareiss 1994; Smith, Lottaz, and Faltings 1995). However, previous systems make no attempt to capture the results of the adaptations for future use. With the manual adapter, our framework also contributes an approach to interactively acquiring adaptation knowledge.

Conclusions

Automatic case adaptation is necessary to enable CBR systems to function autonomously and to serve naive as well as expert users. However, knowledge acquisition problems for the rule-based adaptation methods used in many CBR systems have proven a serious impediment to developing CBR applications that perform their own adaptation.

We have described a framework for characterizing adaptation knowledge in terms of transformations and information search, have discussed how that framework is being used as the basis for a model of automatic learning of case adaptation knowledge, and have sketched an initial implementation of that model.

The model combines reasoning from scratch and case-based reasoning to build up expertise at case adaptation. The aim of this approach is to enable CBR systems to make the transition from adaptation guided by general rules (which may be unreliable and expensive to apply) to adaptation guided by adaptation cases that reflect specific case adaptation experience. Thus our method is a way for CBR systems to learn to become more effective at applying their existing cases to new situations.

Acknowledgments

This work was supported by the National Science Foundation under Grant No. IRI-9409348. This chapter is reprinted with minor revisions from Veloso, M. and Aamodt, A., eds, *Proceedings of the First International Conference on Case-Based Reasoning*, Springer Verlag, Berlin 1995, pp. 229–240.

12 Systematic Evaluation of Design Decisions in Case-Based Reasoning Systems

Juan Carlos Santamaría & Ashwin Ram

Two important goals in the evaluation of artificial intelligence (AI) systems are to assess the merit of alternative design decisions in the performance of an implemented computer system and to analyze the impact in the performance when the system faces problem domains with different characteristics (Aha 1992; Cohen and Howe 1989; Kibler and Langley 1988). Achieving these objectives enables us to understand the behavior of the system in terms of the theory and design of the computational model, to select the best system configuration for a given domain, and to predict how the system will behave when the characteristics of the domain or problem change. In addition, for case-based reasoning and other machine learning systems, it is important to evaluate the improvement in the performance of the system with experience (or with learning), to show that this improvement is statistically significant, to show that the variability in performance decreases with experience (convergence), and to analyze the impact of the design decisions on this improvement in performance. This is particularly difficult in implementations of case-based reasoning (CBR) systems because such systems are typically very complex, as are the tasks and domains in which they operate. However, such an evaluation is essential if one is to go beyond mere empirical observation to the prediction and explanation of empirical results.

In this chapter, we present a methodology for the evaluation of CBR and other AI systems through systematic empirical experimentation over a range of system configurations and environmental conditions, coupled with rigorous statistical analysis of the results of the experiments. This methodology enables us to understand the behavior of the system in terms of the design decisions incorporated into the computational model, to select the best system configuration for a given domain, and to predict how the system will behave in response to changing domain and problem characteristics as it gains experience.

We illustrate this methodology with a case study in which we evaluate a multistrategy case-based and reinforcement learning system which performs autonomous robotic navigation. In this case study, we evaluate a range of design decisions that are important in CBR systems, including *configuration parameters* of the system (e.g., overall size of the case library, size or extent of the individual cases), *problem characteristics* (e.g., problem difficulty), *knowledge representation decisions* (e.g., choice of representational primitives or vocabulary), *algorithmic decisions* (e.g., choice of adaptation method), and *amount of prior experience* (e.g., learning or training). We show how our methodology can be used to evaluate the impact of these decisions on the performance of the system and, in turn, to make the appropriate choices for a given problem domain and verify that the system does behave as predicted.

Background

Two important characteristics of CBR systems are that they are complex and the task domains in which they operate are also complex and often ill-structured. As a result, the behavior of a CBR system has many sources for variability which causes any performance measure defined to evaluate this behavior to have variability as well. This in turn makes it difficult to assess the significance of an observed behavior of the system in a specific situation. Similarly, due to the complexity of the system and problem domains, theoretical analysis of the system performance given alternative decisions and domain characteristics, although desirable, is difficult in many cases (Francis and Ram 1995; Kibler and Langley 1988). However, straightforward performance curves that show how the performance of a system improves over time are not good enough. Although these curves show that the performance improves on specific test problems, they do not provide useful information about why the system works or how specific design decisions affect the behavior of the system, nor can they be used to predict the behavior of the system under different circumstances.

Ablation or lesion studies can be used to analyze the impact of different system's modules in the performance of the system (Cohen and Howe 1988, Kibler and Langley 1988). In such studies, one or more system modules are removed or deactivated to analyze how the performance of the system changes. Although these studies do provide some information about the contribution of different modules to the overall performance of the system, they are based on extreme operating conditions that are often impractical (i.e., one or more modules are set to be either active or inactive). Moreover, design decisions often deal with allocating certain amount of resources to different modules. Due to their nature, ablation studies can only deal with all-or-nothing resource allocation, and cannot be used to investigate resource or other interactions between modules.

As an alternative to these approaches, empirical model fitting and statistical tools can be used to analyze the change in the performance of the system in terms of alternative decisions and domain characteristics. In such an analysis, the system is evaluated through systematic experiments designed to test the impact of various design decisions while filtering out undesirable sources of variability. The results of the experiments are then analyzed using statistical tools. In addition, in CBR systems and other systems that learn from experience, it is important to verify not only that the performance of the system improves with experience, but also that the variability in the performance of the system when solving new similar problems decreases as the number of problems solved in the past increases. Systematic empirical analysis based on statistical tools can also be used to verify the significance of these behaviors and to identify the sources of variability in the behavior of the system.

This chapter presents an evaluation methodology based on well-known statistical tools that can be used to explicitly analyze the merit of a range of design decisions in the performance of a system. The methodology consists of designing experiments to carefully control the variability in the behavior of the system and to obtain empirical performance data over a range of alternative design parameters, representational choices, algorithmic choices, and domain characteristics. This data is used to construct a mathematical model that relates the change in the performance of the system to design decisions and domain characteristics. The model can be used to select the best system configuration for a given domain, to predict the behavior of the system when the domain characteristics change, and to show how (or whether) performance improves with experience.

This chapter is organized as follows. The Evaluation Methodology section describes the proposed methodology. The Case Study section illustrates the methodology through a case study in which the methodology is used to evaluate SINS, a case-based system that performs autonomous robotic navigation. The case study focuses specifically on design decisions that are relevant in CBR systems, although the methodology proposed here can be used for evaluating a wide range of AI systems. The Conclusion summarizes the implications of the methodology for the evaluation of CBR and other AI systems.

Evaluation Methodology

The proposed evaluation method is shown in table 1. It consists of five phases: experimental design, data collection, model construction, model validation, and robustness analysis. During the experimental design phase, the factors that may influence the performance of the system are identified. These factors are classified in two broad groups: *design decisions* and *domain characteristics*. Experiments are designed to measure the performance of the system

1. Experimental Design
2. Data Collection.
3. Model Construction.
4. Model Validation.
5. Robustness Analysis

Table 1. Systematic evaluation methodology.

while systematically varying the factors. In the data collection phase, the experiments are executed and data is collected. During the model construction phase, empirical models that relate the design decisions, domain characteristics, and the performance of the system are constructed. In the model validation phase, the assumptions identified during the model construction phase are verified. In this manner, the models can be used to state valid conclusions about the relationship between the system's performance and the factors (i.e., design decisions and domain characteristics). During the robustness analysis phase, the system is tested under different alternatives for the factors to assess the generality of the results. In addition, for a CBR or machine learning system, learning profile curves are constructed to compare the empirical models with traditional learning curves obtained with the system. These profiles further verify the results and also provide an intuitive feel for the changes in the external performance of the system as it gains experience. Finally, the data collection and analysis at each step may raise new questions and new ideas for continuing the evaluation, perhaps with a different focus or using a different set of factors; this results in iterative use of the methodology until the issues of interest are resolved. The following sections discuss each of these phases in more detail.

Experimental Design and Data Collection

Case-based reasoning systems are typically complex in nature and, like other AI systems, their performance depends on several factors. These factors can broadly be classified into two categories: design decisions and domain characteristics.

Design decision factors are related to the configuration of the system and often deal with allocating resources to different modules within the system. In CBR systems, several factors are of interest: *system configuration parameters*, such as the size of the case library, thresholds for quality of match or distance metrics for retrieval, and other numerical parameters (such as learning rates in machine learning systems); *knowledge representation factors,* such as the choice of representational primitives or the content theory of the domain; and *algorithmic factors,* such as the specific algorithms used for retrieval or adaptation.

Domain characteristic factors are related to problem descriptions and are used to categorize problems in the domain: for example, the difficulty of the problems or the variability in the kinds of problems that the system might face. An additional factor that is relevant to system performance on a given problem is the amount of prior experience that the system has had. If it is feasible to train the system before it is deployed or to hand-code the appropriate experiences, the amount of prior experience can be viewed as another design decision factor for the system designer to consider.

To understand and optimize the performance of the system, it is necessary to assess the role of each factor in the system's overall behavior. During the first phase of our evaluation methodology, factors of interest are identified and experiments are designed to measure the system's performance for different alternatives or *levels*[j] for each factor. A representative sample of system configurations and problem instances is selected, each one with a different set of alternatives for each factor. Several versions of the system are built, each with a different set of choices for the design parameters, representations, and algorithms.

An *experiment* consists of measuring the performance of each version of the system executing on each set of problem instances. Thus, an experiment requires more than a single run; it requires several runs carried out under different conditions (i.e., different configurations of the system, different representational vocabularies, different algorithms for each module, different environmental configurations, different levels of problem difficulty, different order of problems, etc.). Data is gathered from all runs and analyzed using statistical techniques. This allows us to determine not only which factors influence the behavior of the system but under which circumstances and to what extent. (These relationships are captured mathematically in the model construction phase, discussed later.) This information can be used both to understand why the system worked and to select the best system configuration for a given problem domain.

While designing the experiments, it is important to reduce unwanted sources of variability in the system's performance across runs. This ensures that the empirical model attributes differences in system performance solely to differences between alternative chosen factors to the extent possible. If there are other sources of variability in the performance that were not considered beforehand, the model will lose its accuracy and will not be useful in estimating the best design alternatives for optimum system performance. Unwanted sources of variability usually originate by not considering relevant factors in the model or by having a poor experimental design. For example, if the selected sample of problem instances have different levels of difficulty and if the level of difficulty is not considered as a factor, then a poor experimental design might be to measure the performance of two systems configured with a different set of alternatives on only one set of problem instances. If one version of the system solves the easier problems while the other solves the more difficult ones, it will be difficult to assess whether the difference in system performance is due to the different system configurations or to different difficulty levels. To avoid this problem, the experiments should either *balance out* the runs along the factors (i.e., run all system configurations on problems instances with all levels of difficulty), or *block out* the runs along a specific factor (i.e., run all system configurations on problem instances with only one level of difficulty).

The choice about when to balance or to block a specific factor is made by trading off the cost of running experiments against the range of applicability of the results of the empirical model to be constructed. A model is applicable only to the range of problem instances from which it was constructed. Increasing the range of problem instances increases the range of applicability of the model but also increases the number of experiments needed because each version of the system must be run with problem instances that represent the entire range. Due to the fact that factors are often grouped by design decisions and domain characteristics, one practical way to design the experiments is to balance out all the factors related to design decisions and to block out all the factors related to domain characteristics. In this way, a detailed analysis of the merits of the design decisions under specific but representative problem instances can be obtained. Such an analysis allows the selection of the best alternatives for the design decisions considered so that the system's performance is optimum when working under the representative problem instances. Next, during the robustness analysis phase, the generality of the selected "best" system configuration can be studied across different levels of domain characteristic factors.

An approach similar to this use of the robustness analysis phase is described by Aha (1992). He proposes an evaluation methodology designed to understand the effect of different domain characteristics in the performance of learning systems and to derive rules that designers can use to decide when to generalize the results obtained from case studies. In contrast, our methodology is designed to understand the effects of the design decisions on the performance of the system, to determine if the results are significant, and furthermore, to analyze the domain characteristics under which the evaluation study is valid. Thus, our methodology helps us evaluate the theoretical basis for the system and provides a means to select appropriate design parameters for a given application.

At the end of the experimental design phase, the data collection phase is executed. This simply involves running the different versions of the systems on the chosen problem sets and gathering performance data using appropriate performance metrics.

Model Construction

After the experiments are run and the data collected, a mathematical model is constructed to fit and explain the results. Models that relate system performance and relevant factors (i.e., design decisions and domain characteristics) are useful because they provide information about how each factor influences the performance of the system. Such models can serve many purposes, such as predicting what the performance of the system would be under certain conditions of interest, and selecting appropriate system parameters, representations, and algorithms to configure a system for specific situations. The model can also help explain the behavior of the system and thereby provide insight into the theory underlying the design of the system.

Due to the complexity of case-based reasoning systems and the often ill-structured task domains that they operate in, theoretical models that relate system performance and relevant factors are difficult to construct. Instead, the data collected during experiments can be used to infer an empirical model. Empirical models are mathematical expressions based on experimental data and can be constructed using statistical estimation techniques. The basic idea in constructing a model is to assume that there exists a functional relationship between system performance and the relevant factors. The model is a mathematical expression of this relationship.

An example of a linear empirical model is shown in equation 1.

$$Y_i = \beta_0 + \beta_1 X_{1i} + \cdots + \beta_k X_{ki} = \varepsilon_i \tag{1}$$

In equation 1, the results of $i = 1, \ldots, n$ experimental runs are assumed to follow the additive relationship expressed above. In the model Y_i, represents the dependent variable or observed performance of the system for each of the n runs, and the X_{ji} represent the independent variable or alternative values of each of the $j = 1, \ldots, k$ factors for each of the n runs. Note that dependent variables (also known as response variables) may be used to measure not only the external performance of the system according to some metric but also internal behaviors or effects that are of interest. The values ε_i represent the *residual* or error incurred by the model in estimating the observed value Y_i given the values of the X_{ji} for each of the runs. Inferential statistical techniques are used to estimate the values of the β_j coefficients for the given sample.

This empirical model is applicable to a wide range of situations. The response variable Y_i must be a numerical quantity representing either an observed or qualitative variable that measures the performance of the system. For example, for a robot that navigates autonomously, an observed response variable may be the time the robot takes to reach the destination point, whereas a qualitative response variable may be the "smoothness" of the trajectory of the robot on a scale from 1 to 10 as determined by some judge. The independent variables X_{ji} are numerical quantities representing the alternative values of the factors under consideration. These variables may be continuous or categorical. *Continuous variables* represent factors that can be varied continuously, such as the amount of memory given to the system under study (e.g., the maximum size of the case library) or a numerical threshold parameter (e.g., the minimum value of a quality of match metric that is necessary to allow a case to be retrieved). *Categorical variables* represent discrete alternatives, such as different representational vocabularies, different domain theories, or different adaptation algorithms that can be used in various modules of the system.

A widely used inferential statistical technique is regression analysis using least-squared error (LSE) (Neter et al 1989). LSE estimates the model coefficients (the β_j's in equation 1) by minimizing the squared sum of the residuals (ε_i) across the sample. The model coefficients represent the influence of each factor (X_{ji}) on the performance of the system (Y_i). LSE estimation is widely used because of its properties; in particular, the Gauss-Markov theorem establishes that LSE estimators for regression models are the best linear unbiased estimators possible (Weld 1916).

The linear regression model in equation 1 is very general and can incorporate a wide range of smooth functional relations. For example, ablation studies analyze the partial increment/decrement in the system's performance with the addition/elimination of a system component (Cohen and Howe 1988). Such analyses can be performed using a regression model in which categorical variables can take on the values 1 or 0 to indicate whether a system component is present or not. A linear regression model can also be used with continuous valued parameters, such as amount of memory. Finally, quadratic terms or other functional forms can be incorporated into the model because the only restriction is that it must be linear in the β_j coefficients. Thus, the model can capture mathematically the impact of individual design decisions on the performance of the system as well as that of interactions between design decisions. Once the model is created, the best set of parameter values can be selected to optimize the performance of the system. When smooth functional relations do not apply, either the domain of the model is too ample and must be reduced or more terms (e.g., quadratic, cubic, etc.) must be added into the model. This follows from the fact that any functional relationship can be approximated by a series of polynomials with any degree of accuracy as the number of terms of the polynomials increases (Munroe 1963).

A common problem when constructing a model is selecting appropriate independent variables to use from the set of all the possible variables that might be considered. Selecting all possible independent variables in the model may artificially reduce the error between the data and model due to overfitting. One solution to this problem is to consider all the possible subsets of independent variables and select the best model according to a specific criterion. One criterion that is often used is to select the model with the best adjusted multiple coefficient of determination (R^2_{adj}). This coefficient measures the ability of the model to explain the variability of the response variable (Y_i). The greater the R^2_{adj}, the better the model explains the variability of the response variable in terms of the variability of the independent variables. The adjusted multiple coefficient of variation takes into consideration the number of terms (estimated parameters) in the model in such a way that models that include terms to artificially reduce the error have lower R^2_{adj} values.

Model Validation

Any model estimated using an inferential statistical technique relies on a set of assumptions. The validity of the model constructed depends on the extent to which these assumptions hold for a given sample of data. For example, there are two assumptions implied in the additive model of equation 1. First, the residuals are assumed to have zero mean and constant variance across samples. Second, they are assumed to be independent and normally distributed. When these assumptions do not hold, conclusions derived from the model may not be valid. Deviations from the assumption of the residuals having constant variance might lead to overestimates in the ranges of parameter values. This in turn would cause the model to be inaccurate. Small deviations from the assumption of the residuals being normally distributed usually do not create serious problems, but major departures are of concern since the conclusions derived using the model might be incorrect.

To verify qualitatively that the residuals have constant variance, a plot of the residuals against each independent variable and against the fitted response variable is used. A normal probability plot is commonly used to verify the normality distribution assumption of the residuals.

Robustness Analysis

In the final phase of the methodology, alternative levels for the factors are tried and verified against the model. As suggested in the experimental design phase, the experiments in this phase should focus on the factors that are associated with the domain characteristics. In this way it is possible to analyze the sensitivity of the best system configuration as obtained from the model across different domain characteristics, and to verify the generality of the system across a range of problems.

In addition, for a CBR or machine learning system, learning profiles are constructed to further verify the empirical model and to provide an intuitive look at the internal behaviors and external performance of the system as it gains experience. A learning profile is similar to a traditional learning curve, except that it also plots the predicted performance of the system based on the model in order to compare that with the actual performance.

A Case Study

This section describes a case study based on an implemented case-based reasoning system and is intended as an example of how to apply the methodology proposed in the previous section. The case study is based on a detailed and systematic analysis of a system that performs autonomous robotic navigation. The objective of this evaluation is twofold: first, to find a model that describes the relationship between the system's configuration parameters, design decisions, experience level, and its performance as measured by a suitable metric; and second, to evaluate the robustness of the performance of the system under different environmental conditions. The first objective enables us to understand the relationship between the configuration parameters, design decisions, and system performance, to evaluate the merit of alternative design decisions in the behavior of the system, and to verify that the performance of the system continues to improve with large amounts of experience. Moreover, a model that relates the performance metric with the configuration parameters and amount of experience is also useful because it enables us to pick the best system configuration parameters for a given situation and to determine the amount of prior experience (or training) that is necessary to achieve a desired level of performance. The second objective, evaluation of the robustness of the system when performing under different environmental conditions, is useful because it enables us to verify the robustness and generality of the system, that is, whether it is likely that the results obtained will hold when the system runs under different environments.

The following subsections describe in more detail the system we used in this evaluation and how each step in the evaluation methodology was carried out. For the purposes of this chapter, we will focus on a representative set of design decisions that are relevant in many case-based reasoning systems.

System Description

The self-improving navigation system (SINS) is a case-based reasoning system that performs autonomous robotic navigation in unstructured terrains (for a detailed technical discussion of the system, see Ram and Santamaría 1993a; for a discussion of the case-based reasoning aspects of the system, see Ram and Santamaría 1993b). Autonomous robotic navigation is defined as the task of autonomously and safely moving a robot from a source point to a destination point in an obstacle-ridden terrain. SINS uses reactive control methods for navigation coupled with case-based reasoning methods for adaptation and learning during task performance. SINS is implemented on a Denning MRV-III robot and can be used to drive the actual robot as well as a simulation.

It is difficult to evaluate a system such as SINS because its behavior is the result of many factors interacting with each other and because it is designed to work under unstructured terrains. Also, some modules in the architecture perform random actions under certain conditions (e.g., to accomplish exploration behaviors). This causes the evaluation to be even more difficult because random actions increase the variability in the behavior of the system. Thus, as discussed earlier, measuring the performance of the system during a single run (or an ad hoc set of runs) or performing ablation studies does not accomplish the objectives of a systematic evaluation, which are to analyze the impact of the design decisions and domain characteristics on the performance of the system and to select appropriate design parameters for a given application. As discussed below, a systematic statistical evaluation using our methodology can be used to accomplish these objectives.

Briefly, SINS consists of a navigation module, which uses a schema-based reactive control method (Arkin 1989), and an on-line adaptation and learning module, which uses case-based reasoning and reinforcement learning methods (Ram and Santamaría 1993a). The navigation module is responsible for moving the robot through the terrain from the starting location to the desired goal location while avoiding obstacles along the way. A set of control parameters can be used to change the behavior of the navigation module. The adaptation and learning module is responsible for learning control parameters to change the behavior of the navigation module in such a way that the performance of the navigation task is improved. In particular, the adaptation and learning module constructs mappings from sensory input information about the environment to appropriate control parameters that should be used in that environment. These mappings are represented as "cases" that encapsulate the system's navigational experiences.

A case in SINS represents continuous sensory inputs and associated motor schema control parameters over a time window, and recommends appropriate control parameters to use in different situations. Cases are matched not only on the basis of the current instantaneous situation but on the immediate history of situations over a suitable time window. As the system gains experience, it can create new cases by allocating unused memory or it can modify previous cases by updating their content or by increasing their time windows (which changes their temporal extent). Several design decisions affect the behavior and performance of SINS; in this case study, we focus on four that are relevant to the case-based reasoning component of the system. Two of these are system configuration parameters: the maximum number of cases (C) and the maximum case size in terms of the maximum time window over which experiences can be encapsulated (S). These parameters together determine the maximum amount of memory the system can use to store its experiences. When the maximums are reached, the system can use new experiences only to modify the content of the cases if it is appropriate to do so.

The other two design decisions evaluated in this study are categorical decisions: the choice of representational primitives, and the choice of adaptation algorithms. For the former, there are several choices available for the sensory inputs that the learning and adaptation module uses to represent environmental situations. One option is to use sensory inputs with "low-level" information; in the navigation domain, this might involve using ultrasonic sensors to measure the distance of the closest obstacle in the direction of the goal. Another option is to use sensory inputs that encode "high-level" information; for example, using an array of ultrasonic sensors to compute a measure of the density of obstacles surrounding the robot. The former type of sensory input is very specific and may allow SINS to discover the best control parameters the robot may use in specific situations. However, we would also expect that the cases learned by the system to be very specific and not work as well in similar but not identical situations. In contrast, the latter type of sensory input is more generic and may allow SINS to discover good control parameters. However, the learned cases may turn so coarse that the system may not perform near-optimally in most cases.

Another design decision in SINS is the choice of the adaptation algorithm. Every few steps, as determined by a configuration parameter, the adaptation and learning module may recommend new control parameters to the navigation module. To accomplish this, it retrieves the case most similar to the current environmental situation over a recent time window and adapts the control parameters used by the navigation module based on the control parameters suggested by the case. The best values for the control parameters would be those that increase the likelihood of obtaining a positive outcome in the next cycle (as measured by performance metrics such as progress towards the goal or number of collisions with obstacles). In order to learn appropriate control parameters, SINS must "explore" the space of possible parameter values—that is, it must try several values for each environmental situation and learn which values produce positive or negative results. This presents at least two design options for the adaptation method. One option is to select the new values of the control parameters stochastically according to the outcome they have achieved in the past. In this method, values that have produced positive outcomes (or obtained positive rewards) are more likely to be selected than those that have produced negative outcomes. Another option is to select for each control parameter the value that has produced the best reward in the past in any situation. The former adaptation method enforces more exploration and may discover better solutions than the later one. On the other hand, due to the same reason, the latter method may converge faster than the former one.

The performance of SINS depends not only on its design but also on the problem environments in which it is placed, that is, on the domain characteristics. SINS navigates in randomly generated environments consisting of rectangular bounded worlds. Each environment contains circular obstacles, a start location, and a destination location. The location, number, and radius of the obstacles are randomly determined to create environments of varying amounts of clutter, defined as the ratio of free space to occupied space. 15 clutter corresponds to relatively easy environments and 25 clutter to difficult environments. A randomly generated navigation problem in a high clutter world is likely to be more difficult than one in a low clutter world. Thus, an important factor to consider from the domain characteristic group is the clutter value of the environments in which the robot is placed. Finally, because SINS is a learning system, its performance also depends on the amount of previous experience it has had.

To summarize, the performance of SINS varies due to design decisions (system configuration parameters, representational vocabulary, adaptation algorithm), domain or problem characteristics (world clutter), and amount of experience. Moreover, due to the nature of the task and the architecture of the system, SINS can perform differently given the same world and case library. The reason for this is twofold: first, the navigation module includes a behavior which generates random motion to allow the robot to get out of local minima; and second, the adaptation and learning module tunes the navigation module randomly when no appropriate case exists so as to allow the system to explore and discover new regularities. This means that any performance metric used to evaluate the system must be treated as a random variable and statistical estimation techniques should be used to assess its mean value.

The following sections describe two empirical studies. The first study focuses on the categorical design decisions (representational and algorithmic choices), and the second focuses on the continuous design decisions (system configuration parameters) and domain characteristics (problem difficulty). Both studies evaluate improvement in the performance of the system with experience.

Study 1: Choice of Input Representation and Adaptation Method

Experimental Design and Data Collection. The objective of this study is to find an empirical model that describes the relationship between the choice of input representation, adaptation method, and system performance as well as the conditions under the model is applicable. In this study, we evaluated two choices of input representations and two choices of adaptation methods. The input representation refers to the information that the learning and adaptation module of SINS uses to represent and categorize the surrounding environment (situation). The adaptation method refers to the methods by which this module adapts the control parameters suggested by the best matching case to the current situation.

The two choices of input representations studied were the low-level and high-level information types introduced earlier. The low-level information type consists of the following four sensory inputs: *Obstacle-Distance-Ahead, Obstacle-Distance-Behind, Obstacle-Distance-Right,* and *Obstacle-Distance-Left.* Each of these variables provide a measure of the nearest obstacle that impede navigation in the direction towards, contrary to, right of, and left of the direction of the perceived goal respectively. The high-level information type consists of the following four sensory inputs: *Obstacle-Density* provides a measure of the occupied areas around the robot that impede navigation;[2] *Absolute-Motion* measures the activity of the system; *Relative-Motion* represents the change in motion activity over an appropriate interval; and *Motion-Towards-Goal* specifies how much progress the system has actually made towards the goal. Both types of sensory inputs are computed and constantly updated using the information received from the robot's physical sensors (in our case, 24 ultrasonic sensors arranged around the robot every 15 degrees and shaft encoders).

The two choices of adaptation method studied were the stochastic method and the select-best method. The stochastic adaptation algorithm selects control parameter values randomly but favoring to values that lead to positive reward. Specifically, values are selected according to a Boltzmann distribution:

$$P(v) = \frac{exp(w_v)}{\sum_i exp(wi)}$$

where the w_i represent the expected reward for value i. The select-best adaptation method simply selects the value that led to the most positive expected reward in the past (i.e., the value with largest w_v).

To collect data for model construction and analysis, we performed several simulated runs on the system. A run consisted of placing the robot at the start location and letting it run until it reached the destination location. The data for the estimators was obtained after the system terminated each run. This was to ensure that we were consistently measuring the effect of learning across experiences rather than within a single experience.

We evaluated the performance of SINS using the median value of the time it takes to solve a world. The reason for this is that the median is a robust estimator of the mean and is not too sensitive to outliers. Outliers are common in schema-based reactive control since the system can get trapped in local minima points, resulting in a significant change in the behavior of the system. An experiment consisted of measuring the time SINS takes to solve a world across five independent runs under the same conditions (i.e., same conditions but different random seeds) and reporting the median among the five runs as the response variable.

Table 2 shows the design matrix for the study. It consists of a factorial design: two choices for input representation (low-level and high-level), and two choices for adaptation method (stochastic and best). Starting from no prior experience, every setup was exposed to thirty levels of experience, each level

Choice of input representation	high-level / low-level
Choice of adaptation method	stochastic / best-value
Experience Levels	1-30
World Clutter	10%
Replicates	5
Response Variable	Time
Total runs	**600**

Table 2. Experimental design matrix.

being one complete navigation problem. We recorded the outcome of five replications for every level of experience. Thus, the total number of system runs in study was $2 \times 2 \times 30 \times 5 = 600$. The domain characteristics in this experiment were blocked by evaluating all the setups under the same randomly generated 10 percent cluttered world. This allowed us to balance out the effects of the design decision choices and experience level (which were of interest) and block out the effects of other parameters such as world clutter.[3]

Model Construction. The performance of SINS was evaluated by estimating the median time to solve a world. Thus, the model that needed to be determined in this study has the median time (T) as the response variable, and would relate T with the choices of input representation and adaptation method, and with amount of experience. Note that a lower value of T corresponds to better performance on the task. We used the following regressors as independent variables: input representation (I; low = 0, high = 1), adaptation method (A; stochastic = 0, best-value = 1), and experience level (E). We also considered additional regressors, such as the interaction terms IE, AE, and IA. The reason for considering all these factors is to allow for the possibility that interaction terms may explain variability in the response variable better than individual terms. Statistical analysis was used to reveal which of these terms were really significant and should be considered in the final model. Equation 2 shows the complete hypothetical model.

$$T = \beta_0 + \beta_I I + \beta_A A + \beta_E E + \beta_{IE} IE + \beta_{AE} AE + \beta_{IA} IA + \beta_{IAE} IAE + \varepsilon \quad (2)$$

Figure 1 shows the response variable T collected during the experiment. The figure shows that there are mainly two phases as experience increases: a learning phase, where performance improves; and a maturity phase, where performance remains constant. (This is as intuitively expected; recall that SINS is learning to navigate a fixed world because domain characteristics have been blocked in this study.) A single first-order or second-order polynomial

Input representation	Adaptation method	Equation
low-level	stochastic	$\overline{T} = \beta_0 + \beta_E E$
high-level	stochastic	$\overline{T} = (\beta_0 + \beta_I) + (\beta_E + \beta_{IE})\, E$
low-level	best-value	$\overline{T} = (\beta_0 + \beta_A) + (\beta_E + \beta_{AE})\, E$
high-level	best-value	$\overline{T} = (\beta_0 + \beta_A + \beta_{IA}) + (\beta_E + \beta_{AE} + \beta_{IAE})\, E$

Table 3. Design for Experiment 1.

would not be able to fit all the data with enough accuracy in both phases. As described before, there are two ways to solve this problem: either increase the number of terms in the model, or reduce the region of operability of the model. Since there are clearly two phases as experience increases, we decided to use two models, one for each phase.

Table 3 shows the alternative empirical models based on the design decision choices. The terms β_I and β_A measure the change in the intercept of the equation given a change in the choice of input representation and adaptation method, respectively. The term β_{IA} measures the interaction effect of the design decisions on the intercept. The terms β_{IE}, β_{AE}, and β_{IAE} perform the same role but on the slope of the equation. In this context, the slope represents the learning rate of the system, that is, how much the system improves performance (decrease in T) per unit of experience (increase in E).

An all-subsets regression analysis was performed to determine which of the terms in the model are really significant, that is, which terms influence the response variable. In this analysis, all possible subsets of regressors are considered and a model is constructed using each subset. Tables 4 and 5 show the results of this analysis of the models for the learning and maturity phases. We measured the optimality of the model by its R^2_{adj}, the adjusted coefficient of multiple determination.[4] This coefficient measures the ability of the model to explain changes in the response variable by changes in the regressors. Its range is between 0 percent, which means that none of the variation in the response is explained by variation in the regressors, and 100 percent, which means that all of the variation in the response is explained by variation in the regressors. Thus, the larger the R^2_{adj} the more explicative is the model. This coefficient also indicates if we are overfitting the data by introducing more terms that artificially reduce the error in fit between the model and the data.

Tables 4 and 5 show the best model obtained within each subset of constant size or number of variables. In these tables, $\hat{\sigma}$ is the estimated standard deviation of the dependent variable in the model, and R^2_{adj} is the adjusted

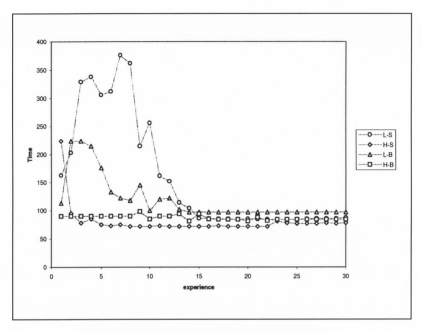

Figure 1. Response variable versus experience level.
The four graphs correspond to low-level representation with stochastic
adaptation (L-S), high-level representation with stochastic adaptation (H-S),
low-level representation with best-value adaptation (L-B), and
high-level representation with best-value adaptation(H-B).

coefficient of multiple determination as discussed earlier. The "x's" show which variables are included in the best model for each size.

During the learning phase, the best model obtained with the all-subset analysis corresponds to the one having six regressors as independent variables (F = 20.04, P-value = 0.000).[5] There is no statistical evidence that the term is significant, that is, there is no evidence that the learning rate is affected by the interaction between the choice of input representation and adaptation method. Table 6 shows the statistical results for each individual parameter in the model for the learning phase as well as the 90 confidence interval estimate of their real values.

The results show that the system configuration that achieves best performance is the one using the high-level representation and the stochastic adaptation algorithm ($T = 51.73$ seconds at $E = 15$ experiences). However, the fastest learning rate corresponds to the system configuration with the low-level representation and the stochastic adaptation algorithm: ($\beta_E = -12.79$ secs./exp.) since changing the level of input representation or the adaptation method re-

No. variables	R^2_{adj}	$\hat{\sigma}$	I	A	E	IE	AE	IA	IAE
1	35.3	66.14	X						
2	45.6	60.64	X	X					
3	52.8	56.48	X				X		X
4	64.0	49.33	X	X	X				X
5	64.5	48.69	X	X	X	X		X	
6	65.9	47.99	X	X	X	X	X	X	
7	65.3	48.43	X	X	X	X	X	X	X

Table 4. Best subsets regression results for the learning phase.

No. variables	R^2_{adj}	$\hat{\sigma}$	I	A	E	IE	AE	IA	IAE
1	50.9	5.61	X						
2	94.1	1.95	X	X					
3	95.0	1.79	X	X			X		
4	96.5	1.50	X	X		X			X
5	97.1	1.38	X	X		X		X	X
6	97.0	1.38	X	X	X	X		X	X
7	97.0	1.39	X	X	X	X	X	X	X

Table 5. Best subsets regression results for the maturity phase.

duces the learning rate (increases the slope). There is a big influence on the intercept (performance with no previous experience) caused by the design decisions. The interaction term (β_{IA}) shows that the amount of change in performance caused by changing one of the design decisions depends on the other design decision. For example, the average change in performance caused by switching from low-level to high-level input representation when using the stochastic adaptation method is $\beta_I = -209.56$ seconds. But, if the same switch is performed using the best-value adaptation method, the average change in performance is only $\beta_I + \beta_{IA} = -113.56$ seconds. In both cases, it appears that using high-level input representations provides a better start in the learning process. There is no statistical evidence ($t = 0.68$, P-value $= 0.499$) to indicate that a change in the input representation improves the learning rate more than a change in the adaptation method (i.e., $\beta_{IE} = \beta_{AE}$).

During the maturity phase, the best model obtained with the all-subset analysis corresponds to the one having five regressors as independent variables ($F = 389.99$, P-value $= 0.000$). There is no statistical evidence that the terms β_E and β_{AE} are significant. This means that there is no evidence that

Coefficients	Value	Std. Error	95% C.I.
β_0	334.19	23.420	(294.99, 373.39)
β_E	−12.79	3.484	(−16.95, −8.63)
β_I	−209.56	28.870	(−257.89, −161.23)
β_A	−132.43	28.870	(−180.78, −84.10)
β_{IE}	7.90	2.868	(3.09, 12.70)
β_{AE}	5.14	2.868	(0.34, 9.94)
β_{IA}	96.00	24.780	(54.51, 137.49)

Table 6. Model coefficients for the learning phase.

there is further learning going on after experience level 15. There is some indication that performance varies with experience in the high-level representation/stochastic adaptation system configuration, but it is positive and small ($\beta_{IE} = 0.53$ secs./exp.). Table 7 shows the statistical results for each individual parameter in the model for the maturity phase as well as the 90 percent confidence interval estimation of the real coefficient values.

The results confirm the hypothesis that the system is in a maturity phase since two terms related with experience are not in the model and the others are statistically significant but with small values. Again, the best system configuration is the one using high-level input representations and the stochastic adaptation method ($T = 73$ seconds). Furthermore, there is an interaction effect in the design decisions on the final performance of the system. For example, the average change in performance caused by switching from low-level to high-level input representation when using the stochastic adaptation method is $\beta_I = -14.07$ seconds. But if the same switch is performed using the best-value adaptation method, the average change in performance is only $\beta_I + \beta_{IA} = -12.67$ seconds. In both cases, the use of high-level input representations provides better performance after convergence. There is statistical evidence that the best-value adaptation procedure causes the final performance to deteriorate by an average of $\beta_A = 11.93$ when the system uses low-level input representations and by an average of $\beta_A + \beta_{IA} = 21.20$ when the system uses high-level input representations. This confirms the hypothesis that the stochastic adaptation method takes longer to converge but arrives at better solutions.

Model Validation. The above results demonstrate the power of our systematic evaluation method: the method enables us to obtain an in-depth understanding of the performance of the system and to make design decisions in a principled manner. However, there are two assumptions that must be verified be-

Coefficients	Value	Std. Error	95% C.I.
β_0	85.07	0.355	(84.47,85.66)
β_I	− 14.07	1.956	(− 15.45, − 12.68)
β_A	11.93	0.502	(11.09,12.77)
β_{IE}	0.53	0.082	(0.39,0.66)
β_{IA}	9.27	2.766	(4.64,13.90)
β_{IAE}	− 0.54	0.116	(− 0.73, − 0.34)

Table 7. Model coefficients for the maturity phase.

fore accepting the proposed models (and associated results) as a valid: the residuals have zero mean and constant variance, and the residuals have normal distribution. The LSE technique relies on these assumptions; thus, since the model coefficients were calculated using this technique we must verify if these assumptions hold. Otherwise, any conclusions derived from the model could be wrong. In particular, violation of the assumption about the residuals having zero mean and constant variance could introduce inaccuracy in the estimation of the model coefficients, and violations of the assumption of the residuals being normally distributed could produce underestimation of the confidence intervals.

A scatter plot of the residuals against the fitted response was used to diagnose changes in variance, and a normal probability plot of the residuals was used to verify the normality distribution of the residuals. The results of each of these two validation techniques are shown in figures 2 and 3 for the learning and maturity phases, respectively. Figure 2a shows a systematic diagonal pattern that appears for the lower values of the fitted response. Usually, the presence of this pattern indicates that additional terms may be required, but in this study this is to be expected since the response is not linear (refer to figure 1). For the purposes of this chapter, we decided to accept this deficiency due to the complications of introducing more terms into the model. Figure 3a shows a constant band of residuals distributed randomly along the horizontal axis. Visually, this appears as a set of dots distributed evenly and randomly across the figure from left to right. When the variability of the residuals is not constant, the band tends to narrow or widen along the horizontal axis. Since this is not the case, we infer that the variance is indeed constant, as is necessary for the model to be valid.

Figures 2b and 3b show normal probability plots of the residuals for the learning and maturity phases. In these charts, the values of the residuals are plotted against their expected value as drawn from a normal distribution. If

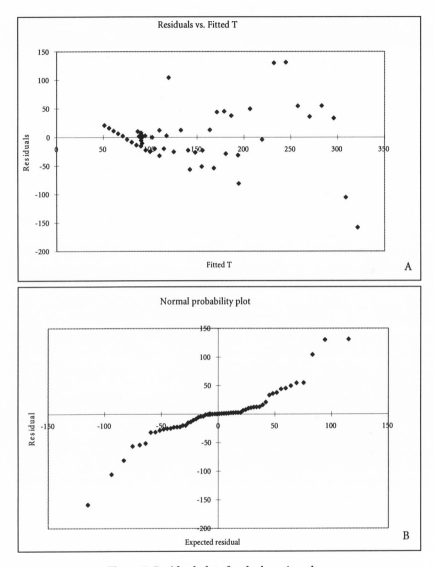

Figure 2. Residual plots for the learning phase.

the residuals are indeed normal, then the plots should show a straight line that crosses the origin. In both models, the residuals have zero mean but there is some departure from linearity, especially in the model corresponding to the maturity phase. The reason for this is that the variance in the maturity phase was very small since the system responded similarly during the five replications at each experience level.

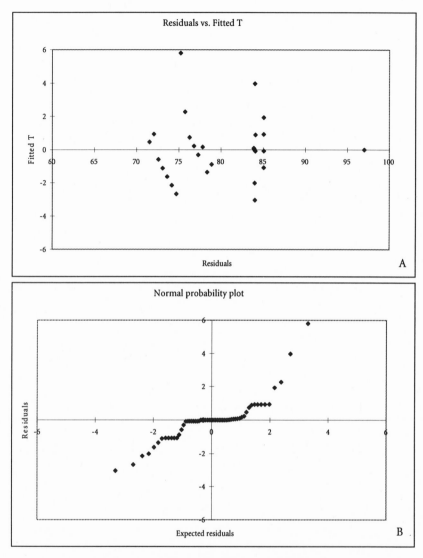

Figure 3. Residual plots for the maturity phase.

Since the two assumptions, residuals with zero mean, constant variance, and normally distributed are not fully satisfied, care must be taken in generalize this result to other 10 percent cluttered worlds. One option at this point would be to repeat the analysis with additional terms, as discussed above. Another option is to repeat the experiments, this time systematically varying the world clutter; this is discussed next.

Choice of input representation	high-level
Choice of adaptation procedure	stochastic
Experience Levels	1–30
World Clutter	7 %
Replicates	5
Response Variable	Time
Total runs	150

Table 8. Experimental design matrix.

Robustness Analysis. A follow-up experiment were designed to evaluate the generality of the system by running experiments with a different set of problems. Since the previous experiments indicated that the best design for the system was to use high-level input representations and the stochastic adaptation algorithm, the system was configured in this manner for the new experiment. The data for the experiment was collected in the same manner as the previous experiment, but with the difference that the system solved a fixed randomly-generated 7 percent cluttered world in every run.

As in the previous experiment, the model that needs to be determined has the median time (T) as the response variable. But in this case, the model relates the response variable with the amount of experience only since the other factors are constant. If such a model is found to be significant (i.e., the model shows that the amount of experience is related to the response variable), we can conclude that the system learns under the new environmental conditions. Furthermore, the coefficient derived from this model can be compared with the respective coefficient in the previous model. If a significant difference is detected, we can conclude that changing the world clutterness from 10 percent to 7 percent affects the learning performance. Table 8 shows the experimental design matrix and equation 3 shows the complete hypothetical model for this experiment.

This model is a simplification of the model in equation 2 where the experience level (E) is the only regressor. Tables 9 and 10 show the statistical results for each individual parameter in the model as well as the 90 confidence interval estimation of its value for the learning and maturity phases, respectively.

The results show that during the learning phase, the learning rate decreased from $-(\beta_E+\beta_{IE}) = 4.89$ secs./exp. to $-\alpha_E = 0.96$ secs./exp. This means that the system decreases the learning rate when solving a simpler world. Additionally, the value of the intercept reduced from $\beta_0 + \beta_I = 124.64$ seconds to $\alpha_0 = 102.97$ seconds. This confirms that that the system is indeed solving a simpler

Coefficients	Value	Std. Error	90% C.I.
α_0	102.97	2.76	$(97.46, 108.48)$
α_E	-0.95	0.30	$(-1.56, -0.35)$

Table 9. Model coefficients for the learning phase.

Coefficients	Value	Std. Error	90% C.I.
α_0	92.71	0.56	$(91.59, 93.84)$

Table 10. Model coefficients for the maturity phase.

world and most of the learning occurs during the early experiences. During the maturity phase, the term α_E is not statistically significant. This means that the system does not improve the performance further after experience level 15, which confirms the hypothesis that it is in the maturity phase.

Study 2: Maximum Number of Cases, Maximum Case Size, and World Clutter

Experimental Design and Data Collection. The second study focuses on continuous design decisions (specifically, numerical parameters) as opposed to categorical ones. The objective of this study is to find an empirical model that describes the relationship between relevant system configuration parameters and its performance as well as the conditions under which the model is applicable. The configuration parameters studied were the maximum number of cases (C) and maximum case size (S). The first parameter limits the number of different cases the system may store in its case library, and the second parameter limits the amount of information a single case can hold. To block the effects of the categorical design decisions, we chose the low-level input representation and the stochastic adaptation method which were kept constant in these experiments.

The data collection in this study was similar to that in the previous study. We chose a randomly-generated 15 percent cluttered performance world on which the system was to be tested.[6] We performed several runs on the system, where a run consisted of placing the robot at the start location and letting it run until it reached the destination location. As in the previous study, the performance of the system was evaluated using the median value of the time it takes to solve a world. We ran different system configurations, each configured using different C and S parameters. The set of runs obtained with each configuration was replicated five times. This allowed us to collect the data re-

Maximum number of cases	15, 25, 35, 45
Maximum case size	6, 9, 12, 15
Experience Levels	1–30
World Clutter	10 %
Replicates	5
Response Variable	Time
Total runs	2400

Table 11. Experimental design matrix.

quired to build a model that relates the system performance with the configuration parameters and amount of experience.

Table 11 shows the design matrix of the experiment. It consists of a 4 × 4 factorial design: four levels for maximum number of cases, and four levels for maximum case size. Each setup was exposed to thirty levels of experience, and the outcome of five replications for every level of experience was recorded. Thus, the total number of experiments in this study was 4 × 4 × 30 × 5 = 2400.

Model Construction. The performance of SINS was evaluated by estimating the median time to solve a world. Thus, the model that needs to be determined for this study has the median time (T) as the response variable; the model relates T with the configuration parameters and amount of experience. A fundamental difference between this model and the one used in the previous study is that the regressors are continuous instead of categorical. This means that the model can be used to predict system performance using values that are not the ones that were used during the experiment. This is an advantage of continuous regressors over categorical regressors. We used the following regressors as independent variables: maximum number of cases (C), maximum case size (S), and amount of experience (E). We also considered additional regressors such as the quadratic terms C^2, S^2, and E^2 and the quadratic interactions CE, SE, and CS. The reason for considering all these factors is to allow for the possibility that interaction terms may explain variability in the response variable better than individual terms. Statistical analysis was used to reveal which of these terms are really significant and should be considered in the final model. Equation 4 shows the complete hypothetical model.

$$T = \beta_0 + \beta_C C' + \beta_S S' + \beta_E E' + \\ \beta_{CS} C' S' + \beta_{CE} C' E' + \beta_{SE} S' E' + \\ \beta_{CC} C'^2 + \beta_{SS} S'^2 + \beta_{EE} E'^2 + \\ \varepsilon \tag{4}$$

where V' is the standardized value[7] of a variable V (i.e., $V' = \dfrac{V - \overline{V}}{\sqrt{\text{var}(V)}}$).

Assuming that the mathematical relationship between the response variable and the independent variables is "smooth", a second order polynomial expression of that relationship, such as the one proposed by the model, is a good approximation. The quadratic terms for the maximum number of cases and maximum case size allowed for the possibility of utility problems, and the interaction terms were included to allow for the possibility of a direct relationship between the response variable and the terms.[8]

An all-subsets regression analysis was performed to determine which of the terms in the model are significant. Table 12 shows the results of this analysis.

The best model obtained with the all-subset analysis corresponds to the one having all the regressors as independent variables ($F = 205.824$, P-value $= 0.000$).[9] Table 13 shows the statistical results for each individual parameter in the model as well as the 95 percent confidence interval estimation of its real value.

Table 14 shows the analysis of variance (ANOVA). The ANOVA table is a statistical tool that it is used to determine the sources of variability in a model. The first column identifies a source of variation, and the second, third, and fourth columns show the degrees of freedom (df), sum of squares (SS), and mean squared (MS) of a source, respectively. The fifth column shows the value of the F statistic which is used to determine the significance of the regression. The sixth column shows the P-value. A high significance value means that the variation in the response variable is indeed explained by variation of the independent variables or regressors.

Considering this model, the optimal system configuration parameters can be found using standard calculus techniques, i.e., by setting the first partial derivatives of the model with respect the relevant parameters to zero. Equations 5 and 6 show the optimal values for C' and S' at a given level of experience.

$$C' = \frac{2\,\beta_{SS}\,\beta_C - \beta_{CS}\,\beta_S}{\beta^2_{CS} - 4\,\beta_{CC}\,\beta_{SS}} + \frac{2\,\beta_{SS}\,\beta_{CE} - \beta_{CS}\,\beta_{SE}}{\beta^2_{CS} - 4\,\beta_{CC}\,\beta_{SS}}\,E'$$
$$= 0.80 + 0.75\,E' \tag{5}$$

$$S' = \frac{2\,\beta_{SS}\,\beta_S - \beta_{CS}\,\beta_C}{\beta^2_{CS} - 4\,\beta_{CC}\,\beta_{SS}} + \frac{2\,\beta_{SS}\,\beta_{SE} - \beta_{CS}\,\beta_{CE}}{\beta^2_{CS} - 4\,\beta_{CC}\,\beta_{SS}}\,E'$$
$$= 0.05 + 0.41\,E' \tag{6}$$

According to these equations the optimal configuration parameter values change with the level of experience. This is due to the interaction terms that exist among those variables. These equations can be used to determine the optimum configuration of the system for a given situation. For example, if

# variables	R^2_{adj}	$\hat{\sigma}$	C	S	E	CS	CE	SE	C^2	S^2	E^2
1	53.8	11.031			X						
2	66.5	9.394	X		X						
3	73.6	8.346	X		X		X				
4	75.7	8.002	X		X		X	X			
5	77.3	7.732	X		X		X	X			X
6	78.8	7.482	X	X	X		X	X			X
7	79.0	7.434	X	X	X		X	X	X		X
8	79.2	7.402	X	X	X		X	X	X	X	X
9	79.4	7.372	X	X	X	X	X	X	X	X	X

Table 12. Best subsets regression results.

the system were going to receive 20 training problems, we might want to optimize the performance of the system at experience level $E = 20$ (i.e., $E' = 0.52$). In this case, we would configure the system using 43 maximum cases ($C' = 1.19$) of size 11 ($S' = 0.26$).

Model Validation. As in the first study, a scatter plot of the residuals against the fitted response was used to diagnose changes in variance and a normal probability plot of the residuals was used to verify the normality distribution of the residuals. The results of each of these two validation techniques are shown in figure 4. Figure 4a shows a constant band of residuals along the horizontal axis. Thus, this chart indicates that the variability of the residuals is constant along the fitted values of the response variable (i.e., median time), which is necessary for a valid model. However, as in the previous study, some diagonal patterns are present. This indicates that a second order polynomial does not perfectly characterize the behavior of the system at certain levels of performance. The values at which this happens corresponds to the values where the system has reached maturity and there is no further learning.

Figure 4b shows a normal probability plot of the residuals. In this chart, the values of the residuals are plotted against their expected value as drawn from a normal distribution. If the residuals are indeed normal, the plot should show a straight line that crosses the origin. Since this is actually the case, we can conclude that the residuals are normal.

Since the two assumptions, residuals with zero mean and constant variance and residuals having normal distribution, hold, the model can be considered valid.

Robustness Analysis. Finally, as before, a follow-up experiment was designed for the robustness analysis phase of the methodology to evaluate the generali-

Coefficients	Value	Std. Error	95 percent C.I.
β_0	72.23	0.78	(70.70,73.77)
β_E	-11.92	0.34	$(-12.58, -11.26)$
β_C	-5.79	0.34	$(-6.45, -5.13)$
β_S	1.97	0.34	(1.31,2.63)
β_{EE}	2.33	0.38	(1.59,3.07)
β_{CC}	2.99	0.42	(2.16,3.82)
β_{SS}	-0.95	0.42	$(-1.78, -0.12)$
β_{CE}	-4.32	0.34	$(-4.99, -3.66)$
β_{SE}	-0.91	0.34	$(-1.57, -0.24)$
β_{CS}	0.74	0.34	(0.08,1.41)

Table 13. Model coefficients.

Source	df	SS	MS	F	P-value
Regression	9	100675.7	11186.2	205.824	7.1E-157
Residual	470	25543.7	54.3		
Total	479	126219.4			

Table 14. ANOVA table.

ty of the SINS approach. In this experiment, we evaluated a specific configuration of the system performing under a different environment. The data for the experiment was collected in the same manner as the first experiment, the only difference being that the agent solved a fixed randomly-generated 20-percent cluttered world in every run. The configuration parameters for the system were selected using the model constructed in the first experiment and to optimize the performance of the system around an experience level E equal to 20, that is, with 43 maximum cases of size 11, as determined earlier.

As in the previous experiments, the model that needs to be determined has the median time (T) as the response variable. But in this case, the model only relates the response variable with the amount of experience since the other factors are constant. The coefficient derived from this model can be compared with the respective coefficients derived in the previous model. If a significant difference is detected, we can conclude that changing the world clutterness from 15 percent to 20 percent affects the learning performance.

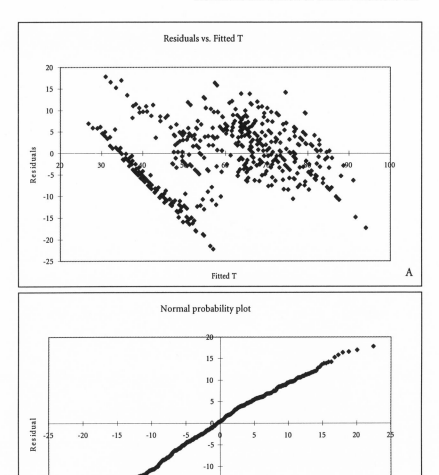

Figure 4. Residual plots.

Equation 7 shows the complete hypothetical model for the second experiment. This model is a simplification of the model in equation where only the experience level (E') is included in the regressors. Table 15 shows the statistical results for each individual parameter in the model as well as the 95 percent confidence interval estimation of its value.

$$T = \alpha_0 - \alpha_E E' + \alpha_{EE} E'^2 + \varepsilon \qquad (7)$$

Coefficients	Value	Std. Error	95% C.I.
α_0	80.2	0.71	(78.57,81.47)
α_E	−2.86	0.48	(−3.84, −1.87)
α_{EE}	2.53	0.55	(1.41,3.65)

Table 15. Model coefficients.

As the model shows, a bigger intercept value is obtained which means that the system indeed needs more time to solve a 20 percent cluttered world. Also, the increased world clutter has a big influence in the rate of learning $(-\alpha_E)$, which is reduced from $-(\beta_E + \beta_{CE}C' + \beta_{SE}S') = 17.30$ secs./exp. to $-\alpha_E = 2.86$ secs./exp. This means that experience does not improve system performance as quickly as for the 15 percent cluttered world or, in other words, the learning rate is higher in the easier world. The acceleration of the learning rate (α_{EE}) does not seem to be influenced by the change of world clutter (i.e., it is in the 95 percent confident interval of β_{EE}).

Learning Profiles. While the above results demonstrate the effectiveness of the SINS approach, it is also interesting to look at the learning profile of the system, if only to provide an intuitive feel for changes in the internal behaviors and external performance of the system as it gains experience. The learning profile of the system can be determined by comparing the model's predictions with traditional learning curves based on the system's actual performance. This is shown in figure 5. The graphs labeled "Median" show the actual time taken by the system (starting with no prior experience or hand-coded high-level knowledge) on a randomly generated 15 percent cluttered world; each point in the graph is the median of five replications with the system configured using the optimal parameters as derived in the previous section. The graphs labeled "Model" show the predicted performance from empirical models. Figure 5a describes the general empirical model along with the error bars for that model. The general model is the performance model derived using the data obtained using the entire range of configurations of the design parameters (equation 4 and table 13). Figure 5b describes the performance model for the specific configuration used in these runs; this was obtained by redoing the statistical analysis for the data obtained from this configuration alone.

As can be observed from figure 5, the performance of the system falls within the general and specific models. The general model has bigger error bars because it must fit the performance of the system over the entire range of configurations. The specific model fits the data better but can only be used to predict the system's performance with this particular system configuration. The results demonstrate that the system does indeed improve its performance with experience, and that this improvement is as predicted by the empirical models derived from the statistical analysis. Furthermore, the performance of the system approaches its optimal level around, which is as expected because, as discussed previously, the configuration parameters used for these experiments were explicitly chosen to optimize performance at that experience level. This provides further evidence for the validity of the analysis.

Discussion

In order to illustrate the kinds of conclusions that can be drawn from this evaluation methodology, let us briefly discuss the above results in the context of the Sins system. The performance of Sins is very complex and depends not only on simple terms but also on their interactions. Study 1 shows that high-level input representations favor learning and enable better solutions than low-level representations. Additionally, study 1 shows that the system using the stochastic adaptation method takes a longer time to converge than the best-value adaptation method; however, once converged, the former arrives at better solutions than the latter. There is no interaction between the choice of input representations and the adaptation procedures. Further study is necessary to find out the effect of the choice of input representation and the knowledge acquired in one world on the performance of the system while solving a different world.

Study 2 shows that the median time taken by the system (when configured with low-level input representations and the stochastic adaptation procedure) to solve a 15 percent cluttered world decreases mainly with the experience level. Increasing the maximum number of cases also improves the performance, but a positive coefficient in its quadratic term may harm the performance for big values. On the other hand, the maximum case size has a positive linear coefficient and a negative quadratic coefficient which indicate that large cases may improve performance as compared to small cases. Negative interaction coefficients indicate that for bigger values of maximum number of cases and case size, the system requires more experiences to start improving its performance. Intuitively, this is to be expected since the more space available to store regularities, the more experience level is required to avoid overfitting and to construct reliable regularities. Finally, the performance of Sins is influenced by the world clutter, the learning rate being the factor subject to the greatest influence.

In summary, the evaluation was useful to verify and understand several aspects of Sins. In particular:

- The evaluation showed that SINS does improve its performance significantly with experience (tables 6 and 13).
- Study 1 showed that the choice of input representation and the choice of adaptation method independently influence the performance of SINS and

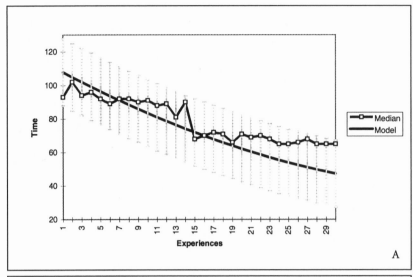

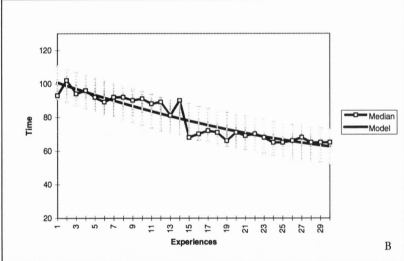

Figure 5. Performance profiles showing median time from actual system runs and predicted time using two empirical models. A is the general model constructed using the data from the entire experiment, i.e., over the entire range of system configurations. B is the specific model constructed using only the data from the specific configuration used in the system runs.

that there are no interactions between these decisions (table 6).

• Study 1 showed that high-level input representations provide a better starting point for learning than low-level input representations. Also, it shows that the stochastic adaptation method takes longer to converge than the best-value adaptation method, but once it does, it arrives at better solutions (tables 6 and 7).

- Study 1 showed that using the regressors (I, A, and E) and their interactions the empirical model can only account for 65.3 percent and 97.0 percent of the variability in the performance of the system during the learning and maturity phases, respectively. This result is important because it captures the limitations of the derived model. Part of the remaining percentage could be explained by introducing more factors or by changing the functional forms of the terms in equation 2; the rest of the variation in performance is due to the randomness in the system.

- Study 2 showed that the performance of the system in a 15 percent cluttered world depends on the selected system configuration parameters, as well as on interactions among them (equation 4 and table 13).

- Study 2 showed the best way to configure SINS in a 15 percent cluttered world for a prespecified level of experience (equations 5 and 6).

- Studies 1 and 2 showed how a change in the environment characteristics, namely cutter, affected the performance of SINS (equations 3 and 7).

- Study 2 showed that using the proposed factors (C, S, and E) and their interactions the empirical model can only account for 79.8 percent (i.e., R^2 = 0.798) of the variability in the performance of the system. Part of the remaining 21.2 percent could be explained by introducing more factors or by changing the functional forms of the terms in equation 4; the remainder of the variation in performance is due to the randomness in the system.

Conclusions

Case-based reasoning systems are typically complex, and the behavior and performance characteristics of such systems are the result of many interacting factors that originate from the many design decisions that go into building them. These design decisions range from numerical system parameters to the knowledge representation scheme chosen to represent the domain and the algorithms and metrics used for matching, adaptation, and other functional modules of the system. Additionally, the tasks, domains, and problems that these systems have typically addressed are also complex and have a significant influence on the behavior and performance of the system. A good evaluation must show not only that a system is performing well; it should also inform us about the performance of the system under various conditions and about learning or improvement in performance with experience. Furthermore, the evaluation must provide insight about how various design decisions influence both performance and learning. Such an evaluation provides an in-depth understanding of the behavior of the system. It allows the researcher to analyze the theory or computational model based on empirical experiments with the computer program, and the system designer and end user to optimize the configuration of the computer program for a given situation of interest. A better understanding of the behavior of the system across domain characteristics also allows the designers to predict the performance of the system under different situations and to determine the conditions under which the system will perform adequately.

In this chapter we proposed a systematic evaluation methodology which enables us to obtain these evaluation objectives for implemented computer systems. The methodology involves identifying the design decisions to be analyzed and designing system experiments which systematically exercise the computer program over the range of design options and problem domains of interest. Based on the experimental results, a mathematical model is constructed that can be used to derive statistically significant conclusions and provide the desired insights into the behavior of the system. The methodology can be used to evaluate CBR systems as well as a broad range of machine learning and other AI systems.

Acknowledgments

We wish to thank Mary Dowling for her comments and suggestions regarding the statistical analysis for the case study, and David Aha, Anthony Francis, Todd Griffith, Mimi Recker, and anonymous reviewers for their comments on an earlier draft of this chapter.

Notes

1. The term *treatment* is also used to denote a level.

2. Note that this sensory input does not provide any information about the distances or direction of the obstacles; it simply measures the density of occupied area around the robot.

3. The choice of the problem world is merely for illustrative purposes and is arbitrary as far as this chapter is concerned. The methodology can be also used to evaluate system performance on a range of problems instead of a single representative problem.

4. The R^2_{adj} is the R^2 value adjusted to take into account the number of parameters in the model. This allows models having different numbers of parameters to be compared.

5. The F statistic is used to determine the significance of the regression. The P-value is the probability determined by F; the lower this value the better the result, since the significance of the regression is $(1 - \text{P-value})\%$ which is 100 percent for P-value $= 0$.

6. As before, the choice of the problem is arbitrary and merely for illustrative purposes. If desired, additional test problems can be introduced and the system tested on each individually or in sequence, although in the latter case additional terms may need to be introduced into the equations in order to account for variability in system performance across problems.

7. Use of standardized values instead of the original values helps to reduce roundoff errors and other problems with multicollinearity between independent variables.

8. Among the three interaction terms only $C\,S$ has physical meaning. The interaction term $C\,S$ is a direct measure of the total amount of memory available to the system. This is an example of a particularly difficult evaluation problem since different design decisions can influence each other under conditions of resource limitations.

9. As before, the F statistic was used to determine the significance of the regression.

13 The Experience-Sharing Architecture:

A Case Study in Corporate-Wide Case-Based Software Quality Control

Hiroaki Kitano & Hideo Shimazu

A vital asset of corporations is the experiences of their employees. Information technology should be deployed to make full use of these experiences. This chapter proposes the *experience sharing architecture* (ESA), a new concept of corporate information system experimentally being deployed at NEC corporation. The experience sharing architecture proposes corporate-wide sharing of experiences using advanced AI technologies, networks, and a graphical user interface, along with algorithmic definition and execution of organizational behavior.

The underlying thrust of the ESA approach is the idea that the case-based system should be viewed as part of a corporate- or department-wide strategic information system to enhance the sharing of experience. Traditionally, CBR systems have been developed as expert systems, to provide solutions to problems (Riesbeck and Schank 1989). Of course, this is still a viable approach. However, the organizational and economic impact would be far greater if the case-based system were integrated into corporate-wide information systems. It could be used as a new medium, to facilitate the distribution of knowledge and experience. This is how we view the role of case-based systems.

CBR systems have traditionally been used as problem-solvers. They store problem-solving cases and the user can query the case-base to find nearest-match cases for new problems. Then, an adaptation process tailors retrieved cases to provide a solution for the user. The basic idea behind this is to replace rule-based expert systems with CBR systems, or to improve them using CBR techniques. This approach provides a problem-specific expert system that can be used in various ways in corporations by accumulating problem-specific, or product-specific, knowledge. While we acknowledge the importance of this approach, we argue that there is an area where CBR techniques can exhibit a far larger economic impact. There are two underlying factors which prompt us to take this view. One of them is the need for a new way of using case-based systems, given the difficulties of case adaptation and the limited impact of domain specific problem-solvers in corporate operations. The other is the practical and emergent need of business management to facilitate the sharing of corporate-wide knowledge.

With regard to the use of case-based systems, we argue that a new way to look at a case-based system is to consider it as a medium, rather than a domain-specific problems-solver, to be used in conjunction with the mainstream corporate information system as a means for employees to share their experience. As we have stated already, using CBR as a problem-solver is still a valid approach. However, we feel that ESA offers a new avenue of research and practical use for case-based systems. This view has three immediate ramifications for the system's design.

First, the media analogy leads to consideration of how the system should be developed, used, and maintained in a corporate environment. Of course, these issues are also common to conventional systems. However, the media analogy clarifies the issue of ecological and organizational embedding of the system. Most attempts to create expert systems and corporate databases have failed because these were not embedded in the behavior of the organization. A clear illustration is the distinction between an automatic teller machine (ATM) and TV or newspapers. Both are highly networked service systems, but exhibit a completely different relationship to our society. TV and newspapers require extensive feedback from viewers and readers to maintain quality of service, whereas ATMs do not.

Second, it requires the contents of each case to be richer than current case representation, which is mainly described in text-based codes. Once we accept the view of the case-based system as a medium, the designer can easily augment the traditional view to incorporate graphical, textual, and sound information to each case. While a formalized data structure is still important for retrieval indexing, the content itself need not necessarily be restricted to frame-like canonical data representation.

Third, more emphasis is placed on how to retrieve and use cases, rather than the adaptation process. One of the central problems in current case-based reasoning is the adaptation process. This process requires extensive domain knowledge to attain adaptation with any acceptable accuracy. However, this requirement contradicts one of the sales points of the CBR, which is that it is good for problems where domain knowledge is hard to obtain or difficult to represent. By viewing the case-based system as a medium, we can focus on how to present cases to the user, rather than how to adapt cases to the problem.

At the same time, there is enormous interest in the business management community about organizational learning, knowledge creation, and the knowledge link. The central issue is how key knowledge and skill can be shared corporate-wide, and how new knowledge can be created. In traditional capitalism, resources such as labor, material, and capital have been the main concern. However, there is increasing awareness that knowledge is a fourth corporate asset. Basically, knowledge is an attribute of the individual. However, the risk exists that knowledge can be lost when a specific individual retires or loses his memory or skill. In addition, knowledge cannot be easily transferred to other employees.

While these issues have been raised and discussed intensively, no definitive methodologies have been proposed so far. In this chapter, we propose ESA as a solution to this problem.

The Experience Sharing Architecture

The experience sharing architecture facilitates the corporate-wide sharing of experiences, thereby promoting organizational knowledge creation (Nonaka 1991), and improving the core skills of the corporation. This is attained through the use of case-based systems integrated with mainstream information systems such as an existing strategic information system (SIS) (Wiseman 1988). While we agree on the importance of an SIS and the effectiveness of the information processing paradigm of corporate behavior, we argue that a new dimension should be added in order to further enhance the power of corporate information systems. This idea perhaps complements the *knowledge highway* concept advocated by American Express, which emphasizes the linkage of knowledge-based problem-solvers.

Since people and organizations learn from experiences (see Badaracco 1991, Ishikura 1992, Meen and Keough 1992, and Senge 1990 for discussion on corporate knowledge creation and organizational learning), collecting, sharing, and mining experiences in the form of a "case" is the best approach to improving knowledge level and organizational skills. There are two types of corporate knowledge: product-specific knowledge and skill-specific knowledge. Product-specific knowledge is a set of knowledge on a specific product. It can easily be expressed in documents such as users manuals and maintenance manuals. Since the mechanisms and behaviors of the designed product are well known, traditional expert systems and case-based reasoning systems can serve as effective problem-solvers. On the other hand, skill-specific knowledge is general knowledge of the skills needed to develop products. For example, creating high quality software is a general knowledge skill that can be applied to a wide range of software products. This type of knowledge is a core skill for the organization. However, this type of knowledge is difficult to transfer, and mostly acquired through individual experience. Consequently, the key question is to find a scheme to effectively transfer skill-specific knowl-

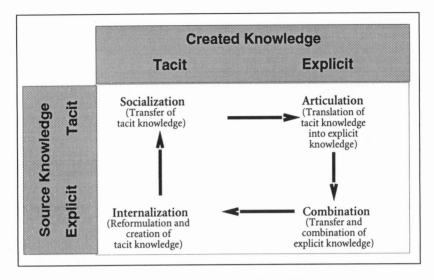

Figure 1. A process of organizational knowledge creation.

edge to other members of an organization.

Badaracco, in his knowledge-link model, argues that there are four major requirements for knowledge to be transferred among organizations (Badaracco 1991): (1) knowledge must be explicitly represented and packaged, (2) an individual or group must be capable of understanding the knowledge, (3) the individual or group must be sufficiently motivated to learn, and (4) no barrier can exist to hamper the transfer of knowledge. Although these requirements are reasonable, they are not met in most corporations. ESA aims to provide a scheme to meets these requirements.

In order to facilitate the transfer of knowledge, and even its creation, we employ Nonaka's theory of organizational knowledge creation (Nonaka 1991) as the organizational theory behind our model. Nonaka assumes the existence of tacit knowledge and articulated knowledge. He observes that organizational knowledge spreads through the process of (1) socialization, (2) articulation, (3) combination, and (4) internalization (figure 1). He argues that articulation and internalization are crucial to improving organizational knowledge.

In the socialization process, unskilled members of the organization work with skillful members, generally in a small group, to acquire the skill on the job. Next, in the articulation process, the group will document the skill, so that some tacit knowledge is articulated. It is not necessary or feasible to articulate every aspect of the skill. However, attempts to document tacit knowledge force group members to communicate in-depth and to reformulate their understanding of the skill explicitly. With a set of documents to represent some aspects of the skill, new knowledge will be created by combining them, and making a detailed analysis. In our model, this is the process of knowledge discovery from the database. A wide range of approaches can be taken for this process. Even the simple construction of a classification tree or the statistical analysis of the data set are surprisingly effective in finding out what is actually going on the field. The fourth process is internalization. New knowledge discovered in the combination process, and cases of other groups are presented to group members, and they then act on the basis of this new knowledge. While cases are raw records of experiences, this process effectively enhances the sharing of experience. It is important, however, that knowledge discovered in the combination process is provided along with the cases. By providing such knowledge, which is relatively conceptual and rule-based, members of the organization can reformulate their conceptual level of understanding, and it enables them to view cases with a new perspective. After this process, the cycle continues from the socialization process in the second cycle to further enhance experience sharing.

By continuing this cycle, Nonaka argues that the quality of shared experience will be improved and that internalization becomes stronger as each individual is entrained by the shared experience.

The next question is how this idea can be implemented in a real organization. First, we must identify which parts can be supported by the system and which parts must be carried out by organizational activities. We have identified that the combination process and part of the internalization process can be supported by the system, and the rest of the cycle needs to be carried out by organizational activities. The basic principle of ESA is to define the system architecture as well as organizational behavior, so that the entire process can be well defined and the system can be embedded in organizational activities.

For the system part, networked workstations and personal computers are deployed so that members of the organization can easily provide their experiences to the system as well as retrieve cases from the case-base. A case-based system is created to handle large number of cases, but not necessarily support the adaptation process. It can be a simple case-base retrieval system requiring users to adapt cases. In fact, this helps internalization of knowledge by forcing them to look into retrieved cases and forcing them think about how to adapt them. In addition, any system with a less than perfect adaptation mechanism is likely to be rejected by users due to mal-adaptation. This design decision makes the system less intelligent, but far more reliable and user acceptable.

For the organization part, a top-down initiative to reformulate organizational activities will be necessary for immediate corporate-wide deployment. However, it is possible to start from smaller business units. It is also necessary to define the workflow to report experiences, collect these reports, create a case-base, and access cases for further activities. This process needs to be institutionalized.

In order to actually implement this scheme, we need a sound development methodology. This methodology is largely divided into two parts: the business process definition and the system development methodology. They are defined in the CASE-METHOD. In the next section, the CASE-METHOD will be described. The CASE-METHOD is a methodology for building and maintaining large scale CBR systems based on the ESA paradigm.

As for the business process definition in the CASE-METHOD, we will further explain how we have carried out this part using a specific example. This is because the best way to define and re-engineer an organizational activity (or, business process) largely depends on the domain as well as the corporate culture. Although the CASE-METHOD provides fairly general guidelines, explanations using concrete examples will help readers understand how the business process was re-defined.

Case-Method: A Methodology for CBR Systems

Despite increasing expectations for using case-based reasoning as a practical approach to building cost-effective problem-solvers and corporate information access systems, no research has been done on how to develop and maintain case-based systems. In the software engineering community—particularly among practitioners—methodology development or selection is regarded as one of the most important development decisions to make.

In general, software development methodologies define how to organize a project, how each development procedure should be carried out, and how to describe interfaces between development processes. Often, the methodology provides automated tools, which support some of the development processes involved (Downs et al. 1988, Wasserman et al. 1983). A number of methodologies have been formulated by mainframe manufactures and by consulting firms. Some of these are AD/Cycle by IBM, Method/1 by Andersen consulting, SUMMIT by Coopers and Lybrand, and NAVIGATOR by Ernst and Young.

If CBR systems are to be integrated into mainstream information systems, a solid methodological support is essential. Unfortunately, however, no methodological support has been provided from CBR community (Acorn and Walden [1992] is a possible exception, but only a part of the entire process has been defined.) Although there are a few methodologies for building expert systems, such as HSTDEK by NASA (Freeman 1987), KEMRAS by the Alvey project, KADS by ESPRIT, and EX/METHOD by NEC, these methodologies are not applicable for CBR system development, because underlying principles are so different between expert systems and CBR.

Consequently, we had to develop our own methodology, optimized for case-based systems. CASE-METHOD was designed to be consistent with methodologies for non-CBR systems, so that the corporate information systems division would be able to use the methodology without major problems. Also, CASE-METHOD was inductively defined based on several CBR projects actually carried out. Thus, CASE-METHOD is already a field-tested methodology.

CASE-METHOD provides how to build and maintain the system to support the organizational knowledge creation. In addition, CASE-METHOD defines a way for organizational knowledge creation to be carried out in the light of modern information technology. It is a methodology to develop case-based systems, as well as a methodology for the knowledge creation cycle.

The Case-Method Cycle

The methodology employs an iterative approach which allows the system to evolve as the process iterates. Figure 2 shows the cycle of system evolution in CASE-METHOD. CASE-METHOD defines the system development process, the case-base development process, the system operation process, the database mining process, the management process, and the knowledge transfer process.

System Development Process: This process employs a standard software engineering approach such as the waterfall model or flower model (Humphrey 1989) as a development methodology. The goal is to design and develop a CBR system that can store and retrieve cases created in the case-base development process.

Case-Base Development Process: The goal of this process is to develop and maintain a large-scale case-base. A detailed procedure is defined to perform analysis, create abstraction hierarchies, and design a relational database (RDB).

System Operation Process: This process defines installation, deployment, and user supports of the CBR system. It follows standard software engineering and RDB management procedures.

Data-Base Mining Process: Data-base mining is carried out using the case-base. Statistical analysis, rule-extraction, and other appropriate techniques are applied. The current model defines how to analyze the case-base using standard statistical procedures and rule extraction using decision trees (Quinlin 1992). This process is a subject of further research.

Management Process: The management process defines how the project task force should be formed, what kind of organizational support should be provided to the project, and what kind of management control should be carried out to obtain a constant flow of high quality cases. We have defined a mixed scheme of bottom-up/top-down control, incentive systems, and central/local controls, and a case filtering committee. This process must be rearranged for each organization.

Knowledge Transfer Process: This process defines methods to transfer knowledge (cases and extracted rules) to related divisions. Network-based

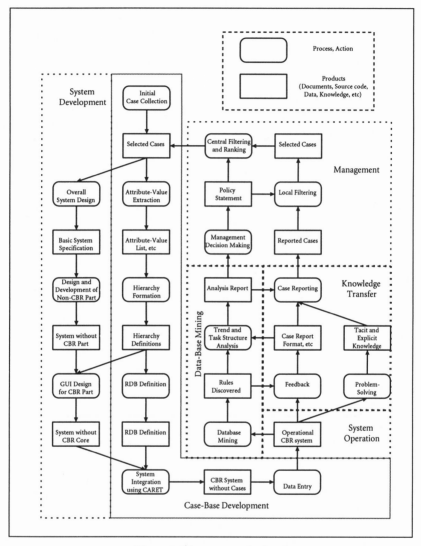

Figure 2. The case-method cycle.

system deployment, incentive systems, management control, and newsletter publications have been defined. In addition, how to create a case report format, which is one of the major means of feed back, is defined.

These processes form one cycle of knowledge creation and system evolution. Because of case structure reformulation in the case base development process and rule extraction in the data-base mining process, the quality of knowledge to be stored and transferred improves as the cycle iterates. When

Part of system	Tools	Process Definition
User Interface	Canae/Yuzu GUI, CAPIT NLI,...	
Case-Base Building	Hierarchy Editor, ...	Case-Method (Case-base building process)
Case-Retrieval	CARET RDB-based CBR Shell	Case-Method (CBR system integration)
Adapation Rule-Based Part	Excore Inference engine, ...	EX/Method, Case-Method
Non-AI Part	CASELAND CASE Tools,...	SEA/I, OMT

Figure 3. Tools and methodologies in the case method.

the system reaches maturity, the system should hold a case-base consisting of appropriately represented and indexed high quality cases and a set of extracted rules specific to the application domain.

Supporting Tools

A set of tools to support the process has been developed. They include the CARET RDB-based CBR shell, the Canae/Yuzu GUI construction kit, a hierarchy editor to help develop concept hierarchies using a graphical interface, the CAPIT case-based natural language interface (Shimazu et al. 1992), which generates seed SQL specifications to be used by CARET, and database mining tools to perform trend and statistical analysis. Figure 3 shows a list of tools for each part of the system development.

Major Process Definitions

In this section we will define the major processes: case collection, attribute-value extraction,hierarchy formation, database definition and data entry, and feedback.

Case Collection

The first phase in the development process requires collecting seed cases. The seed cases provide an initial view of the application domain landscape. For the Software Quality Control Advisor (SQUAD) system, to be described later, the authors started with 100 seed cases, to define a crude case format and data structure. For the new Nation-Wide case retrieval system, another system now being developed to support software engineers in the NEC group, the authors are working on several hundred cases from the beginning.[1] As a start up phase in the project, cases are generally collected in an unstructured and nonuniform style, such as full-text and other domain-specific forms.

From the second cycle, this phase involves the collection of cases which are consistent with the pre-defined case report format, and the filtering of cases so that only cases with minimum acceptable quality will be sent to the next phase. Cases are reported in structured style, using a pre-defined case report form and full-text with specified writing style.

Products of this phase are a set of case report forms, and a set of case reports in full-text.

Attribute-Value Extraction

The goal of the attribute-value extraction phase is to extract all possible elements in case representation and indexing. In the initial cycle, this phase consists of three processes: keyword listing, attribute identification, and value grouping.

The process can be semi-automatic, but a certain amount of human monitoring is necessary, as new keywords and compound nouns must be identified by human experts. Each attribute and value is examined to determine whether or not it is independent from other attributes and values. Ideally, a set of attributes is expected to be a linearly independent set. However, in reality, this is not always possible, thus, some dependency is allowed. However, an excessive degree of dependency makes case representation and indexing less transparent.

Products of this phase are a list of attributes, a list of possible values for each attribute, a thesaurus of keywords to be the value of each attribute, and a set of normalized units for problem description and evaluation.

Hierarchy Formation

The hierarchy formation phase defines relationships among keywords and attributes. For each attribute identified in the previous phase, a set of keywords has already been grouped. In this phase, relationships between keywords are defined, mostly by using *is-a* relations.

The process of defining the relationship is carried out in both a bottom-up and top-down manner. Generally, it starts as a bottom-up process involving sub-grouping a set of keywords, and creates a super-class of one or more keywords. Then, the *is-a* relation will be defined between the created super-class and keywords. One or more superclasses will be grouped and a superclass for them will be defined. Then, the *is-a* relation will be defined between them. This iterative process builds up an *is-a* hierarchy in a bottom-up manner. This bottom-up process creates a minimally sufficient hierarchy to cover values for a set of existing cases. However, it does not guarantee whether the defined hierarchy can cope with unknown, but possible, cases. Thus, the top-down process will be carried out to incorporate a set of classes and values to cover possible unknown cases. In the top-down process, the domain expert checks to determine whether or not all possible subclass are assigned for each class. If possible subclasses are missing, the missing class will be added.

After a set of hierarchies is defined, the relative importance of each attribute and the distance between individual values will be assigned. Ideally, this weight and distance assignment process needs to be carried out, using a sound statistical and empirical basis. However, in many cases, obtaining such statistical data would be unfeasible. In fact, none of the in-house projects is capable of obtaining such statistics, mainly due to the nature of domains and constraints on development and deployment schedules. Also, in some systems, assigning pre-defined weights works against achieving a successful system, particularly when the user's goals for using the system greatly differ, and predefined attribute weights undesirably bias the search space in an unintended fashion. Consequently, decisions on how to assign weights and how to define distance measures must reflect characteristics of the domain and an actual deployment plan.

A product of this phase is a set of concept hierarchies created for each attribute. The hierarchies are assigned with similarities between values.

Database Definition and Data Entry

In this phase, a database definition will be created using the set of hierarchies just defined. There are several methods to map the hierarchy into the relational database. The choice of methods is left to the system designer. However, the CARET case-base retrieval shell supports flat-record style database definition, as opposed to structured indexing (Hammond 1989, Kolodner 1984) due to ease of maintenance. Using an RDBMS is an important factor in bringing CBR into the mainstream information system environment. At the end of these processes, a defined RDB contains a set of cases. The system should be operational after this phase.

Feedback

The goal of the feedback phase is to provide explicit knowledge to case reporters so that the quality of cases to be reported can be improved. In addition, it is expected that by providing the explicit knowledge after extensive knowledge engineering, tacit and explicit knowledge regarding each case reporter can be reformulated in a more consistent manner. This is an important phase in the proposed methodology.

One way of providing feedback is to create a *case report format*. The case report format should be created from the hierarchy used to index the case. There are three major benefits for distributing the case report format.

First, by looking at items in the case report format, case reporters may be able to understand an overall picture of the domain in which they are involved. In the corporate-wide system, the level of expertise the case reporter has may vary significantly; some reporters are not aware of the correct classification applicable to problems and counter measures. Distribution of the case report format is expected to improve the quality of reported cases. In fact, improvement in the quality has been confirmed in the SQUAD system applied to the software quality control domain.

Second, using the case report format reduces data entry cost. Since all attribute-values are covered in the case report format, a simple bulk data entry strategy can be applied to register reported cases. This leads to substantial cost saving, as will be reported later.

Third, by allowing free-form description for items that cannot be represented using the pre-defined attribute-values, new attributes and values can be identified easily and efficiently. These new attributes and values are added to the indexing hierarchies, and the case report format in the next cycle will include new attribute-values.

The product of this phase is a new case report format to be used for reporting cases in the next cycle.

Business Process Definition: A Case Study

In this section we will describe how the business process was re-engineered and redefined using the CASE-METHOD. For our example, we have applied the ESA paradigm to software quality control at NEC Corporation. At NEC, the ability to produce high-quality software is a core skill for the organization. (It should be noted that in the descriptions that follow, there are activities that are tightly coupled with the system development and maintenance process defined in the CASE-METHOD.)

The Software Quality Control Domain

Quality control is an essential element in modern industrial society. High-quality products provide a competitive edge, and assure higher reliability. Software is by no means an exception to this rule. Recent establishment of the ISO-9000-3 standard (ISO 1990) clearly illustrates the need for a high level of software quality control. A major step in improving product quality has been the implementation of a quality control (QC) activity. QC activities have been successfully introduced in many Japanese firms. To implement a QC activity, small groups of workers in the factory and offices meet to discuss how they can improve the efficiency and quality of their work. After discussions, they file a report delineating the problem they have identified, analyzing its status analysis, the measures they took to improve the situation, and the effects of the remedial actions. QC activities have been carried out in virtually every stage in manufacturing processes, and comprehensive and voluminous reports on improvement in quality and productivity have been filed.

Software firms must pay special attention to quality control in order to ensure the success of their product in the marketplace. NEC Corporation is heavily involved in the software business, for it manufactures a wide range of computer systems and telecommunication systems and also provides system integration services. Because NEC's software-related business is increasing significantly, the board of executives and NEC employees agree that software quality control should be given the highest priority within the company.

In keeping with this company policy, NEC established in 1981 a company-wide organizational structure to enforce software quality control (SWQC) (Mizuno 1990). Traditionally, QC activities have been viewed as an important process involving worker participation as well as a substantial means of continuous improvement in production systems. Each reported case provides an analysis of the problem, its possible cause, the corrective measures taken, and the effects of the corrective measures. Each case report consists of a two-page form filled in with major issues in the case. By 1991, over 25,000 quality and productivity improvement case reports had been filed.

Sharing these productivity improvements company wide, however, proved to be difficult. Initially, case reports were stored and filed in book form. Consequently, it was difficult to search through old cases to find problems similar to the one a software engineer was facing. To solve this problem, a corporate database containing the full-text of the case reports was created. Nevertheless, users still found it difficult to search the case reports using uncontrolled keywords and boolean logic formulae. The company considered developing an expert system to solve the problem, but it was determined to be infeasible because no concrete rules could be derived from the cases reported. Consequently, systematic understanding of the domain of software quality control was critically lacking. Since the annual labor investment for case reporting is over 200 man-years, NEC could not afford to disregard utilize reported cases for software quality control.

To solve the problem, we decided to apply the idea of experience sharing architecture in the software quality control domain. The result was the software quality control advisor (SQUAD). The SQUAD project was started in September 1991 after over 3 years of planning. The goal of the project was to develop a software quality control advisor system and a large-scale and corporate-wide case-based system that could improve access to cases reported under SWQC activity, and redefine SWQC activity from knowledge engineering and AI perspectives so that SWQC could be a source of corporate knowledge for software quality improvement. The project was the first one based on the experience sharing architecture concept—a vision of the next generation strategic information systems (Wiseman 1988). In essence, it developed a business process definition that defines how organizations should behave, and a system that facilitates the sharing of experience using AI technologies and networks. The following sections describe details of this project.

Software Quality Control as Corporate-Wide Knowledge Engineering

Our approach was to reformulate SWQC activity as a corporate-wide knowledge acquisition process, and to build and deploy a case retrieval system so that users could easily access reported cases electronically.

The SQUAD system and SWQC activity can be a powerful scheme for organizational knowledge creation. The SWQC activity encourages a certain level of articulation of knowledge, because all participants are supposed to submit reports and forms that describe their improvement activities. Although not all of the reports articulate tacit knowledge, many do. Also, socialization process takes place because participants work together as a group. We have discovered that knowledge acquisition through the group activity is more efficient and effective than individual activity by experts. Although we do not discount the value of well trained experts, it is logistically infeasible to rely on software quality control or productivity experts on a corporate-wide scale. In addition, we consider that each member in each department is a tacit expert in their field, as they have the most experience with the specific task in question.

The knowledge engineering conducted by the SWQC department also augments the level of articulation, and combination takes place when the domain ontology and models are built. Finally, the SQUAD system allows efficient access to the SWQC cases, which enhances internalization of articulated knowledge in different divisions. It should be noted that our knowledge source is case-based, not rule-based. Thus, we are much closer to tacit knowledge than abstract rules.

Establishing the Knowledge Engineering Process

When we established the knowledge engineering process, we made a radical departure from the traditional view of the QC activity. We considered QC activity as a company-wide knowledge acquisition process. Thus, we established a knowledge engineering loop for the SWQC domain. Figure 4 illustrates organizations involved and the process flow. Each SWQC activity group in the entire NEC group submits their case reports. The review committee reviews each case. The review result classifies reported cases into 1 of best cases, 10 of selected cases, and 90 of pool cases. Best cases and selected cases are chosen, based on the quality of analysis, significance of the effects, and universality of the problem. They are considered to be the norm for the case report. Naturally, these cases are given top priority in case-base building, and serve as the

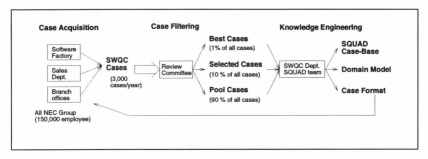

Figure 4. SWQC knowledge engineering loop.

basis of the domain model and the case format definition.

The SWQC activity was started out in 1981 with no substantial case format. The rough case format and the case report category were introduced as SWQC grew into a corporate-wide activity. Recently, we have begun to provide specific feature sets to all participating groups, to help making a standard case report format and improve analysis quality. This is a step-wise cycle. It starts out from a vague standard and provides only top-level features. As knowledge engineering progresses, more detailed feature sets are provided, as we begin to understand the domain model and the features that should be identified. Due to the turnaround cycle, upgrading the case format requires one year at a minimum. Current work is in the end of the fourth cycle in this loop. Only after the third cycle could minimum features be identified, so that it was possible to build a crude case-base. The feature set will be further refined, as this cycle progresses. Consequently, an absolute requirement for case-based systems in this domain is that the incremental modification to the case-base—particularly the indexing features—be accomplished with minimum or no cost.

In order to facilitate the stable flow of high quality cases from nearly all software domains, several organizational measures have been introduced:

Filtering: When knowledge acquisition is scaled up to a corporate-wide level, some case filtering scheme is necessary to select high-quality cases from among all cases with varying analysis quality. This is essential to establish the norm for high quality cases.

Incentive System: This is a management issue for corporate-wide knowledge acquisition. Top-down control has been established regarding the activity framework, awards, symposia, conventions, and other incentive systems. Bottom-up control of operational procedures and system critique scheme has been introduced in order to maintain involvement of the participants.

Feedback: All the best cases and the selected cases have been compiled in a book form, and distributed to all involved sections.

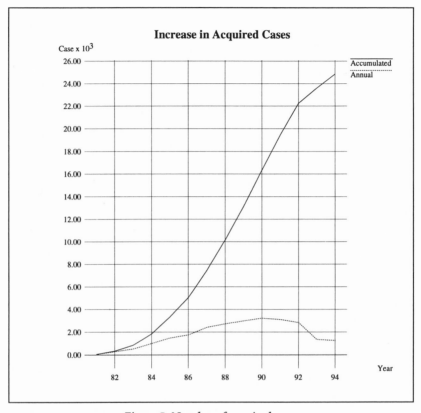

Figure 5. Number of acquired cases.

Distributed Control: Each department hosts internal competitions, so that only qualified cases are reported to the company-wide review committee. This avoids overloading the review committee.

As a result of these measures, the number of acquired cases has increased significantly, and has reached the saturation point. Over 3,000 cases of quality and productivity improvement measures were reported annually, starting in 1989. This figure has decreased to 1,000 cases per year in recent years. The decrease is mainly due to the saturation of cases. Most typical cases are already reported, so the rate of new cases to be reported slows significantly. Over 24,000 cases had been accumulated as of December 1994 (figure 5).

The main point of this part of the project is that the algorithm for case acquisition is essentially executed by people, not by machines. Consequently, it requires organizational support and sustained effort for many years.

Our organizational support has been substantial. The SWQC department was established with 10 full-time employees. This department is responsible for SWQC activity in both traditional and knowledge-engineered processes. Two domain experts are assigned to carry out case-base development. The Case-Systems Laboratory is responsible for overall coordination and methodology development. C&C Information Technology Laboratory is responsible for system development. Substantial management support has been obtained, and the senior executive vice president of NEC was appointed to take full responsibility of the overall activity with close contact to the President and CEO.

The SQUAD System

The SQUAD system is a case-based system developed and maintained using the CASE-METHOD. It is used in the business process that has been redefined based on the ESA paradigm. The central part of this project is to actually implement the ESA paradigm.

System Requirements

As is always the case, real-world deployment imposes various constraints, some of which require major compromises in implementation of the laboratory-level models. The SWQC domain is no exception to this rule. Some of the major requirements are:

Response time: To be a part of a corporate information system, the system should provide fast response time. If a central server approach is taken in the deployment, the potential size of the user group is over 150,000.

Low Development Cost: The development cost should be as low as possible. Although the case-reporting process involves a large number of participants, the process of compiling them into a case-base must be inexpensive. Consequently, the case-base must be built and maintained by one or two full-time employees.

Robustness: The system should allow missing information, inaccurate description, and other erroneous data entries. It is not possible, both for economic and organizational reasons, to force every QC activity group to report cases at a uniform level of accuracy and specificity. It is also not possible for the case-base builder to frequently inquire about details of the reported case.

Flexibility: The system should allow the user a maximum level of flexibility in specifying cues for case retrieval.

Incremental modification: The system should allow an incremental modification of index features for the case-base. As actual products and systems change, the domain itself changes. It is not economically nor logistically feasible to carry out exhaustive knowledge engineering, to identify a well-formed index structure for over 20,000 cases with nearly 3,000 additions

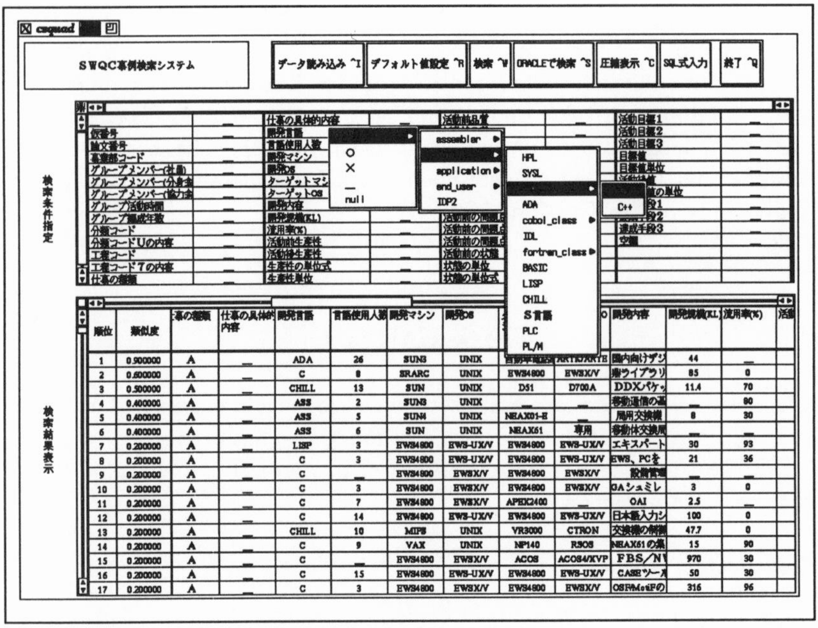

Figure 6. Squad system screen.

every year.

System Architecture

The SQUAD system is a case-based software quality control advisory system. In the current version, the SQUAD system does not involve an adaptation phase. It only has a case retrieval phase for two primary reasons. First, retrieval of cases alone suffices for most advising tasks. Second, the domain is so complicated and ill-formed that any adaptation scheme would require significant development costs. Furthermore, the system behavior would be unstable, because we do not fully understand the nature of the domain. A screen of the SQUAD system is shown in figure 6.

The overall architecture of SQUAD is shown in figure 7. The salient feature of SQUAD is the use of a commercial RDBMS to store and manage case-base. For a CBR shell, we have developed the case retrieval system (CARET). Although we have investigated several commercial CBR shells, none of them supports similarity-based retrieval on an RDBMS.

CARET: RDBMS-based Case Retrieval Shell

The most significant design decision was the use of a commercial RDBMS for

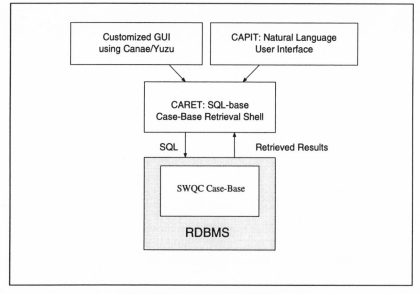

Figure 7. SQUAD system architecture.

the case-base manager. Each case is represented as a record of a relational database table. Use of RDBMS offers several advantages, such as data security, data independence, data standardization, and data integrity. These features are provided by the basic functionality of RDBMS.

The motivation behind the use of an RDBMS is two-fold. First, use of an RDBMS (or a mechanism with equal functionality), was found to be a minimum requirement for CBR systems that are installed on corporate-wide information systems. The main reasons for the requirement are the needs for security control and integrity management.

Second, significant numbers of databases in various domains (built on commercial RDBMSs) are readily available in many corporate information systems. Applying CBR techniques to RDBMSs breaks new ground with corporate information systems, because current RDBMSs only provide relatively primitive (such as only exact match) query capability. Efforts to convert these databases into independent CBR systems, however, are undesirable, because such efforts will inevitably undermine security control, and waste computing resources. In addition, since two separate databases would be created by such a conversion, the integrity of the case-base would not be maintained because mechanisms to automatically reflect changes in the RDBMS to the case-base cannot be installed for technical and security reasons.

Problems in Current Case-Base Management

The concept of case-base management is critically lacking in the current research on CBR systems. This is mainly due to the fact that a vast majority, if not all, of CBR systems have been built as task-specific domain problem solvers. These systems, similar to most expert systems, are detached from the mainstream information infrastructure for a corporation. However, as has been clearly demonstrated in the wide-spread use of data-base management systems (DBMS), data resources management is an essential issue in the corporate information system.

To be more specific, the following issues have not been addressed in the previous studies on CBR systems.

Security Control: In real applications, collected cases include secret information of a corporation or a department. No CBR systems developed so far incorporates any security measures. In the absence of security control, the system cannot be used for highly confidential information where maximum value can be exploited.

Scalability: The efficiency of a CBR application depends heavily upon the number of cases collected. In some real applications, collected cases can increase drastically with time. For example, in the SQUAD system, over 3,000 cases are added into its casebase each year. Since real domains are often very complicated and ill-formed, the use of complex indexing would require significant development costs and the system behavior would be unstable, because the experts themselves do not fully understand the nature of the domain. Thus complex indexing would be beyond control of the system engineers.

Speed: Although various indexing and case-base organization methods have been investigated, only a few studies address the issue of computing cost. Fast case retrieval is an indispensable feature of real-world applications, particularly for very large case-bases.

Interfacing with RDBMSs

Because the use of RDBMSs was found to be the minimum requirement for the CBR systems to be installed as a part of a corporate-wide information system, CARET uses an RDBMS to manage its casebase. CARET generates appropriate SQL expressions to carry out similarity-based retrieval on a commercially available RDBMS, such as ORACLE. There are two constraints imposed by using RDBMS for case-based systems. First, SQL does not support similarity-base retrieval, consequently a mechanism to carry out similarity-based retrieval using SQL must be defined. Second, cases have to be represented as a flat record of n-ary relations. RDBMSs do not includes mechanisms to support the complex indexing schemes seen in most of CBR research. However, this constraint is not necessarily a limiting factor for case representation. We learned through the development of SQUAD that complex indexing schemes

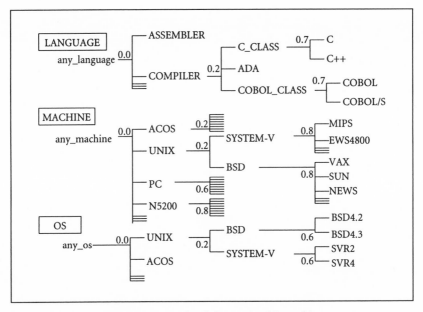

Figure 8. Example of abstraction hierarchies.

are too difficult to maintain, particularly by ordinary engineers. In addition, using a complex indexing scheme hampers retrieval speed on massively parallel machines, due to the huge overhead of the interprocessor communications required to search through indexing structures. A flat record structure is much more suitable for massively parallel machines due to its data-parallel nature of similarity calculation.

In order to create a set of SQL expressions for similarity-based retrieval CARET refers to abstraction hierarchies, as shown in figure 8, to generate a set of values neighboring the value specified by the user. Distance measures between values and the value representing the importance of the attribute are used to assign similarity values to each SQL expression. As a result, a set of SQL specifications, each assigned with a similarity value, is produced. If, for example, a user specified ADA as *language* and VAX as *machine,* the SQL specifications shown in table 1 would be generated and dispatched to the RDBMS.

Coping with Case-Base Modification and
Maintaining User Friendly Query Specification

Critical issues in the SQUAD system include its ability to cope with case-base modification after each knowledge engineering cycle, its robustness against

Rank	Similarity	SQL Specification (only WHERE clause is shown)
1	1.00	(language = ada) and (machine = vax);
2	0.89	(language = ada) and (machine in (sun, news, ...))
4	0.54	(language = ada) and (machine in (mips, ews4800, ...))
3	0.66	(language in (c, c++, cobol, cobol/s)) and (machine = vax);
4	0.54	(language in (c, c++, cobol, cobol/s)) and (machine in (sun, news, ..));
6	0.2	(language in (c, c++, cobol, cobol/s)) and (machine in (mips, ews4800, ...));

Table 1. SQL specifications.

missing information, and its ability to cope with varying query specification levels. The SQUAD system deals with these requirements within a consistent and uniform model, based on a new similarity computing method referring to abstraction hierarchies. Users can specify the value of a feature by selecting specific values such as BSD4.2 or SVR2, or by specifying the class such as BSD or UNIX. Similarity is computed reflecting the uncertainty created by specifying abstract nodes. The same mechanism applies to case entry. When a new case with incomplete data is reported, it can be registered using abstract classes.

Figure 9 illustrates how the case-base, represented in a flat table, can be modified after each knowledge engineering cycle. Initially, only feature F1 is defined in the case-base. Cases with this feature (Case 0001 and 0002) are assigned with 1.0, and a case without this feature (Case 0003) is assigned 0.0. In the second cycle, feature F1 was found to have subcategories: F11 and F12. Due to the lack of specific information for Cases 0001 and 0002, values for these cases on F11 and F12 are assigned as 0.5 for each new feature. In case three subcategories were found, the value would be 0.33. Basically, we assume equal probability distribution regarding which subcategory might be correct. When information is available, either 1.00 or 0.00 will be assigned. Assuming that F12 was found to have a further subcategory in the third cycle, e.g. F121 and F122 in figure 9, the same equal-probability rule is applied for cases which do not have this information. This is a simple mechanism, but it was proven to be effective in coping with changing case structures. Thus, it enables the SQUAD system to cope with incremental modification of case base in each cycle, and maintains reasonably accurate retrieval, even when information is missing.

This mechanism also allows flexible and consistent case retrieval. Each case can be described at any specificity level, and the users can specify a query cue at any level. So far, CBR retrieval methods have assumed that the query, or the cue case, is specified and represented at the same level of abstraction as cases in the case-base. For example, if a feature *tools-used* is specified at the level of a specific name for the tool, the assumption is that the cue case is also specified at this level. Similarity is then computed, using the domain heuris-

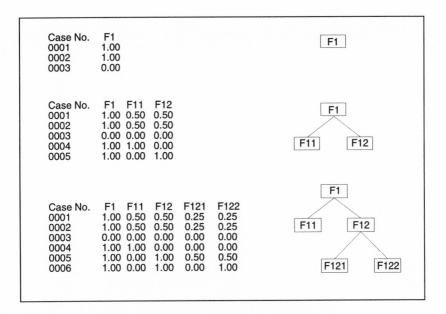

Figure 9. Case-base modification after each cycle.

tics or statistical means. However, the assumption that the user will specify features at the same level of abstraction as the case base is too strong to be implemented in a practical system. For example, users tend to specify kinds of tools (such as *spec-acquisition-case, programming-case,* or *version-control-tool*), rather than specific names for tools (such as *prospec, sea/i,* or *life-line*). By the same token, cases collected do not necessarily contain information at the same abstraction level.

This is illustrated in figure 10. The figure shows an example of user query selection and two cases. A typical query is specific for some of the features, but not for other features. However, for example, the query should return case-1 with the highest similarity, because the only difference in between Query and case-1 is the specificity of features selected. Actually, all selected items in the query and case-1 are subsumed in other selected features, in one way or the other.

For example, the query specifies F1, F222, and other features. case-1 and case-2 match F1, because the feature F1 value for case-1 and case-2 is 1.0 (See figure 9). On the other hand, F222 would have a lower similarity score, because only partial information is provided for case-1 and case-2. In fact, the similarity score between F222 and F22 is 0.5. F222 and F21 have a similarity score 0.0, because case-2 has the feature F21 which implies the F22 value is 0.0. In this example, assuming equal weight distribution, the similarity score

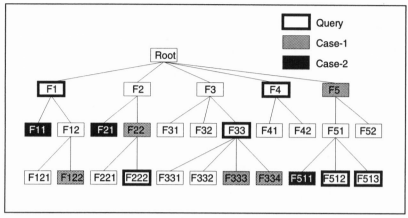

Figure 10. Examples of feature selection by user.

for case-1 and case-2, for the query, are 0.305 and 0.167, respectively.

Similarity-based Retrieval Using SQL

In this section, we'll look at case retrieval using nearest neighbor and generating SQL specifications with similarity measures.

Case Retrieval using Nearest Neighbor

CARET uses nearest neighbor retrieval, instead of the indexing-based methods which have been studied in most CBR research (Cain et al. 1991, Cook 1991, Kolodner and Thau 1988, Veloso and Carbonel 1991). Typically, a similarity between the query case (Q) and a case (C) in the case-base ($S(Q,C)$) is the weighted sum of similarity of each attribute:

$$S(Q,C) = \frac{\sum\limits_{i=1}^{n} W_i \times s(Q_i,C_i)}{\sum\limits_{i=1}^{n} W_i}$$

where W_i is a weight of the attribute, $s(Q_i,C_i)$ is a similarity between the value of the i-th attribute of the query case (Q) and a case in the RDB (C).

Traditional implementations would compute the similarity value for all records, and sort records based on their similarity. However, this is a time-consuming task as computing time increases linearly as the number of records in the case-base (C : *cardinality* of the database) and as the number of

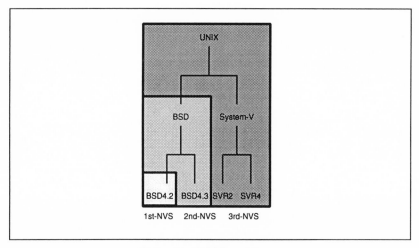

Figure 11. Neighbor value sets.

defined attributes (D : *degree* of the database). This results in time-complexity of $O(C \times D)$. Application of this implementation strategy for an RDBMS would be foolish because every record would have to be retrieved to compute similarity, and the processing cost would be intolerable.

The challenge here is to discover an algorithm to perform the nearest neighbor algorithm using SQL and efficient enough to be practical. The following sections describe such an algorithm and report on its performance using the deployed system.

Generating SQL Specifications with Similarity Measures

Similarity Definition using an Abstraction Hierarchy: Similarity between values is defined using an abstraction hierarchy, shown in figure 8. It is defined for each attribute in a flat table such as language, machine, and OS. In this example, the similarity between C and C++ is 0.7. Similarity between the input query and each case in the case-base is calculated by referring to the similarity of values in each attribute.

Creating Neighbor Value Sets: For each attribute, CARET refers to the abstraction hierarchies, as shown in figure 11, to generate a set of values neighboring the value specified by the user. For example, assume that the user specified BSD4.2 in the hierarchy shown in figure 8. BSD4.2 is an element of the first-order neighbor value set (1NVS). BSD and BSD4.3 are elements of the second-order neighbor value set (2NVS), and UNIX, System-V, SVR2, and SVR4 are elements of the third-order neighbor value set (3NVS). Such sets are created for each attribute.

Set	Language	Machine
1NVS	ADA	VAX
2NVS	C, C++, COBOL, COBOL/S	SUN, NEWS, ...
3NVS		MIPS, EWS4800,...

Table 2. NVSs for ADA and VAX.

Suppose the user specified VAX for an attribute *machine* and ADA for an attribute *language* in the hierarchies in figure 8. Table 2 shows NVS sets.

Enumerating the Combinations: Next, all possible combinations of neighbor values are created from the n-th order neighbor value sets. Figure 12 illustrates how such combinations are created. This example assumes that the user specified values of attributes *language* and *machine*. All combinations of values under attributes *language* and *machine* will be created. Weights of attributes (0.3 for *language* and 0.4 for *machine*) and the similarity measure (such as 1.0, 0.2, 0.5 assigned to each value set) are used to assign similarity between a combination and the problem definition specified by the user.

Using the neighbor value sets from the previous example, combinations shown in Table 3 are created.

Assigning Similarity Value: For each combination, a similarity value will be assigned using similarity between values of attributes specified by the user and values of combinations created in the previous stage. Calculation is similar to weighted nearest neighbor, except that not all attributes are involved. The CARET algorithm does not compute attributes not specified by the user. Whether the user specified the attribute or not is shown in a mask matrix (M), which is a one-dimension matrix whose size is equal to the degree of the case-base. The matrix element will be 1, if the user specified the value of the attribute i. Otherwise, M_i will be 0. The formula to calculate the similarity is as follows:

$$S(Q,F) = \frac{\sum_{i=1}^{n} M_i \times W_i \times s(Q_i, F_i)}{\sum_{i=1}^{n} M_i \times W_i} \tag{1}$$

where F is a combination of NVSs and F_i is the i-th attribute of the combination. It should be noted that similarity is calculated between the user specified attributes and a combination of NVSs, which are the seed of SQL specifications. In essence, the similarity is computed between the user's specification and the SQL specification. This contrasts to traditional methods which compare the query and each instance of a case. For example, the simi-

```
and(language(ada),  machine(vax))
and(language(ada), machine(or(sun, news, ...)))
and(language(ada), machine(or(mips, ews4800, ..)))
and(language(or(c, c++, cobol, cobol/s)),  machine(vax)
and(language(or(c, c++, cobol, cobol/s)), machine(or(sun, news, ...)))
and(language(or(c, c++, cobol, cobol/s)),machine(or(mips, ews4800, ..)))
```

Table 3. Combination created.

larity of a combination, (["C"], ["MIPS, ..."]) to the query case is 0.2. This is because only the attributes *language* and *machine* are involved (the user specified only these attributes), whose weights are 0.3 and 0.4, respectively, and similarity between ADA and C is 0.2 and that of VAX and MIPS,... is 0.2.

Thresholding and N-Best Match: When there are too many combinations, translating all combinations and dispatching all SQL specifications is inefficient and wasteful. Methods to limit the number of SQL specifications to be created are necessary in real deployment. Two approaches are incorporated in the CARET system.

The first method is the N-Best match. CARET dispatches SQLs starting from the highest similarity score, and counts the number of cases retrieved, stopping the retrieval when the number of retrieved cases exceeds a predetermined number.

Second, a threshold can be set in order to dispatch SQL specifications which are sufficiently similar to the user's problem specifications. SQL specifications below threshold will not be created.

Generating SQL Specifications: Each combination is translated into corresponding SQL specifications. Since SQL does not involve the similarity measure, the value assigned in the previous process is stored in the CARET, and is referred to when the query results are returned.

The only SQL command type used here is the SELECT-FROM-WHERE type. Its form is:

> SELECT field-i, field-j, ...
> FROM case-base table
> WHERE field conditions ...;

This means "Select records in a case-base table which satisfy specific conditions in the WHERE clause, and return the value of the requested fields in the SELECT clause from the selected records".

Each element in a specific combination is translated into a certain condition expression of SQL. For example, *machine(vax)* is translated into *(machine = vax)* which means that the attribute *machine* must be *vax*.

```
SELECT *
FROM CASE-TABLE
WHERE (LANGUAGE in (C,C==,COBOL,COBOL/S))
AND (MACHINE = VAX);
```

Figure 13. Generated SQL.

Factors	Query-1	Query-2	Query-3
Length of Query	1	2	3
Depth of Tree & 3	2 × 3	2 × 2 × 2	
Width of Tree	16	16+12	8+8+9
Number of Generated SQL	3	6	4
Cases Matched	158+4+199	0+0+11+0+0+94	2+0+0+0

Table 4. Characteristics of queries.

language(or(c,c++,cobol,cobol/s)) is translated into *(language in (c,c++,cobol,cobol/s))*, which means that the attribute language must be *c, c++, cobol,* or *cobol/s*. Then, each condition expression is connected with logical-AND operators. For example, *and(language(or(c,c++,cobol,cobol/s),machine(vax))* is translated into *(language in (c, c++, cobol, cobol/s)) and (machine = vax)*.

As a result, the SQL specification is produced. An example of the generated SQL is shown in figure 13.

Performance Evaluation

Performance of the SQUAD system has been evaluated. The experiments were carried out on a SUN SparcStation-2 using Oracle version 6 installed on SunOS version 4.1.2.

Figure 14 shows the response times measured for three user queries, and various sizes of case-bases. The three queries are:

Query-1: LANGUAGE = C
Query-2: (LANGUAGE = ADA) and (MACHINE = VAX)
Query-3: (PROBLEM-TIME-BEFORE-QC = SYSTEM-GENERATION-TIME) and
(PURPOSE-TIME-OF-QC = SYSTEM-GENERATION-TIME) and
(CHOSEN-METHOD = CHANGE-OF-PROCESS-SEQUENCE)

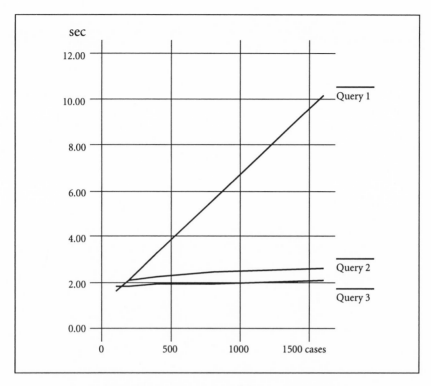

Figure 14. Response time of three user queries.

For the query-2, SQL specifications and their similarity values as shown in Table 1 are derived.

Characteristics of each query are shown in Table 4. "Length of query" refers to the number of conjunctive clauses in the WHERE section. "Depth of tree" shows depth of abstraction hierarchy of each attribute. "Width of tree" is the number of terminal nodes of the abstraction hierarchy of each attribute. "Number of Generated SQL" is the number of SQL queries generated and actually sent to the RDBMS. "Cases matched" shows number of cases matched in each query. 158+4+199 should be read as 158 matches with the first SQL, 4 matches with the second SQL, and 199 matches with the third SQL. These numbers are measured with a case base that contains 800 cases.

The scalability of the algorithm has been tested by increasing the number of cases in the case-base up to 1,600. Response time (in real-time, not in CPU time) are shown in figure 14.

Query-1 returned the major part of cases in the case-base, resulting in slower response time due to retrieval of these cases. The response time of the query-1 increases linearly as the size of the case-base increases. Indexing methods for the commercial database systems are not effective for reducing response time in such cases. Also, most of the time is spent on retrieving matched cases, rather than matching itself.

Fortunately, however, users generally specify queries in a detailed manner. An empirical analysis using the SQUAD system discovered that the average number of specified attributes for each retrieval was 3.4 out of 75 features. This detail helps the RDMS to constrain search and results in dramatically shorter query time. The second and third queries confirm this observation.

The second and the third query show a nearly constant time response regardless of the size of the case-base. This consistency is due to the fact that SQL specifications are specific enough to constrain the search by the RDBMS. Since the system provides fast response time, it suffices for most tasks.

A brief analysis of the performance results sheds light on the behavior of the system. There are two major factors which affect retrieval speed. These are: number of SQL specifications actually dispatched to the RDBMS, and number of cases retrieved.

The maximum number of the SQL specifications that can be created is decided by a number of attributes specified by the user and the depths of the tree of the specified attribute (equation 2).

A larger response time is required when larger numbers of cases must be retrieved. The number of cases retrieved depends upon the specificity of the SQL specifications.

Query-1 resulted in longer response time than query-2, and query-3 because a larger number of cases had to be retrieved. Query-2 and query-3 attained faster response time because the SQL specifications were specific.

Discussion

In this section, we will discuss the effects of a corporate-wide information system and the system development workload and cost.

Corporate-Wide Impact

It is extremely difficult to assess the effects of a corporate-wide information system because its effects are by nature, hard to quantify. However, we have obtained a rough estimate of effects of the activity by conducting a series of surveys for software-related sections.

The summary of the surveys indicates that our project has already attained an estimated pay-off of over one hundred million dollars per year in 1991. This includes both SWQC and the SQUAD system itself. The activities are so interrelated, however, that it is not possible to isolate the effect of SQUAD system itself. However, we estimate 10-15 percent of the benefits are derived from the SQUAD system. As such effects accumulate, the net effect is considered to be on the scale of many billions of dollars.

System Development

The application of CASE-METHOD resulted in a significant reduction of the system development workload, as well as a significant reduction in system development costs. For this kind of system, the expected workload for the development of the entire system (but excluding a knowledge-base) is about 10 man-months. However, the system was completed with less than 4 man-months of workload. Since this workload includes successive upgrading of the CARET CBR shell itself, the real workload for SQUAD itself is estimated to be about 1.5 man-months. Since CARET has reached a well-defined state, we expect the next system can be built with 1 man-month of workload. There are two major contributing factors for this workload reduction.

First, the use of an RDBMS in CARET offered a significant workload saving over building a specific case-storage mechanism. All necessary functionalities and performance-tuning facilities have been provided by the commercial RDBMS.

Second, Canae/Yuzu—a GUI construction environment—dramatically reduced the workload needed for user-interface development. Since SQUAD uses menus and tables extensively for the user interface, predefined parts of the user interface eliminated the need for coding these parts. Our assessment indicates that the user-interface development workload was reduced to 1/10.

Case-Base Building and Maintenance

Application of the methodology resulted in qualitative and quantitative change in case-base building and maintenance.

On the quantitative side, we observed a reduction in the workload for building case-bases from cases reported from various divisions. Before the methodology was introduced, the case report format was free form, and consisted of about 20 items. Although one domain expert had been working full time on case-base building, it took almost 6 months to add 1,500 cases. Thus, processing the more than 3,000 reported cases each year took an entire year. By introducing the methodology described in this chapter, the workload began to decrease. After a fourth cycle, the total workload was reduced to 0.5 man-months for 1,500 cases, or 1/12 of the initial workload. At this cycle, the number of attributes used reached 130. Figure 15 shows the history of workload reduction. Thus, total system development cost and maintenance cost have been reduced dramatically (figure 16).

There are qualitative effects as well. As the number of attributes and possible values increases, more cases are covered by a set of values which are already on the case report form. Our current coverage is over 95. Thus, the

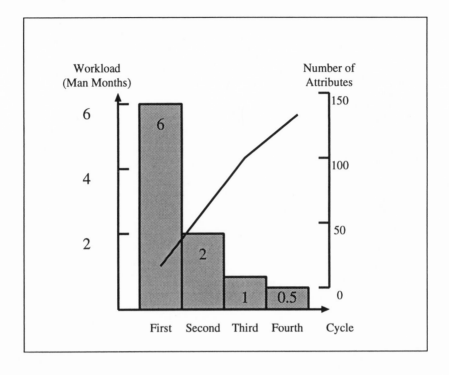

Figure 15. Casebase building workload

process of case-base building has become a simple data entry task that can be automated in the next step. Some cases continue to require special handing, however—such as those that cannot be covered by the values and attributes defined in the case reports. A knowledge engineer on the development team analyzes and registers these cases. At the same time, new values or new attributes are added to the case report form so that the coverage can be increased in the next cycle.

Furthermore, quick turnaround for data entry has enabled the SWQC division to carry out detailed analyses of the new cases, thus enabling the SWQC division to inspect the quality of cases, using the extra time gained by its workload reduction.

Conclusion

It took us almost a decade to establish a corporate-wide process of case acquisition, which provides a stable flow of up-to-date cases of software quality

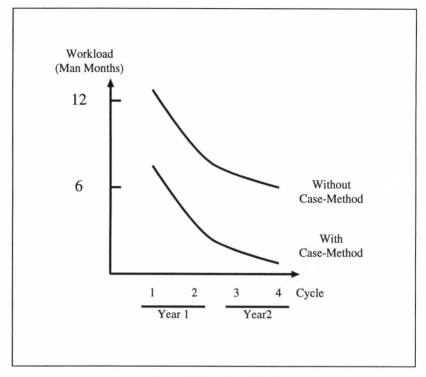

Figure 16. Total workload.

control and productivity improvement. The current statistics indicate that this process offers quality and productivity improvement over a hundred million dollars each year. The net effects could easily exceed many billions of dollars. Application of CASE-METHOD for the development of the SQUAD system substantially reduced the development and maintenance cost. These results support the concept of experience sharing architecture.

There are several findings which we wish to share. First, the successful corporate-wide deployment of an AI system must involve organizational efforts, as a part of the algorithmic loop in the system in a broad sense. This includes a strong commitment from top-level management.

Second, the system should be flexible and robust enough to cope with the incremental and changing nature of the corporate structure and corporate activities. Sophisticated algorithms and AI theories are not always necessary; sometimes, these technologies even harm the system. The important decision is to identify the appropriate technology for the given task.

Third, a solid methodology is essential. It is a powerful driving force to promote system development using the most efficient procedure. It also helps ensure the quality of the system developed.

Fourth, use of an RDBMS for case-base retrieval enables us to explore data-base management techniques built into the RDBMS. Our new method for conducting similarity-based retrieval using SQLs is highly consistent with existing mainstream corporate information systems, and thus highly acceptable to MIS staff for full scale deployment.

In summary, the experience sharing architecture presented in this chapter is a promising approach toward the next-generation corporate information system.

Acknowledgements

We would like to thank Dr. Mizuno, Dr. Fujino, Mr. Saya, and Mr. Kai for continuous support for this project. We would also like to thank all the NEC employees who have engaged in this project for a decade, and continue to participate in this endeavor in one way or the other. This chapter is based on Kitano et al. (1992), Kitano et al. (1993), and Shimazu et al. (1993).

Notes

1. The Nation-Wide system stores and retrieves implementation techniques that are useful in particular situations. These include methods to speed up database retrieval for specific configurations (which is important because there is no general theory available), and methods for re-designing a data-base schema to reflect specific user requirements.

14 Case-Based Reasoning: Expectations and Results

William Mark, Evangelos Simoudis, & David Hinkle

C ase-based reasoning makes certain key claims, both as a research approach and as an implementation technology. Using CBR tests these claims and provides new insights. In our research we have focused on how CBR can be applied with other technology approaches, both in learning and in problem-solving. In our system- building efforts we have seen CBR as part of an overall solution strategy, using it when it seemed to offer significant advantage. This chapter describes three CBR experiences in different domains, employing different software technologies, and with different expected roles for CBR. In each case we discuss why case-based reasoning was chosen as an approach, our expectations for the role and value of CBR in the system, how these expectations evolved as the system was developed and deployed, and finally what results were achieved.

As with any other technology, case-based reasoning brings with it a set of expectations for researchers, systems developers, and users. These expectations arise from explicit claims about the technology, and evolve through research and experience. The Lockheed Martin Artificial Intelligence Center creates, adapts, and deploys AI and other advanced software technologies. For the past several years, case-based reasoning has been part of our portfolio, both as an area of research and as an approach to building systems for our various customers. In this chapter we discuss our experience with case-based reasoning, highlighting three projects: an application for which CBR seemed to be a "natural" approach, a research effort to see how CBR could be applied to a diagnosis problem, and a commercial system for which CBR technology was a differentiator in our proposal and in our eventual implementation.

Expectations

Before we examine the projects individually, we will briefly discuss our initial expectations of CBR technology in general, based on the claims that its practitioners have made for it.

Problem-Solving Efficiency

The traditional view of reasoning in artificial intelligence is that problems are solved by specializing and composing abstract operators. The base set of abstract operators is determined in advance, though of course new compositions are automatically generated and used by the system to solve specific problems. We were seeking technology that would increase the "chunk size" of the knowledge that the system uses to address problems. In the case-based paradigm, reasoning is a process of recalling one or a small set of concrete cases that have actually produced results on some input. Composition may still be required if the recalled cases solve only parts of the current problem, but the elements being composed are substantial sub-solutions. There should be considerable advantage in not having to create (and always re-create) time-consuming derivations based on composing abstract operators. We therefore expected CBR to be the most efficient way to solve at least some problems.

Automated Knowledge Base Growth

The derivation of solutions by composition is what gives "traditional" systems their breadth and flexibility. In case-based reasoning breadth and flexibility are achieved in two ways: 1) the system automatically adds to its case library, giving it a larger repertoire; and 2) the system automatically creates new recall paths for accessing its cases by creating new indices. We therefore expected CBR to provide new approaches for reducing problem-solving brittleness and for creating systems that automatically improve and adapt over time.

We were also interested in the insights CBR provided as a learning paradigm, i.e., CBR's focus on learning in terms of automatically acquiring and organizing specific domain knowledge. We hoped that CBR could be combined with empirical and explanation-based approaches to make learning technology more useful in large scale application systems.

Use in Not-Fully-Formalized Domains

Case-based reasoning allows problem solving in domains whose knowledge has not been fully formalized. Much domain knowledge is difficult to represent adequately because of incomplete understanding of the domain itself, lack of expressiveness of representation languages, or simply the sheer volume of knowledge in the domain. Case-based reasoners do not depend on fully modeling the content of cases, which need only be records of past behavior in unanalyzed form. Instead, CBR relies on knowledge of when to recall and use the cases. We thought that this different emphasis on required knowledge would allow us to address domains in which other approaches had not been feasible. We saw the CBR element as part of an overall system, with, for example, cases being used to focus on important features of a problem, while other methods might be used to solve subproblems defined by those features.

Also, a major problem in reasoning in many domains is the need to deal with uncertainty resulting from imprecision of source information, or the need to make decisions before all relevant information can be examined. Case-based reasoning offers a way to refocus the problem of dealing with uncertainty based on incomplete information by having the reasoner rely on what has worked in the past. Rather than computing confidence in a proposed solution based on the composition of knowledge with extrinsically assigned uncertainties, the case-based reasoner simply chooses among solutions that have worked in the past in "similar" situations. Once again, reasoning is pushed into similarity determination, including any reasoning about the certainty of the similarity assessment. We thought that this shifting from reasoning about uncertainty to similarity determination might help to organize our approach to solving problems in which uncertainty is an issue.

Reduced Construction Costs

A frequent claim for case-based reasoning is that case knowledge can be directly acquired and used in a system, while in other approaches knowledge must be analyzed and manipulated to form rules, models, etc. The idea is that in at least some parts of some domains, knowledge is "naturally" structured as cases that can be straightforwardly translated into equivalent or closely approximate computer representations.

Since we shared the common view that knowledge acquisition and maintenance are the major investments in building knowledge-based systems, we looked forward to CBR as an approach for significantly reducing the cost of knowledge-based system development.

A "Natural" Application

One of Lockheed's manufacturing processes uses an autoclave (a large convection heater) to cure composite parts (Hinkle and Toomey 1994). Autoclaves are expensive resources; maintaining a high level of throughput of parts through the autoclave is critical to managing manufacturing time and cost. Maintaining throughput is complicated by the fact that the curing process is sensitive to the layout of the parts and also to intrinsic part properties such as size, shape, and material. A further complication is that the parts waiting to be processed are given priority rankings depending on whether they are required for work in progress, assemblies that need to be completed soon, replacement parts, etc.

Autoclave loading is thus a task that requires considerable expertise in choosing among the waiting parts and arranging them into a "layout" that

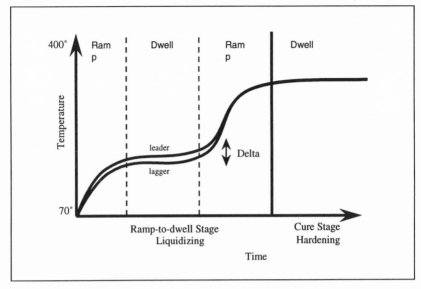

Figure 1: Thermodynamic-profile.
Curve indicates the mold temperature of the hottest and coolest parts while
curing in the autoclave. Parts exceeding a 30° delta may need to be scrapped.

will keep the throughput of high priority parts as high as possible while still ensuring that all the parts follow the correct thermodynamic profile (see figures 1 and 2). If a part goes outside the correct profile, it may be damaged and need to be scrapped.

Autoclave layout planning was being done manually: expert operators created new layouts based on their experience with the success or failure of previous layouts. A new layout was created by selecting the previous layout that matched the largest number of high priority parts in the queue. Any remaining places in the layout were then filled in with lower priority parts or left unfilled. Considerable expertise and judgment were required to adapt previous layouts based on allowable "fill-ins" that would not violate the implicit constraints that made the previous layout successful in the first place.

Determining an individual autoclave load is part of the overall autoclave scheduling task: making sure that the parts waiting to go through the autoclave are configured into a series of loads that best meet the needs of the overall production process (see figure 3).

Autoclave scheduling was being handled as a two-phase process. A formal schedule was generated based on experience. This was considered to be useful as a general guideline. However, the *real* schedule was hammered out every week in a meeting in which the project managers, fabrication managers, au-

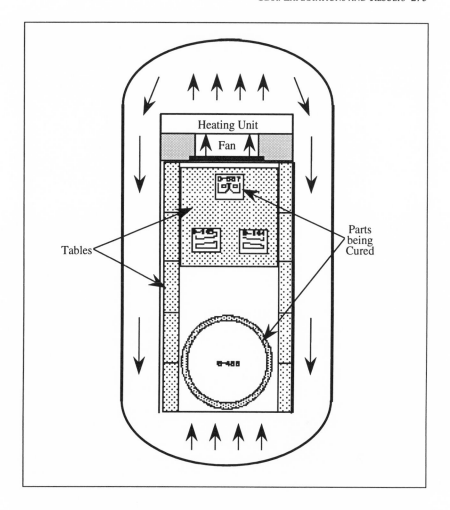

Figure 2: Autoclave. Arrows indicate the airflow's path down the exterior auto-clave chamber, and back through the central autoclave chamber where it cures the parts.

toclave managers, etc. lobbied for resources until a compromise was achieved.

The goal of the Clavier system was to provide interactive support for auto-clave operators throughout the autoclave scheduling process. The idea was to use previous cases to propose individual load configurations and to build multi-load plans. One of its key perceived advantages within Lockheed was that the program would learn, becoming more and more competent as it automatically acquired new cases.

When we began the Clavier project in 1989, case-based reasoning was rela-

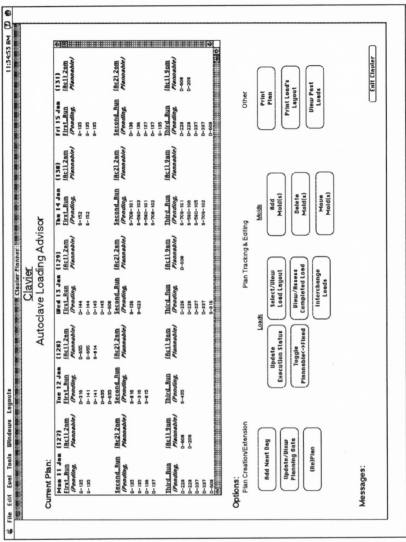

Figure 3. Clavier Planner/Scheduler interface showing a five-day schedule of three autoclave loads per day.

tively new as a technique for implementing a system that provides some economic value. We chose the autoclave domain because we thought that it was a "natural" application of case-based reasoning: the operators already used cases, which were to some degree documented. During the development of the Clavier system, we also considered rule-based technology, thermodynamic modeling, and inductive learning as candidates for the autoclave loading task, but none of them proved practical (Hinkle and Toomey 1994).

Why Case-Based Reasoning?

When we first investigated the autoclave loading problem, it became apparent that a form of case look-up was already in use. We felt that we could build a system that automated the current method using reasonably well understood case-based reasoning techniques. Existing cases would be compared against the list of parts to be processed according to a "best match" criterion. The matching criterion is based on the number and priority of parts that match the parts in a particular case (see figure 4). Unmatched parts in the chosen case would be filled with the highest possible priority parts from the list according to "similarity" criteria based on the part and its spatial context in the layout (Barletta and Hennessy 1989).

The initial choice of case-based reasoning as a technology for this application was therefore straightforward: it was a direct mapping of the current approach. The cases already existed, allowing knowledge engineering costs to be minimized. The system was a direct replacement for manual look-up, to be used by the same operators who currently performed this task. The system's graphic user interface was designed to mimic the form of the current records. "Training costs" would therefore be minimal. The implementation was for a standard Apple Macintosh to keep capital costs low.

Expectations

We expected Clavier to show clear—and measurable—benefits to the Lockheed manufacturing process. Layouts created with Clavier would show marked improvements in reliability and efficiency (curing the most high-priority parts in the least time). Furthermore, we expected these improvements to increase steadily over time because of the cumulative nature of Clavier's knowledge base.

Assuming success on the autoclave layout task, we expected Clavier (or Clavier technology) to expand into the larger scheduling task, eventually finding application in the large scale manufacturing process that includes autoclave management as one of its tasks.

We expected that it would be easy to evaluate Clavier's effectiveness—an important consideration given our desire to expand Clavier's role in Lockheed manufacturing. Clavier's results would initially be evaluated by autoclave loading experts to make sure that the results did not violate known principles of part compatibility and positioning. After that, we felt that Clavier's results would be directly measurable against existing autoclave throughput records.

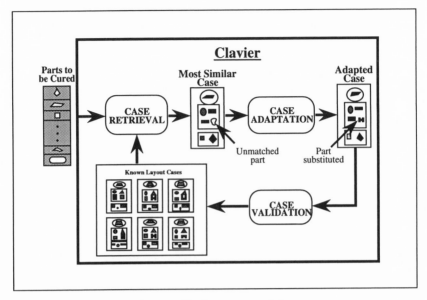

Figure 4. Clavier system task flow.
Production schedule of parts prompts retrieval of best matching cases.

Evolution

As it turned out, although we had records for all of the layouts used during the past year, we could not use them directly. The record keeping was inadequate to determine validity for many of the layouts. We needed to review the records with domain experts to verify which layouts were valid and which were invalid. From the set of layouts the experts considered valid, we developed a core set of cases covering all the parts that needed to be manufactured. We used this as our initial case base.

Clavier was successful in finding correctly matching layouts most of the time. Sometimes, however, operator assistance was required to adapt an old case to the production problem at hand. As originally proposed, the Clavier system was to automatically adapt the closest matching case and present the adapted layout to the operator for verification. Unmatched parts in the chosen case were to be filled with the highest possible priority parts from the list according to "similarity" criteria based on the part and its spatial context in the layout (Barletta and Hennessy 1989). This proved to be too difficult due to the complexity of determining thermodynamic compatibility from a part's spatial context. Instead, we reversed the roles, asking the operator to manually adapt the cases, while giving Clavier the responsibility of validation.

If an exact matching case cannot be found, Clavier presents the closest matching cases. The user then decides how to modify a chosen case. After the user makes a modification, Clavier validates the new configuration by comparing it with similar valid and invalid cases. If the load is predicted to be valid, the system proceeds to generate the description of how to configure the molds within the autoclave. If the system predicts that the load might be incompatible (because of similarity to an invalid load), it suggests alternative configurations that are similar but valid. If the system strongly believes that the load will be incompatible, it suggests ways of breaking the single load into multiple valid loads. In this case Clavier sacrifices some of the load's efficiency in order to decrease the risk of part defects. After the load has been cured in the autoclave, the operator tells Clavier if the load was successful. The annotated new case is then stored in the library, allowing the system to expand its expertise.

It was initially expected that case base growth would level off after about two years; final case base size was predicted to be around 300 cases. During the first two years, as expected, the case base did grow quite rapidly to approximately 300 cases. However, the case base did not stop growing, and now contains more than 600 cases. This is primarily due to the dynamic nature of the manufacturing process and the continuous refinement of the case base.

While our sample of past loads was classified into two categories, valid and invalid, the true situation is actually a little more complicated. Loads in which a mold goes outside the allowable thermodynamic profile are clearly invalid. However, even loads that do stay within the thermodynamic profile may still be classified invalid based on how close they came to going outside the profile (i.e., how risky they are). In addition, how much risk the operators are willing to take depends on whether there are less risky alternatives. For example, if a new load is developed that is similar to, but less risky than, a load currently classified as valid, the new load will be added to the database and the old load will be reclassified as invalid. What this means in practice is that the validity of a load is not strictly Boolean and can change over time.

Results

Clavier was the first fielded commercial application of case-based reasoning technology, and has been in continuous daily use at Lockheed's Composites Fabrication facility in Sunnyvale, California, since September 1990. Two to three autoclave loads are cured per day in this facility, all of which are selected through operator consultations with Clavier.

Clavier ensures that high quality load configurations are used for manufacturing composite parts, even when experienced autoclave operators are unavailable. This consistent level of expertise is critical to producing high quality parts and maintaining the production schedule. There are now five operators and two support personnel who regularly use the system as part of their daily routine for the generation of autoclave load configurations and other reports.

If a mold goes outside the correct thermodynamic profile, a discrepancy report must be issued and the part must be manually inspected at a cost of $1,000. If the part is flawed and must be scrapped, it costs an average of $2,000, and in some cases $20,000 to $50,000. Since Clavier came on line, discrepancy reports due to incompatible loads have been virtually eliminated, saving thousands of dollars each month.

One important additional benefit of Clavier is that it has clearly demonstrated, both to management and the technicians on the shop floor, the power of knowledge-based systems. Since Clavier's initial fielding, we have gone on to develop several other knowledge-based applications for use in other stages of the manufacturing process.

Research in Fault Diagnosis

Diagnosis is an area in which AI technology has been applied for many years with considerable success. Our goal was to extend existing approaches to address domains in which scale, complexity, and adaptability were the major drivers. Our intent was to advance the state of the technology, and our approach was to conduct the research in the context of a specific problem domain. We focused on improving the diagnosis and recovery of faults in large multi-station machine tools. Rapid recovery from machine faults (malfunctions and unexpected conditions) is essential in manufacturing operations. In particular, the growing use of just-in-time material handling in manufacturing requires that downtime for any piece of equipment be minimized.

An effective fault recovery process in this domain must establish how the equipment entered into the identified fault state, and must prescribe a safe exit from the fault state. Modern milling machines are equipped with self-diagnosis capabilities that allow them to identify the source of 20% to 40% of the problems that occur during their normal operation, and to suggest actions to the operator that result in an appropriate solution. For the remaining problems, a field-service engineer has to be dispatched to the customer's site by the equipment's manufacturer.

The field-service engineers have varying degrees of experience. In order to minimize down-time a customer usually prefers a senior engineer. As a result, these engineers are severely oversubscribed, leading to customer dissatisfaction. This problem can be alleviated through the use of a knowledge-based system that provides the junior engineers access to the senior engineers' problem-solving expertise. The system would have to deal with the scale and complexity of real machine tools, and would have to be easy to modify and maintain. Our goal was to build and test a knowledge-based system to be used by junior field service engineers.

Why Case-Based Reasoning?

Field service engineers are required to document all of their service calls. The required report has three entries: (1) the customer-provided description of the problem, (2) problem-related information obtained during the fault recovery process, and (3) the repair action performed by the engineer to recover from the fault, including the milling-machine parts that had to be installed and/or replaced. The contents of the first and third entries are always recorded because they are used by the milling-machine manufacturer for billing the customer. The content of the second entry depends on the experience and diligence of the engineer. Senior engineers tend to provide detailed descriptions of the problem-solving process they follow. Junior engineers tend to be very brief and often omit providing an explanation.

After looking through a large number of field service reports, we determined that:

- The same types of faults occur again and again.
- Field engineers identify fault states via a feature-and-precedent-based classification process.
- In most cases established solutions to particular problems can be reused.

Based on these observations, we felt that milling-machine fault recovery was an appropriate domain in which to apply case-based reasoning, with field service reports being used as cases.

Expectations

We had two expectations with this work. First, that it would be easy to create a large case base from the data recorded by the field service engineers. The milling-machine manufacturer had a corpus of 10,000 such records, which we felt would be adequate for creating a large case base. We especially wanted to experiment with the effectiveness of the CBR method at large scale.

The issue of scale led us to our second expectation: that we would need automated means to index cases. The problem-solving efficiency of a CBR system is based on its ability to rapidly retrieve the most appropriate cases for each new problem. In order to expedite the retrieval process, CBR systems organize their case base using indices. Index-creation is a major issue in any CBR system. During index creation, the system tries to identify the case features that characterize the new case and establish its appropriateness for a class of situations.

The goal is to define the most general class of retrieval situations, as long as no situation in the class violates the set of conditions that made the case effective in the first place. If the indices are too specific, the case would not be retrieved in situations in which it was actually applicable. If the indices are too general, the case would still be retrieved and applied even though critical conditions were violated. For our domain, over-generalization would lead to the worst system behavior, because it could drastically increase the machine's downtime if an inappropriate case were applied.

Unfortunately, the conditions that determine whether a case is appropriate are usually not initially observable. They must often be inferred from the surface features of the case. Our idea was to use explanation-based learning techniques to create generalized indices from surface features (Barletta and Mark 1988). Both rule-based and model-based reasoning can be used to implement explanation-based indexing. We decided to use a model-based reasoning approach because we believed that we could obtain a partial structural, behavioral, and functional model of the milling machine.

The explanation-based reasoner would use the model to establish inferential links from features of a case to known classes of faults. The resulting inference chain would constitute an explanation of how those features were relevant. These "known to be relevant" features, generalized to the extent supported by the model, would then become the primary indices of the case—necessary conditions for the case to be applicable. Features not determined to be relevant according to the model would become secondary indices, used to choose between cases that were deemed applicable based on primary indices. (Secondary indices could not be discarded because the models were assumed to be incomplete.) We felt that this approach made good use of the domain knowledge we thought we could acquire and represent. We were also motivated by the potential usefulness of the approach for other applications.

Evolution

Construction of the case base for the system took a very different course than we had expected. We were initially provided with a set of 100 problem reports. We first tried to analyze these reports on our own. However, because of the terseness of the cases and the various domain-specific terms and abbreviations used in the cases, we needed the assistance of an expert field service engineer. But the engineer decided to use the contents of the cases to create new prototypical cases rather than to fill in the details of the provided problem reports because the cases contained no contextual information. Customer support engineers are evaluated based on the number of customer problems they are able to address, not the amount of detail they provide for every problem they solve. Consequently, they often do not include details, i.e., the context, of the problem. As mentioned earlier, the information they always record is useful primarily for accounting purposes and not for future problem-solving. Since the expert could not re-create the details of the partic-

```
(case1
    (problem-features (machine-type t-30) (year-of-manufacture 1989)
        (control-type cnc) (tool-changer-state stuck)
        (machine-drive-type dc) (tachometer-condition dirty))
    (repair-plan ((replace tachometer) (adjust gain))))
```

Figure 5. Part of a prototypical case

ular problem-solving experience (episode), he used the available information to create prototypical cases.

In the process he relied not only on the milling machine's structure and behavior model, but also on his own heuristic knowledge, gained from many years of experience. Part of one of the prototypical cases created by the engineer is shown in figure 5.

While creating these prototypical cases, the expert was able to provide a partial model of the milling-machine components referenced in the problem reports (e.g., tachometer, tool changer, etc.). A high-level view of the model is shown in figure 6.

In the process of working with the engineer to create the prototypical cases and model, we developed a good understanding of the feature space. The initial set of cases was incorporated into a retrieve-and-propose CBR system we implemented, called CABER (Simoudis and Miller 1993).

Retrieve-and-propose systems are a specialization of the retrieve-and-adapt CBR systems (Kolodner 1991). The general CBR paradigm calls first for cases that appear similar to the problem at hand to be retrieved from the case base, and then for the solution plan associated with the best of the retrieved cases to be adapted, if necessary, so that it can fit the particular characteristics of the new problem. The application of CBR technology to a variety of real-world domains has shown that adaptation is a domain-specific operation necessitating the development of problem-specific techniques. Also, even within a domain, adaptation methods have been a collection of ad hoc techniques; consequently users do not feel comfortable with automated adaptation systems. On the other hand, case retrieval is a rather well understood task, that generalizes across domains and that has been successfully automated for case bases of varying sizes. For this reason, we chose to follow the pattern of the latest generation of CBR systems, especially the ones that have been used in real-world applications, by automating the retrieval operation and then presenting the retrieved cases to the users to adapt (Kolodner 1993).

The purpose of indexing is to provide paths for quickly accessing the cases in the case base. This is done by identifying each stored case by only a subset

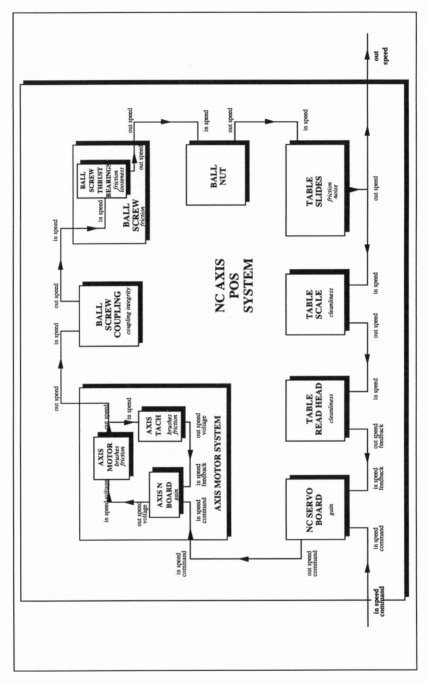

Figure 6. A partial view of milling-machine model used by the CABER system.

of the features that describe it, and by further organizing these features into data structures that decrease the search cost, e.g., trees. Indices serve in case bases the same purpose they serve in general purpose databases. Indices are very important when the case base is large and is expected to grow further. If the case base is small, and if each case is described by a small number of features, comparing each feature of each stored case against the new problem is not expensive. Therefore the computational cost of creating, organizing, and maintaining indices and index structures can be avoided.

Since the initial set of cases available for this domain was small, as was the number of features included in these cases, and the obtained model not adequately detailed, cases in the first version of CABER were not indexed using explanation-based indexing. Indeed, the first set of cases did not have to be indexed at all. Instead, the nearest-neighbor retrieval algorithm (Duda and Hart 1973) was used during retrieval. The nearest-neighbor algorithm is the simplest of the case-retrieval methods. It calls for the full comparison of every feature of all the stored cases and the new problem.

After an initial experimentation phase during which the resulting prototype was shown to the expert, we were provided with an additional 250 problem reports. Again, we had to use the expert to interpret the cases and provide us with additional prototypical cases. With the expert's assistance, we created 40 additional prototypical cases and expanded the milling-machine model. Reduction from 250 problem reports to 40 prototypical cases was due to both the overlap of some cases, and to a lack of problem-solving details recorded in many of the problem reports.

Encoding these cases required that we expand the represented feature space, which grew from 30 to 100 features. Due to the increase in the size of the case base and in the size of the feature space, we decided to index the entire set of cases using explanation-based indexing. Since the feature space was still relatively small, we decided to organize the created indices in a flat structure.

Results

One of the major lessons of CABER was that the organization and reasoning needs of the CBR component changed significantly during the course of system development. We decided that the best result of CABER would be a shell that embodied what we had learned from building CABER. We therefore generalized our CABER experience in knowledge acquisition and analysis of retrieval and learning operations to create a case-based fault recovery shell called REPRO (for *re*trieve and *pro*pose).

REPRO is a tool kit for fault recovery system builders that provides automated assistance for the development of retrieve-and-propose case-based systems. REPRO's design is based on two hypotheses.

Hypothesis 1: The characteristics of an application domain may necessitate the use of different retrieval and learning algorithms during a case-based expert system's life cycle.

Existing commercial CBR shells do not provide for such selections, especially if they need to be made during the middle of the expert system's life cycle. Instead, they incorporate one or two predefined algorithms (e.g., nearest neighbor) that are hardwired into the expert system under development. However, existing commercial CBR shells do provide adequate case representation and storage facilities for the needs of a case-based expert system. Such facilities need not be duplicated by shells such as REPRO. For these reasons, REPRO is layered on top of the ReMind™ CBR shell.

Hypothesis 2: The selection of the appropriate algorithms should be based on a methodology that takes into account the characteristics of domain knowledge and the characteristics of algorithms.

The development of a case-based reasoning system is comprised of four design processes: (1) selection of a case retrieval algorithm, (2) selection of a case adaptation algorithm (not necessary for retrieve-and-propose systems), (3) selection of a learning algorithm, and (4) creation of a seed case base. The selection of the appropriate algorithms is difficult because it is driven by the interrelation between the retrieval, adaptation, and learning functions, the characteristics of the application domain (e.g., available knowledge, size of feature space, etc.), the tasks to be performed by the CBR system (classification, design, monitoring, etc.), and the contents of the case base. Our goal for REPRO was to systematize and build in some of the required domain and algorithm analysis for retrieve-and-propose systems

Our analysis of the fault recovery domain is based on the generic task methodology (Chandrasekaran 1988). Fault recovery begins with a set of symptoms that describe a fault, as well as other features establishing the fault's context. The goals of fault recovery are to: (1) identify the fault's type, and (2) execute a plan whose actions can eliminate the fault. Therefore fault recovery consists of two generic tasks: *classification* and *plan instantiation*. In REPRO, both tasks are mapped into the retrieve-and-propose method. In particular, given a set of cases that contain pre-classified faults, the retrieve-and-propose method tries to retrieve the best case and use its contents to propose a classification for the new fault. In retrieving the case, it also proposes the best plan for the user to execute.

Our analysis of the learning and retrieval operations was based on the needs of the domain and the characteristics of the algorithms involved. In its simplest form, the learning task performed by a CBR system consists of storing new cases in the system's case base (rote learning). In our framework for fault recovery applications, a new case needs to be incorporated into the case base for one of three reasons: (1) a new fault type has been identified, (2) a new set of features that are indicative of a known fault type has been identified, or (3) a new plan for repairing a known fault type and a known set of features has been identified.

As discussed in relation to CABER, the retrieval operation required for a CBR system depends on the size of the case base and the characteristics of the cases it contains. As with the first version of CABER, if the case base and the number of features per case are relatively small, the nearest neighbor algorithm may suffice. However, for larger case bases or more complex cases, nearest neighbor comparison becomes computationally prohibitive.

The computational cost of case retrieval can be reduced in two ways. First, through reasoning with appropriate domain knowledge during retrieval (Koton 1988c, Simoudis and Miller 1990). For example, the system CASCADE (Simoudis 1992) uses knowledge about the cost of establishing the value of each attribute in the process of determining which case to retrieve. Second, by organizing the case base through indices and employing a retrieval algorithm that can utilize the created indices.

The creation of indices is part of the overall learning task. After the index is created, it is incorporated into the case base together with the case it organizes. Associated with index creation are two other subtasks: index organization and index maintenance. Index organization refers to the way indices are organized in the case base once they are created (e.g., hierarchically, in flat structures, etc.). Index maintenance refers to the modifications that must be performed on indices (e.g., specialization, or generalization) to increase their effectiveness in organizing cases.

Deciding whether or not to generate indices for the cases of a case base, is based on both domain-specific and domain-independent characteristics. For example, if the case base is small (e.g., less than 20 cases), grows very slowly over time (e.g., less than one case per month), the number of features making up each case is small (e.g., less than six features), and feature acquisition is not expensive, then the cases do not have to be indexed in the case base. However, there also are instances where the case base is very large and the cases still need not be indexed because of either the classification task the system performs, or the use of massively parallel hardware, for example, the MBRtalk system (Stanfill and Waltz 1986). The selection of algorithms is, therefore, driven by the interrelation of the learning and retrieval tasks as well as the characteristics of the application domains.

Furthermore, algorithms may be combined in order to achieve acceptable retrieval performance. For example, index-driven retrieval may return a subset of the case base on which nearest neighbor retrieval is then performed.

REPRO is targeted for the knowledge engineer who is expected to cooperate with domain experts to develop retrieve-and-propose fault recovery systems. It can be layered on top of commercial CBR shells, allowing it to take advan-

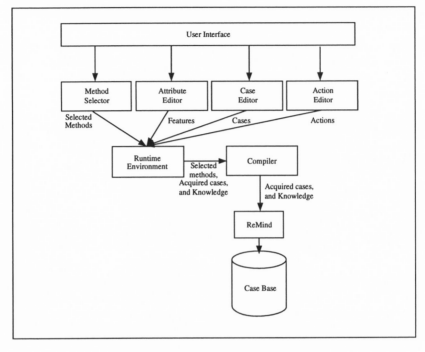

Figure 7. REPRO's architecture.

tage of efficiently implemented and well tested generic retrieval, indexing, and data storage capabilities, in the context of a tool kit of specific methods to be used by the knowledge engineer as necessary.

REPRO consists of the following components: method selector, attribute editor, action editor, case editor, runtime environment, and compiler, as shown in figure 7.

REPRO provides the knowledge engineer with:

- The capability to define the feature space of a domain and create a seed case base.
- A structured way of initially selecting a set of index creation, organization, maintenance, and retrieval methods.
- A structured way of satisfying the requirements of each selected method for explicit domain-specific knowledge. This knowledge expresses the interrelations among the features, and methods for their acquisition.
- The ability to experiment with the chosen methods and select different ones as the system evolves.
- The ability to compile the development system into a runtime system that can be used as a stand-alone application.

Development of a case-based fault recovery system using REPRO is performed through the following steps:

1. The knowledge engineer uses the method selector to select one or more of the index creation methods incorporated in REPRO, as well as an index organization method and a retrieval method for each selected index creation method.

2. The knowledge engineer represents the explicit domain knowledge that is required by each selected method using the action editor. The attribute and case editors are used to create a seed case base that is stored in ReMind's database. The state of REPRO with the knowledge it contains about the expert system under development can be saved, creating application-specific versions of the shell.

3. Each case is indexed under all index creation methods that have been selected by the knowledge engineer and each index is organized using the selected index organization methods.

4. The knowledge engineer uses the runtime environment to exercise the system with a set of test cases. During this testing process the knowledge engineer may try different index creation, organization, and retrieval methods.

5. Once the performance of the system on the test set is deemed satisfactory, the knowledge engineer uses REPRO's compiler to create a runtime version of the case-based fault recovery system.

Copies of the REPRO application can then be made and distributed to users. Updating and refining of the system can be made through the application-specific version of REPRO. REPRO has been distributed to a number of organizations for use in the development of prototype CBR systems.

A Commercial Test

The growing complexity of products, especially in the computerized on-line services arena, has greatly increased the job complexity of customer support representatives. For example, support representatives must often have knowledge not only of the products their company offers, but also of the third-party products that the customers require to make their company's products work. At the same time, there is enormous pressure to minimize service costs, giving rise to a pattern of hiring junior support representatives who are subsequently trained on the job and are complemented with a few senior representatives.

One approach to dealing with the cognitive overload of junior customer representatives is to provide them with automated support. In fact, this approach is widespread in practice, with the support technology ranging from information retrieval to knowledge-based systems. We have developed a case-based help desk system, Expert Help Desk System (EHDS) for a major financial institution. Our system supports junior representatives in helping customers over the telephone with their problems in using home banking software systems such as Intuit's Quicken™. Support takes the form of automated classification of the problem based on its symptoms, and automated prompting of the service representative with instructions for what the customer needs to do to resolve the problem.

Why Case-Based Reasoning?

We chose a case-based reasoning approach because problems in this domain appeared to recur with great frequency and because identifying the appropriate solution to a problem could easily be formulated as a classification process based on features and precedents. Moreover, a senior customer support representative had developed a corpus of prototypical cases for one class of problems that we believed could be used to form a seed knowledge base. We were even more confident of the viability of the CBR approach because it has been successfully applied to help desk domains (see Simoudis and Schutt 1993).

Expectations

We had three expectations with this work. First, that the corpus of knowledge provided by the senior customer representative would enable the quick development of a case base. We were initially provided with 50 cases that addressed the modem connectivity problems that represented 60% of the technical calls received by the particular help desk.

Second, because the corpus of knowledge was provided in the form of prototypical cases, we expected that a pure case-based reasoning system would be sufficient for addressing the problem. In particular, through knowledge acquisition sessions with the expert we determined that the similarity assessment knowledge for these cases was very simple, and that at most one or two cases were always appropriate for each of the problems that the prototype system was going to address.

Third, we expected that commercial case-based reasoning shells would enable the rapid development, deployment, and incremental improvement of the system. Given that problem classification is the key task for customer support representatives, the major component of any case-based expert help desk system is the case retriever.

As discussed in relation to REPRO, since case retrieval is a well-understood operation that can generalize across application domains, it has been possible to incorporate generic case retrieval capability into CBR shells. Such shells (e.g., Inference Corporation's CBR Express™, Cognitive Systems Inc.'s Re-Mind, etc.) provide a simple case representation scheme (usually in terms of attribute-value vectors), a case repository (a flat file or a relational database, e.g., Oracle®), one or two index-creation schemes, (e.g., inductive index-creation), and corresponding retrieval methods (e.g., tree-traversal, nearest neighbor). We chose CBR Express to implement our help desk application.

Evolution

Within one week we prototyped a stand-alone system that included ten of the provided cases, stored in a flat file. The initial prototype was well-received by both the help desk's representatives and management. Our tasks were then to enhance the case base and to interface the CBR system with a relational database management system that would store both the cases and customer data. We also needed to provide junior support representatives with a mechanism to escalate difficult problems to the senior representatives. Finally, we needed to provide senior representatives with the ability to write new cases and to store them in the case base, where they would be automatically indexed and integrated with the rest of the case base.

The CBR system we developed has two types of components: a problemolving component that the customer support representatives use to solve problems that clients report, and a case authoring component that experts can use to write new cases for problems that customer support representatives cannot solve. The architecture of each of these components is shown in figures 8 and 9.

Associated with every attribute in CBR Express is a question that is used during the problem-solving session to obtain the attribute's value during problem solving. The retrieval algorithm of CBR Express, a variant of nearest neighbor, always asks the first unanswered question of the case that is considered most relevant at each iteration, given the available information. Since the nearest neighbor algorithm is executed after each question is answered, a question from a different case may be asked at each iteration. One limitation we encountered was that there was no way for prior-probability information to affect the retrieval process. As more cases were entered into the case base and cases started sharing attributes and therefore questions, this operation presented problems. The customer support representatives are supposed to follow one case (line of reasoning) until the case proves to be inappropriate for the problem at hand. To resolve this problem, we had to modify the retrieval algorithm of CBR Express. This modification forced the retrieval algorithm to pursue a single line of reasoning until the case was confirmed or eliminated, and was essential to solving the focus-of-interaction problem.

In fact, we found that CBR systems have an advantage in addressing the focus-of-interaction problem that has been examined in the context of rule-based systems. Since a rule-based system's knowledge has been broken up into distinct rules to allow compositional problem-solving, the system must use some extra-knowledge-base mechanism to control the way in which

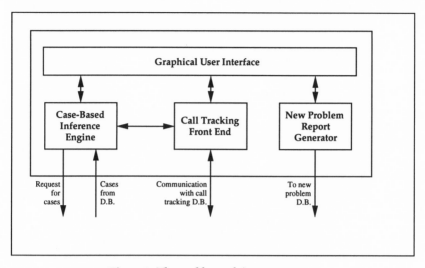

Figure 8. The problem solving component.

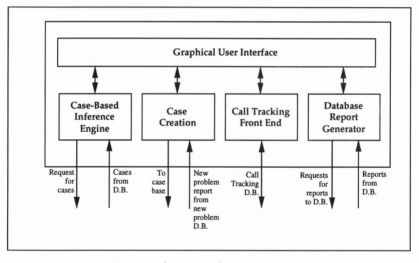

Figure 9: The case authoring component.

these rules are used to interact with the user. For example, a system like MYCIN must add additional meta-rules or use ad hoc mechanisms to control the order in which problem-solving rules are used to ask data-gathering questions of the user (Buchanan and Shortliffe 1985). In CBR the structure of the case includes the context in which a particular piece of knowledge is used. This context provided the required focus of interaction in the help desk application.

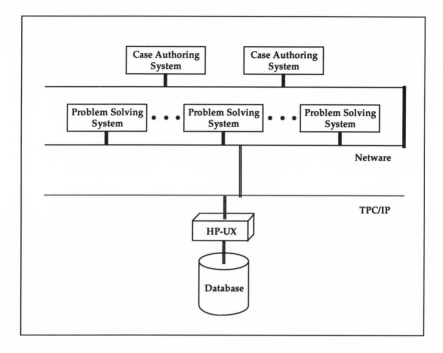

Figure 10. The computing infrastructure of the financial help desk CBR system.

An application system does not operate in isolation; it is always part of a larger solution environment. Our help system had to interface with customer databases, as well as be able to access knowledge that was stored in relational databases running in a distributed environment. Significant engineering effort was expended in tuning the databases so that cases and collateral data could be retrieved as quickly as possible regardless of the number of simultaneous users that access the other databases in the environment. We also needed to have scaleable performance as more users were added to the system. This implied that the case indices had to be mapped to database indices and to obey the restrictions imposed by database indices.

Results

The system is currently running in a real help desk environment on a 24-hour, 7-days a week basis. It is being used by 25 customer support representatives who are organized in two levels of seniority; 15 are junior support representatives, 10 are second level support representatives, with several of those being experts. The number of users is expected to grow to approximately 200 support representatives.

Our system architecture is currently meeting the case retrieval performance demands of the environment. As the system matures, the case base will be continually monitored to validate content and organization.

Conclusions

The three systems that we have described here are very different in terms of intent, domain, implementation approach, and user community. Nonetheless, we have some conclusions that we believe generalize across the individual efforts.

Cases Are a Good Representation, But They Don't Come For Free

Knowledge in the form of cases may not be readily available in most domains. For some "natural" domains, such as Clavier's domain of autoclave loading, they are available. However, the information available in many other domains, even if it is caselike in the informal sense of episode records, legal cases, etc., must be thoroughly analyzed and reformulated in order to make it into CBR-ready cases. The cases required for CBR technology, at least as it exists today, must be created by knowledge engineers—the domain knowledge does not "come that way." However, the pre-existing "protocases" of a domain are extremely useful in facilitating the acquisition of knowledge: they guide the knowledge engineers in determining what questions to ask the expert, and provide them with a domain vocabulary through which they can interact with the expert. The existing information also helps the expert in articulating case knowledge, as well as other types of knowledge, (e.g., models), because it provides a context-setting framework.

One question that is frequently asked of knowledge-based systems, including CBR systems, is: what percent of the domain is represented in the system? We did not find case-base size to be a particularly useful measure for answering this domain-coverage question. Counting cases is no better than counting rules or concepts, because the details of indexing and retrieval determine issues of applicability and generality. Case-base size should only be considered a very rough measure of coverage. As with other approaches, there is no clear internal knowledge metric; the system's knowledge should be measured by its externally observable performance on tasks. For example, coverage can be evaluated by field testing on a random sample of problems.

We did find that the case representation produced as a result of the knowledge acquisition effort offers significant advantages in terms of explainability (it is relatively easy to show domain experts and other stake holders what the system knows) and maintainability (cases, unlike rules and model fragments, interact with each other in only limited ways, thus allowing bugs to be more easily detected and corrected).

In summary, we have consistently found that creating a CBR system in a new domain requires a full-scale knowledge acquisition effort of the usual sort: designing an appropriate organization, representation, and set of reasoning methods; putting the knowledge into the designed framework; and debugging and refining the knowledge base in close interaction with domain experts. Casting the knowledge base in terms of cases does not automatically create useful knowledge base metrics, but it is useful for explaining the system, for making some debugging easier, and for making it possible for users to extend the system without intervention from knowledge engineers. On balance, in appropriate domains, CBR systems can be prototyped and built faster than rule-based systems. In some domains where rule-based systems are not feasible (such as Clavier), CBR can prove to be a valuable alternative (Hinkle and Toomey 1994).

Adaptation Is for Users

One of our consistent findings was that automated adaptation of cases was not feasible. The required depth of domain understanding consistently forced us into ad hoc approaches that had very limited coverage. Even when these approaches did apply, the results could not be justified to skeptical users. Simply trying an automatically adapted case to see if it would work was not possible in any of our domains due to the cost of failure. The usual justification for a case is that "it has worked before" (or, for prototypical cases, that "this class of things has worked before"). Ad hoc automated adaptation invalidates this justification, and leaves no well motivated explanation to replace it.

On the other hand, we found in Clavier that users are very willing to participate in the adaptation process. The CBR system's ability to present near-misses or other forms of context to help the user create new cases was seen as very valuable. Use of the system to validate the adapted case by comparison with similar cases that had worked before was very well accepted—even when, as in Clavier, the users were well aware that the comparisons were being performed only at the level of surface features. As with other knowledge-based system technologies, success in CBR adaptation is achieved by creating the right shared task environment between the system and the user.

CBR Offers Interesting Integration Opportunities

We assumed from the outset that CBR technology would be only a part of the overall solution to the problems we were trying to solve. Our experiences bear this out and show how critical it is to integrate the CBR technology with the rest of the solution environment.

As shown in CABER, CBR integrates well with other knowledge-based reasoning approaches. But CBR also marries very naturally with other aspects of the "solution environment," both software and human. For example, large CBR systems (like any other application) must coexist with the other systems and data of the enterprise. The total enterprise environment is usually distributed over highly heterogeneous computing infrastructures. Any integration task of this nature poses enormous engineering challenges. CBR's contribution is to provide a clean conceptual interface with the rest of the world. For example, cases are data structures that fit well into conventional data base representation schemes. The CBR system can thus interact with the rest of the enterprise environment in terms of the well-defined interfaces of existing data base management systems.

Of course, human beings are also part of the enterprise environment, and CBR offers interesting opportunities to integrate into human problem-solving processes as well as software environments. In Clavier, for example, human operators had to be intimately involved in the process of creating new autoclave loads. The fact that Clavier represented loads as cases provided a clear mapping between what the user recognized as coherent objects (individual loads) and what the CBR system recognized as coherent objects (cases to be added, indexed, modified, or deleted as such). This mapping was reified in the system through Clavier's presentation of each case as a load diagram (a visualization of parts in their actual spatial configuration). Similarly, in both CABER and in the help desk application, both user and system share a common view of the objects that can be created and manipulated. We found this clear conceptual mapping to be a crucial part of integrating the CBR system into the human environment.

15 Goal-Based Scenarios: Case-Based Reasoning Meets Learning by Doing

Roger C. Schank

There has always been a great deal of lip service given to the idea of learning by doing, but not much has been done about it. In fact, John Dewey remarked in 1916, in his book *Democracy and Education:*

"Why is it that, in spite of the fact that teaching by pouring in, learning by passive absorption, are universally condemned, that they are still so entrenched in practice? That education is not an affair of "telling" and being told, but an active constructive process, is a principle almost as generally violated in practice as conceded in theory. Is not this deplorable situation due to the fact that the doctrine is itself merely told? But its enactment in practice requires that the school environment be equipped with agencies for doing ... to an extent rarely attained."

There are two important reasons why learning by doing isn't our normal form of education. First, it is quite difficult to implement without "doing devices." How can we teach history by doing? What does it mean to teach literature by doing? In many cases, it is difficult to define what *doing* might mean with respect to a given subject and to attempt to implement a realistic sense of doing in a classroom setting. When there are "doing devices" available, it is easier to implement learning by doing. Driving can easily be taught in a learning-by-doing manner, for example, because students can reasonably be placed behind the wheel of a car. This can be done because cars are relatively inexpensive and relatively safe. When this is not the case, when the necessary equipment is too expensive or unsafe, or where there is no equipment at all, learning by doing is usually abandoned as a teaching philosophy. There is, of course, another reason why learning by doing isn't the primary teaching model in the schools. Educators and psychologists have not really understood why learning by doing works, and thus are loathe to insist upon it. They can't say exactly what it is that learning by doing teaches. They suppose that it teaches real life skills, but what about facts, the darlings of the "drill-them-and-test-them" school of educational thought?

To consider learning by doing from a psychological point of view, we must think more about learning in real life, which is, of course, the natural venue of learning by doing. There is, after all, something inherently artificial about school. Natural learning means learning on an "as needed" basis. In such a learning situation, motivation is never a problem, we learn because something has caused us to want to know. But school has no natural motivation associated with it. Students go there because they have no choice. The same is true of most training situations. Trainees don't usually elect training. And, while they may well choose their jobs, they can hardly know that they need certain information in order to do their jobs better. They can only know this because they are told. Training rarely comes after someone has done badly at his job. Businesses try to anticipate such situations, to avoid mistakes on the part of their employees. Thus, they provide training in anticipation of real problems and employee-perceived needs. This concept, of training in anticipation of need, is an important reason why businesses are often ineffective in training.

One of the places where real life learning takes place is in the workplace, "on the job." The reason for this seems simple enough. Humans are natural learners. They learn from everything they do. When they watch television, they learn about the day's events. When they take a trip, they learn about how to get where they are going and what it is like to be there. This constant learning also takes place as one works. If you want an employee to learn his job, then, it stands to reason that the best way is to simply let him do his job. Motivation is not a problem in such situations since employees know that if they don't learn to do their job well, they won't keep it for long.

Most employees are interested in learning to do their jobs better. One reason for this is, of course, potential monetary rewards. But the real reason is much deeper than that. If you do something often enough, you get better at it— simple and obvious. When people really care about what they are doing, they may even learn how to do their jobs better than anyone had hoped. They themselves wonder how to improve their own performance. They innovate. Since mistakes are often quite jarring to someone who cares about what they are doing, people naturally work hard to avoid them. No one likes to fail. It is basic to human nature to try to do better and this means attempting to explain one's failures well enough so that they can be remedied. This self-correcting behavior can only take place when one has been made aware of one's mistakes and when one cares enough to improve. If an employee understands and believes that an error has been made, he will work hard to correct it, and will want to be trained to do better, if proper rewards are in place for a job well done.

In general, most businesses are aware that the more experience an employee has with a given situation, the more effective he is in that situation. It would seem to follow, therefore, that the best way to teach anybody is to let them work on a job that requires the skills we are trying to teach. This is a bit circular since it means letting an employee attempt to use skills that we know he doesn't have in order to teach him those skills. The best way to learn how to do a job is to simply try doing the job, with no preparation in particular, but with an expert available for help as needed. Although this is the best way to learn from the perspective of the employee's natural learning process, it might well not be the preferred choice of either the employee or the employer.

Employers have to be very tolerant to allow learning by doing to be the dominate teaching method for training because of the potential for costly errors made by novice employees. Most employers are unwilling or unable to do this. Employees don't really want to do this either. People are afraid of public failure, and nothing could be more public than failing on the job.

One obvious answer is the use of simulations for training. The best of the current simulators built for training purposes are the air flight simulators. Modern flight simulators are phenomenally real. Inside, they look like cockpits down to the last detail. They bounce and rattle and jolt, and what you see out the window are pictures that accurately portray whatever airport you select from whatever perspective your airplane would be putting you in at the moment. It looks like the real thing. It feels like the real thing. And so, you can take off and land at will, going in and out of your favorite airports. You can try things out and see what happens. You can crash and try to figure out what you did wrong. After enough time, you can teach yourself how to fly. Of course, it helps to have someone next to you whom you can ask for help, and it also helps a great deal if the person beside you is not in a panic about his own imminent demise because of your inadequacies as a pilot.

In the use of a simulation of this type, what exactly is learned? That is, when someone learns by doing, what is it that he is learning? It is important to answer this question for two reasons. First, we want to know if a student or trainee has learned whatever it is we were supposed to be teaching him. To know this, it is important to know what we were intending to teach him. Second, there will be times when learning by doing will be difficult to teach. If what was to be learned in this fashion could be taught by some other means, we will indeed try. It is critical then to understand what is learned so that we don't make the mistake of teaching something else, like facts, and assuming that this kind of teaching will be an effective substitute.

To begin to think about what learning by doing actually teaches, consider the following:

Suppose I decided to open a school that taught about the art of dining. Some people know good food and good wine and we might ask what is it, exactly, that they know? This domain is a good one to discuss because it is one with which everyone is somewhat familiar and is one for which there do not exist prejudices about what one "should know." There is no cultural literacy movement in the world of fine dining. So what could we teach in such a school?

We could teach how to order in a restaurant; how to select a wine; how to understand what is likely to be good in a particular place; how to eat certain foods, and so on. But it would indeed seem rather foolish without getting to eat. If you want to know what Korean barbecue, sushi, chestnut puree, or truffled egg tastes like, you've got to eat it. If you want to know whether the sushi you had was typical of what sushi should taste like, you have to have sushi a second time. If you want to know the extent to which freshness matters in sushi, you have to eat sushi that isn't fresh and then eat some that is especially fresh. To gain this experience in a restaurant means asking about when the sushi was made, when the fish was bought, when it was caught, and so on.

In short, learning about food means eating it, thinking about what you ate, eating things like what you have already eaten in order to contrast one experience with another, and asking questions to determine other information that may help you make sense of your experiences. Still, this doesn't tell us exactly what it is that we are learning when we are learning by doing. It does tell us one important thing we are doing, however. We are acquiring experience. Experiences, or cases, are a critical element in understanding what is learned when one learns by doing.

When we eat sushi for the first time and then feel we want to understand all the possibilities for sushi, both good and bad, we know that this means eating more sushi. It may also mean eating sashimi, and eating rare tuna in an restaurant that grills tuna steaks. The more we eat, the more we become experts on the possibilities with respect to raw fish.

To put this in terms of case-based reasoning, a learner is interested in acquiring sufficient cases such that he can learn to detect nuances. He wants to be in a position to compare and contrast various experiences. To do this, he needs to have had those experiences, and he needs to have properly labeled those experiences. This labeling process is what we refer to as indexing. Indexing means taking an experience and giving it a name. So, we might call an experience of eating sashimi "sushi without the rice leaves blander taste experience due to lack of contrast in textures." Or, we might call eating sashimi "sushi without the rice." There is no right way to index, but it is clear that the former index is richer than the latter and thus is likely to lead to better remindings. In other words, someone who had used the former index might get reminded of other foods where rough and smooth textures are found in the same bite. One conclusion here is that if you want to know about food—eat. Someone telling you about how something tastes, in effect, giving you a vocabulary for describing tastes, is not of great value. The experiences that build up a knowledge base cannot be obtained vicariously. One must have experiences, not hear about them. The reasons for this are simple. Hearing about them means that the teller has crystallized his own experiences, shortened them, summarized them, and in effect has taken from them the material of indexing, the stuff from which we can build our own index. One cannot index on someone else's experience largely because that experience, as transmitted, will omit many of the details that are the fodder for indexing.

How we index cases is highly idiosyncratic. Indexing has a great deal to do with learning in that what we learn from an experience depends entirely on the indices that we assign to that experience.

Apart from cases and indices to cases, what exactly is learned when one learns by doing?

For many educators, this might seem to be an unimportant question. As long as students learn to do what they were trying to do, they have learned the right stuff. We need not ask exactly what they have learned unless we are seriously interested in what learning is all about. Of course, if we wish to design new educational systems we must be interested in precisely this question. It is all too easy for United Airlines to say that they know how to train pilots—they use flight simulators and allow their pilots to learn by doing. Similarly, any parent can say that he knows how to teach a teenager to drive: Sit him or her behind the wheel, grit your teeth, and let them go.

The problem is that it isn't all that easy to know what you are trying to teach all the time, and it is often tempting to preach rather than teach. Just because someone can fly an air flight simulator does not mean that you'd trust him to deal with any extraordinary situation. When you have taught your child to drive, you nevertheless fret each time he takes the car out for a spin. Can he handle wet conditions? What about drinking and driving? We cannot anticipate every possible condition in a simulator; lectures about the evils of drinking and driving may not necessarily teach the lesson.

What are the implications of this for education? We must, as best as we can, teach students to do things, rather than having them be told about what others have done. Learning is the accumulation and indexing of cases and thinking is the finding and consideration of an old case to use for decision-making about a new case. Critical to all this is the process of expectation failure and explanation. To make thinking beings, we must encourage explanation, exploration, generalization, and case accumulation. How do we do this?

Recently, in a graduate class of mine, which has in it a few undergraduates, we were discussing learning. The students were making a variety of assertions about learning which caused me to wonder whether we were all talking about the same phenomenon. I asked various members of the class what they had learned recently. One told me that he had learned that a wok will rust if left overnight with the cooking residue in it. Another told me that she had learned that cheap paint doesn't work as well as expensive paint. Another told me that she had learned that she could buy cough medicine across the street and didn't have to walk a long way for it as she had thought. Another told me that he had learned that I liked to sit in a certain place in the classroom. Another said that he had learned how to handle himself better in certain social situations. These learners were all graduate students.

The undergraduates, on the other hand, noted that they had learned various facts such as certain events in history or certain methods of calculation in mathematics. Why the difference? The graduate students were much older than the undergraduates. They had more daily concerns because their environment was not as sheltered as the undergraduates. In addition, the undergraduates were engaged in the process of getting As by learning what they were told. The graduate students were trying to find out about their new environment, living in new houses, cooking for themselves, trying to understand what was expected of them in graduate school. The graduate students were being forced, both in school and in life, to think for themselves. What method were the undergraduates using for learning? Basically, they were copying what they were told. The graduate students were, on the other hand, experimenting, hoping to find out what was true by trying things out and attempting to make generalizations about what might hold true in the future.

All of this tells us that learning is essentially a discovery process. We are all natural learners. As babies, we discover things by ourselves before we can be told. Even when we understand enough to be told, we still need to try things out for ourselves. The understanding cycle—expectation failure – explanation – reminding – generalization—is a natural one. No one teaches it to us. We are not taught to have goals, nor to attempt to develop plans to achieve those goals by adapting old plans from similar situations. We need not be taught this because the process is so basic to what comprises intelligence. Learning is a natural act.

How do we enhance learning? One way to enhance learning is by doing. If you want to learn about food and wine you have to eat and drink. If you want to learn how to drive, you have to drive. If you want to learn to fly a plane, you need to, at least, fly a simulated plane. What does this tell us about training and education then? It tells us that we need to try and recall, when designing a curriculum, what it is we are trying to get students who had been through that curriculum to do. To put this another way, we need to transform all training and education so that it looks, feels, and is like doing.

This brings us back to the question of what would then be learned if all training and education were, in fact, doing. We have so far said that cases and indices to cases are learned in this way. But something more important and, unfortunately, considerably less interesting from an intellectual point of view is learned this way as well. To see what we mean here let's return to teaching a teenager to drive.

It is easy to agree that certain cases would be learned while driving. For example, I recently was waiting at a red light at an intersection and, when the light turned green, decided not to go forward. I decided to wait because I was crossing a four lane road and a bus was in the lane third farthest from me and was blocking my view of the lane that was farthest away. Although the light was with me, it had just changed and there was always the possibility that a car was running the light and I wouldn't be able to see it. As it happened, that was exactly what took place. My caution averted a serious accident. That caution was based on many prior cases of seeing people run red lights. My experience was quite useful.

Now, of course, we want young drivers to have enough experiences that they could make similar judgments. We all know that drivers are much more cautious after an accident. We hope that our teenage will not need to have an accident or near accident in order to acquire reasonable judgment, but we know that this is unlikely to be the case. We just hope they won't get hurt as they learn.

So, they are learning cases, but what else are they learning? Of course, they are learning how forcefully to press the brake, how to accelerate in the proper way, how to stop at a stop sign, how to enter a highway, how to turn the wheel, and other mundane things that experienced drivers never think about and have difficulty articulating when attempting to teach their teenage children. It is actually quite hard to say how to press the brake. We can try, but all we have are words and these are as useless here as they are in describing how tuna sushi is different from yellowtail.

What We Learn When We Learn by Doing

In a book that laid out the primacy of goals in comprehension (Schank and Abelson 1977), an idea that was critical to understanding how humans decide what to do and understand what others do was developed in some detail. I am referring to the concept of scripts. Simply speaking, scripts were intended to account for the human ability to understand more than was being referred to explicitly in a sentence by explaining the organization of implicit knowledge of the world that one inhabits. Thus, when John orders sushi, we assume that he is in a Japanese restaurant; we know he might be seated at a sushi bar; we know that he is probably using chopsticks and not a fork; and, we can even assume that he is drinking Japanese beer. We assume these things because we know the sushi bar script. If we do not know this script, we cannot make such assumptions and thus might have difficulty understanding various sentences that refer to things we might be assumed to know.

Scripts enable people to understand sentences that are less than complete in what they refer to. When we hear "John ordered sushi but he didn't like it" we know that this sentence is referring to eating and to John's reaction to a type of taste sensation that he has never had before. We know this because of what we know about restaurants (the restaurant script) and because of what we know about a small specification of the restaurant script, namely "sushi tasting." When we hear that "John flew to New York, but he was very unhappy with the meal" we now must invoke the airplane script to understand it. We do not imagine he flapped his arms to get to New York, nor that he was in a flying restaurant. We can explain what happened to him by saying "well, airline food isn't very good" because we know the details of the airplane script and those details include that kind of information.

How do we come to know such scripts? The answer to this is very simple. We learn them. We learn them by practicing them over and over. We can learn them as children, by being taken to a restaurant many times and gradually learning each step of the restaurant script. We can learn them through expectation failure by seeing an aspect of a script fail to be true (chopsticks instead of forks, for example) and explaining the difference to ourselves, creating a new Oriental restaurant addendum to that portion of the everyday restaurant script. And, we can learn them as adults, by, for example, going on our first airplane ride, trying to understand its script and gradually modifying our understanding with each subsequent trip.

It is this last aspect of the learning process that is most important for education. When we go on an airplane trip for the first time, or indeed, when we do anything for the first time, we are highly dependent upon finding a reminding, that is, finding some prior experience that will help us understand the current situation. Reminding is the process by which case based reasoning takes place. When we attempt to understand anything, we do so by attempting to find something in our memories that looks sufficiently like it so as to be helpful in processing. The reminding process allows us to learn by causing us to constantly compare new experiences to old ones, enabling us to make generalizations from the conjunction of the two experiences.

Now, one of two things happens during this comparison process. Either we realize that the new experience is significantly different from the one that we have compared it to, or we realize that it is really very much like it. (I will ignore gray, in between, cases here.) When a new experience is found to be different from our prior closest memory, we must create a new case for it. We can use our prior knowledge of trains to help us out on our first airplane ride, but we soon realize that while the comparison may have been helpful for initial processing, airplanes are cases of their own. We can index airplanes in terms of trains, but eventually we will treat them as a new thing entirely.

We may not know to do this initially, of course. How can we know on one airplane ride not to treat it as a specialization of train travel? But on our tenth airplane ride, we will cease to need that comparison. Instead, in trying to compare each airplane ride to each other, we will have created an airplane script that predicts what airplane rides are like in general, including information that states that one should not expect much of a meal. This is, of course, the other aspect of the comparison process. Finding a new experience to be a lot like an old experience allows us to build the script.

So, we either use new cases as new material to add to our library of cases or we use new cases to help build up our detailed script knowledge. We can, of course, decide that our new case is of no interest whatever because it is exactly what we have experienced many times before. In that instance, no learning occurs at all. We shall consider further the significance of new case acquisition within the learning by doing context later on. Now, we need to discuss further the significance of scripts in learning by doing.

In Schank and Abelson (1977), scripts were described as very large structures that covered whole experiences. The restaurant script, the airplane script, the hospital visit script, and even the car accident script were discussed and are typical of the extent to which we believed that script-based, that is routinized, behavior dominated the performance of actors in these scripts and also accounted for our ability to understand events that take place within the context of these scripts.

In Schank (1982), I recognized that what I was calling scripts were structures that encompassed similar aspects and that the independence of these structures in memory would not account for the fact that learning could take place across such structures. Thus, for example, one might pay for a restaurant meal, an airplane ticket, and a hospital visit in much the same way, that is, by going to a person seated behind a desk, presenting a credit card, signing and taking the receipt. Of course there are differences in paying in each situation, so one could argue that human memory would want to treat these as completely different entities, but this is unlikely. It is unlikely because, if one found that one had misunderstood how to sign the credit card receipt in one situation, learning how to do it properly in the next situation would be generalized across all the situations by a reasonable person.

The recognition that memory was made up of independent scenes such as "paying" that could be assembled in memory by larger memory structures made clear that entities such as restaurants served more as memory organization packets (MOPs). Thus, the MOP restaurant included scenes such as "paying" or "ordering" or "being seated," which, with the exception of some of the variables contained in the restaurant's version of "paying" or "ordering" were not substantially different from MOP to MOP. It thus became clear that scenes were major memory items, that scenes were "colored" by different MOPs in different ways, and that MOPs collected together various scenes in particular orders.

While the details of all this may not be important for our purposes here, certain aspects are very significant for understanding how learning works. Learning can, of course, take place in any memory structure. Memory structures are, by their very nature, meant to be alterable. However, when we learn about something that takes place in a restaurant, we need to know whether what we learned is about restaurants per se (and thus we need to alter the restaurant MOP), or about some aspect of restaurants that has significance beyond restaurants such as "paying" (in which case we need to alter what we know about a scene), or something that just happened to occur in a restaurant and has nothing to do with the MOP or scene in which it occurred (so we must alter what we know about some more abstract MOP, such as embarrassment or romance, that might have been operating at the same time in the same place).

What has happened to scripts in all this? Actually, they are still there. There are many highly routinized packages of events that are quite specific without any particular application beyond their immediate purpose. In Schank (1982) we said that scenes packaged scripts, that is, one scene might contain many small scripts. The difference between my use of the term in 1977 and in 1982 was one of scope. A 1982 version of script might be looking at the menu, putting ketchup on the hamburger, brushing one's teeth, or parking the car. These scripts seemed, unfortunately, not to be very interesting. Further it was easy to forget the new use of the term and people who used the term script continued to think of the 1977 variety. This matters a great deal as we shall see. So, I would now like to rename the 1982 scripts, calling them micro-scripts, thus making clear the smallness of their scope.

The reason why all this matters is that the object of learning in learning by doing is the acquisition of micro-scripts. The skills to which we refer when we ask about people's abilities almost always refer to micro-scripts. Let me explain.

Our abilities are bound up in micro-scripts. When we say we know how to do something, we are often referring to one or more micro-scripts that we have acquired over the years. These micro-scripts are often quite unconscious. We cannot easily describe what we know to someone who doesn't have the right micro-script. They often consist of very low-level skills that we have practiced many times over the years. An important point here is that this practice almost never takes place for its own sake. We practice micro-scripts solely because we are constantly pursuing the same goal again and again. We never use a micro-script except in service of a goal.

Two good examples of a micro-script are "setting up a VCR for taping" or "sending electronic mail." I know how to do both of these things. Many people do not. I have had to learn each many different times. In the 25 years that electronic mail has existed, I have had to use probably ten different systems. Although I was told how to use each, I rarely remembered what was said long enough to try it out. When someone watched over my shoulder as I did it, I could do it, but then I would forget by the next try. In short, I learned how to use electronic mail by using it. I am quite adept at the two systems I now use, although I probably don't know all the features of either. Nevertheless, if you asked if I had the skill of using these two systems, the answer is clearly "yes." It should be obvious that I have no interest in how these systems work in any way. I do have interest in sending and receiving mail, however. The goal of sending and receiving mail caused me to try the systems until I got good at them. These trials were held in the course of use, not as outside practice. To put it simply, I learned the e-mail micro-script by doing the e-mail micro-script — this is learning by doing.

A more common example is the use of the VCR. I got one of the first VCRs, and have had maybe ten of them over the years for various reasons. They all have different ways of setting up a recording, and I can operate all of them. I find them annoying to use, but I like to record and watch movies, so I have learned each system. If I am away from any of them for very long, I tend to forget how they operate. I know some generic stuff about how they work and this can help me re-learn what I need to know. But when I have relearned the micro-script I cannot do it quite efficiently. Micro-scripts tend to decay in memory if they are not used. But still, you could say that I have the skill of recording on my VCRs. I have learned those skills by doing them.

I am mentioning all this for a simple reason. Education ought to be, in principle, about learning cases and micro-scripts. We want students to know the exceptional cases from which they can learn and make judgments on their own about new situations. And we want students to know how to do things, to have sets of skills. But when we talk about the skills we want students to have, we often get confused by what we mean by the term, talking about what we want students to know, or how we want students to comport themselves and not about what we want them to do.

Students need to acquire micro-scripts so that they can perform the actions contained in them. However, micro-scripts are, almost by definition, very dull. Teaching them as objects in themselves, as things to be learned independent of what knowing them can do for you, is very difficult to do. On the other hand, students will easily acquire micro-scripts if they are acquired in the natural course of the pursuit of a goal that is of interest to the student. Micro-scripts must be taught in the service of a goal, or to put this more clearly, they ought not be taught at all. They need to be learned naturally in the course of the pursuit of a goal. This is what learning by doing is all about.

How to Do It: Skills as Micro-scripts

A proper teaching environment should contain all the skills that the curriculum designer wanted to teach, and then put them into some natural situation around which a set of actions culminating in a desired conclusion can be constructed. We can call such a set of actions a scenario. A goal-based scenario (GBS) allows a student to play one or more roles in a single or group situation that culminates in the accomplishment of some goal. That goal should be readily identifiable and seem real to the student. The goal can actually be real (like driving or repairing a car) or only be play-acting (like running a simulated company and attempting to beat the competition). In either case, the student must care about achieving the goal in order for the scenario to have any educational value. The scenarios can take as long as the designers want them to, from a day to a year. They can be built in software or partially instructor led, or completely paper-based. Case libraries are an important part of such a scenario. When a student has difficulties in achieving subgoals on the way to the main goal of the scenario, a teacher, whether real or electronic, needs to intervene. Such intervention is often in terms of a case, related as a well-told story, presented to the student immediately after a problem is encountered and the student indicates the need for help. Such case-based intervention can be in software, in video, or on paper. In chapter 5, Burke and Kass describe a system that does this.

The curriculum redesign process begins with an understanding of what skills are to be learned. Assessing what is a skill and what is not a skill is critical to this process. For this reason, understanding skills as micro-scripts is quite important. It is all too easy to see anything and everything as a skill. Certainly, reading, mathematics, management, and getting along with people are often talked about as being skills. But they are certainly not micro-scripts. They may be comprised of many micro-scripts—certainly this is the case for reading and mathematics. And, indeed, there may well be micro-scripts for management and getting along with people. But identifying precisely of what actions such micro-scripts are comprised can be quite difficult. It is, in fact, part of the art of the curriculum design process to determine what exactly it is that people know when they are reputed to have a skill such that the micro-scripts that comprise such a skill can actually be practiced.

There are three broad classes of micro-scripts. Looking at micro-scripts according to this classification can help us understand more about them. These classes are *cognitive, perceptual,* and *physical.*

The examples we have used so far have been primarily cognitive micro-scripts. Cognitive micro-scripts naturally have a physical component (if they didn't nothing would ever happen). Thus, the VCR micro-script is mostly a prescription about what to do in a cognitive sense, the physical aspect being no more than button pushing. The skill of button pushing is not a particularly interesting one, nor is it the difficulty that would-be VCR programmers encounter that makes them incapable of getting the right program taped at the right time. The difficulties they encounter are cognitive, in knowing which button to push when, not in knowing how to push the button. Similarly, the e-mail micro-script involves only mouse clicks and keyboard strokes at the physical level. All cognitive micro-scripts have a physical component, although that physical component is quite often rather uninteresting and the knowledge of how to do it quite independent of the micro-script in question.

Purely physical micro-scripts do indeed occur—typing and button pushing on a remote control device being two of them, for example. More interesting ones are bicycle riding, brake pedal pushing on a car, or tooth brushing.

Perceptual micro-scripts involve the recognition of things, such as recognizing individual people, noticing dangerous situations, or the perceptual part of hitting a baseball.

When we say that someone has a skill in the sense of skill that is appropriate here, we mean that he has a micro-script that might involve a primary cognitive micro-script and some physical and perceptual ones as well. This distinction is not that important here and we shall use the term micro-script to refer to a mental entity which might actually involve a mix of all three types of micro-scripts. Thus the following definitions apply:

> *A cognitive micro-script refers to knowledge about use.* This knowledge is usually consciously available. That is, a person in possession of that knowledge can talk about it. If the sentence "John knows how to use X" makes sense for a given X then X is a cognitive micro-script.

> A physical micro-script refers to knowledge about operations. This knowledge is not usually consciously available. That is, a person in possession of a physical micro-script may not be able to talk about it. If the sentence "John knows how to operate an X" makes sense for a given X then X is a physical micro-script.

> *A perceptual micro-script refers to knowledge about observations.* This knowledge is not usually consciously available. A person in possession of a perceptual micro-script may not be able to talk about it. If the sentence "John knows how to recognize an *X*" makes sense for a given *X* then *X* is a perceptual micro-script.

As we noted above, we are referring to what is commonly meant by skills. The problem with this word, and why we feel the need to avoid it, is that the word has no clear definition—nearly anything can be a skill. We can say, for example, that someone is a skilled negotiator or is skilled at cooking. When we talk about skills, we are often referring to what we believe a person "knows how to do." Unfortunately, this can mean just about anything at all. Any human action or capability can be referred to as a skill, so the word offers us very little to go with if we want to teach skills. We are left in the position of saying that we want to teach just about anything.

What exactly is the problem here? Why shouldn't memorizing a list of biological terminology be a skill, for example? By any definition, it would be a skill, of course, since one could require it of students, some would be better than others, and we could say that they were more skilled in biology and give them a better score on an exam than those who were less skilled. But looked at in terms of micro-scripts, it becomes clear that the skill involved is a cognitive micro-script involving memorization. If we wanted to teach this micro-script, we would have to teach someone how to memorize, so that they became good at memorization rather than becoming good at biology.

One problem with the word "skill" is that we can say "John knows how to do mathematics" or "John knows how to do biology" and still feel comfortable that we are talking about skills because we are talking about knowing how to do something. The illusion is that mathematics or biology are a kind of thing one can learn to do. We might expect our employees to know how to do systems installation or to manage other employees, for example. But, although these may seem like skills, in each case they are really collections of a large number of micro-scripts. This becomes clear when one thinks about teaching someone to do any of these things.

You can't teach students to do biology, but you can teach them to dissect a frog (a physical micro-script), or relate diet components to biological functions (a cognitive micro-script), or interpret chemical equations (a perceptual micro-script). In fact, even these micro-scripts are likely to made up of many smaller micro-scripts (such as knife handling).

Similarly, you can't teach someone to do mathematics, but you can teach them addition (here changing a cognitive micro-script into a perceptual one over time), or how to prove a theorem in plane geometry.

In business, this means we have to stop thinking about teaching management techniques, or communication methods. Why? Because these are not micro-scripts. They tend to be taught the way high school biology is taught, as facts to be memorized, which as I have said, is only relevant to teach if memorization is the micro-script you want students to master. But if we want students to get good at managing or communicating we have to do something else.

There is an important difference between a skill that is teachable and a skill set that is, by itself, not teachable. Whatever doing biology or managing employees might be, these things cannot be only one skill. They are collections of various, possibly quite unrelated, micro-scripts. If we confuse micro-scripts to be learned with simple headings that we have used to describe skill sets, we will cause the courses we design to lose their focus.

Recognizing the skill set to which a micro-script naturally belongs is critical to curriculum redesign. If one did need to learn some type of calculation to learn to do biology, for example, two very different ways to approach this problem exist. We could separate these skill sets in traditional ways, requiring a course in mathematics prior to biology, for example. This is pretty much what schools do today and it has disastrous consequences.

The first problem with this method is that by grouping these skills separately we risk losing the student's interest. By making a biology student take chemistry or calculus we risk killing off a budding biologist by making him focus on subjects that may not interest him and at which he may not have much talent. A second risk is that much of what else is taught in such prerequisites may not be at all germane to the needs of the biology student. What makes up a coherent course in mathematics is likely to be determined by someone who has an agenda other than helping the biology student be a good biologist. Finally, as a consequence of this, the aspects of mathematics most of interest to a biologist might be little dwelt upon by the mathematician. In fact, a biologist is likely to be the real expert when it comes to the mathematics he uses on a daily basis. The mathematician is more likely to understand, and therefore teach, the theory behind the necessary mathematics rather than the practice of such mathematics.

This problem is even more critical in the relationship between academic psychology and human resource management. It is all well and good to propose that psychology majors are good prospects for being human resources specialists. But if they are good prospects, it can only be because of their inherent interest in the subject, not because of what is taught in psychology courses. In the popular image, psychology majors have learned about how to get along with people and understand human relations. In reality, psychology majors have learned how to be miniature academic psychologists. They have learned how to run an experiment, how to do the relevant statistical analyses, and how to appreciate the various sub-specialties in academic psychology, none of which have much to with how to understand or get along with people better.

What should be done is to break down traditional academic lines and teach micro-scripts on an as needed basis. Doing this allows for the creation of goal-based scenarios that entail the learning of many different and often unrelated micro-scripts in the pursuit of a goal. To put this another way, a micro-script is something that fits into the following situation:

a1: I need John to do X

b1: John doesn't know how to do X

a2: Well, then teach him how to do X

b2: That's easier said than done; learning to do X requires experience

Part of the point here is that, in business especially, one wouldn't have the above dialogue where X is "human resource management." In that case, a1 and b1 make little sense. X might be "to fire somebody," however. In that case such a dialogue might make sense. Further, it also makes sense that one can't learn to fire somebody except by firing somebody. This is the best way to spot a micro-script. If one can't learn to do it without actually doing it in practice, it isn't a micro-script. What this suggests, of course, is that the best way to teach a micro-script is in practice situations. If one wanted to teach "firing someone," practice scenarios would be constructed in which such talents could be learned, and experiences could be gained before one tried it out for real.

Looked at this way, biology is not a micro-script, but dissecting a frog properly is. Physics is not a micro-script, but performing a calculation needed in a physics experiment is. Managing people is not a micro-script, but making sure that an order is sent out on time is. Writing a report is a set of micro-scripts. Computer programming is composed of many micro-scripts (learning how to do a loop, for example, is a micro-script, as is writing that loop in C). Reading a financial report involves a multiplicity of micro-scripts. Playing a musical instrument involves multiple micro-scripts. In short, if one has to learn to do something, and it is relatively easy for an expert to tell whether or not one has done it properly, then we are talking about a micro-script or a natural grouping of micro-scripts.

Confusion arises when we talk about major job classifications as if they are skills, when in fact they comprise numerous micro-scripts that are often quite difficult to define. For example, being the president of a large company could be talked about as if it were a skill. Upon closer examination, however, it is clear that such a job must be comprised of many different micro-scripts. It is determining which ones exactly make up such a job that gets everyone confused. A company president ought to be able to talk to the press, make his board of directors see his point of view, get the most effort out of his immediate subordinates, and so on. Some of these may be micro-scripts learned on the job, micro-scripts learned at other times but applied in a new place, or brand new actions, taken for the first time, invented by the user, which will eventually become micro-scripts if they continue to be of use.

When we attempt to determine where the needed micro-scripts lie, we may well discover that not only is this a difficult task because of the normal English language use of the term "skill," but it is also difficult because of the way in which courses have traditionally been taught. We are quite used to courses in biology, or economics, or history, or psychology. Since the content of these courses is rarely looked at from a micro-script-related point of view, their definition is usually quite micro-script independent. Courses, after all, usually involve a number of issues that have nothing to do with micro-scripts at all.

First, courses almost always involve grades. This often means tests with quantifiable measures, which more often means measures of vocabulary (often called concepts) rather than measures of actual achievements. Sometimes, tests will test micro-scripts. (This frequently happens in mathematics, for example). But most of the time tests are oriented towards getting a student to reiterate the teacher's point of view, which is not a micro-script (except in a kind of perverted view of the term).

Second, courses tend to try to make the student into a kind of mini-scholar of the field in question. Teachers are afraid that their students will have been in an English literature course and not have read Dickens, or have been in a philosophy course and not know Plato, or in an economics course and not know Malthus. Thus, most courses have a serious bent towards history of a particular field. This comes at the expense of time spent on micro-scripts, that is, how to actually do anything is ignored, and, more important, tends to shift the focus towards scholarship. Such a shift towards scholarship means that courses will have a heavy emphasis on facts. (The "literacy lists of the field" are big here.) So, knowing what a particular scholar said and being able to reconcile his view with particular conditions or with the views of an opposing scholar becomes the meat of such courses and of the tests that provide the grades for such courses.

The emphasis becomes one of reading about a subject (and being able to argue in a scholarly way about that subject) rather than doing that subject. Thus, philosophy courses don't ask the students to "do philosophy" but to read about those who have done philosophy. In the case of philosophy this may not seem so bad. There have been great philosophers, the world does not change all that much in the really important issues, and an argument could be made that all the important things have been said already. Even so, the micro-scripts of philosophy, which I take to be original reasoned thought and argument, are only peripherally taught if they are taught at all.

But matters become much worse when the courses under discussion are in fields where the great thoughts have clearly not all been thought and where much remains to be learned. Two fields that come to mind are economics and psychology. Students are asked to read the great works but not to do much of anything except spit back what they have read. The argument is that they should be learning to "do economics" or to "do psychology" but it is not at all clear what this might mean. The fact that this is not clear is part of the problem.

Of course, one can be cynical about such fields and say they contain no micro-scripts to be taught. But people engaged in such work do employ a number of micro-scripts, although they are often associated with other subject areas, such as statistics. The problem is twofold. First, just because practitioners can do good work in their field is no reason to suppose that they understand how they do what they do well enough to be able to teach the micro-scripts that they have. Second, even if they did know how to teach those micro-scripts, it would still be reasonable to ask if that micro-script is worth learning for the student who only wants to take one or two courses in psychology or economics. After all, wouldn't the students be better off with a survey of work in the field without attempting to teach them micro-scripts that take a very long time to learn and which they may never use?

This, then, is the essence of the argument. In education in general, there is a choice between a survey of past works in a field, or learning how to be a practitioner in that field. My argument is simple. Survey courses tend to teach to the test, emphasize the point of view of the instructor, leave students years later with very little memory of what they had learned in order to pass the test, and are generally a waste of time.

Micro-scripts on the other hand are testable in simple ways, are not biased towards the teacher's point of view, remain with students for a very long time, and provide a framework into which the work of the great masters of that skill can best be appreciated. Further, and this is the main point, mastery of micro-scripts builds confidence, is much more easily motivated in school, and the process tends to get students to think about what they are doing.

As an example, let's consider musical education. The argument here is that musical education ought to begin with learning to play an instrument and that, after the many micro-scripts relevant to an instrument have been learned, students will be better able to appreciate the work of musicians who have gone before them. By the same reasoning, if we want students to understand music theory, they should have to create some music first.

Now this may not seem like such a radical idea, since many music schools do exactly this. But such a point is often devalued as we get to higher education, where music scholars are often clearly differentiated from musicians, and it is the former who teach the courses. Further, high school courses, and even elementary school courses, often perpetuate the biases of university level music professors, thus creating non-learning-by-doing courses in a subject area where the set of micro-scripts are as easily definable as is ever possible.

Many elementary schools are smarter than this and teach kids to play anyway. The same is not true, unfortunately, in subjects considered more central to a child's education. We don't let children just do physics. In fact, we hardly even know what that means. We do let students do math, because we know what that means, but we lose track of why we are doing it. One reason, I suspect, is that schools really like to teach micro-scripts when they can identify them. They are easy to measure and thus fit well into our test oriented society.

But what happens when a micro-script is hard to identify? We know we want students to be able to read and understand, but it isn't all that easy to tell when students actually have the requisite micro-scripts to do so, especially when the material they are reading doesn't interest them. But it is easy to tell if a student can solve a quadratic equation, and it is a cognitive micro-script, so schools emphasize mathematics. The point is that while identifying relevant micro-scripts is indeed difficult, one should be wary of teaching any micro-script one can identify just because it is in fact something easy to teach. We need to teach micro-scripts, but they must be relevant micro-scripts. This means knowing the answer to what one can do with that micro-script. The things that one can do with algebra are far too limited for anyone to justify teaching it for practical reasons, so it is usually justified as a way to teach reasoning (although there might be better means available for doing so). It is a good idea, therefore, to know what micro-scripts one needs for what real purpose before one goes about designing a curriculum.

The Idea of Curriculum

Schools are full of curricula, that is, agreed upon sets of courses that constitute what the designers of curricula feel that their students must learn to be "qualified" in a given subject. The French curriculum covers certain aspects of French language, culture, and history as deemed appropriate by the designers of that curriculum. The mathematics curriculum covers certain material in the third grade, certain parts of geometry in high school and so on. When colleges say they require four years of mathematics, they mean that they require study in certain particular aspects of mathematics, to be studied over the course of a certain number of years, with certain tests at the end. There is some variation in these curricula from school to school, of course, but not all that much, especially when a standardized test looms at the end.

The idea of a curriculum is that a school has the right, indeed the obligation, to say what should be learned about a given subject. And therein lies the rub. There is a serious problem with the idea of a curriculum.

From the arguments so far stated, we know that a curriculum ought to be no more than a collection of micro-scripts to be acquired. Because real knowledge comes from doing, and micro-scripts are what are acquired in doing, then it follows that any curriculum, course, or teaching program should be no more than, and no less than, a set of exercises that allow students to acquire a micro-script in the natural way that micro-scripts are acquired, that is, by practice. Of course, there is the issue of motivation. No one will learn a micro-script, much less practice one, unless there is real motivation to drive what may be real work. Take for example, the micro-scripts mentioned earlier, programming your VCR and sending e-mail. Neither of these are intrinsically rewarding activities. Learning to do them comes from the results they bring. This means, to a course designer, that the results they bring need to be brought to the fore, serving as real motivation to acquire the micro-script.

Under this light, the idea of curriculum becomes very clear. Micro-scripts enable people to do things. To motivate a student to learn a micro-script, one of three things needs to be true. Either the student must find the result of the micro-script to be intrinsically rewarding, or the micro-script must be part of a package of micro-scripts which are intrinsically rewarding, or the micro-script must enable learning another micro-script.

Many micro-scripts can be grouped together to accomplish a goal even if no one of them would naturally stand alone. The classic restaurant script which I later reclassified as a restaurant MOP (see Dynamic Memory, Schank 1982) is a collection of micro-scripts (such as ordering or paying). Driving a car is a collection of micro-scripts (such as engine starting, braking, or lane changing). Playing baseball is a collection of micro-scripts (such as fielding a ground ball to your left, hitting the curve ball, or sliding). No one of these things is ever done for its own sake. No one feels the need to pay a restaurant bill without its surrounding micro-scripts having taken place. No one decides to slide into a base (unless they are practicing) in the absence of the need to. Nevertheless, all these things take practice, and one can learn to do them so that one is quite skilled at various subtleties that might arise.

I have referred in other works to ordering and paying and scenes and said that MOPs package scenes. One should not confuse scenes with micro-scripts, although it is quite easy to do so. Remember that I am using the term micro-script in order to avoid using the wider term "skill." By micro-script I do indeed mean one aspect of the word skill and it is that aspect that is relevant when thinking about the difference between scenes and micro-scripts. There is a paying scene which has within it a paying micro-script which might be no more than the skill of knowing how to fill in the credit card slip properly. The scene has other properties (such as the presence of the waitress and the use of a little plastic tray) that have nothing to do with the micro-script at all. The micro-script refers to the set of actions one learns as part of one's role within a scene.

We do not often refer to these micro-script by themselves. While one might say that one knows how to make toast, change a tire, or program a VCR, it is less usual to say that you know how to start a car or pay the check. Nevertheless, these are all micro-scripts. The second category of micro-script, the one that one never brags about, is part of the packaged micro-scripts that one learns simply because it is part of the package. The package itself is worth talking about. So, one can say that one is good at playing baseball or that one is a good human resource manager, but there is no one micro-script associated with these so-called abilities. It becomes obvious, therefore, that they are not abilities at all. Rather they are names for packages of micro-scripts, no one of which may be worthy of comment.

Nevertheless, each micro-script, whether in a package or not, has the same properties. One needs to learn them by practicing them. When one decides to teach them, however, one must bear in mind their important differences. The ones that stand alone, that are intrinsically rewarding, can be taught by themselves. One can learn to make toast or program a VCR in the absence of any other activity or motivational issue. One learns it to learn it. This is simply not true of packaged micro-scripts. A sliding lesson may be fun for someone who is intrinsically rewarded by getting dirty, but very few people want to take a credit card signing lesson, and no one takes a braking lesson in the absence of an entire driving lesson. Micro-scripts that are part of packages must be taught within the context of those packages. We shall see why this matters later on.

Another situation arises when micro-scripts are learned in order to do something else. Now, clearly each micro-script in a package can be learned in order to do something beyond the micro-script, and so can micro-scripts outside of packages, and the packages themselves. That is, one can learn a micro-script that is intrinsically rewarding in order to learn another that is also intrinsically rewarding. Or one can learn a package that has a goal as part of a larger package that accomplishes a different goal. The idea that a micro-script is only useful in that it relates to a distant goal is the critical idea in an understanding of what should be meant by curriculum.

We might all agree, for example, that being able to calculate square footage of an area is a useful skill that any adult might need. Schools therefore assume that such skills should be taught, but they place such instruction in a course of mathematics. I am arguing that the concept of micro-script makes clear that there should not be any courses in mathematics in the early years of school. Rather, mathematics micro-scripts, of which the calculation of square footage is one, need to be taught in a meaningful curriculum. The reason that this must be so is that square footage calculation is not intrinsically rewarding, nor is it a part of a package of micro-scripts that depend upon each other like restaurants and driving. It is a quite independent micro-script that no one wants to learn for its own sake and thus presents a serious motivational problem.

One possibility in such a situation is to reconsider whether it is in fact important to learn the micro-script at all. But once one has decided that it is important, the curriculum designer would need to find a situation in which this micro-script must be learned in order to accomplish another goal that is rewarding. Thus, if the calculation of square footage is important to learn we might embed the learning of it within the attempt to plan and build a house. This calculation would need to be made many times in a such a situation and would be learned in that way. If this situation is rewarding for the student then the student will indeed learn the relevant micro-scripts. If, on the other hand, no situation can be found that is rewarding for the student that naturally contains this micro-script it is reasonable to assume that this micro-script isn't all that important for the student to learn. Not every student will master every micro-script that we determine he should know.

The same is true in business. If we determine that reading a financial report, a package of micro-scripts, is important to know, we must find a context in which that knowledge matters. Giving the student a decision to make in which the various micro-scripts in reading a financial report come into play can make all the difference between a student really acquiring the relevant micro-scripts and his simple learning them in order to pass a test. One thing is important to remember here. It is not simply a question of finding the context in which the micro-scripts come into play, they must come into play quite often. Practice is a very important part of micro-script acquisition. Here again, this does not mean repetition of the same micro-script again and again as is done in drill and practice situations in school. It does mean finding repeated situations in the curriculum in which the same micro-script is of use so that the practice does not seem like practice. If you want someone to become a good driver, the issue is not having him drive in circles, but giving him a job which requires repeated driving in a non-artificial way.

The concept of a goal-based scenario, then, is that it is a means by which micro-scripts can be acquired where the micro-scripts (or packages of micro-scripts) themselves are not intrinsically rewarding, but where the situation has been set up such that every micro-script is acquired because the student can see that he will need that micro-script in order to accomplish a different goal that it enables. The student, in this scheme, must be aware of the progression of goals. He must want to accomplish the goal that drives the scenario itself, he must understand the subgoals that lead to the accomplishment of the final goal, and he must understand how each micro-script helps him accomplish the various subgoals necessary. Creating meaningful curricula means creating goal-based scenarios that comprise micro-scripts that have been determined to be important to learn.

The Role of the Teacher

In designing a curriculum, it is important to understand that the aim is to provide enough relevant experiences that allow for the acquisition of micro-scripts and for thinking about difficulties that do not result in practiced, script-based solutions. Further, it is important to provide some guidance through those experiences so that the student can know the difference. That is, the student needs to know when more practice is required and when an exception has occurred and more thought is required. It is not important that a student figure out everything for himself. A teacher can suggest new data to consider, new experiences to try, and, when asked, can answer questions by providing facts that cannot be readily inferred or attained through repeated experience.

The role of the teacher is to be an exposer of knowledge. Learning by doing entails trying things out, formulating hypotheses and testing them. But, a student cannot do this in a vacuum. The teacher should be there to guide us to the right experiences. The teacher should also be there to answer a student's questions, or at least, to listen to his questions and perhaps suggest ways that he could discover the answer himself. Curiosity comes from trying things out, from failing on occasion, from explaining why, and from trying again. This is what any goal based scenario must entail.

How do we know, under such a scheme, that the student knows all that he needs to know about a given situation? We don't. But we shouldn't care that much either. A good teacher should have as his goal exposing his student to enough situations that the student will become curious enough to take his learning into his own hands. In other words, the role of the teacher in a goal-based scenario is to open up interesting problems and provide tools for solving them when asked by the student to do so. The accomplishment of the goal should be its own reward. The curriculum must be oriented towards, and satisfied with, the idea that a student will learn what they need to in order to accomplish goals. Hopefully they will have become curious and acquired both oddball cases and routine micro-scripts along the way.

If we abandon the idea of easy measurement of achievement, then we can begin to talk about exciting learners with open-ended problems and we can begin to create educational goals such as learning to think for oneself. Of course, such things are difficult to measure, but one cannot help but feel that we'll know it when we see it. Under this view, the problems of how we teach and how education is delivered become far more important than one might initially imagine. Actual content may not be the issue at all since we are really trying to impart the idea that one can deal with new arenas of knowledge if one knows how to learn, how to find out about what is known, and how to abandon old ideas when they are worn out. This means teaching ways of developing good questions rather than good answers.

To understand something about why goal-based scenarios matter, let's take a subject which could be taught in either the traditional way or in a more reasonable way, and play with the idea. Consider wine, for instance. I happen to know something about wine, which is an adult subject; that is, one not normally formally taught except to adults who have specifically requested such training and have typically paid money for it after work.

Let's go to wine school. Not a real wine school, but a wine school where the instruction is done in a way similar to that done in the schools or in many formal training programs.

We would start our instruction in wine by handing out four texts. One would be a geography text, teaching about where Burgundy is and where the wine growing regions of the United States are, talking about Virginia, New York, and Texas wineries, for example. The second would be an agricultural text. It would teach about the various grapes, where which is grown and why, discussing soil conditions, climate issues, optimal grape pricking times, and so on. The third would be a text about the wine making process. Fermentation, storage, blending, and such would be included, as well as a discussion of the wine business, including who owns which chateaus and so on. The fourth would be a history text, answering such questions as: What kind of wine did the Romans drink? Who invented the cork stopper? How were issues of proper storage discovered? Why do the British prefer to drink Bordeaux? Which wine growing regions of France were there in Roman times?

After instruction in these various areas, we would begin testing. What was the best year for Bordeaux in the last 30 years and why? Who owns Chateau Margaux? When did Mouton-Rothschild achieve first growth status? What grapes are grown in Oregon and why? What was the first French-American joint venture in wine growing? Can you identify the Chateauneuf du Pape region of the Rhone valley on a map?

What is wrong with this picture? Nothing, I think. It is the way schools teach most subjects. Schools teach information that can be tested. How will they know if you have learned anything if they can't test you? So, they must teach something testable. The tests drive the curriculum, and people lose sight of the original purpose. Notice that no micro-script (save those of memorization or reading) would really be involved at all in such a course. The goals of the student, which presumably had something to do with drinking rather than the acquisition of facts, were ignored. In general, I don't think that such a school would stay in business long. Students would vote with their feet. If students in school or training programs could vote with their feet in the analogous situations, they most certainly would.

The school that would stay in business would not involve lectures about wine. Teaching about wine means drinking wine, not memorizing facts about wine. Drinking with some help from someone who knows more than you do means that you will learn something. Being able to compare one wine to another, having many different experiences to generalize from, means being able to create new cases (a particularly great wine would be remembered, for example) and new generalizations (seeing a common property that all wines from a certain place or year had in contrast to others from different places or years, for example).

Over time, a learner becomes curious about a wider range of issues. Learning entails, among other things, knowing what questions to ask. This means having gotten enough cases or micro-scripts that one can begin to wonder about them, seeking out new cases and refinements on micro-scripts such that new knowledge can be acquired. It is only in this context that the acquisition of facts is of any interest at all. To put this another way, facts can only be acquired in a way that they will be useful if those facts are sought after by the student for reasons of satisfaction of curiosity.

It took me a long time of wine drinking before I began to wonder about Rhone wines, or the British preference for Bordeaux (they used to own it.) I know about when Chateau Margaux changed hands because the quality has changed dramatically (down and then back up) the last two times that that occurred and I really like Chateau Margaux and need to know which years to avoid. I visited the famous Chateau Margaux and really appreciated the place and the wine I tasted there, but would not have if I hadn't liked the wine in the first place. A shrine isn't a shrine unless it means something to you. I know where Bordeaux is now because I had to find it on a map in order to get to Chateau Margaux. I drank Bordeaux for years without really knowing anymore about the region of Bordeaux than that it was in the southwest of France somewhere. All these facts would have been meaningless and easily forgotten had I simply been told them at the wrong time. The right time was when I wanted to know them, a time that could only have been determined by me and not a teacher.

Processes

Apart from any micro-scripts that we may wish to impart to a student, all students, in virtually all contexts, need to be able to engage in certain processes, no matter what their particular lives are like. If there is a sine qua non of education it must be these universal processes, not a set of particular facts. It is our contention that there are three processes that are more important than any others and that any curriculum must teach them. However, it is critical that they be taught indirectly, embedded in scenarios that are otherwise intended to teach micro-scripts and cases. The three processes are communications, human relations, and reasoning.

Every student, indeed every adult member of society, needs to be constantly learning how to communicate, how to get along with and understand others, and how to think. These processes are learned quite naturally when students are part of teams attempting to accomplish goals. What does it mean to learn these processes? Clearly, learning a process is different than acquiring a micro-script. A micro-script can be easily described as a set of steps and those steps can be practiced so that they become routine and require little or no thought to execute. Since micro-scripts are prescriptions for action we can meaningfully talk about their execution. The same is not true of processes.

We cannot say that someone knows how to do human relations. We can say they know how to communicate or how to reason, but it is very difficult to specify what we mean when we say such things. Clearly we are not talking about micro-scripts here. It would be very difficult to specify a set of procedures that form a package called "communication." Being able to get along with others or think about a new problem may have some executable procedures but it also seems to entail a great many more fuzzy concepts, such as being nice or trying unusual solutions, that are a great deal more difficult to quantify.

The word process here sheds little light on these phenomena in the same way that "skill" shed little light on what it was that we wanted people to know how to do. As with "skill" the word "process" can encompass too much. There are many phenomena that can be called processes. There are political processes, economic processes, scientific processes, and so on. What these ideas have in common is that they refer to complex sets of forces that come into play that require more of their participants than a simple knowledge of how to execute certain procedures. The phenomena they represent are complex and often not given to clear procedures that can be guaranteed to work. There is one way to send e-mail and program the VCR. There are known solutions to braking a car, riding a bike, or making toast. But for what we have been labeling processes there are often no good answers or many good answers. What answers there are are not executable procedures but rules of them, general strategies to try that may or may not work under the particular circumstances that have arisen. For this reason, it might be better to describe the substance of what we want people to learn about these phenomena as *participation strategies*.

Thus, we can restate what is learned in a goal based scenario as micro-scripts, cases, and participation strategies in various processes that are contained within the scenario. An ideal goal-based scenario would involve many people participating as part of a team, a complex environment in which to work, and a need to report the results. Such a scenario would cause participants to have to develop strategies for getting along with other team members, reasoning about the complex domain, and communicating the results.

Learning by doing, when one is talking about processes, means inventing for oneself strategies that work within the processes that one is involved in. When we asked what was learned in learning by doing earlier we recognized that the same mental structures we had always used were active here as well and that our old idea of scripts and packages of scripts was entirely relevant to learning by doing. In effect, learning by doing modifies existing memory structures at the lowest level described in Schank (1982).

Now we must ask where participation strategies for processes fit into this scheme. The answer is again to be found in Schank (1982). This becomes clear when one considers what a participation strategy actually looks like. Let's consider a few. Some good ones for human relations might be:

If you want someone to like you, ask for their help

If you are in charge of someone, be firm but treat them as an equal

Some good ones for reasoning might be:

In order to attack a new problem, try to see it is an instance of an old problem

In order to find a solution, hypothesize a world in which the current problem wouldn't exist

Some good ones for communication might be:

Never say everything you know in one speech

Always write in an easy to read, unpretentious style

One thing that should be obvious here is that these rules are most certainly not always right. Their opposites could also be right under certain circumstances. Further, they are accumulated by experience, by actually trying to engage in processes. Thus, they have all the characteristics of what were referred to as thematic organization packets (TOPs) in Schank (1982) and have been referred to as indices in several subsequent books (Schank 1986, and Schank 1991a in particular). These strategies are developed from particular cases. Cases provide data for generating abstractions, store exception episodes to warn of problems with existing knowledge structures, and provide a starting point for future comparisons (Schank 1982).

Thus, no matter what else a course is intended to teach, if it has a format that includes using a group, it will also cause human relation strategies to be developed individually, by each participant, that, like TOPs are domain independent. If the course includes open-ended problem solving, it will teach strategies having to do with reasoning simply by force of having to engage in these strategies. If the results of any of this needs to be communicated, strategies for communication will be developed. These three processes, and how to engage in them, should not be explicitly taught. They will be learned by the very best method of all: by having students experience the processes for themselves.

Within the context of a group that is working within a scenario, the issue of human relations comes up quite naturally and must be worked out. Communications would be part of working within the group as well as part of communicating the work of the group to outsiders. Any scenario should have to have enough unsolved problems in it that reasoning would need to take place on a regular basis. The idea is never to explicitly teach these processes within a course, but simply to engage in them during the course of action included in the scenario. However, explicit instruction by experts ought to be available, from specialists, when difficulties arise, handled on an as needed basis.

Though the three processes listed above are critical for any learning situation and are also critical to learn in and of themselves, it is imperative that they not be taught directly. For some processes this is not a problem since they have never been taught directly, thus there is no existing bad stuff to undo. With other processes we are not so lucky. It is common enough for students to be taught principles and theories as a substitute for actually engaging in a process. We see this with the Pythagorean theorem, for example. It is taught simply because it is a principle of mathematics, a mathematical generalization, that students can easily grasp. It is not taught to enable students to do anything. Similarly, students learn facts about language, as opposed to improving how they use language. These ideas are of great importance to schools, since they are much easier to test than the more subjective issue of how well a student engages in a process.

Even when principles are worth knowing, despite the fact that they usually have no practical use, they are extremely difficult to learn without having, in some sense, discovered them oneself. Parents lament that they wish their children could learn from their own experiences, but there is a very good reason why children cannot learn from their parent's experiences. As we learn we generalize from our experiences. Only when these generalizations are grounded in actual cases will our memory of a bad or good result reinforce the rule that has been learned.

We really want to teach students reasoning. But there is a big difference between letting them create their own theories and, when these theories seem to fail, allowing them to consider other "official" theories in order to see if they work, and teaching those official theories directly. In the former case the student's own thinking provides a motivation to learn more. In the latter case, the official theories are objects of learning in themselves. The argument here is that it is simply not important to learn the official theories unless one wants to learn to do physics. But, with children, the goal must be to teach reasoning, creativity, argument, and such, not physics. Every goal-based scenario constructed to teach various skills, must, first and foremost, teach communication, human relations, and reasoning.

The reason learning by doing works is that it strikes at the heart of the basic memory processes that humans rely upon. Human memory is based in scripts and the generalization of scripts. We learn how to do things and then learn how what we have learned is wrong and right. We learn when our rules apply and when they must be modified. We learn when our rules can be generalized and when exceptional cases must noted. We learn when our rules are domain bound or when they can be used independent of domain. We learn all this by doing. In other words, we learn all this by constantly having new experiences and attempting to integrate those experiences, or more accurately the memory of those experiences, into our existing memory structures. This integration process relies upon new data. This data is provided by experience. When new data are simply told to us, we don't know where in memory to put them because we don't really understand the use of that data. When we experience the data ourselves, we also experience, at the same time, other sights, sensations, feelings, remembrances of goals achieved, goals hoped for, and so on. In other words, we have enough context to help us to know how to characterize what we have learned well enough to find a place for it in memory and we begin the generalization and exception process.

It follows, then, that what we learn when we learn by doing will be details of how to accomplish something in a particular domain (a micro-script); strategies that are independent of domain (process participation strategies); and the cases that stand alone as exceptions awaiting possible future integration into the memory system. Learning by doing works because it impacts all these important memory issues.

Learning by Doing Versus Learning by Cognizing

Learning by doing allows for the natural acquisition of micro-scripts that supply a learner with a set of individual or packaged executable procedures that, if practiced, will be of use for as long as necessary. Also, rules of thumb about how to function in the course of various complex processes are acquired while engaging in these processes. We have mentioned, and will discuss in detail later on, the acquisition of cases that serve as exceptions to executable procedures and strategies for behavior while engaging in various processes.

All this leaves open the question of knowledge. Is this all there is to knowing? Is this all there is to useful knowing? If it is the case that the above items are all that can be learned by doing, is there some other method by which other types of knowledge is acquired? Or is the picture of what is acquired in learning by doing still incomplete?

To begin to understand this issue better, let's consider some kinds of knowledge that do not fit easily into the three categories mentioned above, namely, executable procedures, participation strategies, and exceptional cases. To make this easier to think about, below is a list of what might normally be considered to be some knowledge that an intelligent, literate, adult might have that does not readily fit into any of these categories:

Richard Daley is the mayor of Chicago, following the path set for him by his father.

Michael Jordan may well be the best basketball player who has ever lived.

It is the freshness of the fish that matters most in determining the quality of sushi.

1970 was a great year for Bordeaux and the wines of that year are still drinking well.

Kurt Vonnegut was an author esteemed by the children of the 1960s who still seems relevant today.

George Bush used the Gulf War as a political instrument for his own re-election but it didn't seem to help.

In 1841 the U.S. had three different presidents.

The Balkans have been a hotbed of trouble ever since the Ottoman Empire caused one ethnic group to be divided into two religions.

If you want to get ahead in life, follow your natural instincts and ignore the advice of your compatriots.

One way to get rich is to never spend a dime.

If you want people to like you ask for their advice.

When looking at knowledge of this kind, two issues are: When would one acquire this knowledge? and When would one use this knowledge? One could stretch the definitions of the three types of knowledge acquired in learning by doing to include some of the information listed above, but by and large they would be real stretches. One could argue that these are cases or rules of thumb or procedures, but they seem to be much more like the kinds of static knowledge that people can call up as needed. And therein lies the key to understanding what this type of knowledge is about.

It is important to make a distinction in any discussion of knowledge between that which is implicit and that which is explicit. The types of knowledge that we have been discussing in the context of learning by doing are, for the most part, quite implicit. Most people cannot tell you how to send e-mail or program their VCRs or how to tie a tie or change a tire. It is a lot easier to show you because the memory for such procedures is in the procedures themselves. We do not know how to talk about this kind of knowledge because that knowledge is not encoded in memory apart from the procedure for executing it.

Similarly, while we can tell a good story that indicates an exceptional case that we know, we cannot say exactly why that case has come to mind. The indices that are used are not always accessible. We know we were reminded of it by something that we just heard, and we may be able to make vague references to some of what reminded us of what we knew, but, although the case itself is explicit memory, what we know about the case that makes it relevant is often implicit and difficult for us to actually state. This is why people often tell stories and leave out the point. The point is typically implicitly encoded.

And, in the same way, participation strategies are often nearly impossible to explicitly state. We rarely know how we behave or why we behave that way. We treat people the way we do, communicate the way we do, and reason the way we do, without thinking about it very much at all. When we do try to make conscious our behavior in such situations, we often have a poor picture of what we actually are doing and how others perceive what we are doing. Often we are the last people to be able to say how we thought of something or why we said something or why we treated someone the way we did. In general, participation strategies are entirely implicit in memory.

But the information listed above is quite explicit in memory. We know that we know that kind of stuff, and can call it up at will. But how did we learn it and why would we want to know it? Let's start with the first example:

Richard Daley is the mayor of Chicago, following the path set for him by his father.

It is fairly obvious how one might come to know such a fact. As I write this, I am in Chicago, and simply by virtue of being here, I am aware of who the mayor is. Further, most Americans were aware of Mayor Daley's father when he was mayor because Chicago and the first Richard Daley played a significant role in the politics of the 1960s. I feel quite certain I did not acquire either of these facts in a classroom. No one taught them to me, yet it seems convoluted to attempt to make an argument that I learned them by doing.

What exactly would I have been doing when I learned them? It seems obvious to me that two good choices are either watching television or reading the newspaper. In a broad sense, I suppose, one could argue that watching and reading are something one can do and so I learned these facts by doing as well. However, it seems to me that we miss the real issues entirely by adopting such a stance. The real issue has to do with the way that such material is absorbed into memory. If the way such material is absorbed does not actually matter, then it would follow that the current strategy of teaching facts by having students memorize them would be one that is perfectly plausible. Since I clearly do not believe this to be the case, it behooves me to explain why the method of absorption matters and what that method might have been.

Consider the hypothesis that reading and watching television are, in fact, two ways in which information can be absorbed into memory. I am writing this in the morning, following my normal routine of spending an hour reading the Chicago *Tribune* and the New York *Times*. I read a long story on the front page of the *Tribune* about a small child who died. I do not now re-call the name of the child or much about the circumstances of her death. That I remember this article at all is simply a recency effect; it will soon be gone from my memory. There was more than one story on the firing of the manager of the New York Mets and the hiring of a new one in both papers. I read all of them because I am a fan of the Mets. At this moment I could tell you a great deal about this event because I have been following it and I care about it. I do not particularly remember the actual articles that I read, but I can safely say that I have absorbed many of the details of them into my memory. How long they will stay there is quite unclear. The Mets have hired and fired managers before, and while I can probably name most of them, my memory is faulty and the details are likely to be wrong.

I also read in the *Times* today an account of a murder being tried in Louisiana involving a Japanese student who was looking for a Halloween party and unfortunately knocked on the wrong door. I had seen an interview with some of the murderer's neighbors a day or two ago on TV and I was struck with their equating the right to shoot someone who knocks on your door with the American way of life. I have heard about the murder and the current trial on and off since it happened and was interested today in the de-fense attorney's account of the events that portrayed the Japanese student as acting oddly. It is clear that I have learned something from the collection of articles and stories that I have seen.

In fact, we can learn from what seems to be passive absorption, even if we don't understand exactly how we can or can't do so. The key issue is that we remember what matters to us. In order to understand why we learn what we learn, and how we learn it, we must understand that motivation is a phenom-enally important part of the puzzle.

This is not just an issue of simply motivating learners to want to learn something. The motivation of which I speak is internally generated. The kind of motivation relevant here comes from knowledge goals, not externally gen-erated goals (like grades or cookies). In order to make explicit knowledge your own you must have understood the need for that knowledge at the time of its appearance. In other words, explicit awareness of one's knowledge goals is one key to the absorption of explicit knowledge. It is by no means the only relevant aspect of the absorption of knowledge however.

Acquiring Explicit Functional Knowledge

Let me introduce here the concept of *explicit functional knowledge* (EFK), which is knowledge that we know we can use. To put this another way, if you find out the answer to something you have always wanted to know, it is un-likely that you will forget that knowledge. On the other hand, if I tell you something that you did not want to know, that you can find no obvious need to know, it is unlikely that that knowledge will remain with you for very long.

The idea behind EFK is that, parallel to the physical learning by doing that drives the learning of the three types of knowledge mentioned earlier, there is a cognitive learning by doing that is going on as well. The doing here has nothing to do with physical actions. Rather, it is centered on the mind's desire to build up a functional knowledge base. The creation of this knowledge base is what drives curiosity and is what makes us human. We shall dub this process learning by cognizing.

To better understand learning by cognizing, we must reconsider learning by doing. Learning by doing has, as its core premise, the idea that goals drive learning. When someone wants to accomplish something, they are forced to pay attention to the detailed actions that accomplish the goal. If they want to go somewhere by car, they must learn many details of driving. We have termed these micro-scripts. We know that not all micro-scripts are physical. There is a cognitive dimension to the micro-scripts that we learn. Nevertheless, the goals are physical—to go someplace, to operate a piece of equipment, to behave properly in a situation so as to get someone to do something that you want.

Sometimes, however, goals are completely cognitive. Or to put this another way, the goal is to know something. Whereas it seems obvious that higher order animals can learn micro-scripts because they too have physical goals, it is less obvious that animals other than humans have knowledge goals. In any case, humans do seem to have such goals. And they often do not seem to be in any way in service of a physical goal. When a small child asks why the sky is blue, he is not hoping to use that knowledge to help him to do something. When I want to know who the new manager is for the New York Mets, I will indeed use that information, but my use is mostly cognitive. I will use that information to help me understand what the Mets are doing, or to converse with other baseball fans about the Mets. The notion of use here is purely cognitive and differs from that of the term use in learning by doing.

Nevertheless, the analogy is direct. *Learning by doing works because the natural physical goals that people strive to achieve cause a need to acquire micro-scripts in order to achieve them.* These micro-scripts are reinforced by practice and combine together to allow us to become adept at complex physical activities. Similarly, *learning by cognizing works because the natural cognitive goals that people strive to achieve cause a need to acquire knowledge in order to achieve them.* This knowledge is reinforced by repeated use and combines together to allow us to become adept at complex cognitive activities.

The activities to which I am referring here revolve around thinking and communicating one's thinking. I cannot think about how Chicago is being run if I do not know anything about its government. I can only understand how good a basketball player Michael Jordan was by watching him and comparing him to others. In order to do this I have to care about basketball, or athletic prowess, or excellence or something like that. Caring about such things is a mental activity grounded in the need to know more. Or, to put this another way, learning by cognizing entails asking and answering questions about the observed world in order to come to conclusions about it. Having a knowledge goal means having a question and seeking its answer either by observation or by asking someone who might know.

There can be many reasons to want to know something. One reason might be to supply a cognitive piece to a micro-script to enable you to be able to do something. Another might be to supply a piece of knowledge that will enable you to be able to know something. EFK is of two basic types, therefore. If we need to know something in order to do something, we are talking about physical EFK. If we need to know something in order to know something else, we are talking about cognitive EFK.

The reason to make this distinction and to put it in this way is related to teaching. It has always been easy for schools to identify knowledge that they wish students to have and then to begin a program to impart that knowledge by telling it to them and asking them to tell it back on a test. Similarly, we can make students learn to do certain micro-scripts properly, without giving them any understanding of why they might need such a micro-script, causing them to forget the new knowledge as soon as a test is finished. When one is talking about learning by doing, the proscription is clear: never teach anyone to do anything that they didn't want to learn to do in the first place. If micro-scripts are acquired in the service of real goals that students actually have, they will not be forgotten.

The same is true of learning by cognizing. We cannot acquire new knowledge unless we truly wanted that knowledge. As in learning by doing, the issue is that goals have to be real. We cannot tell a student something and expect them to remember it, unless they wanted to know it in the first place. Now, it is clear that this is wrong if we take a literal view of remembering. We can force students to memorize information for long periods of time, especially if we give them mnemonics such as alphabetical cues or rhymes. All this does, however, is enable them to tell that information to themselves each time so that they can hear it again. It does not enable functional recall of that knowledge.

Recalling information functionally means being able to recall it at the precise moment that it might be of use, and this entails having learned it with respect to its use in the first place. To ensure that this happens easily the knowledge to be acquired must be learned in terms of its potential use. This is fairly difficult to achieve in school for the rather simple reason that much of what schools want students to know has no actual use. Even when that information does have use, the schools have often long since forgotten what it was. To see what I mean here, let's consider the functionality of the knowledge that I wrote down earlier and see how it can be broken down into the following classes:

Useful for understanding a domain:

> Richard Daley is the mayor of Chicago, following the path set for him by his father.

> Michael Jordan may well be the best basketball player who has ever lived.

> The Balkans have been a hotbed of trouble ever since the Ottoman Empire caused one ethnic group to be divided into two religions.

Useful for making day to day decisions:

> It is the freshness of the fish that matters most in determining the quality of sushi.

> 1970 was a great year for Bordeaux and the wines of that year are still drinking well.

Useful for understanding life:

> Kurt Vonnegut was an author esteemed by the children of the 60's who still seems relevant today.

> George Bush used the Gulf War as a political instrument for his own re-election but it didn't seem to help.

> If you want to get ahead in life, follow your natural instincts and ignore the advice of your compatriots.

> One way to get rich is to never spend a dime.

> If you want people to like you ask for their advice.

Trivia:

> In 1841 the U.S. had three different Presidents.

We shall refer to these knowledge types as *domain knowledge, decision-relevant knowledge, life knowledge,* and *trivia*. When attempting to impart knowledge to students, the rules of thumb for how to best do this relate to the knowledge type we are hoping to impart. As with learning by doing and for the same reasons, learning by cognizing is best done within the context of a goal-based scenario. Let's consider these types one at a time.

Domain Knowledge

A person wanting to participate in a domain of expertise, city government, for instance, must know something about the subject at hand. This much seems obvious. But when it comes to translating this rule of thumb into an understanding of what should go on in a classroom, it is easy to get confused. Why not simply teach people about the domains they need to be conversant with? Why not simply tell them what we want them to know about city government? The answer is: Because they will learn the information better if they can actually use it. This means we must ask ourselves what uses we anticipate for any domain knowledge we believe students should know.

This question is not always so easy to answer. In our example, a citizen would need to know how to deal with the government on various occasions. To do this he might want to know who his representatives are in government and how he can petition them. Of course, he could always find this out when the occasion arose, again learning by doing. What exactly would be the difference between learning about governmental process in a GBS that allowed one to play roles in a scenario about government, and learning by cognizing with respect to the same situations?

One answer is that the distinction between learning by doing and learning by cognizing is a rather fine one and that they are really two sides of the same coin. One problem with this answer is that it is indeed possible to be an expert on something without ever having actually done anything at all. For example, I know a great deal about history, knowledge acquired entirely from reading and talking about it. I've never studied history formally, have never written any papers, or done anything (not that I know what that would mean for history) in history. But I do know a lot of stuff. Clearly, I have learned this stuff by cognizing, but what exactly does that mean? How can we make that natural process take place in a more formal educational setting?

The answer seems to be that reading and discussing can be all that is actually done and something good can come out of it. I say this with some trepidation since it is this view that is behind all the problems in today's educational system. We all know that reading and discussion works to some extent, and since it is so easy to implement we settle for a school system based on that. So I hesitate to say that it has its place after all. What is its place then?

One of the things that works in school, sometimes, is the attempt to get students to "do the reading" for the next day. In the usual implementation of this idea, a reading is assigned and students know that the class the following day will be based upon that reading. They know that they may be called upon to say something about what they have read during that discussion. For some students this serves as sufficient motivation for reading the material. They do not want to be embarrassed in front of the class. Many students live in fear of being called upon by the teacher, having to answer a question about what they should have read. For some this fear is sufficient cause to do the reading. For others, they devise ways to deal with their fear and avoid the reading altogether.

One would be hard pressed to call the goal of "learning the information for reasons of not being embarrassed" a genuine knowledge goal. But what practical difference does it make? Either way the student reads, discusses, and learns new material, or does he? The claim here is that while knowledge goals can be induced they cannot be required. When I learn about what is happening with my favorite sports team, it is possible to imagine that the scene is much the same as with an assigned reading. I know there is going to be some discussion soon about what is going on with my team and I don't want to be embarrassed by not knowing the latest information. Many people go the latest movies for this reason—they know there will be discussions of them at parties and such and they don't want to be out of the conversation. Indeed fear of embarrassment can cause many people to learn about their government, literature, history, and many other subjects, simply because they do not want to be embarrassed. Recently, I heard Vince Coleman, a black player on the Mets, say he had never heard of Jackie Robinson. He apparently was not embarrassed by this, but most New York Met fans were.

For most people, avoiding this kind of intellectual embarrassment can serve as motivation in school and out, for wanting to know things. Why does this matter here? When one wonders where knowledge goals come from, one must remember that human beings are social animals. They need to interact with others and verbal interaction is an important part of the social scene. Nearly everyone fears doing badly in such situations, and so they do what they have to to avoid embarrassment. This indicates that there really is a knowledge goal that comes about because of fear of embarrassment. The question we need to address is: "Is there a more positive version of the same kind of knowledge goal?" When does someone want to acquire knowledge for reasons other than fear of embarrassment?

We talked earlier of explicit functional knowledge that is of value in achieving a goal. We know that there is stuff we need to know about how to do things, the knowing of which will help us get what we want. Physical EFK is the knowledge we need to do physical things. But what is avoiding embarrassment? It doesn't seem to have much to do with functional knowledge. What is the function? Avoiding embarrassment isn't much of a goal, nor does it seem to make much sense to talk about the knowledge necessary to do that since that knowledge could be of any sort in any place or time. Nevertheless, people do learn for this reason. The question is, how long do they retain information acquired in order to avoid embarrassment?

The answer to this must depend upon the issue of subsequent use. We have argued against the idea that memorization can be a way to acquire new knowledge. Obviously, we know a person can acquire knowledge in this way. That knowledge will remain with that person for some amount of time, depending on how thoroughly they were drilled. The problem is that knowledge learned in this way is usually only accessible in the way it was learned. Thus, it is not of great use in real life because it was not acquired in relation to any actual activity that might occur.

The story is different with knowledge acquired for the purpose of discussion of that knowledge. No matter whether that knowledge was acquired in order to avoid embarrassment, if it is indeed used in subsequent discussions, then those discussions would certainly reinforce that knowledge and begin to cause new knowledge from the discussion to be associated with it. In other words, we can learn by cognizing and discussion is one way of cognizing. The method used by the schools would be just fine if reading-based discussion allowed continual themes to be followed, allowed time for genuine reflection, encouraged the formation and explication of divergent opinions, and ensured that the initial subject matter was of interest. Let me explain why this matters.

Continual Theme

One thing that differs between my acquiring the latest information on the New York Mets and a student learning about ancient Greece by reading Homer is that I am continually interested in the Mets. I always want to know about them and am not boning up for a particular exam. Thus, I do think about them, have thought about them, and will think about them. The knowledge I acquire about them is EFK, where the function is thinking about and perhaps conversing about the Mets. When a student who reads Homer does so because he is enrolled in a course in classic literature, he is, unless he is planning on being a scholar of the field, being poorly educated. Here again the problem is traditional courses as opposed to GBSs.

It is very important that any course of study focus on the attainment of a goal that is realistic, achievable, and germane to the interests of the students involved. The GBSs we have mentioned so far have tended to be physical in the sense that the goal was a performance goal that usually involved a physical component. Clearly, there need be no physical component to a GBS. There can be purely cognitive GBSs. Such GBSs would entail the pursuit of a goal that involved understanding a thematically coherent body of material and being able to discuss and argue for some propositions entailed within that material that is germane to one's own goals. Courses like this already exist. But sometimes they are actually quite difficult to differentiate from courses that are more or less parodies of what we have been saying here.

There are, quite typically, many courses in any school curriculum that superficially might look to be in line with what we have suggested for a cognitive GBS. For example, a literature course that has as its unifying theme that all the authors to be read were ancient Greeks, might ostensibly be portrayed as a cognitive GBS. One could claim that the goal of the course was understanding and being able to argue for some thesis or other that stemmed from one or more of the books to be read. The difference between such a literature course and a cognitive GBS revolves around the reasons that the works were being read in the first place. A cognitive GBS would first allow the student to decide what goal he was trying to pursue for which reading these books might be helpful. For example, something a student was trying to understand about life or about history might be the goal. Then the material to be read would be chosen by the student such that that material was germane to the student's goal. The task of the student in reading the material would be to gather what the student needed from the material to help him make a decision, understand a complex issue, or deal with whatever the student's actual goal was. For example, if a student had to make a decision about how the Greek government of a certain period were to be run, he might read the literature of the period in order to understand the issues and make an appropriate decision. In such a case, we would expect the organizing theme of the material to be read to be the issues covered by the material, rather than the fact that all the authors were Greek. Thus, it is the goal of the student that is the organizing theme in a cognitive GBS, rather than the course organizational themes current today in most curricula that group material around some concept of "literacy." Typically such courses concern themselves with attempts to make the student "literate" in some area (like the classics) rather than attempting to get the student to know something he actually may have wanted to know. In other words, if the motivation for reading were not avoiding embarrassment at one's lack of knowledge in a given area, but the honest attempt to know more about a subject matter that concerns you, the results could be quite worthwhile.

This means that the theme of any cognitive GBS would revolve around an issue that was of concern to the students in the GBS, and was likely to continue to be of concern after the GBS was over. We can discuss Greek authors all you like, but if what we discuss is not relevant to the issues with which I am concerned, and if what we discuss never occurs again in my life, and if what we discuss varies wildly from discussion to discussion, I will forget what we have talked about. If, on the other hand, we are discussing issues that concern me, and will continue to concern me, and that build with each additional reading, providing more evidence for varying points of view, I will remember what we have read and discussed.

There are teachers who conduct classes in this way and there are courses that are constructed in this way, typically in English and history departments in some of our better high schools. They are to be commended for doing it right. In general however, even these courses tend to end in the dreaded exam. In a cognitive GBS, the final measure must still be *performance*, in this case performance in being able to adopt and defend a point of view, citing evidence for one's position. There is nothing radical here. This method is quite typically used in graduate schools, for example. Domain knowledge is learned in this way. The function of such knowledge is to enable one to think better about a subject of interest. This is the only way such knowledge should be learned, since it doesn't matter what one knows, it matters how one can put together a coherent argument for a point of view.

Genuine Reflection

Any purely cognitive GBS must revolve around the act of reflection. When I listen to stories about Mayor Daley I am considering issues of government that affect me. I might wonder who to vote for; that might be one reason to listen to the mayor talk. But I also might want to have an opinion on a political subject. When a new tax bill is passed and all the people I know are talking about it, I want to throw in my two cents. Part of this may be the embarrassment factor again, but part of it also is a concern for how the new taxes will affect me. I might want to call my accountant and ask his advice, or I might simply get angry and attempt to better understand the political alliances that exist in the country. I might view it all as a giant soap opera that is very entertaining, or as a puzzle to be solved about economics.

No matter why we choose to follow the political issues that are reported daily in the media, the physical performance goal of voting is not all that compelling a reason to spend much cognitive time on these issues. We follow these issues because they are interesting to think about for a variety of reasons. The key point is that we do think about them. Thus, any cognitive GBS needs to allow time for thinking, for working out one's own arguments, for gathering one's own information, and for forming new generalizations. The EFK acquired during such a period of reflection is acquired mostly through reasoning processes. We can hear about Serbian actions in Bosnia, but we must come to some conclusion about them before we can engage in the next important steps in a cognitive GBS.

Divergent Opinion

When reflection has occurred and a conclusion has been reached, it is time to engage in discussion with others. Discussion with others is a key aspect of learning by cognizing. It is very easy to come to conclusions that don't hold water when reasoning on one's own and it is thus very important to test one's conclusions with others and to attempt to poke holes in the arguments of others who have reached opposite conclusions. Again, some schools and courses do allow students to do these things and they are to be commended for that. Unfortunately, there is often a feeling, even in the most enlightened courses, that there is in fact a right answer and that the student needs to be led by the teachers to the place where this right answer can be properly viewed.

The reason that this is problematic is not only that there probably isn't a right answer, but, more important, that a course shouldn't be focusing on the transmission of answers as its goal. The goal of a cognitive GBS is not to teach the facts of the domain of interest but to teach reasoning within that domain of interest. The knowledge itself doesn't matter since that knowledge will be acquired quite naturally in daily routines if the learner is both capable of reasoning in that domain of knowledge and has acquired a basic understanding of that domain. That basic understanding should not come from spoon feeding answers or memorization of facts, but from participating in continued conversations based upon reflections that the learner has made on his own. These could only have happened in the first place if the learner was personally interested in the subject and was ready to reflect upon it. Thus, a cognitive GBS must have a discussion period, unbiased by assumptions of what constitutes the correct argument, that allows each student to voice the conclusions reached during the reflection period and to attack those reached by others.

Subject Matter of Interest

One real issue in the design of cognitive GBSs that examine a domain of knowledge is the selection of that domain. We cannot simply allow domains to be chosen because they interest the school board, or the college board, or even the teacher. Inherent in a cognitive GBS is the idea that the student had the interest that would drive the domain being taught prior to entering any course. To put this another way, to learn by cognizing, one must be motivated to think about the subject in the first place. A course in the history of Bosnia might have little attendance in the ghetto, but a course in dealing with violence, which could easily have Bosnia as one of the places under study, might have a great deal of relevance because the students are likely to have already been thinking about that subject.

Since the kinds of facts that make educators proud can be learned within a multiplicity of contexts, the trick in any cognitive GBS is to find a domain of interest that truly excites a student and then introduces cases that are applicable to that domain that contain the material that the teacher feels must be known. Thus, if we want students to know about Columbus, we can design a cognitive GBS that is about exploration, intended to interest students who want to see new worlds, in which they can discuss how best to do that. Within that context accounts of Columbus' voyages can be read. Students would pick up EFK about problems in exploration that would be grounded in a variety of cases of interest to those who feel that knowing about Columbus is somehow part of being an American. Nevertheless, and more important, the students would learn to think about exploration by discussing issues of which they have become aware via reading with their peers.

Day-to-Day Decision Making

It seems obvious that the way to teach the EFK that is part of day-to-day decision making is to allow students the opportunity to make decisions. This argues for the creation of environments in which students make many decisions that they would not ordinarily get to make. In particular, they need to be allowed to make contrastive decisions, that is to choose one thing one day and then make alternative choices the next, in order to learn the detailed level of nuance that is part of good decision making.

An example I cited earlier was in knowing how to select the right year of a wine to order. The trick to doing this is rooted in bad experiences. If everything turns out well, it is difficult to learn much from a decision one has made. To learn to drink wine, and to wind up with EFK about specific years in Bordeaux, one must acquire many expectations and many expectation failures, each allowing one to discriminate better. In order to make proper day-to-day decisions one must know what to expect as the outcome of each decision. To see this in the case of wine, imagine a small baby at its mother's breast. It may not know what to expect the first time it starts to suckle, but after a number of tries at getting and receiving milk from its mother, the baby will be quite surprised if one day it gets chocolate milk. A baby would cry in this situation, not because it wouldn't like chocolate milk, one would suppose it would, but because of expectation violation. Children learn to adapt to all kinds of things by noting expectation failure and adjusting to it. A baby may cry the first time it is exposed to something new, when it had expectations to the contrary, but the baby will quickly adapt.

Let's imagine that instead of chocolate milk the baby suddenly finds itself drinking Chateau Mouton-Rothschild 1966. No one will find Mouton-Rothschild to be a great wine if it is the first wine they have ever drunk. Before you can discriminate great wine, you have to have first drunk wine. Very few of us drink our first glass of wine and rave about the experience. Wine is, after all, not what you expected. Few of us like our first taste of wine or beer or anything alcoholic, for that matter. We all know that we have to learn to develop a taste for such things, but what does it mean to "develop a taste?" The first time we have a new experience, we only have prior experiences to work with. If we want to learn important discriminations in a taste, for instance, it is helpful if those discriminations are rather on the fine side. If the discriminations are rather gross, then little will be learned from the connoisseur's point of view. If everything happens the way you expected it to happen, you may well be happy, but you won't learn a thing.

Many young people get their first taste of alcohol in college. They drink beer indiscriminately, taking whatever is offered. They often don't wonder if they liked the stuff, they are not drinking it because of the taste. What should such a student expect? What is the beer going to taste like? What can we predict about what the student might be thinking before he tastes his first beer and what would you predict that he might think afterwards? These are very important questions for understanding EFK because knowledge is only built upon prior knowledge.

The novice beer drinker could only have had one of two basic expectations. Since expectations come from prior generalizations, we can only expect what we already have experienced. We have to have a basis of comparison, and this comes from the prior experience that we have chosen as the best expectation we can muster at the time. One might guess, for example, that this student would expect that either beer tasted like soda, the thing it most resembles physically in the experience of a student, or it that it tastes like some other alcoholic experience, such as wine drunk at a religious ceremony.

Some of the expectations that such a student might have would be quite reasonable. For example, he might expect a liquid, for example, perhaps a non-poisonous, possibly slightly nourishing liquid, probably a refreshing-on-a-hot-day kind of liquid. When I drank my first beer I remember being surprised that it was bitter and wasn't sweet. What kind of criticism is it of beer to say that it isn't sweet? All alcohol had been sweet before in my experience, so I expected sweet.

Every time we experience an expectation failure, we need to explain it so that it doesn't keep happening. You can't go through your life always expecting there to be a parking lot on the corner of Fourth and Maple. The day they start construction on a new office building on that corner, you must decide whether this is temporary, like a carnival—maybe it will go away—and if it isn't, you begin to update your expectations. No elaborate explanation is needed; in fact, we can explain it simply by saying to ourselves that, yes, buildings do tend to get built where parking lots once were. But when they tear down a beautiful old house to make way for a parking lot, a slightly more elaborate explanation must be constructed, one that talks about the insensitivity of our times, perhaps, or maybe one about the money needed to repair a grand old structure is just too much for anyone. But when expectations fail horribly, when beer just doesn't taste anything like Coca-Cola®, we have no explanations that are satisfactory. What can you say? Beer just isn't Coke®, and it isn't sweet wine. When this happens, we create a new category.

Once that is done, we are on our way to becoming an expert. The next time someone serves us a beer, we can announce proudly that Miller just doesn't have the flavor of Budweiser®. In fact, pronouncements like that, made by amateurs after having had only two beers in their life, are usually quite accurate. You remember your first beer and can easily distinguish the taste of the second from the first. After having drunk hundreds of beers of many different sorts, it becomes harder and harder to distinguish one from the other. You just have too much information. Unless, of course, you are paying attention, careful attention. You have to care about what you are going to learn in order to learn anything at all.

Now imagine such a new expert beer drinker, tasting his first glass of champagne. He should expect something beer-like. Champagne even looks like beer. Now suppose that the champagne drinker likes champagne a great deal and drinks a lot of it, getting drunk and then later getting sick. What can the student learn from this experience? One serious problem in learning to make day-to-day decisions is understanding the results. Deciding which generalization to make, and thus which new expectation to generate, when one is dealing in a complex environment, requires knowing more than you actually can know on your own.

Suppose that we go to eat in a fine restaurant that serves Thai food. You have never eaten Thai food before, you like the meal, but the next day you are sick. Should you avoid Thai food in the future or just that restaurant or just squid, which you ate there for the first time? Or should you never go out to eat with the people who took you to that restaurant? In real life, we have no easy answers to such questions. In science, we can run an experiment and control the variables. You can eat at another Thai restaurant, you can go back to the same one and avoid the squid, and you can also go out to another restaurant that is not Thai with the same company. But you are really unlikely to do all this, and even if you did, it would prove nothing. Suppose you got sick at the non-Thai restaurant. Does that really mean that the company made you sick? And suppose that you ate the squid, and it was okay. Does that mean it was okay the first time, too? Being scientific in real life is very difficult, and, in fact, none of us tries to be. We just make the generalizations that we want to make anyway.

It takes some time to make an expert on anything. To make a wine expert out of our novice beer drinker one would have to expose him to some wine of any sort and then, gradually, keep adding new information. We still can't give him Chateau Mouton-Rothschild because although he might notice the difference between some table wine and the Mouton, he wouldn't know what he was noticing. Our beer drinker, even one who now likes wine, too, wouldn't notice anything about the Mouton other than that he liked it. Changes in expectations cannot happen overnight. In order to get ready to appreciate the Mouton he needs to create complex knowledge structures that pertain to wine. Contained within such structures are the detailed expectations about smell, color, and various aspects of taste that one must compare and contrast in order to come up with a new idea, a modification of the existing expectations within the knowledge structure. New ideas are inherently modifications of old ideas.

Being able to add new information without regard for the old information it replaces might seem appealing on the assumption that we have empty spaces in the mind that would somehow be filled up by the new stuff. But how would we ever find the new information we have just added? For information to be useful you must know how to find it.

Imagine adding a new book to your library. You might as well not own it if you place it somewhere and forget where. In a small enough library, you could count on stumbling upon it, but as the library got larger, it would be necessary to have an effective indexing system that would allow you to find something on the basis of some scheme connected to important information about what is contained in the book, such as its author or its subject matter. Similarly, a new fact must be placed somewhere in the mind. People are not usually aware that they place new facts, experiences, ideas, and such some-place in memory, but in a metaphorical sense, they do. There may not be actual spots where one can find George Washington, but there has to be an indexing scheme that allows one to hear "President, wore wig, had wooden teeth, chopped down cherry tree" and to know instantly who we are talking about. But how does this work? Labels such as "wooden teeth" are indices used by the mind to retrieve information.

In order to appreciate and detect the differences in Mouton Rothschild one must have a place to put that information. That place would need to stand in relation to other places that store information about wine and would be in terms of features of the wine that were be gathered over time by lots of tasting. The effect of this tasting is to gather together a set of features that are of use in day-to-day decision making that are grounded in actual experience. The value of all feature collection is to be able to say, when tasting a 1959 Mouton, that it is better than the '61 but not as good as the '59 Latour. Of course, you might not care enough about wine to say this, nor have enough knowledge to say it, but if you both cared and had the relevant experiences, you would want to be able to say it. The only way to do this is to be continually re-examining and re-using the features that you have previously used. To do this, you must have myriad expectations and be able to deal with the failure of those expectations. When expectations fail, you must be able to explain why. This is the basis of learning. If you want to know how 1959 Mouton-Rothschild tastes, therefore, drinking a bottle of it isn't all you need to do. You need to work up to it with lesser wines, taste both younger and older wines, taste wines of the same year of chateaus of equivalent quality, and taste other Moutons. If you fail to do this, you will taste the wine, but you won't learn a whole lot from the experience.

In order to get good at making decisions then, students need to make a great many of them. A cognitive GBS must allow students the opportunity to make numerous decisions and to discuss those decisions with other students. The purpose of the discussion is to encourage the collection of features and ways of talking about those features that help one discriminate between choices. Students must not only be allowed to choose, they must also reflect on why they chose the way they did. To do this they must be able to defend their choices and to do this they need to be able to articulate the features of a situation that caused them to make the decisions they did.

Understanding Life

Teaching the EFK that is part of understanding life is rather complicated. One problem is that unlike domains of knowledge discussed above, there is little agreement on the facts. Another problem is that unlike day to day decision making, there is no program of ordered decisions that can be gone through to arrive at nuances of knowledge. For example, let's return to the two adages cited above:

> If you want to get ahead in life, follow your natural instincts and ignore the advice of your compatriots.
>
> One way to get rich is to never spend a dime.

They are both neither true nor false, and neither can be learned in any ordinary sense of learning. Nevertheless, people feel that they "know" such things and that they were learned in "the school of hard knocks."

It is fairly obvious that generalizations made over the course of a lifetime about strategies for success are not likely to be best taught in a short course that proposes to simulate life conditions. Any such course would be naturally slanted towards the generalizations that the teacher wanted made and would thus fail to teach the key issue. The issue with respect to such generalizations is not knowing them but making them. You can have opinions on what makes for a happy life, or healthy children, or great wealth, or any other subject which has been reduced to myriad proverbs, and I may have a different opinion. There are no right answers in this regard. There are only beliefs that individuals have and beliefs that various subcultures have. What is important is learning to make these generalizations in the first place, or to put this another way, to observe life and learn from it.

Put this way, it seems clear that the teaching issue here can be addressed by having students reason about situations and discuss their conclusions with others, defending their points of view. The discussion would need to revolve around the rationale behind those generalizations, not around the generalizations that were formed by a student. The lessons are in the reasoning processes themselves, not in the biases and belief systems of the participants. As it turns out, a good venue for doing this is the reading of literature. But I say this with some trepidation.

The problem is that literature courses invariably are taught with respect to issues of writing, appreciation of classical authors, detection of themes of various time periods, and deconstruction of the text, among other things. I am suggesting that literature (and for that matter, movies) has value in the presentation of life situations and the possibility for discussion of what the right course of action might be in those situations. In other words, in a course in "life" one needs to discuss issues that come up in life. The best way to do this is to experience life vicariously in a variety of formats and situations and then have the teacher, who would be a "reasoning teacher" in this case, not a literature teacher, help students formulate points of view about proper courses of action and about life themes. This process happens quite naturally out of school all the time. When teenagers discuss movies they often dwell on life themes, but without guidance and in the non-intellectual stance often taken by teenagers, they might dwell on the baser issues and not learn as much about life as they might with the help of a teacher.

The same course of action pertains to business. There are fewer business movies and less business literature, but there are some examples of these genres. Even so, there are classic business cases that students often consider for reasons different than we are discussing here. What we are suggesting is that general business themes are best taught by seeing examples rather than by preaching. Thus, when a company wishes to teach its employees that honesty is the best policy in business, they tend to preach it. But teaching is better than preaching. Teaching in this case means allowing students to read about or see depictions of sample situations that illustrate possible courses of action and then allowing them to discuss the possibilities. To some extent this is done in business ethics courses today, but often these revolve not around reasoning the right course of action but learning the fine points of the law.

Learning from Experience: Case Acquisition

We learn micro-scripts when we learn by doing; we learn participation strategies when we participate in a process; we learn explicit functional knowledge when we learn by cognizing; and in each of these three types of learning we learn cases. While it may seem that knowledge, strategies, and micro-scripts are critical aspects of what we know, and they surely are, they do not have the overwhelming importance in the formation of unique individuals with distinct personalities, opinions, and reasoning abilities as does the acquisition of a case base.

When people are confronted with new situations they tend to attempt to see them as old situations, ones they have dealt with previously, so that they can copy behavior that has worked for them in the past. Typically, this sort of case based reasoning tends to be a version of the old concept of a script. When one has been in a restaurant many times before, one needn't ask existential questions about what to do next or why each role player is doing what he is doing. Scripts save processing time and energy. We do what we have done before. The difference between cases and scripts is really just one of the overarching generality and ubiquity of the script. Everyone has more or less the same McDonald's script because the world over one McDonald's is like another. We can assume that our knowledge about how to operate in them is not individualized in any interesting way.

I cannot assume that everybody has the same Lutece or Taillevant scripts, however. Most people have not been to these places. However, if they did eat there, their behavior would only differ from each other in small ways. The fancy restaurant script can be inferred rather easily, and most people can adapt their prior restaurant scripts to help out. Thus, when a particular script is unavailable, the usual strategy is to find the closest possible script and use it.

The distinction between cases and scripts is not that great. The reason for this is that when a new situation is encountered, and the best possible old script is used to help out, the understander will still recognize that a new situation has been encountered. So, when our first time diner at Taillevant has to resort to using the script that he had for the best restaurant in his home town to help him understand how to behave, either one of two things will happen. Either he will find that certain stuff works (e.g., "You will be handed a wine list and will be expected to order wine which will be poured out for the orderer to taste first") or he won't. When his rules fail (when he sends back the chocolates that arrived with the coffee saying he didn't order them) he will begin to acquire a new case.

People acquire new cases because the old script they were using didn't work all that well. We would expect our first time diner at Taillevant to remember and tell the story of his dining experience. Further, we would expect that, if he should find himself at Taillevant again, he would not make the same errors he made the first time. He would have learned from experience. Learning from experience manifests itself as the acquisition of a new case which has been added to memory.

Two questions that can be asked at this point are: Where in memory is that case added? and what form does the case take in memory? These questions matter because their answers will tell us how learning from experience actually takes place and what kinds of learning from experience can take place.

When a script is being formed in memory, it owes its existence to repetition and continued use. No script is formed when a given behavior is done only once, or in any case done quite rarely. Further, even if there is a great deal of repetition, lack of continued use would kill the script. (How many people could go back to sixth grade and recall the classroom routine that was at one time a script for them?) Since repetition and continued use matter so greatly in script formation, it seems obvious that at the time of the initial encounter with a new experience, memory could not possibly tell the difference between a script and a case.

Thus it stands to reason that scripts and cases are the same thing as far as processing of new information is concerned. To put this another way, human memory is full of processing structures. These structures tell us what to expect next from other people who are acting in a situation and what to do next in response to those actions. We have described in Schank (1982) how MOPs are formed as containers for aspects of such processing structures such that larger structures can be put together from smaller structures. Thus, knowledge of how to act in a fancy restaurant comes from what we know about paying, ordering, tasting wine, and so on, some of which are particular to fancy restaurants and some of which come from what we know about contracting for services. The MOP is an organizer of scenes which contain the processing rules for particular situations.

But where do cases fit in this scheme? In Schank (1982) we said that cases were found as wholes when they were labeled (or indexed) by TOPs which were explanations of situations that were couched in the language of goals and plans (see also Schank 1986). Also, we indicated that cases were sometimes stored as exceptions to expectations within scenes in a MOP. Thus, cases are to be found in two places in memory in the scheme presented in Schank (1982). First, they are inside scenes, stored as exceptions, waiting for confirmation that their exception was normal and that they should be generalized into new scenes or new parts of scenes. Second, they are labeled by TOPs, stored in terms of certain goal interactions, and planning situations that might occur.

What does this tell us about learning? Obviously, learning takes place when an existing memory structure needs to be modified. We learn because some processing structure got it wrong, that is, an actor did not do what was expected of him, or an action we did turned out badly (or unexpectedly well).

If we learn by modifying memory structures, then it stands to reason that we cannot learn anything much if we do not have processing structures to modify. In other words, we can only learn a new case when the old case we were using for processing turned out not to work. Since expectations need to fail in order to acquire a new case, we need expectations in the first place or we won't learn much. Since expectations only exist inside scenes in MOPs and inside planning strategies in TOPs, and these are derived from previous cases, a clear educational strategy emerges.

Any educational scheme must focus on creating expectations in the mind of the learner and then presenting cases which cause those expectations to be modified. Since the expectations that are critical here are those contained in scenes in MOPs and in planning strategies in TOPs, it is clear what must be done in any learning situation. In order to learn a new case, a similar case must already exist in memory. Further, that case must make a prediction about what will happen, which turns out to be wrong. The new case can then be understood in terms of a partial match to the old case and in terms of explanations that need to be created by the learner to account for the differences between cases. In other words, there is an art in presenting new cases to a student. New cases must follow in a particular way from previously presented cases. They must modify expectations built up by the prior case. There can be no new cases without prior partially matched cases.

The reason for this comes from the two questions cited above. Where do we put a new case? The answer is that new cases are stored in relation to the aspect of the old case that failed. Since a new case needs to be stored in memory in order for it to be learned, we would hope that it would be stored someplace where it could be found some other time. This can only happen when cases are stored in terms of expectations that are activated by situations. If a case is stored independent of an expectation linked to a situation, nothing would cause it to come to mind during active processing.

The second question above was: What form does a new case take? The answer is that it simply copies most aspects of the old case from which it was derived and adds an exception that is true under certain circumstances, and it notes those circumstances. Thus, it has the effect of causing detailed discriminations in expectations to be made that allow a learner to detect nuances of difference in a complex situation.

The lesson for education here, then, is that one can only learn from experience if the experience one is having is strongly related to an experience one has already had. Since so much of education fails to understand this key point, and since allowing students to learn from experience is so critical to education, we shall now explain carefully exactly under what circumstances learning new cases from experience can work and under which circumstances it will not work.

While educators often understand the significance of presenting cases to their students, they often fail to understand the significance of the ordering and timing of the cases they present. So, business and law schools which use case methods of teaching fail to recognize the errors they make in case selection, case size, case ordering, and other factors that severely affect students' abilities to absorb the material. The goal, after all, is that students remember the cases, storing them in a way that assures their retrieval at a relevant time later in life. In order for this to happen, particular attention must be paid to the memory issues that mitigate their absorption.

The key error that most case-organized courses make is the preference for temporal ordering over thematic ordering. Temporal ordering of cases occurs when cases are presented in a serial order determined by the time in history when the case actually occurred. This is the worst possible ordering of cases that could exist because it totally ignores the issues of partial matching of prior cases that enables new cases to be stored in terms of the expectation failures of old cases since no expectation failures occur.

Creating properly organized courses based on cases depends on making sure that each case sets up the next. That is, every case needs to provide its understander with new expectations, some of which fail in subsequent cases. It is easy to misunderstand the concept of cases setting up cases. Why couldn't the case of what happened in 1810 set up the case of what happened in 1815? Isn't that one case setting up another? Of course it is in the temporal sense, but it might not at all be a set up in the thematic sense. The issue is whether the material in the second case builds on the expectations set up in the prior case by confirming some and violating others. This distinction, between cases that build on each other and those that merely follow each other, is central to the goal of having a student remember not only the cases but also the principles those cases exemplify.

There are many possible orderings of cases and decisions on what makes cases appropriate besides temporal ordering that are of concern here. In general, any syntactic ordering or selection criteria (e.g., one from this type and one from that type, or all the cases that involve fire engines) will make for a course that violates the principles that underlie memory's ability to absorb new information. The ordering and selection must be made according to the following maxims:

1. No case before its time
2. Any new case must violate expectations from prior cases
3. Cases should relate to actions
4. Cases should have the potential to change behavior

We will now consider these maxims one at a time.

No Case Before Its Time

It is tempting to tell children stories that are of general interest. Thus, one can tell of George Washington chopping down the cherry tree or of Paul Revere's ride because these are stories of the culture to which children can relate. But when we consider that we are trying to do more than entertain, such stories need to be more than simply appealing to children. They also must be germane. The question is, of course, germane to what?

Perhaps the best way to illustrate the issue here is with reference to the story "The Boy Who Cried Wolf." Typically, parents tell this story when a child has complained about some actions on the part of another child when it turns out that there really wasn't much of a problem and the complainer had exaggerated or just plain lied. This story is not such a fascinating story, and probably is told by parents at just the time that they perceive that it is needed.

This pattern of just in time story telling is one that parents and teachers know to be the right thing to do in ordinary life situations, but it is violated all the time in educational settings. This happens because someone simply wants to tell a story for some reason, or more commonly, because that story has been mandated to be told by some curriculum committee at some specified time in the school year. When this happens two bad things occur.

First, the listener is often bored. Frequently, listeners find themselves distracted when they have no need for what they are hearing. One must be ready to hear a story, to receive a lesson, or to read a book. The same message told before its time is often completely ignored by a person who might revel in that story at some later time (or might have loved it at some earlier time.) If we want listeners to remember what they are being told, they must want to hear what they are being told. "Want" means in this case, the presence of an active expectation, question, or curiosity about some life strategies that happens to be addressed by the new story (or case).

The second problem is that the listener, having no clear need for the story, is left to determine the point of the story for himself. This means that a listener is left thinking about why George didn't like trees or wanted to eat cherry pie, or why Paul Revere didn't use his car or what the roads were like in those days. While it is fine for listeners to speculate on aspects of a case that they find interesting, the intended "lesson" of the story fails to come across and, more important, the entire story is unlikely to be remembered at all unless the listener does a remarkably good job of creating his own idiosyncratic lesson.

This same problem occurs in business situations when a classic case is told to an audience that could not possibly appreciate its point. Left to memorize the point, the trainees have no clue what to do with this memorized point and they fail to link it to actual behaviors that they have had on the job. Sometimes they cannot do this because the company that is training them is giving them training prior to their doing the job, which considering what I have been saying here is absolutely ludicrous from a memory and expectation point of view. How can they learn something that relates in no way to any expectation that they have ever formed? But even when expectations have been formed and when a trainee has worked on the job, the new cases that he hears about often relate to situations in some future job for which he has no expectations. The trainee is thus left with cases and no place to put them, which means he will soon forget them.

Any New Case Must Violate Expectations from Prior Cases

The particulars of what case is best presented when are important to work out. The right thing to ask about the right time to tell the cherry tree story is, "After what case should the cherry tree case be presented?" One possibility, a very good one indeed, is that this (and all other cases) are presented only after the listener has taken some action that shows he is in need of the case (lying, in this example). This point shall be elaborated further in the next maxim. Here we address the issue of what to do when the only medium available is the presentation of cases.

The ordering of cases in a continuous presentation of cases requires that each case address some expectation in a prior case. Put this way, the cherry tree case would have to be presented after a case about lying and getting away with it if it were part of a course on honesty in relationships. Or it could be presented after the case of Cain and Abel if it were part of a course on managing hostility in children. I am actually not trying to make a joke here at all, but rather to bring up a significant issue. There is no way to say when the cherry tree case ought to be presented in the absence of an understanding of what kind of course it was a part of. What is absolutely wrong is that it be used as a case in American history since it tells us nothing whatever about American history. It might be part of a course in Washington's character. This could be useful in setting up expectations about his honesty that might be built upon or violated in a subsequent story about his adult behavior, but I have never heard such a story and certainly have never heard of it being told for that reason.

This bears on the ideas brought up earlier of the thematic organization of cases in a course. Cases cannot be easily remembered if they are not part of some organized set of expectations about a certain class of behaviors. It may be appealing to tell Paul Revere and George Washington stories to children who may well respond to them as children respond to any well told story. But if we want children to remember what they have been told and put that story to use in some way, they need to be told with some coherent themes in mind, building each new point on an expectation set up by a prior case.

Cases Should Relate to Actions

Of course, the best teaching relates to actual behaviors, not passive listening. This is what learning by doing is all about. Not all learning can be learning by doing, but when possible this must be the first method of teaching. This does not mean, however, that cases must only be actually experienced to be learned. We can absorb cases that are told to us if they are told at the right time. The question is, "What is the right time?"

Expectations are created by both cases and by behaviors. When you see a man enter a store with a gun in his hand, you expect a robbery. This is somewhat different from reading about the same situation. You still expect a robbery, but you are not afraid and are not wondering what you should do next. The prior situation is, of course, far more memorable. Nevertheless, one can tell a case in either situation. Ideally, in a teaching situation, we want to set up the robbery with the student as a player in the scene so that it feels real. The more real it feels the more memorable it will be. Then, any teaching we wish to do involving a new case can be understood in terms of the case that has been set up in a realistic way. The listener is ready to hear about the second case after experiencing the first. In some sense, the second case will be remembered as part of the first, so the more memorable the first, the more likely that the upcoming case will be remembered as well.

Cases Should Have the Potential to Change Behavior

This maxim is, of course, quite critical. Learning is about behavior change after all. Thus, what we need to do is remember that when a case is told (after a doing experience, for example) we want the listener to have to act upon the lesson of the new case immediately. That is, if the case being told is how someone died in a robbery attempt because they threatened the robber, then we want the next experience to cause the learner to have to make a decision about how to deal with the robber. Or, to put this back to cherry trees, if there isn't a situation presented where the learner needs to choose between lying and telling the truth the lesson will be lost.

It follows from this that cases must be followed by actions of some sort. If the actions are purely cognitive, and all a listener needs to do is say what he would do, we run the risk of having students parrot right answers independent of real visceral decision making. Students can learn to say the right answers but can they learn to do them? This can only be found by alternating cases with actions in some way.

Conclusion

Learning by doing works because it teaches implicitly rather than explicitly. Things that are learned implicitly need only be experienced in the proper way at the proper time. In order to make classrooms into learning-by-doing experiences we need to allow students to be in situations that are germane to their interests.

What students learn when they learn by doing often remains implicit. Micro-scripts, participation strategies, explicit functional knowledge, and lessons from cases are often the kind of knowledge that people don't really know they have. The knowledge comes up when they need it and people can sometimes explicitly state what they know. Educators are often confused by the fact that people can explicitly state what they know. In fact, they are so confused by this that they pervert the education system so that it will highlight the explicit stating of what one knows rather than highlight the behavior that would indicate the presence of implicit knowledge. We must turn this state of affairs around if we are to ever really change education.

16 Making the Implicit Explicit: Clarifying the Principles of Case-Based Reasoning

Janet L. Kolodner

This chapter, based on a talk I gave in 1993 at the AAAI summer workshop on case-based reasoning, is an attempt to dispel several common misconceptions about case-based reasoning. As I collected examples of case-based reasoning systems around that time, I was delighted to find how many fielded efforts there were, the diversity of those systems, the size of some systems, and the ingenuity some had used in devising simple, elegant, and working indexing schemes. But as I reviewed case-based reasoning-related papers, I found that while case-based reasoning had caught on, many authors were throwing around CBR terminology, criticizing CBR, and making claims about CBR without understanding it well.

A whole series of papers I was asked to review made misleading claims and statements, some written by people who should have known better. Some claimed, for example, that indexing couldn't do the job it was supposed to do; others claimed that retrieval algorithms were too slow for CBR to be viable; and so on. My response to such claims was to question how they chose their indexes, exactly which retrieval algorithms they were using, why they made their representations too complicated to use, and the like. But I realized that while I could ask these questions of and educate the few people whose papers I reviewed, I couldn't reach everyone that way. And I worried that I was seeing only the tip of the iceberg.

It was clear to me that the case-based reasoning community had not done a good enough job yet of articulating its principles and assumptions to the outside world. Those of us who have been part of the development and history of CBR know its underlying assumptions in our guts. They form the basis for heated and deep discussions we have with each other. We are often good at passing those assumptions down to our students, but we hadn't been very good at articulating them explicitly to the rest of the artificial intelligence and cognitive science communities. My fears were that some CBR critics would do a better job of addressing the broad AI and cognitive science communities than we were doing and that if our lack of articulation led to failures of those in industry to success-fully build systems, then a CBR backlash would be created. I urged the CBR community to think about case-based reasoning: where it comes from, what its assumptions are, and what the things are that we only know deep in our guts. In short, I said, we needed to make sure the implicit was made explicit.

My talk, and this chapter, are an attempt to do that: to uncover and clarify common misconceptions about case-based reasoning, focusing in particular on indexing and representation issues and on case-based reasoning's implied cognitive model. My intention is to address three audiences: those who build case-based applications, cognitive scientists, and the broad AI community. For builders of case-based applications, I hope to provide some concise state-ments and short lists of things that define the essence of CBR and its underly-ing conceptual foundations and assumptions, the things that will allow them to use the methodology as it is meant to be used. For cognitive scientists, es-pecially those engaged in defining cognitive models at the architectural level, I hope to provide some insight into the functions a cognitive architecture needs to carry out to engage in real-world reasoning and the ways those func-tions are guided by reasoning tasks. For the AI community, my intention is simply to make case-based reasoning's assumptions clear enough so that oth-ers, besides CBR's inventors and developers, can replicate results, understand claims, and compare and contrast CBR methodology, assumptions, coverage, applicability, and potentials with those of other approaches.

Two warnings are in order before proceeding. First, some of what you'll read here is dated. I've tried to put all the things that might be dated in the past tense. I think most remain fresh. My apologies in advance if I'm wrong about that. Second, the chapter has little in the way of introduction to case-based reasoning. Those who are not familiar with CBR will want to read this book's tutorial chapter on case-based reasoning (Chapter 2) before reading this chapter. Those who will get the most out of this chapter, I think, are peo-ple who have become confused in trying to understand CBR deeply, especial-ly those who have tried to grapple with what is confusing.

I continue by briefly presenting some of the things I found out in collecting systems for my book (Kolodner 1993)—the good and the bad, the surprising and the expected. Then, I collect up the misconceptions. The bulk of the chap-ter is an attempt to articulate those parts of CBR's paradigm that address each.

Setting the Stage: Early 1993 Accomplishments

As of early 1993, case-based reasoning had caught on. In late 1992, when I put together the appendix of my book (Kolodner 1993), I included descriptions of about 75 systems. Six months later, I had heard about 30 more systems, and

I'm sure there were many more that I didn't know about. Systems' tasks and domains ranged from help desks of various kinds to autoclave configuration to design aiding to stock screening, and more, some of which our community had not previous thought about. Some systems were fully automated; some helped human problem solvers. In 1993, there were three commercially-available shells for building case-based systems; today there are more.

Some efforts were very interesting. For example, the NEC corporation in Japan had a 20,000 case library on software testing called SQUAD (Kitano and Shimazu [Chapter 13 of this book]; Kitano, et al. 1992). A partial matching algorithm allowed their software debuggers to use the case library as a database when they encountered a new bug they needed to fix. They queried the case library in SQL, and the system retrieved similar software bugs and their fixes. They were very proud of their parallel algorithms—even with 20,000 cases, the system was apparently quite fast. They used a nearest-neighbor search to find matches. Their major message to the rest of us was that if you want a case-based advisory system to work on a large scale, then you need to make sure you have the support staff available to make it work. Their case entry staff included over a dozen people.

Perhaps the most surprising thing I discovered about applications was that many real applications were successfully using very simple indexing procedures. The most common way of retrieving appropriate cases was to use the equivalent of an inverted index to pull out cases that shared features with a new situation. Then a numeric nearest-neighbor matching algorithm was used to choose cases that matched best. Many of those taking this approach were choosing the terms for their inverted indexes wisely. Many were recognizing that the reason they could make this method work was because what is important doesn't change much from situation to situation. The method is simple, even simplistic, but for fairly narrow real-world applications where there aren't more than several hundred cases, it works just fine.

I was also pleasantly surprised by the extent to which many developers of the fielded systems showed a good understanding of the role of situation assessment. *Situation assessment,* which precedes search, means interpreting a new case or query and elaborating its representation to bring its description more in line with what might be stored in the case library, thereby enabling relevant cases to be recognized even if they are represented differently. I read many reports of interactive case retrieval systems where the search was iterative and the user changed the specification as items were retrieved and evaluated for applicability. Those who understood this issue well, I think, were those with experience using information retrieval systems.

Developers were finding that building case-based systems took less time than building equivalent rule-based ones, and people liked advice-giving systems better than autonomous expert systems. In short, there was much to be excited about.

Early 1993 Misconceptions

On the other hand, there were many efforts that made me concerned. Apparently, we hadn't been explicit enough about what our terminology meant or what our assumptions were. This led to a whole variety of misinterpretations and nonsensical claims, some of which are listed below. I leave them anonymous.

1. "I've got a new role cases can play. They can act as integrators of lots of different kinds of knowledge."

2. "My system is just like a case-based reasoning system. After solving a problem, it creates specific operators based on all the operations it did and stores all of them. It doesn't have to figure out anymore how to apply its operators."

3. "With my parallel system, no indexing is needed.... Of course, we still need a theory of how to assign importance values and how to allow them to change with context."

4. "In my system, we use conditional probabilities to determine what to retrieve. With my parallel system that makes decisions using conditional probabilities, no indexing is needed.... Of course, there is still more work needed to discover how to assign conditional probabilities well."

5. "In the first pass of my scheme, surface features are used to find cases that partially match. Then, in the second pass, we do more expensive reasoning, choosing out those cases that match on deeper features."

6. "But I can't support this as psychologically plausible. All the experimental evidence shows that people are reminded only on the basis of surface features."

7. "We've all had the experience with case-based systems that when the case library is small, retrieval is fast, but that after it grows, retrieval gets so slow that case-based reasoning isn't viable anymore."

8. "That's a nice looking system, but until you tell me you have retrieval algorithms that can select from among 20,000 cases, I can't take it seriously as a real-world system."

There are a variety of misconceptions embedded in these statements. The first two comment on the content of cases; the first author discovered anew that cases chunk and integrate, the second one missed the point that cases chunk and integrate. The last statement's author comments erroneously on what makes a case-based system useful, missing the point that for many applications, a relatively small case library suffices.

The remainder of the statements are about indexing and retrieval. Authors of the third and fourth statements misunderstand what the term "indexing" means. They assume it means "pointer." While the CBR community began by using the term indexing to refer to pointers, the term has been used more recently (since 1988) to refer to labeling that allows useful and efficient access. The author of the fifth statement misunderstands the relationship between surface features of a case and features that might be predictive. He assumes both are the same. They are not. More deeply, he misunderstands the qualities of a good index. The author of the sixth statement also misunderstands what makes a good index; he further misunderstands what an indexing scheme is and how vocabulary for indexing might be chosen (by people and for machines). His statement misinterprets the relationship between experimental findings about analogical reasoning (collected in the very controlled lab) (e.g., Gentner 1987, Gick and Holyoak 1984) and common observations about people using cases to reason (collected in the street). Experimental findings on analogical reasoning have been carried out in laboratory situations far too controlled for a general statement about the role of derived or deep features in reminding to be culled from them. The person who wrote the seventh statement clearly misses the intent of indexing schemes: to guide retrieval and make it efficient. He further misunderstands the relationship between organizational schemes and retrieval algorithms. As we all learned in data structures classes, organizational schemes need to match retrieval needs, and retrieval algorithms are chosen to complement organizational schemes. This fellow wants the scheme for his small system to work universally.

Nor, alas, are all misconceptions about case-based reasoning illustrated in these statements. Left out of this set are a whole variety of misconceptions about the relationship between case-based reasoning and learning.

Clarifying the Misconceptions

I continue by addressing the misconceptions illustrated above and attempting to clarify them.

What Is a Case?

The basics of the answer to this question can be found in the tutorial chapter in this book (Chapter 2). A case, which generally represents a concrete situation, integrates a multitude of complex information in a very concrete way. Cases always include a situation description, and usually include three other parts (Kolodner 1993, Chapter 5): (1) a description of some problem or question or failed expectation that arose in that situation, (2) a description of the way that problem or question was addressed or the way the failed expectation was explained, and (3) a description of the consequences, results or outcome of addressing the problem in that way. Moreover, cases connect these pieces to each other. The richer the parts and the richer the connections between them, the more useful a case can be. A case might represent a single point in time, or it can represent a time slice of any size.

Important in this description of a case are several things. A case chunks together information concerning problems, responses to those problems, and effects of those responses. This is because effective reuse of an old experience generally requires comparing and contrasting a new situation to an old one to determine if indeed the old experience brings light to bear on the new one. The more that is known about an old situation, the better a reasoner can determine whether the old experience is relevant and what to glean from it. Particularly important in determining if an old experience is relevant are knowing how its solution achieved its goals (i.e., the connections between the situation description and the solution or response) and whether the solution achieved its goals (i.e., the outcome of the situation and the relationship of the outcome to what was expected).

Thus, a case stores enough content and context so that when recalled later, its useful and interesting lessons can be extracted. For example, in building the Buckhead branch library in Atlanta, the architect had to figure out how to get enough natural light into the long narrow space while still making stacks of books available to users (problem description). He made the back wall (narrow side of the building, south-facing) out of glass and made it two stories high, opening up to a view of the Atlanta skyline, put awnings of a certain kind up to keep out the heat and glare of the sun, put the stacks along the long sides of the space, located the reading space down the center, and located the information desk and office space at the front (where little natural light gets in) (solution or response). The result is a well-lit and pleasant reading area and a naturally-lit stack area (the natural light comes from above the stacks). It works well for a small branch library that caters mostly to adults, but does not allow for a separated children's area or accommodate specialized or noisy spaces (outcome or effects). This case teaches several lessons: one way to get light into a long narrow space, one way to mitigate heat and glare from south-facing windows, and so on. Those lessons can be extracted from the case to the extent that the case includes and connects together relevant descriptors of the situation, problem, response, and effects related to each.

The example also makes clear that while cases might be about application of an individual operator, more often they are about the effects of a long line of reasoning and several related decisions. It is the record of that long line of reasoning, the situation in which it was used, and its effects that allows a reasoner to take shortcuts as it reasons. Rather than having to derive reasoning steps from individual operators, it often can reuse solutions that were derived previously or reuse the old means of reaching a solution.

The combination of integration, concreteness, and connection to an experienced event differentiates a case from other kinds of information chunks. The author of statement 1 understood cases to be connected to experienced events and to be concrete; somehow he missed their integrative nature. The author of statement 2 also misses the importance of their integrative nature: in creating operators from a case and storing each individually, he keeps his operators separate from the content and context that might help a reasoner to determine their usefulness, and he requires his reasoner to recompute its reasoning steps and solutions for each new problem. While his reasoner can find its operators more easily and apply them in more appropriate situations, it still must choose its operators one at a time.

What Does "Indexing" Mean?

An index in a book is a pointer to a page. An index in a database is a pointer to a record. An index in a case library is sometimes implemented as a pointer to a case, and indeed, the earliest implementations were pointer implementations. But that was back in the early 1980s, and a dozen years later, pointers are only one way to implement indexes; there are other ways as well:

• Assign importance values to dimensions of a representation and prefer as better matches cases that match on more important dimensions.

• Label cases with their important or defining sets of features and choose cases that match on those sets of features over those that match on others.

Perhaps "indexing" was the wrong term for the "accessibility problem," but we're stuck with it. "Indexing" means more than assigning pointers; "the indexing problem" refers to the whole set of issues inherent in setting up a memory and its retrieval processes so that the right cases are retrieved at the right times.

People criticize pointer schemes for being too restrictive, or as being too hard to compute, so they want to do away with them. But the indexing problem isn't solved when you do away with pointers; rather, the problem is moved to a different part of the system. The same conceptual questions still need to be addressed. The authors of statements 3 and 4 are confused about exactly this issue.

Accessibility depends on a combination of processes and representations: situation assessment, recognition of what is important about a case, search functions, similarity metrics, vocabulary, and matching functions. Different implementations divide the work in different ways among these processes. A parallel system divides the work differently than a serial one because search can work differently.

Several parallel schemes (e.g., Kettler, et al. 1993, Kitano, et al. 1992), for example, make multiple incremental queries to memory, since each query is fast. Rather than using pointer structures within the case library, their situation assessment and/or matching procedures do the majority of the work. Queries are formed incrementally by situation assessment procedures. A series of queries is made, each derived from the last, until an appropriate case is found. In one scheme, queries include only salient descriptors, so anything that is found during search is deemed relevant and usable. In another scheme, queries contain both important and not-as-important descriptors, and matching procedures analyze the retrieved cases to see which might be relevant and useful. What might have been embedded in the pointer schemes in previous implementations is embedded in the knowledge used by situation assessment procedures and in the knowledge used by matching functions.

What Kinds of Features Make Good Indexes?

In other words, which features are the important ones to match on to retrieve useful cases? Authors of statements 5 and 6 don't understand the answer to this question. The "indexes" of a case, sometimes called its "labels," sometimes its important features, are those combinations of features that distinguish it from other cases, because they are predictive of something important in the case. The "indexing problem" means finding labels for cases such that each case will be recalled whenever appropriate in the future. In addition to being predictive of something important, indexes need to be concrete enough to be recognizable and abstract enough to make a case useful in a variety of future situations.

This poses a potential problem, however, since some predictive features are hard to recognize. To make retrieval efficient, we need our indexes to not only predict but also to correspond to features that are either available, easy to compute, or that are computed in the natural course of reasoning. Hammond (1989c) calls these "easily available" features. But one shouldn't index by all easily available features, only those that pass the test of being predictive.[1]

Notice the words used to describe good indexes: predictive (of something important or useful), recognizable, provide discrimination, provide coverage, …. The case-based reasoning view of indexing sees these as the important issues in choosing indexes. We focus on what makes a feature useful as an index in defining goodness of features for indexing. Thus, when we hear people argue about using surface features, deep features, structural features, pragmatic features, thematic features, and so on, we get confused. Those descriptors describe where a feature lies in a representation or what its content is. But the same content might be useful for indexing in some situations and not so useful other times. For example, the hair color of a job applicant might be important if that applicant is applying for a modeling job but it isn't at all important if the applicant is applying for a computer programming job (Kolodner 1984). While hair color is easily available in both situations, it is relevant only to the first. So we tell our colleagues who talk about surface features, deep features, structural features, and so on, to choose from among all of those for good indexes, but make sure the indexes have the properties we've told you are important.

So what's wrong with indexing by "surface features" (statement 5)? Since surface features are merely what's available without inference, they may not be predictive at all. Often, it is some interpretation of the surface features that predicts. Indexes correspond to those features of a situation that, if we see them again, predict some important aspect of the rest of the situation. There may be inference required to analyze a situation and figure out what it really represents. Once that interpretation is done, it is easy to index the case based on its interpretation. And, to find a usefully-matching case in memory, it may be necessary to at least begin to interpret a new situation to derive more meaningful features before attempting retrieval (situation assessment). The necessity of interpreting or assessing before attempting retrieval was made clear in CASEY (Koton 1988b). The most relevant and useful cases in making a diagnosis often had little or nothing in common at the level of surface features. Thus, indexing by surface features on the first pass and deeper ones later on might completely miss important cases.

As to the statement about people indexing only on surface features (statement 6), anyone who goes back and examines those experiments will find that they test only novice subjects, those who don't know enough about the domain to do situation assessment well. Without the knowledge necessary to carry out situation assessment well, only surface features are available for reminding. As the novice-expert literature shows, however, interpretation by novices is quite different than interpretation by experts (Chi et al. 1981, Larken et al. 1980). Thus, one would expect quite different remindings from those who are more expert in an area. Our claims about useful indexes are claims about the indexes a knowledgeable expert would formulate. As the analogical reasoning community begins to take this claim more seriously, I believe we will see much controlled experimental evidence showing that many of our claims about preferred choice of indexes hold up as quite consistent with people. And as more of our community better explores the evolution of indexes (as has been done in e.g., CELIA [Redmond 1991]), we will provide better foundation for running those experiments.

Where does Vocabulary for Indexing Come From?

This is a complicated but important issue. In answering the previous question, I stated that the most easily available features are those that are computed in the natural course of reasoning. Many are from the domain vocabulary. But which pieces of the domain vocabulary, the level of detail at which concepts are represented, and the degree to which relationships between domain terms need to be represented are a function of the needs of the reasoner. One thus chooses vocabulary for indexing by taking into account both the domain being reasoned about and the reasoning tasks being performed.

Some indexing vocabulary is specific to a domain; other indexing vocabulary cuts across domains. We find cross-domain vocabulary by considering both the similarities across domains and the needs of generic reasoning tasks. If we understand the variety of reasoning tasks, it can help us to choose indexing structure and terms that go beyond individual domains. I'll discuss this issue in more detail in the next section.

How Important Are Retrieval Algorithms?

Retrieval algorithms are very important, and one of the open questions in CBR. For very large case libraries, we don't yet have a set of tricks up our sleeves for making retrieval fast. On the other hand, we have many methods for making it fast enough in situations that are not as drastic (Kolodner 1993, Chapter 8). If retrieval algorithms aren't working fast enough, it could be that they haven't been implemented well enough or that indexes have not been chosen well. We don't have all the best algorithms yet, but there are some people who are making what we have work for very large case libraries (see, e.g., Kitano and Shimazu, [Chapter 13 of this book]). Given that, it requires only a bit of care and ingenuity to make them work for smaller sets of cases. The author of statement 7 didn't do his homework. He assumed the retrieval scheme that he used for his small case library was universally appropriate. He probably could have solved his problem by looking at the algorithms and organizational strategies that have been proposed. All that being said, the CBR community does need to get together with the people who know algorithms and search (e.g., IR people) and figure out how to make search more efficient.

How Many Cases does It Take to Have a Useful System?

The answer to this question depends on the domain. The author of statement 8 might have in mind a domain that requires 20,000 cases for coverage. But there are many domains where hundreds of cases work just fine, and available retrieval methods work just fine for those. A case library doesn't have to be very large to be very useful. For example, MIDAS's (Domeshek, et al 1993) case library of 36 cases performed better on a trade-off analysis than people had performed without the system.

The Conceptual Underpinnings

Unfortunately, pointing out and clarifying these misconceptions still misses many of case-based reasoning's conceptual underpinnings. Learning to do something well requires knowing the concepts and facts involved and also knowing when and how to apply them. So, while I addressed misconceptions, I haven't addressed my audiences well enough yet. I need to be far more concrete than I've been so far if I want all of those in my audience to be able to take a "case-based reasoning" approach to new problems.

What I want to do in this section, then, is to try to uncover the tacit knowledge that the CBR community shares. Our tacit understanding of CBR has three parts: basic assumptions about the world that underlie case-based reasoning's philosophy and approach, the component processes, and central tenets. After presenting the basic assumptions and process, I'll discuss the ins and outs or case-based reasoning's tenets, concentrating, as I did above, on issues of case representation, index selection, and indexing vocabulary. While we tend to agree about the assumptions and processes, we are still arguing about many of the tenets, and I will try to present the discourse we are having about those topics.

Assumptions about the World

Underlying case-based reasoning is a set of assumptions about the world that guide the approach:

1. *Regularity:* The world is mostly regular; the same actions executed under the same conditions will tend to have the same or very similar outcomes.

2. *Typicality:* Things tend to repeat; a reasoner's experiences are likely to be typical of future experiences.

3. *Consistency:* Small changes in the world require only small changes in the way we interpret the world and only small changes in solutions.

4. *Ease of adaptation:* Though things don't repeat exactly, differences tend to be small, and the small differences are easy to compensate for.

Clearly, not all problems in all domains are regular, repetitive, consistent, or easy to adapt to. But the world as a whole is regular, and things recur in typical ways. This is what makes it possible for us to learn to get around in the world. Case-based reasoning begins with these assumptions in mind and looks to explain reasoning as, primarily, a set of processes that work well in a regular consistent world, and, secondarily, processes that are adapted from those to work in harder situations.

Processes

Case-based reasoning means recalling one or several previous cases and reasoning based on those. Figure 1 shows case-based reasoning's component processes.

First comes retrieval, the first step of which is situation assessment or interpretation, the process of interpreting or understanding a situation and figuring out what is important to its representation. This leads to search. Retrieval processes use partial matching procedures to determine which of the cases in the case library can be most useful to the reasoner.

Once a case or cases are retrieved, they can be used. An old solution might

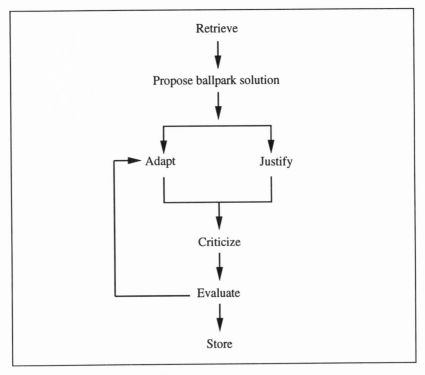

Figure 1. The case-based reasoning cycle.

be adapted to solve a new problem; pieces of several old situations might be merged to create a new solution; predictions might be made on the basis of an old situation; an old and new situation might be compared and contrasted to determine important issues to focus on or what needs to be adapted, and so on. Use of cases for reasoning leads to interpretations and/or solutions that affect the way we or our systems behave.

Next is action based on those inferences, which leads to results. If results are different than expected, there is a need to explain discrepancies, which leads to learning. Many things can be learned: a new case, a new knowledge structure, new knowledge learned through explanation, a new way to index, and so on. Learning processes range from simple inductive procedures that collect up similarities to complex processing aimed toward generating and generalizing explanations. Learning must be attempted even when knowledge is incomplete.

Of course, the processing isn't as sequential as what I've presented. Situation assessment and search processes can work hand in hand with each other. Case manipulation might require retrieval of additional cases. And so on. But the diagram makes explicit the major processes and their relationships to each other.

Tenets

Aside from arguing about whether I've captured the relationships between all the processes, I think most of the CBR community would agree with the analysis of CBR so far. The arguments begin after we try to tease out the tenets, or tacit beliefs, on which CBR's processes rest. Let me simply list some of these:

1. Cases are primary in reasoning, and processes that manipulate cases are *the* crucial reasoning methods.

2. Reasoning is more a process of "remember and modify" than "decompose and recompose".

3. Access to cases (reminding) is *the* number-one issue, implying several other important things, that the best representations of cases are those that allow relevant similarities between cases to be recognized; that identifying, in a new or old situation, what it is important to focus on is crucial; and that representation and reasoning are intimately connected to each other.

4. Learning and reasoning are intimately related to each other; one shouldn't approach one without taking the other into account. Failure is especially important as a trigger to learning—both failure of actions and failure of expectations.

This list still doesn't look all that controversial to most people in the CBR community. But while on the surface, each tenet looks well-enough defined, they all begin to look fuzzy around the edges when we try to be more specific about what they mean. It is this fuzz that our community needs to make clearer. This presentation represents my first pass at attempting to make the fuzz explicit. Certainly more work is needed. I'll go through the assumptions one by one.

Cases

> Cases are primary in reasoning, and manipulation of cases is *the* crucial reasoning problem.

This was certainly the original assumption in case-based reasoning, but in fact, some of the research most central to case-based reasoning's core uses knowledge structures more general and abstract than cases in the same ways cases are used. For example, SWALE (Kass and Leake 1988, Kass, Leake and Owens 1986) uses XP's (explanation patterns). XP's are derived from cases, but they aren't cases themselves—they are large-scale patterns that work similarly to cases. AQUA (Ram 1991 1993) uses both abstract XP's and specific cases. One of SWALE's XP's, for example, states that one explanation for an athlete dying of a heart attack after exertion is that there was an unknown defect in the athlete's heart and the exercise right before the heart attack overwhelmed that defect. There are some concrete concepts in this XP (e.g., heart attack), but other concepts are more general (e.g., athlete), some are pretty abstract (e.g., heart defect, exertion, exercise), and the whole explanation pattern is just that—a pattern extracted from one or several cases.

What, then, is the real tenet here? Is it that large-scale patterns are primary?

No, a focus on large-scale patterns is not specific enough. In model-based reasoning, for example, large-scale patterns are important also, but the large-scale patterns used in model-based reasoning are quite different than those used in CBR. The way models have been used by the model-based reasoning community, they cover all options (e.g., what are the different things that somebody might do with this doorknob?). Cases seem to cover only one option at a time (e.g., when the doorknob was turned, then such and such happened; when the doorknob was pulled, then ...).

But clearly some large-scale patterns can function like cases. Where do we set the boundaries? My first set of boundaries discusses how much such a pattern can cover:

Chunks that cover one type of situation at a time can function like cases.

This requires us, of course, to say what a "type" is. We might want to go back to the assumptions for this. Cases, we said there, are used for reasoning because, in general, the world is regular and consistent. We believe individual events will repeat in regular ways. Cases represent states of the world that, if responded to in the same way each time, will tend to result in a similar new state each time. Based on this assumption about the world, a large-scale pattern (generalization, chunk) that represents a situation that is likely to repeat and where the response to the situation would be about the same each time, can function the same way a case can. Going back to representing models, we would use cases to represent states of the system that, if responded to in the same way each time, would result in the same new state. Thus, a case-based approach to representing models would separate out the different paths through the model and represent each path as a chunk rather than including the whole model in one large-scale chunk.

But we still haven't dealt with the issue of how abstract a representation can be and still function like a case. A generic device description is not as concrete as a description of an individual device, but it is relatively concrete, and one can treat it as one treats a case, comparing and contrasting generic device descriptions to each other or adapting the description of one device to create a description of a new one (e.g., as KRITIK (Goel 1991, Goel and Chandrasekaran 1992) does). In other words, they play a role similar to cases in reasoning; they are concrete enough to easily reason about them. My analysis of SWALE's and AQUA's XP's and my analysis of model representation leads me to the following treatment of the abstractness of useful, or primary, large-scale patterns.

Chunks that can function like cases in reasoning can be concrete or abstract, *but* if abstract, they must still be *operational.*

Of course, now we must deal with what "operational" means. To me, operational chunks are those that require only instantiation and adaptation to be usable. If much inference involving chaining and branching is needed, then the chunk is not easily usable and certainly is not usable using case-based processes; therefore it can't play the same role in reasoning that cases do.

We can restate the first assumption, then, to refer to a more broad class of knowledge representations as primary in reasoning: those that cover a type of situation in a concrete enough way that they can be easily used or applied. These, we claim, are the primary knowledge sources used in everyday reasoning, and processes that manipulate these structures, we claim, are the crucial reasoning process we need to focus on and explain. Case manipulation processes include, but are not restricted to, adaptation, merging, and comparing and contrasting. Note that we do not claim these are the only types of representations, nor that their manipulation is the only type of reasoning a system or person needs to do, but only that these are the preferred representations and processes since they are the easiest to reason about and the most concretely applicable.

Some now will ask what cases are for if more general knowledge structures can function like cases as well. Others will now ask about the role of MOPs (Memory Organization Packets, Schank 1982). Case-based reasoning derived from dynamic memory, and MOPs are the means of representing a dynamic memory. Some MOPs are concrete enough to be applied as just described, but some are far more abstract. Whatever the level of concreteness or operationalization of an abstract representation, it will never carry with it predictions that are as concrete and specific as those that come from cases or individual instances themselves. MOPs, models, and other abstractions play an important role in reasoning. They organize cases and they carry predictions. Their predictions are generally less complete and more abstract than those that come from cases. Thus, while they are sometimes the best we have, and they can sometimes be used as easily as cases, they are not good enough by themselves to guide reasoning, nor are they as efficient as cases for guiding very specific inferences.

Some may see an implication here: that everything should be represented in a MOP-like way—cases tied to small-scale integrated abstractions. I don't think I want to go that far, but I do want to claim that all knowledge important for efficient reasoning should most certainly be represented in case-like ways. Case-based systems typically represent three types of knowledge this way:

• The way things work
• How things are done
• What happened when

But carrying case representation to its new limits, we should represent not only simple situations as cases attached to MOPs, but we should also situate any knowledge whose applicability depends on context with the contexts in which it is used. Two other kinds of knowledge come to mind for me here:

(1) the use of design principles, and (2) reasoning strategies IDEAL (Bhatta et al. 1994) begins to do the first. MEDIC (Turner 1994) and META-AQUA (Ram and Cox 1994) begin to do the second.

A caveat: Am I telling you that every case-based reasoning system needs to represent its cases using MOPs? Most certainly not. In his talk at the AAAI–93 CBR Workshop, Kris Hammond identified several approaches to case-based reasoning. Some are trying to take the theoretical implications of the approach to its limits. The systems built under this approach need to take all claims about representations seriously and study their implications and consequences. These systems should represent cases in conjunction with MOPs. But many people are engaged in trying to implement applications. These systems need to take those pieces of the theory that seem key and implement those pieces in ways that work efficiently. Since our computer implementations don't yet correspond to what our minds can do, our working systems may not use MOPs at all.

Reasoning

> Reasoning is more a process of "remember and modify" than "decompose and recompose".

Does this claim mean that we never advocate decomposition? No. Clearly, some problems are large enough or complex enough that they have to be broken into parts to be solved.

And what does this principle mean for case-based reasoners that are only part of the system, such as CASEY (Koton 1988b), ROUTER (Goel et al. 1994), and PRODIGY (Veloso and Carbonell 1993a, 1993b)? In each of these systems, the case-based reasoner collects up and reuses the experiences of a rule-based or model-based reasoner that works by decomposing problems until the available operators apply.

Operationally, this principle has the following implications:

- Systems should be designed to decompose only when necessary, and then they should use a case-based approach to figure out how.

- Decomposition should not be considered straightforward. It is a reasoning process that requires deliberative decision making. Mistakes might be made while decomposing, as mistakes are made in carrying out all deliberative processes. Ways of decomposing might need to be altered over time; learning processes might need to concentrate on decomposition failures. Meta-AQUA, for example, uses and combines many learning strategies; it uses a case-based reasoner to figure out how and when to put them together, allowing it to become a better reasoner over time.

- Make CBR primary and let the other components of a system revolve around it (a true-faith approach in Hammond's construal). JULIA (Hinrichs

1992), for example, needs a reason maintenance system to carry out some of its tasks, a goal scheduler because it needs to decompose sometimes, and a constraint propagator to hold its pieces together. But JULIA is primarily a case-based reasoner. Those other components are there to serve CBR.

- If the case-based component is only a piece of a bigger system (as, e.g., in CASEY, PRODIGY, and ROUTER), then apply these principles to at least the case-based component and examine their implications for the rest of the system. (a hard-core implementation approach according to Hammond). For example, one might give the goal scheduler and decomposer a strategy of trying to apply CBR to the current task or problem, decomposing it into smaller pieces only when the case-based reasoner has no case that applies to the whole big chunk.

Reminding and Indexing

> Access to cases (reminding) is *the* number-one issue, implying several other important things, that the best representations of cases are those that allow relevant similarities between cases to be recognized; that identifying, in a new or old situation, what it is important to focus on is crucial; and that representation and reasoning are intimately connected to each other.

This principle, like the first, is clearly incomplete. Even in a true-faith case-based reasoning system, cases are not the only source of knowledge. The best illustration of that comes from an example from my creativity project (Wills and Kolodner 1994 [Chapter 4 in this book]). In this project, we are taking a case-based approach to understanding creativity. One of the ways we've collected data is that my associate, Linda Wills, participated in a mechanical engineering design class, recording everything that went on in her work group. In one session, when students were trying to figure out how to cushion an egg to keep it from breaking, one of the students suggested embedding it in an orange. She had clearly never had the experience of embedding anything in an orange and using it for cushioning, so why the orange? In other instances, people talked about how different devices work or would work. One student explained why the orange might work by making reference to a shock absorber in a car. Another time students considered ping pong ball shooters as a model for something they were designing.

These students recalled plenty of cases along the way, but clearly they were also recalling things that were not cases. Accessibility to the whole variety of sources of knowledge that can help with prediction and inference is important to good reasoning. We might better state this principles as follows:

> Access to relevant knowledge is *the* number-one issue....

The inference we make from this is that indexing is important not only for cases, but also for other knowledge in memory—knowledge of objects, adaptation strategies, models, facts and so on. All are needed to reason; all must be accessible. When fact bases are large, they, too, must be well indexed to make their contents easily accessible. Retrieval and indexing are the key to knowledge access, whether access is to cases or otherwise.[2]

I want to use this insight to move back to defining what indexing is. The purpose of indexing is to make cases and other knowledge accessible at relevant times. Whatever the form of indexing, it needs to allow correspondences between stored cases or knowledge and new situations to be easily recognized. That requires, at some level, being able to identify relevant similarities. Whatever the representational form, the indexing problem is the problem of deciding which features and combinations of features to pay attention to in determining relevance or usefulness of some stored case or other piece of knowledge.

The authors of statements 3 and 4 understand indexes as pointer representations, but they don't understand the full implications of the indexing problem. Both told us that their parallel implementations didn't have to worry abut indexing. When you continue reading these papers (and others that claim that indexing isn't important), however, they always tell you that they are left with the problem of where the importance values or conditional probabilities or whatever else come from. What they don't understand is that those issues are the indexing problem. Importance values and conditional probabilities are two ways of representing the importance or relevance of features to such decisions. In systems that use those schemes for representing importance, the indexing problem means figuring out what values they should take on.

But we still are skirting the issue of exactly how we can determine which features and combinations of features are the important ones in determining relevance. What guidelines are there for choosing an indexing vocabulary? In his talk at the workshop, and in his chapter (15) in this book, Roger Schank gives us some clues about how we can figure this out. But we first need to consider what the purpose of a case-based reasoner is. We build case-based reasoning systems, and we describe people as case-based reasoners. Yet the goals of our systems and the goals of people are not to collect cases. Rather, our own goals and those of our systems are to get around in the world—to perform the tasks we need to carry out. Cases are collected as a byproduct of getting around in the world. If our goals are to get around in the world, they we need to choose indexes for cases that allow that to happen well. Cases, then, are indexed as a byproduct of the reasoning that needs to be done, based on predictions about how they might be used in the future.

Case-based reasoners, whether people or machines, function in task contexts; their reason for being is to accomplish sets of goals by carrying out a variety of tasks. Given the goal-driven nature of reasoning, it makes sense for indexes to be chosen such that they will allow a reasoner to achieve its goals and carry out its tasks more easily in the future. It makes sense, then, for representational vocabulary to match processing needs. The best indexing vocabulary is drawn from the concepts that naturally come up in the course of carrying out reasoning tasks (Kolodner 1993, chapters 4, 6, and 7). They match the needs of the reasoner and are drawn from a combination of the vocabulary describing the domain the reasoning is about and the vocabulary the reasoning task uses.

We can see this relationship most clearly when we look at the universal index frame (UIF) (Schank and Osgood 1990). The UIF, developed by Roger Schank and his students, records concepts derived in the normal course of understanding stories about social situations. It provides a set of dimensions and vocabulary for indexing that captures the concepts that understanding processes consider when they are understanding these kinds of goal-based situations. Understanding and acting in such situations requires tracking the goals and plans of participants and their interactions. Reasoning processes make inferences about these features and based on these features as a natural part of the way they work. These are the things the UIF records: goals, plans, and their interactions. Some vocabulary comes from the domain a story is about (e.g., in a post office story, stamps are often bought). Other vocabulary comes from the reasoner's needs and inferences as it is understanding a story (e.g., the need to know whether a chosen plan is likely to achieve the stated goal gives rise to the need for vocabulary items that express goal/plan relationships (plan is likely to achieve goal; plan is unlikely to achieve goal); the need to predict if resources are used well gives rise to a need for vocabulary items that express resource use (plan is likely to use more resources than available)). Such indexing makes it easy to recognize similarities across domains . When one indexes based on natural reasoning processes, it is easy to recognize the applicability of an old situation to a new one—both are described according to the same vocabulary—one based on processing needs.

It turns out that the UIF wasn't universal—it covered only intentional (social) situations. And when filled in, the index frame wasn't good enough as an index—it held too much in it and therefore didn't discriminate well enough. But it did turn out to be an excellent framework for describing cases at a level of detail from which indexes could be chosen.

We've been trying to apply this lesson in my lab as we develop indexing vocabularies to support our design projects. We've been working in a variety of domains and are aiming for a scheme that covers all of them. Our understanding of design processes has allowed us to come up with five dimensions of an indexing scheme for design stories that cuts across a variety of design domains (Griffith and Domeshek 1996 [Chapter 3 in this book]): functional subsystem the story is about; physical part it is about; issue it addresses; stakeholder it pertains to; and lifecycle stage it is about. We've applied the scheme to architectural design and to airplane hydraulic system design, among other domains. Of course, the particular vocabulary items are different for each. Building designers refer to different subsystems and different issues than do airplane designers. But the scheme applies to design stories from across design domains just as the UIF covers intentional situations in a variety of domains.

This discussion is not meant to imply that indexing vocabulary needs to be consistent across systems or unchanging over time. Some vocabulary may be idiosyncratic to different reasoners, each of which have different interests and goals. Some of the vocabulary will be derived over time as a reasoner discovers misconceptions that keep it from getting around as well as it could and new nuances that could help it perform better. It is important, of course, for systems that need to communicate with each other, especially across domains, to be able to translate from a communicating partner's vocabulary into their own. This is one job of situation assessment procedures. Over time, two communicating systems might adapt their indexing and descriptive vocabularies to match each other better.

The conclusion is this: Taking representation seriously means also taking seriously what those representations will be used for. Representations that make sense with respect to processing are the key to good reminding, knowledge access, and adaptation.

Learning

Learning and reasoning are intimately related to each other; one shouldn't approach one without taking the other into account. Failure is especially important as a trigger to learning—both failure of actions and failure of expectations.

I've said almost nothing about learning up to now, so why include it at the tail end of the paper? The reason is that CBR's ties between reasoning and learning have important implications for both case representation and indexing.

Recall that learning, in a CBR system, is primarily a byproduct of other reasoning processes and is triggered by the needs of reasoning processes. The reasoner's most pressing need is generally to perform effectively and efficiently in the world. This requires learning from analysis and examination of its experiences. Integration with the outside world is thus a crucial part of the paradigm and a crucial part of what should be represented in cases.

Does that mean that every case-based reasoning system needs to learn and that every case-based reasoning system needs to try out its solutions and get feedback from the world? I'd like to propose two answers, one for research systems, the other for fielded systems. For research systems, I must insist that the systems learn through some connection to the world. The connection might be an oracle (we tried this out and here's what happened) or it might be a real connection with sensors and effectors. If there is no ability to experience real-world lack of predictability, then the investigation will be too impoverished to provide critical analysis. CBR is built on the assumption that the world is regular; we are also aware that there are many unpredictable things that happen in the world. If our systems are to model real-world cognition, they must be prepared for real-world contingencies as well being able to deal with real-world regularities.

The answer for fielded systems is different but based on the same principle. Because we can't predict every real-world possibility, it is important that systems be piloted and tested in real-world situations. While every fielded system might not learn and every fielded system might not be intimately connected to the world, each should be designed taking into account what we know about the world, and each should have a significant learning phase as part of its development. Every fielded system should be piloted on real problems with collection of real feedback, with the results of this feedback integrated back into system. This will allow capturing in a system's representations and indexes those things that are learned through trial experience that are useful to the system's functioning.

Furthermore, looking at the conditions in which learning is triggered can guide us in determining the content of cases and indexes. Learning is often triggered by failure or failed expectations. These arise because of lack of knowledge, incomplete knowledge, or inability to anticipate response in the world. Some kinds of knowledge, if available, mitigate failure.

One reason for failure is inability to distinguish between several competing alternatives. This implies, among other things, that case representations should include outcome information. A system whose cases cover only the problems and responses of situations will be able to repeat the responses used earlier, but it will not be able to distinguish which of several alternative responses is best in any new situation without first trying the alternative out. A system whose cases, in addition, keep track of what happened as a result of carrying out some response will be able to reason about the relative goodness of one alternative over another by using outcome information from the old cases to predict outcome in the new situation.

Even better is for cases to capture an analysis of outcomes. Analyses of outcomes, if they represent why an outcome came about, will allow the reasoner to judge whether a past outcome is likely in the new situation.

Another reason for failure is inability to predict that a suggested alternative will fail, and a reason for inefficiency is consideration of too many possible courses of action. The implication here is that case-based systems should reason based on both successful and failed cases. Successful cases can suggest avenues to pursue. Failed cases, especially, those whose conditions are quite similar to successful ones, allow a reasoner to recognize the conditions under which a suggested alternative should be abandoned and to guide its reasoning away from the kinds of solutions that are likely to be flawed.

Yet another reason for failure is inability to predict a solution's behavior when carried out in the world. This implies that case-based systems should index their cases in ways that allow them to both come up with solutions and anticipate their potential for success.

Concluding Remarks

What should be taken away from this chapter? Those in the CBR community should see this as a first attempt at uncovering our tacit knowledge and in making the implicit explicit. This chapter is only a beginning to articulating the paradigm, the methodology, and the cognitive model. We need to be more aware of what our assumptions are, discussing them among ourselves and articulating them explicitly to the outside world. Case-based reasoning has the potential to change a lot in the way we look at intelligence and cognition. That change has already started. In order to reach full potential, we need to articulate case-based reasoning, its underlying assumptions, its conceptual foundations, and its implications in ways that the rest of the community will appreciate.

I hope those from the outside who are reading this take away two insights, first, the importance of focusing on representation and knowledge access both in building systems and in addressing new problems, and second, the notion that seeing case-based reasoning as a driver of cognition rather than an add-on allows us to look at important issues (such as chunking and knowledge access) in new and useful ways.

Notes

1. There's a difference, by the way, between "easily available" features (described in the previous paragraph) and "surface" features, but the principle relates to both: surface features make good indexes to the extent that they are predictive of something important or useful.

2. There's a challenge related to this, one I posed at the talk in summer, 1993: I'd like to see someone take a case-based approach to what Doug Lenat is doing with CYC. How would it be different? The major difference is that it would take access of knowledge (indexing) seriously.

17 What Next? The Future of Case-Based Reasoning in Post-Modern AI

Christopher K. Riesbeck

Case-based reasoning, (CBR)once the rallying point for anti-rule revolutionaries, has become an increasingly accepted part of the modern artificial intelligence toolbox. For example, a recent report on the ARPA/Rome Planning Initiative included several examples of large AI systems that involved several rule-based and case-based reasoning subsystems interacting to solve complex real-world problems (Fowler et al. 1995). Most calls for papers in modern AI conferences include CBR as one of the relevant topics.

Some may view this acceptance and proliferation of systems as success for CBR. On the other hand, some of us view it as a sign that the revolution has been co-opted, that the real point of CBR has been lost. Of course, this then raises the question, "What is the real point of CBR?"

In this chapter, I will argue that the real shift in AI has yet to come, and that CBR was just the opening act. The argument will proceed by answering the following questions:

- What is the point of case-based reasoning?
- What is (the point of) AI?
- What's the future of AI?
- What is the role of CBR in that future?

What Is the Point of Case-based Reasoning?

The original point of case-based reasoning was that people really don't think all that much, they remember, in both senses of the word "remember." First, we remember the things we do, including the thinking we do. Second, most of the time we don't need to think, we just have to remember what we thought before (Schank 1982). The first point was an obvious but revolutionary idea when first presented. It was obvious in that of course people remember what they do, but revolutionary in that virtually no problem solvers and story understanders did it. The primary exceptions were in planning, where some planners stored plans under the goals they achieved, usually for efficiency. Most machine learning programs, interestingly enough, did not remember the examples that they saw, only the generalizations that could be inferred from those examples. While they changed their behavior as the result of their experiences, they didn't remember those experiences.

At Yale, we found it particularly embarrassing to realize that our story understanders would do exactly the same thing no matter how many times they read the same story. They never got bored, they never realized that one story contradicted another, they were never reminded of Mary's burnt hot dog when reading about John's overcooked hamburger. This was intelligent story understanding?

The second point was—and remains—more controversial. How often do we really think and how often do we just re-use? The claim in Riesbeck and Schank (1989) was that people rarely "think," in the sense of performing the logiclike inferencing common to most AI systems. Rather, people respond to new situations by reusing memories of similar old situations.

> Real thinking has nothing to do with logic at all. Real thinking means retrieval of the right information at the right time (Riesbeck and Schank 1989, p. 9).

For example, repeat trips to Burger King® are handled by reusing memories of previous trips to Burger King®, if any, or by adapting memories of trips to McDonalds®, if any, or by trying to apply memories of other kinds of restaurants, repairing the expectation failures that result, and remembering those repairs for future reuse.

Early development of CBR systems focused on this reuse of real memories. Such systems began with retrieved cases, i.e., memories of past experiences, and adapted them to fit new situations. For example, Simpson's Mediator (Kolodner and Simpson 1989) retrieved and adapted cases of mediations, Hammond's Chef (Hammond 1989c) retrieved and adapted complete recipes, and Kass, Leake and Owens' Swale (Schank et al. 1994) retrieved and adapted old explanations to explain new anomalies. All of these systems used adaptation processes that *replaced* inappropriate details in retrieved cases with details from the current situation. The adaptation process was often quite complex and rulelike, leading many of the early researchers to propose case-based methods of doing adaptation and repair.

Old habits die hard, however, and as the use of CBR became more widespread, it began to take on a more rulelike flavor. Most modern CBR systems do not use episodic cases. It's much more common for them to retrieve "abstract cases" that are generalizations of real cases. These abstract cases are retrieved and applied by refinement processes that *add* details from the current situation, rather than replace details of old situations.

Some researchers have characterized case-based reasoning as "rule-based reasoning with very big rules." This comment only really applies to this modern "abstract CBR." Old-fashioned "true CBR" has two central processes not found in rule-based reasoning or abstract CBR:

- *Partial matching:* in true CBR, you don't find a matching case, you find the case that matches *best.* No case matches exactly in all details. Patterns may be used to organize and store generalizations about cases, but they are not themselves considered to be cases.

- *Adaptation:* in true CBR, you don't apply a case by filling in the details, you have to decide which details to throw away, which to replace, and which to keep.

Partial matching implies adaptation. If you allow the retrieval of cases that don't match the input situation exactly, you need adaptation to resolve the discrepancies. In short, abstract CBR starts with a template for an answer, and fills it in, while true CBR starts with an old answer, then works its way towards a good answer. This difference will become relevant when we discuss the role of CBR in the future of AI.

To summarize: the original point of CBR—the radical point—was to replace reasoning with the recall and adaptation of episodic knowledge.

What is (the Point of) AI?

Everyone has their own definition of AI and reasons why the other definitions don't work. A fair number of them are discussed in Russell and Norvig (1995), who then provide their own definition, which will be discussed shortly. I'd like to motivate my own definition by contrasting it to the following three very typical definitions:

> Artificial intelligence (AI) may be defined as the branch of computer science that is concerned with the automation of intelligent behavior (Luger and Stubblefield 1993, p. 1).

> *Artificial Intelligence:* The field of research concerned with making machines do things that people consider to require intelligence (Minsky 1986, p. 326).

> Artificial intelligence is the study of mental faculties through the use of computational models (Charniak and McDermott 1987, p. 6).

The first and second definitions focus on the term "intelligent." The problem with focusing on intelligence is that many of the most interesting tasks in AI are those that any jerk can do (walk, talk, nod appropriately during a lecture, and so on). Furthermore, there are activities, such as equation solving, or even simply multiplying very large numbers, that are considered to require intelligence if done by a human, but which, when performed on a computer, are not considered to be AI.

The third definition, perhaps in an attempt to be sensitive to the apparent irrelevance of intelligence, generalizes AI to cover any mental activity at all. But this seems to go too far, making AI a vehicle for any kind of psychology, and leaving out all the AI programs that bear no connection to modeling human cognitive processing.

In short, all of these definitions have the same basic problem: they include many things that are not AI, as it's conventionally construed, and exclude many things that are AI.

A New Definition of AI

My definition of AI comes at it from another angle, by focusing on what most people really want:

> Artificial intelligence is the search for answers to the eternal question: *Why are computers so stupid?*

That is, AI is a repair process. Cognitive science has, among others, the goal of understanding "what is intelligence?" AI has the goal of understanding "what is computer stupidity, and how can we get rid of it?"

AI as a repair process immediately explains the following oft-noted phenomenon: If it works, it's not AI any more. This effect occurs because once computers stop being stupid in that particular way, further work is not repairing the stupidity, but solving some other problem, e.g., making the process faster.

Focusing on repairing stupidity also explains why getting computers to do simple tasks like walking and talking seem more like real AI than tasks requiring great intelligence, for example:

- Not understanding simple sentences in context is stupid. Ergo, natural language understanding research is AI.
- Not being able to solve equations is not stupid. Ergo, numerical analysis is not AI.
- Not recognizing your own hand in front of your own face is stupid. Ergo, computer vision research is AI.
- Not learning from experience is stupid. Ergo, machine learning and case-based reasoning are AI.

There are some controversial implications of this definition:

- Not being able to play chess well is not stupid. Ergo, computer chess is not AI.
- Not being able to prove theorems is not stupid. Ergo, theorem proving is not AI.

- Not being an expert is not stupid. Ergo, expert systems are not AI.

I claim however that in fact the definition is right in these conclusions. These areas are AI by historical inertia. That is, the initial research was AI, but, like optical character recognition and symbolic equation solving, the AI motivation has long since been superseded by other goals. In particular:

- Building the world's best chess player is no more AI than building a video game.
- Building a powerful theorem prover is no more AI than building an equation solver.
- Building an "intelligent" job-shop scheduler is no more AI than building a normal job-shop scheduler

Saying that these things are not AI has nothing to do with whether they are worth doing. Being AI is not better or worse than not being AI. The goal of defining AI is not to make value judgments, but to 1) explain to ourselves and others what the point of AI is; 2) explain what makes the field coherent, i.e., how AI people working on very different problems can actually have something to say to each other; and 3) provide a vision as to where AI should go next.

With this definition, the answer to (1) is that as computers become ubiquitous in modern society, so do the effects of computer stupidity. More and more people are encountering stupidity in word processors, spreadsheets, payroll programs, Web browsers, educational software, and so on. The costs and dangers of computer stupidity are increasing daily. The point of AI, then, is to reduce those costs and dangers.

The answer to (2) is that the solutions to the many examples of stupidity come down to a small number of common basic techniques, such as explicit knowledge structures and case memory.

The answer to (3) is the topic of the next section.

What's the Future of AI?

I have a vision of *post-modern AI*. Obviously, this presumes a definition of modern AI. Fortunately, such a thing exists.

Modern AI: Intelligent Agents

In 1995, Russell and Norvig's *Artificial Intelligence: A Modern Approach* appeared, with the following statement:

> The unifying theme of the book is the concept of an *intelligent agent*. In this view, the problem of AI is to describe and build agents that receive percepts from the environment and perform actions (p. vii, [italics in original]).

Russell and Norvig use this theme to structure their textbook from beginning to end. Rather than simply reviewing the standard sequence of topics (search, knowledge representation, rule-based inference, etc.), everything is described in terms of how it can help build an autonomous intelligent agent.

Intelligent agents are indeed what most people, both inside and outside the field, probably view AI as being about. Robot vehicles, expert systems, chess players, automated text understanders, even software robots cruising the 'net—these all seem to qualify as intelligent agents. There's still that tricky bit about "intelligence," but we could reword the above to be "the problem of AI is to describe and build agents that aren't stupid." So let's assume that describing and building intelligent agents defines modern AI. What's wrong with that as a unifying goal for a field? Why do we need postmodern AI?

Problems with Intelligent Agents

I claim that there are two primary problems with making the development of autonomous intelligent agents the primary goal for AI:

- Intelligent agents are so far off that the goal doesn't help decision making in the here and now.
- Intelligent agents are not even what we want computers to be for a great many situations.

The goal of autonomous intelligent agents is too distant to drive near-term research and development. Viewed from the standpoint of this ultimate goal, all hard AI problems are of equal importance. It provides no guidance, no roadmap in trying to determine where the next big push should go. As a result, research decisions are made on the basis of where we are, rather than we want to be next. Someone with an inference engine will work on making it faster, adding new capabilities to it, or finding a new application for it. Someone with a natural language parser will make similar choices for it. It's hard to know what's really the best problem to tackle next, because the ultimate goal is so far off.

The intelligent agent theme is also inappropriate because it ignores a key difference between computers and people: computer programs rarely act as independent agents. They are components in larger systems in ways that people never are, except metaphorically. A computer in a car or a server on a network is not a free-standing entity. The communication protocols are far more rigid, and requests for real-time service far more demanding, than anything people can handle, or that an intelligent autonomous agent should want to put up with.

But if intelligent agents are both a distant and somewhat unnecessary goal, what should be the driving goal for AI?

Post-Modern AI: Intelligent Components

Following the textual form of Russell and Norvig, here is my theme for post-modern AI:

> The unifying theme of this chapter is the concept of *intelligent components*. In this view, the problem of AI is to describe and build components that reduce the stupidity of the systems in which they function.

That is, the goal should not be intelligent systems. The goal should be the improvement of how systems function through the development of intelligent parts to those systems. For example, I don't want an automated librarian. I want a library search program that isn't stupid. I want one that knows concepts, not keywords, that won't find James Cook when I'm researching great chefs in history. Central problems in post-modern AI are cases of stupidity that are common and severe across a large class of systems.

Though I've not seen the term "post-modern AI" before, much of this alternative view of AI can be found in other writings. For example, Chandrasekaran wrote the following in an editorial for *IEEE Expert* "AI, Knowledge, and the Quest for Smart Systems:"

> The public's definition of a smart product has nothing to do with ... the AI community's long-held goal of developing a general purpose intelligence. The public does not expect a smart system to do everything that people do. It does expect a smart product to be flexible, adaptive, and robust (p. 2).

If we differ, it would be on two points. First, I claim that the proper adjective isn't "smart" but "not stupid." For many reasons, some rational, some not, people don't want machines to be smart, but neither do they want them to be stupid. Second, I claim that this is not just a change in how AI should be applied in the real world, but in how the field of AI should define its ultimate goals and select strategies for achieving those goals.

Another point that distinguishes post-modern AI from modern AI is what each area means by "integration." Consider figure 1, taken from an article on an expert system for a data acquisition and control system for an electrical utility (Pfau-Wagenbauer 1993). The original caption said "The expert system *integrated* with Scada" [italics mine]. In the United States, this kind of integration leads to school bussing. That is, the systems reside in "separate but equal" areas, but they don't really have to talk to each other very much. This is exactly the level of integration that one would expect if the expert system is an autonomous intelligent agent. Integration for agents means "communicates with."

In post-modern AI, the AI becomes an invisible part of the overall system. In this, I am inspired in part by a vision articulated by Allen Newell at a panel, held at IJCAI–81, celebrating the twenty-fifth anniversary of the 1956 Dartmouth Conference. At one point, the participants were asked to predict the future of AI. Most gave the standard answer: intelligent thinking computers.

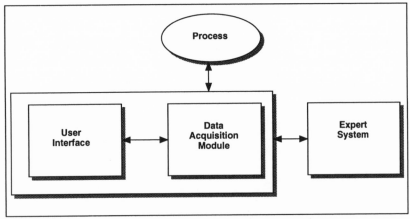

Figure 1. Integrating intelligent agents into other systems.
(Pfau-Wagenbauer, 1995, p. 13)

Newell had a different view. He envisioned not a single intelligent entity, but "a cognitive city," where traffic lights understood the flow of traffic and street lamps knew when people stood below them. His examples, at least as I remember them, are paradigmatic cases for post-modern AI. The goal is not "smart" appliances and cars that talk to us. The goal is street lamps that don't waste electricity on totally deserted sidewalks, and traffic lights that don't turn green for streets closed for construction. That is, the primary goal is to develop systems that aren't stupid, not systems that are intelligent. The intelligence that makes systems not stupid will be as unremarkable in those systems as it is in people.

Examples of Intelligent Components

I will now describe a few examples of intelligent components in systems built at the Institute for the Learning Sciences, in order to illustrate the differences between the intelligent agent and intelligent component approach, some of the different demands intelligent components must deal with, and some of the techniques that work well for intelligent components. The third item will bring us to the future of CBR.

The Casper Parsing Component

The Casper system was developed at the Institute for the Learning Sciences for North West Water, a privatized British water utility, to teach their customer service representatives (CSRs) how to diagnose water quality problems (Kass 1994a).

Casper was built by first designing a number of scenarios, e.g., a customer with a water problem caused by rust in a hot water tank, another with a problem caused by the mains (hydrants) being flushed recently, and so on. Then content analysts determined all the relevant questions, both good and bad, that a novice CSR might ask in those scenarios. Finally, actors playing customers recorded answers to those questions. A scenario usually has several hundred such question-answer pairs.

A student, playing the part of a customer service representative, interacts with the pre-recorded customers. To ask a question, a student can use a menu-based "question constructor." This is however somewhat unnatural and interrupts the flow of the dialog. Alternatively, the student can simply type what they want to say. Casper then lists the questions it has that best match the student's input, and the student either picks one, tries again, or uses the menus.

The student input is "understood" by an *indexed concept parser* (Fitzgerald, 1995), an intelligent component that works as follows: 1) The stored questions are indexed in advance by the sets of the basic concepts those questions refer to. 2) The student input text is mapped to a set of index concepts. 3) The stored questions are sorted by how well their index sets overlap with the input index set, and the best matches are presented. Full details appear in Fitzgerald (1995).

The key points for our purposes are as follows.

There's enough AI to avoid being stupid:

· Matching is done on concepts, not words
· Ambiguous words and phrases are handled smoothly
· Matching takes into account ISA relationships between index concepts
· The scoring algorithm gives more weight to matches between less commonly seen concepts.

There's only a little AI here:

· The concepts and stored questions have no internal structure.

The needs and capabilities of the system determine the scope and power of the parser:

· The system needs the stored question closest to what the student wanted, therefore, the job of the parser is to find that question, and no more.
· The system needs only very simple concept structures and inference rules to connect student actions to scenario events and tutoring responses, therefore, the parser must make do with very limited knowledge representations.
· The system is a feasible solution only if content analysts, not programmers, can maintain and add new scenarios easily and quickly, therefore, the pars-

```
IF the student makes a diagnosis of the problem
   AND there is not enough evidence for it
   THEN
      1. Ask the student to justify his or her diagnosis.
      2. Explain why the diagnosis is premature.
      3. Ask the student to retract the diagnosis statement.
      4. Help the student with the next problem-solving step.
```

Figure 2. A critiquing rule example, summarized in English.

er has to be no harder to maintain than the rest of the system.

In short, on the one hand, the job of the parsing component is made harder by the fact that Casper needs reliable and robust handling of real user inputs, with serious limitations on how much knowledge is present in the system. On the other hand, the job of the parsing component is made simpler by the fact that the system requires only the selection of stored questions, not the generation of novel meaning structures.

The Casper Critiquer

There are many kinds of mistakes students can make in Casper. Some are mistakes in reasoning, such as coming to a conclusion unjustified or even inconsistent with the existing evidence. Some are mistakes in procedure, such as asking leading questions like "Is the water tea colored?" or performing some action before it makes sense.

Responses to classic student mistakes are generated in advance by content experts. These responses consist of text and video commentary on various actions, as well as stories of what happened when CSR's made similar mistakes in real life.

Mistakes are recognized by the Casper tutoring module, an intelligent component that selects an appropriate pre-defined response, based on the type of mistake, and where in the task it occurred. An example of a critiquing rule, summarized in English, is depicted in figure 2. Full details appear in Jona (1995).

The key points for our purposes are:

There's enough AI to avoid being stupid:
- Causal and diagnostic rules make the obvious connections, e.g., "rusty pipes cause rust flakes in water which causes brownish water," and "black bits in water implies possible flaking lead pipes."
  - Evidence rules catch the obvious mistakes in hypothesis formation, such as

failing to eliminate all other likely possibilities, or having only weak evidence for a conclusion.

There's only a little AI here:

• The critiques are basically canned templates.

The needs and capabilities of the system determine the scope and power of the critiquer:

• The system needs the most relevant of the pre-defined critiques retrieved at the right time. Therefore, the critiquer doesn't have to generate critiques, but it does have to avoid finding obviously irrelevant ones.

• The critiquing rules must be maintainable by the same people who maintain the rest of the system.

In short, on the one hand, the critiquing component has to be reliable and robust enough to help, rather than annoy. On the other hand, the critiquing component does not have to do anything more than what Casper needs, which is to point out mistakes that Casper knows about, and get the student back on track.

Casper differs from a classic intelligent tutoring system in several ways. First, Casper is not a model of a tutor, but of an environment. The environment has been modified to make learning easier, but the simulated environment remains the focal point. Second, Casper is not a domain expert. Casper has a crude causal model of the domain and of the diagnostic task. Finally, Casper does not try to model the student. It has only a simple ontology of actions and mistakes. In short, the *system* Casper is not intelligent. It does, however, have some not-so-stupid components, namely the parser and the critiquer.

The Creanimate Parser

Creanimate (Edelson 1995) is a program developed to get children to understand how the particular features and behaviors of different animals relate to the kinds of goals those animals have. Creanimate does this by engaging a child in a dialog about designing a new animal, based on modifying some existing animal, and showing lots of short, interesting videos about animals and the things they do.

One component of Creanimate is a DMAP parser (Martin 1993) that maps short phrases typed by students to internal frame structures, e.g., from "find female spiders" to find-mate (Fitzgerald 1995). As in Casper, the job of the parser isn't to construct meaning structures, but to find the most relevant existing concepts in memory. Full details appear in Edelson (1993) and Fitzgerald (1995). The key points for our purposes are:

There's enough AI to avoid being stupid:

• The parser can map the words such as "chase after gazelles" to the underlying concepts for hunting gazelles.

- Taxonomic relationships link points such as using speed to catch gazelles to using speed to catch prey in general.

  There's only a little AI here:
- The videos are "black boxes" to the rest of the system. There's no image processing or detailed representation of the events in the videos.
- There's no model of the student.

  The needs and capabilities of the system determine the scope and power of the parser:
- All "understanding" means here is finding the point stored in Creanimate closest enough to what the student meant to keep the dialog coherent.
- The parser must be maintainable by the same people who maintain the rest of the system.

In short, on the one hand, the parsing component has to be reliable and robust enough not to interfere with the flow of the dialog. On the other hand, the parsing component does not have to do any more than get to something Creanimate can talk about that's consistent with what the student just said.

Select and Adapt: The Secret of Intelligent Components

On the one hand, life is hard for intelligent component designers. They're not in control of what the component gets, what it has to produce, or how fast it has to produce it. Even worse, a component can only require a level of engineering and maintenance work commensurate with the value the component adds to the system as a whole. For example, the lexicon and knowledge representation aspects of the parsing components in Casper and Creanimate had to be relatively easy to engineer and maintain, because parsing was not a central component of those systems. Creanimate represented knowledge with a hierarchical frame system that the parser could take advantage of. Casper did not need such sophisticated representations. Therefore a parsing component had to be designed that could make do with less, because the effort and skills required to create such representations was more than the parsing component was worth.

On the other hand, designing an intelligent component can be orders of magnitude simpler than designing an intelligent agent, because of strong limitations in the needs and capabilities of the rest of the system. Thus, the parsing component in Creanimate didn't have to understand everything a kid could type, only those things that referred to concepts that Creanimate knew about. The parsing component in Casper didn't have to understand everything a customer service representative might ask, only those questions that Casper was prepared to handle.

Recognizing and taking advantage of the limits and capabilities of the bigger system is the secret of building intelligent components that are robust and

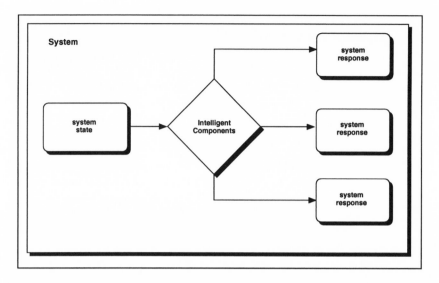

Figure 3. Integrating intelligent components into other systems.

successful. Artificial intelligence, like linguistics and computer science, has too long been concerned with being able to generate potentially infinite sets of responses In fact, many real systems are like Casper and Creanimate. They have very few things they can do. The problem is getting from a very large number of situations to the most appropriate response.

The key problem for systems like Casper and Creanimate is *selection,* not construction. That is, the job of the parser was not to construct a meaning, but to help the system select the most appropriate pre-defined response template, from a relatively small set. The job of the critiquer was to select the most appropriate pre-defined critiquing templates.

Figure 3 shows how an intelligent component is integrated, and is intended to contrast directly with figure 1. In figure 3, the component is an integral part of the larger system. The job of the component is to help the system choose a response good enough to meet the system's needs in a timely fashion. Figure 3 is, I believe, an accurate abstraction of how the parsers and critiquing components discussed earlier are integrated into Casper and Creanimate.

Select and Adapt Versus Generate and Test

There are two arguments for select and adapt rather than the classic AI paradigm of generate and test for intelligent components.

First, many systems have a finite set of possible response branches that they can follow, e.g., *x, y* and *z.* If a component generates (constructs) representational structures, then the rest of the system has to map those structures to branch *x, y* or *z*. Such mapping is extra run-time work for the system, and extra build-time work for the system maintainers. The rules or tables that perform the mapping are one more place where things can break, and one more reason not to use "that AI stuff."

An intelligent component that *generates* responses, in other words, forces the rest of the system to become smarter, in order to understand those responses. A component that *selects* from the responses built into the system adds no extra effort to the rest of the system.

The second problem with generate and test is one of timeliness. It's often hard to put time-bounds on generative processes. Two general methods of generation are 1) assembly from parts, and 2) refinement from templates. If you prematurely stop either process, you get an incomplete, nonfunctional solution.

A selection processes, on the other hand, can be designed to start with a default complete answer. The answer may be wrong, but nothing is missing. Given more time, it can be replaced with better solutions, or the bad parts modified. At any point in time, there's an answer available. One might call this a "shoot first and ask questions later" approach.

Chess playing programs (whether they're AI or not) have this capability because they're always selecting moves from the set of possible legal moves. If you stop a chess program early, there's some move it can give that's the best choice so far. You could write a chess program that started with strategic goals (control center, reduce threat), and refined them into particular moves, but then you would no longer be able to interrupt it and ask it to move immediately.

In order for select and adapt to avoid the same problems as generate and test, adaptation has to be carefully limited. Many CBR systems avoid adaptation entirely. They are problem solving assistants that simply retrieve relevant prior examples for a human user to consider when solving some problem. The Casper and Creanimate systems also needed no adaptation after retrieving a stored question or concept. The Casper critiquer and the Creanimate dialog manager only had to instantiate text templates to create bridging introductions to the canned videos.

Ideally, then, two properties should be true of select and adapt algorithms used in intelligent components:

- The selection process should be an "anytime" algorithm (Dean and Boddy 1988) that quickly retrieves a real answer. It can replace that answer later with a better one, but it's never at a loss for some answer.
- The adaptation process, if needed, should be quick and never leave the adapted answer in an unusable state for very long.

CBR is a Select and Adapt Algorithm

CBR systems inspired by research on human reminding, i.e., the truest of the true CBR systems, typically have an "anytime" capability. That is, they find some answer almost immediately, then, given more time, they adapt it, or replace it with a better reminding. Examples of such systems include MEDIATOR (Kolodner and Simpson 1989), Protos (Bareiss 1989a) and Swale (Schank et al. 1994).

Saving and reusing adapted answers helps to overcome the strong limitations on adaptation just described. Even though any particular adaptation episode may be limited because of time and resource constraints, over time better and better answers are constructed, because later adaptations begin with the results of previous adaptations and repairs.

An early example of this is in CHEF (Hammond 1989c). CHEF's adaptation rules were probably more complex than appropriate for a small intelligent component, but they were still quite limited. Most plan step interactions were simply not recognized, such as the fact that stir frying beef and broccoli together might lead to soggy broccoli because of the water generated from the cooking beef. However, when those interactions led to execution failures, the repaired recipes, e.g., cook beef and broccoli separately, were stored in memory and made available to later problem solving situations. Thus, even though the adaptation process in CHEF was too limited to catch such interactions in general, common interactions were learned and added to the system's repertoire.

Case-based Intelligent Components

Case-based intelligent components, as illustrated in figure 4, select (and optionally adapt) system responses from an indexed store of response selections that is dynamically extended as the system runs over time.

I believe that there are some simple ways in which practical case-based components can be developed right now, but that the role of intelligent component also suggests some significant research problems. In the short term, I see three feasible kinds of case-based intelligent components: First, generalized situation-response caches, using surface feature indices to provide simple caching of answers to apply old answers to new situations that "any moron" would see are the same. Second, case memories for knowledge-based intelligent systems, including rule-based ones, using the deep feature indices already present in the larger system. Third, embedded browsable case bases, using topic indices and inter-case cross-links to support user-driven retrieval.

Situation-Response Caches

Caching responses to commonly asked requests is a well-known technique that is common in low-level processes, like disk accesses, but under-used in higher-level software. Caching reduces a major form of stupidity, namely redoing the same work every time a problem is solved, no matter how many times that kind of problem has already been solved.

One reason why caching is not used in systems supporting human problem solving is that as situations become more complex, the likelihood decreases of

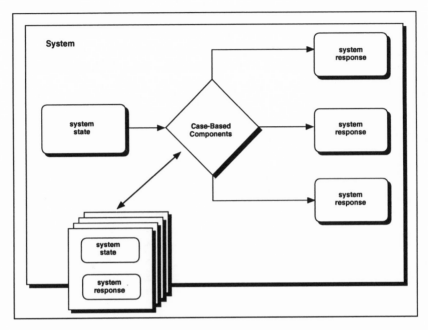

Figure 4. A case-based intelligent component.

seeing exactly the same situation again. This of course is what partial matching and adaptation in CBR is supposed to solve. Often the differences between two situations can be inferred to be irrelevant, using just a little bit of knowledge.

The inferencing needed to do the partial matching (and adaptation, if required) must be limited, otherwise the development and maintenance costs of adding a case-based cache will outweigh the benefits. For this reason, I think that approaches using surface features are currently the most appropriate. Several inductive techniques for case-based learning are discussed in Aha (1991), and a partial matcher for dealing with noise in DNA sequences is described in Shavlik (1991) These and similar approaches allow cases to be stored and retrieved with very little knowledge engineering effort. They extend exact-match caching to handle situations that are "obviously" the same. Such approaches are of course limited to very narrowly scoped case bases, but this is often exactly the kind of case base a larger system is generating.

Case Bases for Intelligent Systems

Case bases for intelligent systems are feasible because the representational work has already been done for the rest of the system. Adding the CBR component does not significantly increase knowledge maintenance needs. An early example of an adjunct system is Casey (Koton 1988c), where a CBR system ran in conjunction with a model- based diagnostic system.

One potential stupidity in this kind of system is spending more time adapting a retrieved case than would have been required to solve it using the rules. JUDGE (Riesbeck and Schank 1989) and PRODIGY (Veloso and Carbonell 1991) give two very different approaches to guessing when it isn't worth using a case.

Browsable Case Bases

Browsable case bases achieve feasibility by paring the notion of CBR to the bone. ASK systems (Ferguson et al. 1991), for example, are browsable corporate memories in which there is not only no adaptation, but no retrieval as well! Instead, there's a case-base, partially indexed with topics and richly indexed with inter-case links. The end user uses the topics to "zoom" to an initial case and then follows the links to other cases. The links in ASK systems are based on conversational coherence principles, but intercase links of some form are part of many early true CBR systems, such as MEDIATOR (Kolodner and Simpson 1989) and Protos (Bareiss 1989a).

ASK systems provide some of the "job aid" memory of a case-based retriever, in a form that allows systems to be built and maintained by content analysts, rather than AI programmers or knowledge engineers.

Research Goals for Case-Based Intelligent Components

Looking to the future, I see several research areas for CBR relevant to making CBR feasible for intelligent components in non-intelligent systems.

Indexing

Indexing in CBR tends to be either a major effort or almost no effort at all. Systems using surface features, as described above, require little knowledge engineering, but don't support cases from multiple domains. Systems like Swale (Schank et al. 1994) use fairly complex, inferred features as case indices, in order to support retrieval of the most relevant case from very disparate domains. This of course requires significant representational effort.

A research area then is broadening the range of case bases that can be indexed without incurring development and maintenance costs greater than the value added by the broader range. Such research includes the development of well-defined indexing methodologies, to lower the costs of developing and applying indexing vocabularies; libraries of indexing vocabularies, (and here I believe that many libraries of specific vocabularies will be more useful than a few libraries of very abstract concepts); and semi-automated indexing assistants, to assist indexers in applying indices to large case bases. One example is described in Osgood and Bareiss (1993).

Adaptation

Adaptation has always had a mixed status in CBR. On the one hand, adaptation is the "reasoning" part of "case-based reasoning." Furthermore, most early CBR work focussed on the development and application of adaptation strategies, such as parameterization and abstraction/respecialization (Riesbeck and Schank 1989). On the other hand, adaptation is usually the weak link in a CBR system. Adaptation techniques are hard to generalize, hard to implement, and quick to break. Furthermore, adaptation is often unnecessary. The originally retrieved case is often as useful to a human as any half-baked adaptation of it.

For intelligent components, adaptation techniques have to be far more robust than they currently are, far easier to define and support, and of far greater value to the system as a whole. Furthermore, the techniques have to work incrementally, so that there's an answer available any time one is asked for. For example, an adaptation technique that removes all details specific to the old situation before replacing them with details from the new situation would not be suitable, because the partially empty case would not be a usable intermediate answer.

A research area then is the development of incremental adaptation techniques. As with indexing vocabularies, I personally believe that developing libraries of fairly specific techniques is of greatest value.

An interesting approach to try is splitting adaptation techniques into quick fixers that rapidly fix problems in a retrieved case, and optimizers that remove inefficiencies in the results produced by the quick fixers. For example, when a recipe that chops vegetable is applied to situation calling for two vegetables, the quick fixer creates a recipe with two chopping steps. The quick fixer then calls its associated optimizer to see if the two chopping steps can be merged. The key point though is that the recipe with two steps is available for use, if the rest of the system needs it. The quick fixer makes sure that the adapter isn't so "stupid" that it doesn't even realize it has to chop two ingredients.

Conclusion

The argument above can be summarized as follows:

- AI should focus on the development of intelligent components rather than intelligent agents, because 1) we need systems that aren't stupid more than systems that are smart, and 2) we need nearer-term objectives than autonomous intelligent agents to focus current AI research strategies.
- Select and adapt is a better control structure for intelligent agents than generate and test.
- CBR's future is in the development of intelligent components that select and adapt true cases from dynamic memories.

18 Bibliography

Aamodt, A. 1994. Explanation-Driven Case-Based Reasoning. In *Topics in Case-Based Reasoning*, eds. S. Wess, K. Althoff, and M. Richter, 274–288. Berlin: Springer Verlag.

Aamodt, A., and Plaza, E. 1994. Case-Based Reasoning: Foundational Issues, Methodological Variations, and System Approaches. *AI Communications* 7(1): 39–52.

Acorn, T., and Walden, S. 1992. SMART: Support Management Automated Reasoning Technology for Compaq Customer Service. In *Innovative Applications of Artificial Intelligence 4*, 3–18. Menlo Park, Calif.: AAAI Press.

Aha, D., ed. 1996. *Artificial Intelligence Review* (Special Issue on Lazy Learning). Norwell, Mass.: Kluwer. Forthcoming.

Aha, D., ed. 1994. *Proceedings of the AAAI-94 Workshop on Case-Based Reasoning.* Technical Report WS-94-01. Menlo Park, Calif.: AAAI Press.

Aha, D. W. 1992. Generalizing from Case Studies: A Case Study. In Proceedings of the Ninth International Conference on Machine Learning, 1–10. San Francisco, Calif.: Morgan Kaufmann.

Aha, D. 1991. Case-Based Learning Algorithms. *Proceedings of the DARPA Case-Based Reasoning Workshop,* 147-158. San Francisco: Morgan Kaufmann.

Aha, D., and Branting, K. 1995. Stratified Case-Based Reasoning: Reusing Hierarchical Problem Solving Episodes. In Proceedings of the Thirteenth International Joint Conference on Artificial Intelligence, 384–390. Menlo Park, Calif.: International Joint Conferences on Artificial Intelligence.

Aha, D., and Ram, A. 1995. Preface. Adaptation of Knowledge for Reuse: Papers from the 1994 Fall Symposium, v. Technical Report FS-95-04, American Association for Artificial Intelligence, Menlo Park, Calif.

Aha, D.; Kibler, D.; and Albert, M. 1991. Instance-Based Learning Algorithms. *Machine Learning* 6:37–66.

Allemang, D. 1993. Review of the First European Workshop on Case-Based Reasoning (EWCBR-93). *Case-Based Reasoning Newsletter* 2(3), December 22.

Alterman, R. 1988. Adaptive Planning. *Cognitive Science* 12:393–422.

Alterman, R. 1986. An Adaptive Planner. In Proceedings of the Fifth National Conference on Artificial Intelligence, 65–69. Menlo Park, Calif.: American Association for Artificial Intelligence.

Althoff, K.-D., and Wess, S. 1991. Case-Based Knowledge Acquisition, Learning, and Problem Solving for Diagnostic Real-World Tasks. In Proceedings of the European Knowledge Acquisition Workshop, 48–67. Glasgow, Scotland: EKAW.

Althoff, K.-D.; Barletta, R.; Manago, M.; and Auriol, E. 1995. *A Review of Industrial Case-Based Reasoning Tools.* Oxford, U.K.: AI Intelligence.

Anderson, J. R. 1983. *The Architecture of Cognition.* Cambridge, Mass.: Harvard University Press.

Anick, P., and Simoudis, E., eds. 1993. *Proceedings of the 1993 AAAI Spring Symposium on Case-Based Reasoning and Information Retrieval,* Technical Report WS-93-07. Menlo Park, Calif.: AAAI Press.

Arcos, J., and Plaza, E. 1994. A Reflective Architecture for Integrated Memory-Based Learning and Reasoning. In *Topics in Case-Based Reasoning,* eds. S. Wess, K. Althoff, and M. Richter, 289–300. Berlin: Springer Verlag.

Arkin, R. C. 1989. Motor Schema-Based Mobile Robot Navigation. *International Journal of Robotics Research* 84:92–112.

Armengol, E., and Plaza, E. 1994. Integrating Induction in a Case-Based Reasoner. In Proceedings of the Second European Workshop on Case-Based Reasoning, 243–251. Chantilly, France: EWCBR.

Ashley, K. 1990. *Modeling Legal Argument: Reasoning with Cases and Hypotheticals.* Cambridge, Mass.: MIT Press.

Ashley, K., and Aleven, V. 1991. A Computational Approach to Explaining Case-Based Concepts of Relevance in a Tutorial Context. In *Proceedings of the Case-Based Reasoning Workshop 1991,* 257–268. San Francisco, Calif.: Morgan Kaufmann.

Ashley, K., and Rissland, E. 1987a. Compare and Contrast, a Test of Expertise. In Proceedings of the Sixth National Conference on Artificial Intelligence, 273–284. Menlo Park, Calif.: American Association for Artificial Intelligence.

Ashley, K., and Rissland, E. L. 1987b. But, See, Accord: Generating Blue Book Citations in HYPO. In Proceedings of the First International Conference on AI and Law, 67–74. New York: Association for Computing Machinery.

Auriol, E.; Wess, S.; Manago, M.; Althoff, K.-D.; and Traphoener, R. 1995. INRECA: A Seamlessly Integrated System Based on Inductive Inference and Case-Based Reasoning. In *Proceedings of the First International Conference on Case-Based Reasoning,* 371–380. Berlin: Springer Verlag.

Badaracco, J. 1991. *The Knowledge Link.* Cambridge, Mass.: Harvard Business School Press.

Bain, W. 1989. JUDGE. In *Inside Case-Based Reasoning,* eds. C. Riesbeck and R. Schank, 93–140. Hillsdale, N.J.: Lawrence Erlbaum.

Barber, J.; Bhatta, S.; Goel, A.; Jacobsen, M.; Pearce, M.; Penberthy, L.; Shankar, M.; and Stroulia, E. 1992. AskJef: Integrating Case-Based Reasoning and Multimedia Technologies for Interface Design Support. In *Artificial Intelligence in Design,* ed. J. Gero, 457–476. Norwell, Mass.: Kluwer.

Bareiss, R., ed. 1991. *Proceedings of the DARPA Case-Based Reasoning Workshop.* San Francisco, Calif.: Morgan Kaufmann.

Bareiss, R. 1989a. *Exemplar-Based Knowledge Acquisition: A Unified Approach to Concept Representation, Classification, and Learning.* San Diego, Calif.: Academic.

Bareiss, R. 1989b. The Experimental Evaluation of a Case-Based Learning Apprentice. In Proceedings of the Case-Based Reasoning Workshop, 162–167. Chantilly, France: EWCBR.

Barletta, R. 1994. A Hybrid Indexing and Retrieval Strategy for Advisory CBR Systems Built with REMIND. In Proceedings of the Second European Workshop on Case-Based Reasoning, 49–58. Chantilly, France: EWCBR.

Barletta, R., and Hennessy, D. 1989. Case Adaptation in Autoclave Layout Design. In *Proceedings of the DARPA Case-Based Reasoning Workshop*, ed. K. Hammond, 203–207. San Francisco, Calif.: Morgan Kaufmann.

Barletta, R., and Mark, W. 1988a. Explanation-Based Indexing of Cases. In *Proceedings of the Case-Based Reasoning Workshop 1988*, 50–60. San Francisco, Calif.: Morgan Kaufmann.

Barletta, R., and Mark, W. 1988b. Explanation-Based Indexing of Cases. In Proceedings of the Seventh National Conference on Artificial Intelligence, 541–546. Menlo Park, Calif.: American Association for Artificial Intelligence.

Barr, A.; Feigenbaum, E. A.; and Cohen, P. 1981. *The Handbook of Artificial Intelligence*. Reading, Mass.: Addison-Wesley.

Bartsch-Spoerl, B. 1995. Toward the Integration of Case-Based, Schema-Based, and Model-Based Reasoning for Supporting Complex Design Tasks. In *Proceedings of the First International Conference on Case-Based Reasoning*, 145–156. Berlin: Springer Verlag.

Bell, B.; Kedar, S.; and Bareiss, R. 1994. Interactive Model-Driven Case Adaptation for Instructional Software Design. In *Proceedings of the Sixteenth Annual Conference of the Cognitive Science Society*, 33–38. Hillsdale, N.J.: Lawrence Erlbaum.

Bento, C. 1994. A Similarity Metric for Retrieval of Cases Imperfectly Explained. In *Topics in Case-Based Reasoning*, 92–105, eds. S. Wess, K. Althoff, and M. Richter. Berlin: Springer Verlag.

Berger, J. 1995a. ROENTGEN: A Case-Based Radiation Therapy Planner. Ph.D. diss., Computer Science dept., University of Chicago.

Berger, J. 1995b. Using Past Repair Episodes. Unpublished manuscript.

Berger, J., and Hammond, K. 1991. ROENTGEN: A Memory-Based Approach to Radiation Therapy Treatment. In *Proceedings of the DARPA Case-Based Reasoning Workshop*, ed. R. Bareiss, 203–214. San Francisco, Calif.: Morgan Kaufmann.

Bhansali, S., and Harandi, M. T. 1993. Synthesis of UNIX Programs Using Derivational Analogy. *Machine Learning* 10.

Bhatnagar, R. K. 1989. Construction of Preferred Causal Hypotheses for Reasoning with Uncertain Knowledge. Ph.D. thesis, Dept. of Computer Science, University of Maryland.

Bhatta, S., and Goel, A. 1993. Model-Based Learning of Structural Indices to Design Cases. Presented at the IJCAI-93 Workshop on Reuse of Designs, Chambery, France, 29 August.

Bhatta, S.; Goel, A.; and Prabhakar, S. 1994. Innovation in Analogical Design: A Model-Based Approach. In *Artificial Intelligence in Design*, ed. J. Gero, 57–74. Norwell, Mass.: Kluwer.

Birnbaum, L. A. 1986. Integrated Processing in Planning and Understanding. Ph.D diss., Dept. of Computer Science, Yale University.

Birnbaum, L.; Collins, G.; Brand, M.; Freed, M.; Krulwich, B.; and Pryor, L. 1991. A Model-Based Approach to the Construction of Adaptive Case-Based Planning Systems. In *Proceedings of the DARPA Case-Based Reasoning Workshop*, ed. R. Bareiss, 215–224. San Francisco, Calif.: Morgan Kaufmann.

Blevis, E., and Kass, A. 1991. Teaching by Means of Social Simulation. In Proceedings of the International Conference on the Learning Sciences, 45–51. Charlottesville, Va.: Association for the Advancement of Computing in Education.

Blumenthal, B. 1990. *Replaying Episodes of a Metaphoric Application Interface Designer.* Ph.D. diss., Artificial Intelligence Lab, University of Texas at Austin.

Boden, M. 1990. *The Creative Mind: Myths and Mechanisms.* New York: Basic.

Böerner, K. 1994. Structural Similarity as Guidance in Case-Based Design. In *Topics in Case-Based Reasoning,* eds. S. Wess, K. Althoff, and M. Richter, 197–208. Berlin: Springer Verlag.

Brachman, R. J. 1985. An Overview of the KL-ONE Knowledge Representation System. *Cognitive Science* 9:171–216.

Bradtke, S., and Lehnert, W. G. 1988. Some Experiments with Case-Based Search. In Proceedings of the Seventh National Conference on Artificial Intelligence, 133–138. Menlo Park, Calif.: American Association for Artificial Intelligence.

Branting, L. K. 1991a. Building Explanations from Rules and Structured Cases. *International Journal of Man-Machine Studies* 34:797–837.

Branting, L. K. 1991b. Integrating Rules and Precedents for Classification and Explanation: Automating Legal Analysis. Ph.D. diss., Computer Science Dept., University of Texas at Austin.

Branting, L. K. 1989. Integrating Generalizations with Exemplar-Based Reasoning. In Proceedings of the Eleventh Annual Conference of the Cognitive Science Society, 139–146. Ann Arbor, Mich.: Cognitive Science Society.

Branting, L. K., and Aha, L. 1995. Stratified Case-Based Reasoning: Reusing Hierarchical Problem-Solving Episodes. In Proceedings of the Fourteenth International Joint Conference on Artificial Intelligence, 384–390. Menlo Park, Calif.: International Joint Conferences on Artificial Intelligence.

Branting, L. K., and Porter, B. 1991. Rules and Precedents as Complementary Warrants. In Proceedings of the Ninth National Conference on Artificial Intelligence, 3–9. Menlo Park, Calif.: American Association for Artificial Intelligence.

Bratman, M. 1987. *Intentions, Plans, and Practical Reason.* Cambridge, Mass.: Harvard University Press.

Buchanan, B. G., and Shortliffe, E. H. 1985. *Rule-Based Expert Systems.* Reading, Mass.: Addison-Wesley.

Buckley, C. 1985. Implementation of the SMART Information Retrieval Retrieval [sic] System, Technical Report, 85-686, Dept. of Computer Science, Cornell University.

Building Diagnostics. 1988. Post-Occupancy Evaluation: New Bedford County Courthouse, CBR85-ISTU, Office of Programming, Division of Capital Planning and Operations, Boston, Mass.

Burke, R. 1993. Representation, Storage, and Retrieval of Stories in a Guided Social Simulation. Ph.D diss., Dept. of Electrical Engineering and Computer Science, Northwestern University. Also Technical Report, 50, Institute for the Learning Sciences, Northwestern University.

Burke, R. 1992. Knowledge Acquisition and Education: A Case for Stories. Presented at the Symposium on Cognitive Aspects of Knowledge Acquisition, Stanford, Calif., March, 1992.

Burke, R., and Kass, A. 1992. Integrating Case Presentation with Simulation-Based Learning-by-Doing. In *Proceedings of the Fourteenth Annual Conference of the Cognitive Science Society,* 629–634. Hillsdale, N.J.: Lawrence Erlbaum.

Burstein, M. 1989. Analogy versus CBR: The Purpose of Mapping. In *Proceedings of the DARPA Case-Based Reasoning Workshop,* ed. K. Hammond, 133–136. San Francisco, Calif.: Morgan Kaufmann.

Bylander, T.; Allemang, D.; Tanner, C.; and Josephson, J. 1991. The Computational Complexity of Abduction. *Artificial Intelligence* 49:25–60.

Cain, T.; Pazzani, M.; and Silverstein, G. 1991. Using Domain Knowledge to Influence Similarity Judgement. In *Proceedings of the Case-Based Reasoning Workshop.* San Francisco: Morgan Kaufmann.

Carbonell, J. G. 1986. Derivational Analogy: A Theory of Reconstructive Problem Solving and Expertise Acquisition. In *Machine Learning: An Artificial Intelligence Approach, Volume 2,* eds. R. Michalski, J. Carbonell, and T. Mitchell, 371–392. San Francisco, Calif.: Morgan Kaufmann.

Carbonell, J. G. 1983. Learning by Analogy: Formulating and Generalizing Plans from Past Experience. In *Machine Learning: An Artificial Intelligence Approach,* eds. R. Michalski, J. Carbonell, and T. Mitchell, 137–162. San Francisco, Calif.: Morgan Kaufmann.

Carbonell, J. G., Blythe, J.; Etzioni, O.; Gil, Y.; Joseph, R.; Kahn, D.; Knoblock, C.; Minton, S.; Pérez, A.; Reilly, S.; Veloso, M.; and Wang, X. 1992. PRODIGY 4.0: The Manual and Tutorial, Technical Report, CMU-CS-92-150, School of Computer Science, Carnegie Mellon University.

Chandler, T. 1994. The Science Education Advisor: Applying a User Centered Design Approach to the Development of an Interactive Case-Based Advising System. *Journal of Artificial Intelligence in Education* 5(2): 283–319.

Chandler, T., and Kolodner, J. L. 1993. The Science Education Advisor: A Case-Based Advising System for Lesson Planning. Presented at the World Conference on Artificial Intelligence in Education, Edinburgh Scotland, August.

Chandrasekaran, B. 1994. AI, Knowledge, and the Quest for Smart Systems. *IEEE Expert* 9(6): 2–5.

Chandrasekaran, B. 1990. Design Problem Solving: A Task Analysis. *AI Magazine* 11(4): 59–71.

Chandrasekaran, B. 1988. Generic Tasks as Building Blocks for Knowledge-Based Systems: The Diagnosis and Routine-Design Examples. *Knowledge Engineering Review* 3:183–219.

Chapman, D. 1987. Planning for Conjunctive Goals. *Artificial Intelligence* 32:333–377.

Charniak, E., and McDermott, D. 1987. *Introduction to Artificial Intelligence.* Reading, Mass.: Addison-Wesley.

Chi, M. T. H.; Feltovich, P.; and Glaser, R. 1981. Categorization and Representation of Physics Problems by Experts and Novices. *Cognitive Science* 5:121–152.

Cohen, P. R. 1989. Evaluation and Case-Based Reasoning. In Proceedings of the Case-Based Reasoning Workshop, 168–172. Chantilly, France: EWCBR

Cohen, P. R., and Howe, A. E. 1989. Toward AI Research Methodology: Three Case Studies in Evaluation. *IEEE Transactions on Systems, Man, and Cybernetics* 19(3): 634–646.

Cohen, P. R., and Howe, A. E. 1988. How Evaluation Guides AI Research. *AI Magazine* 9(4): 35–43.

Cook, D. 1991. The Base Selection Task in Analogical Planning. In Proceedings of the Twelfth International Conference on Artificial Intelligence. Menlo Park, Calif.: International Joint Conferences on Artificial Intelligence.

Cox, M. 1994. Machines That Forget: Learning from Retrieval Failure of Mis-Indexed Explanations. In *Proceedings of the Sixteenth Annual Conference of the Cognitive Science Society,* 225–230. Hillsdale, N.J.: Lawrence Erlbaum.

Cunningham, P.; Bonzano, A.; and Smyth, B. 1995. An Incremental Case Retrieval Mechanism for Diagnosis, Technical Report, TCD-CS-95-01, Dept. of Computer Science, Trinity College.

Cuthill, B. 1992. Situation Analysis, Precedent Retrieval, and Cross-Context Reminding in Case-Based Reasoning. Ph.D. diss., Dept. of Computer Science, University of Connecticut. Also Technical Report, CSE-TR-92-3, Dept. of Computer Science, University of Connecticut.

Dean, T., and Boddy, M. 1988. An Analysis of Time-Dependent Planning. In Proceedings of the Seventh National Conference on Artificial Intelligence, 49–54. Menlo Park, Calif.: American Association for Artificial Intelligence.

DeJong, G., and Mooney, R. 1986. Explanation-Based Learning: An Alternative View. *Machine Learning* 1:145–176.

de Kleer, J., and Brown, J. 1984. A Qualitative Physics Based on Confluences. *Artificial Intelligence* 24:7–83.

Dewey, J. 1916. *Democracy and Education: An Introduction to the Philosophy of Education.* New York: Macmillan.

Domeshek, E. 1992. Do the Right Thing: A Component Theory for Indexing Stories as Social Advice. Ph.D. diss., Dept. of Computer Science, Yale University. Also Technical Report, 26, Institute for the Learning Sciences, Northwestern University.

Domeshek, E. A., and Kolodner, J. L. 1993. Using the Points of Large Cases. *Artificial Intelligence for Engineering Design, Analysis, and Manufacturing* 7(2): 87–96.

Domeshek, E. A., and Kolodner, J. L. 1992. A Case-Based Design Aid for Architecture. In *Artificial Intelligence in Design 92,* ed. J. S. Gero, 497–516. Norwell, Mass.: Kluwer.

Domeshek, E. A., and Kolodner, J. L. 1991. Toward a Case-Based Aid for Conceptual Design. *International Journal of Expert Systems* 4(2): 201–220.

Domeshek, E.; Kolodner, J.; and Zimring, C. 1994. The Design of a Tool Kit for Case-Based Design Aids. In *Artificial Intelligence in Design,* ed. J. Gero, 109–126. Norwell, Mass.: Kluwer.

Domeshek, E.; Herndon, M.; Bennett, A.; and Kolodner, J. L. 1994. A Case-Based Design Aid for Conceptual Design of Aircraft Subsystems. In Proceedings of the Tenth IEEE Conference on Artificial Intelligence for Applications, 63–69. Washington, D.C.: IEEE Computer Society.

Doorenbos, R. B., and Veloso, M. M. 1993. Knowledge Organization and the Utility Problem. In Proceedings of the Third International Workshop on Knowledge Compilation and Speedup Learning, 28–34.

Downs, E.; Clare, P.; and Coe, I. 1988. *Structured Systems Analysis and Design Method.* New York: Prentice Hall.

Doyle, J. 1979. A Truth Maintenance System. *Artificial Intelligence* 12:231–272.

Duda, R. D., and Hart, P. E. 1973. *Pattern Classification and Scene Analysis*. New York: Wiley.

Edelson, D. 1993. Learning from Stories: Indexing and Reminding in a Socratic Case-Based Teaching System for Elementary School Biology, Technical Report, 43, Institute for the Learning Sciences, Northwestern University.

Etzioni, O. 1993. Acquiring Search-Control Knowledge via Static Analysis. *Artificial Intelligence* 65.

Fabel-Consortium. 1993. Survey of FABEL, FABEL Report 2, Gesellschaft für Mathematik und Datenverarbeitung mbH, Sankt Augustin.

Faries, J., and Schlossberg, K. 1994. The Effect of Similarity on Memory for Prior Problems. In *Proceedings of the Sixteenth Annual Conference of the Cognitive Science Society*, 278–282. Hillsdale, N.J.: Lawrence Erlbaum.

Ferguson, W.; Bareiss, R.; Birnbaum, L.; and Osgood, R. 1992. ASK Systems: An Approach to the Realization of Story-Based Teachers, Technical Report, 22, Institute for the Learning Sciences, Northwestern University.

Ferguson, W.; Bareiss, R.; Osgood, R.; and Birnbaum, L. 1991. ASK Systems: An Approach to Story-Based Teaching. In Proceedings of the 1991 International Conference on the Learning Sciences, 158–164. Charlottesville, Va.: Association for the Advancement of Computing in Education.

Fikes, R. E., and Nilsson, N. J. 1971. STRIPS: A New Approach to the Application of Theorem Proving to Problem Solving. *Artificial Intelligence* 2:189–208.

Fikes, R. E.; Hart, P; and Nilsson, N. 1972. STRIPS. *Artificial Intelligence:* 189–208.

Fink, E., and Veloso, M. 1994. Formalizing the PRODIGY Planning Algorithm, Technical Report, CMU-CS-94-123, School of Computer Science, Carnegie Mellon University.

Firby, J. 1989. Adaptive Execution in Complex Dynamic Worlds. Ph.D. diss., Technical Report YALEU/CSD/RR 672, Computer Science Department, Yale University.

Fischer, G. 1993. Turning Breakdowns into Opportunities for Creativity. Presented at the International Symposium on Creativity and Cognition, Loughborough, U.K.

Fitzgerald, W. 1995. Building Embedded Conceptual Parsers, Technical Report, 63, Institute for the Learning Sciences, Northwestern University.

Forbus, K. 1988. Qualitative Physics: Past, Present, and Future. In *Exploring Artificial Intelligence: Survey Talks from the National Conferences on Artificial Intelligence*, ed. H. Shrobe, 239–296. San Francisco, Calif.: Morgan Kaufmann.

Forsythe, D., and Buchanan, B. 1989. Knowledge Acquisition for Expert Systems: Some Pitfalls and Suggestions. *IEEE Transactions on Systems, Man, and Cybernetics* 19(3): 435–442.

Fowler, N.; Cross, S.; and Owens, C. 1995. The ARPA-Rome Knowledge-Based Planning and Scheduling Initiative. *IEEE Expert* 10(1): 4–9.

Fox, S. 1995. Introspective Reasoning for Case-Based Planning. Ph.D. diss., Computer Science Dept., Indiana University.

Fox, S., and Leake, D. 1995a. Learning to Refine Indexing by Introspective Reasoning. In *Proceedings of the First International Conference on Case-Based Reasoning*, 431–440. Berlin: Springer Verlag.

Fox, S., and Leake, D. 1995b. Modeling Case-Based Planning for Repairing Reasoning Failures. In *Proceedings of the 1995 AAAI Spring Symposium on Representing Mental States and Mechanisms*, Technical Report WS-95-05, 31–38. Menlo Park, Calif.: AAAI Press.

Fox, S., and Leake, D. 1995c. Using Introspective Reasoning to Refine Indexing. In Proceedings of the Thirteenth International Joint Conference on Artificial Intelligence, 391–397. Menlo Park, Calif.: International Joint Conferences on Artificial Intelligence.

Fox, S., and Leake, D. 1994. Using Introspective Reasoning to Guide Index Refinement in Case-Based Reasoning. In *Proceedings of the Sixteenth Annual Conference of the Cognitive Science Society*, 324–329. Hillsdale, N.J.: Lawrence Erlbaum.

Francis, A. G. 1995. Sibling Rivalry. *The Leading Edge: Magazine of Science Fiction and Fantasy* 30:79–102.

Francis, A., and Ram, A. 1995. A Comparative Utility Analysis of Case-Based Reasoning and Control-Rule Learning Systems. Presented at the Eighth European Conference on Machine Learning (ECML-95), 25–27 April, Heraklion, Crete, Greece.

Francis, A., and Ram, A. 1993. Computational Models of the Utility Problem and Their Application to a Utility Analysis of Case-Based Reasoning. Presented at the Workshop on Knowledge Compilation and Speed-Up Learning, Amherst, Mass., June.

Freeman, M. 1987. HSTDEK: Developing a Methodology for Construction of Large-Scale, Multi-Use Knowledge Bases, NASA Conference Publication 2492, NASA/Marshall Space Flight Center, Houston, Tex.

Garland, A., and Alterman, R. 1995. Preparation of Multi-Agent Knowledge for Reuse. In Adaptation of Knowledge for Reuse: Papers from the 1995 Fall Symposium. Technical Report FS-95-04, 26–33. Menlo Park, Calif.: AAAI Press.

Gentner, D. 1987. The Mechanisms of Analogical Learning. In *Similarity, Analogy, and Thought*, eds. S. Vosniadou and A. Ortony. New York: Cambridge University Press.

Gentner, D., and Forbus, K. 1991. MAC/FAC: A Model of Similarity-Based Retrieval. In *Proceedings of the Thirteenth Annual Conference of the Cognitive Science Society*, 504–509. Hillsdale, N.J.: Lawrence Erlbaum.

Gero, J., and Maher, M. 1993. *Modeling Creativity and Knowledge-Based Creative Design*. Hillsdale, N.J.: Lawrence Erlbaum.

Gick, M., and Holyoak, K. 1980. Analogical Problem Solving. *Cognitive Psychology* 12.

Goel, A. 1991. A Model-Based Approach to Case Adaptation. In *Proceedings of the Thirteenth Annual Conference of the Cognitive Science Society*, 143–148. Hillsdale, N.J.: Lawrence Erlbaum.

Goel, A. 1989. Integration of Case-Based Reasoning and Model-Based Reasoning for Adaptive Design Problem Solving. Ph.D. diss., Dept. of Computer and Information Science, Ohio State University.

Goel, A., and Chandrasekaran, B. 1992. Case-Based Design: A Task Analysis. In *Artificial Intelligence Approaches to Engineering Design, Volume II: Innovative Design*, eds. C. Tong and D. Sriram, 165–184. San Diego, Calif.: Academic.

Goel, A., and Chandrasekaran, B. 1989. Case-Based Design: A Task Analysis. In *Proceedings of the DARPA Case-Based Reasoning Workshop*, ed. K. Hammond, 100–109. San Francisco, Calif.: Morgan Kaufmann.

Goel, A.; Ali, K.; Donnellan, M.; Garza, A.; and Callantine, T. 1994. Multistrategy Adaptive Navigational Path Planning. *IEEE Expert* 9(6): 57–65.

Golden, K.; Etzioni, O.; and Weld, D. 1994. Omnipotence without Omniscience: Sensor Management in Planning. In Proceedings of the Twelfth National Conference on

Artificial Intelligence, 1048–1054. Menlo Park, Calif.: American Association for Artificial Intelligence.

Golding, A., and Rosenbloom, P. 1991. Improving Rule-Based Systems through Case-Based Reasoning. In Proceedings of the Ninth National Conference on Artificial Intelligence, 22–27. Menlo Park, Calif.: American Association for Artificial Intelligence.

Goldstein, E.; Kedar, S.; and Bareiss, R. 1993. Easing the Creation of a Multipurpose Case Library. In *Proceedings of the AAAI-93 Workshop on Case-Based Reasoning*, Technical Report WS-93-01, 12–18. Menlo Park, Calif.: AAAI Press.

Gómez de Silva Garza, A., and Maher, M. 1996. Design by Interaction Exploration Using Memory-Based Techniques. *Knowledge-Based Systems* 9(1). Forthcoming.

Goodall, A. 1995. Supplier Profile: AcknoSoft International. *AI Watch* 4(2): 15–19.

Goodman, M. 1989. CBR in Battle Planning. In *Proceedings of the DARPA Case-Based Reasoning Workshop*, ed. K. Hammond, 264–269. San Francisco, Calif.: Morgan Kaufmann.

Hammond, K. J., 1993. Actualized Intelligence. Presented at the AAAI–93 Workshop on Case-Based Reasoning, 11–12 July, Washington, D.C.

Hammond, K. J., 1989a. Opportunistic Memory. In Proceedings of the Eleventh International Joint Conference on Artificial Intelligence. Menlo Park, Calif.: International Joint Conferences on Artificial Intelligence.

Hammond, K. J., ed. 1989b. *Proceedings of the DARPA Case-Based Reasoning Workshop*. San Francisco, Calif.: Morgan Kaufmann.

Hammond, K. J. 1989c. *Case-Based Planning: Viewing Planning as a Memory Task*. San Diego, Calif.: Academic.

Hammond, K. J., 1986a. CHEF: A Model of Case-Based Planning. In Proceedings of the Fifth National Conference on Artificial Intelligence, 267–271. Menlo Park, Calif.: American Association for Artificial Intelligence.

Hammond, K. J., 1986b. Case-Based Planning: An Integrated Theory of Planning, Learning, and Memory. Ph.D. diss., Dept. of Computer Science, Yale University.

Hammond, K. J., and Seifert, C. 1993. A Cognitive Science Approach to Case-Based Planning. In *Foundations of Knowledge Acquisition: Cognitive Models of Complex Learning*, eds. S. Chipman and A. L. Meyrowitz, 245–267. Norwell, Mass.: Kluwer.

Hanks, S., and Weld, D. 1995. A Domain-Independent Algorithm for Plan Adaptation. *Journal of Artificial Intelligence Research* 2:319–360.

Hanney, K.; Keane, M.; Smyth, B.; and Cunningham, P. 1995. Systems, Tasks, and Adaptation Knowledge: Revealing Some Revealing Dependencies. In *Case-Based Reasoning Research and Development*, eds. M. Veloso and A. Aamodt, 461–470. New York: Springer Verlag.

Haton, J.-P.; Keane, M.; and Manago, M., eds. 1995. *Advances in Case-Based Reasoning: Second European Workshop*. Berlin: Springer Verlag.

Hayes, P. 1985. Naive Physics 1: Ontology for Liquids. In *Formal Theories of the Commonsense World*, eds. J. Hobbs and R. Moore, 71–107. Norwood, N.J.: Ablex.

Hayes-Roth, B. 1995. Agents on Stage: Advancing the State of the Art of AI, Knowledge Systems Laboratory Report, KSL 95-50, Knowledge Systems Laboratory, Stanford University.

Hayes-Roth, B., and Hayes-Roth, F. 1979. A Cognitive Model of Planning. *Cognitive Science* 2:275–310.

Hennessy, D., and Hinkle, D. 1992. Applying Case-Based Reasoning to Autoclave Loading. *IEEE Expert* 7(5): 21–26.

Hinkle, D., and Toomey, C. 1994. Clavier: Applying Case-Based Reasoning to Composite Part Fabrication. In *Innovative Applications of Artificial Intelligence 6*, 54–62. Menlo Park, Calif.: AAAI Press.

Hinrichs, T. R. 1992. *Problem Solving in Open Worlds: A Case Study in Design*. Hillsdale, N.J.: Lawrence Erlbaum.

Holyoak, K. 1985. The Pragmatics of Analogical Transfer. In *The Psychology of Learning and Motivation*, ed. G. Bower, 59–87. New York: Academic Press.

Hua, K., and Faltings, B. 1993. Exploring Case-Based Design—CADRE. *Artificial Intelligence in Engineering Design, Analysis, and Manufacturing* 7(2): 135–144.

Humphrey, W. 1989. *Managing the Software Process*. Reading, Mass.: Addison-Wesley.

Hunter, L. 1990. Planning to Learn. In *Proceedings of the Twelfth Annual Conference of the Cognitive Science Society*, 261–268. Hillsdale, N.J.: Lawrence Erlbaum.

Hunter, L. 1989. Gaining Expertise through Experience. Ph.D. diss., Computer Science Dept., Technical Report, 678, Yale University.

Hunter, K. M. 1986. "There Was This One Guy": Anecdotes in Medicine. *Biology in Medicine* 29:619–630. Also in 1991. *Doctors' Stories: The Narrative Structure of Medical Knowledge*, 69–82. Princeton, N.J.: Princeton University Press.

Ihrig, L., and Kambhampati, S. 1994. Derivation Replay for Partial-Order Planning. In *Proceedings of the Twelfth National Conference on Artificial Intelligence*, 992–997. Menlo Park, Calif.: American Association for Artificial Intelligence.

Inference Corporation. 1995. Inference Forms Knowledge Publishing Division, Press Release, 17 November.

Ishikura, Y. 1992. *Title in Japanese* (Building Core Skills of the Organization). Tokyo: NTT Publishing.

ISO. 1995. Guidelines for the Application of ISO 9001 to the Development, Supply, and Maintenance of Software, DIS 9000-3, ISO, Washington, D.C.

Jabbour, K.; Vega-Riveros, J. F.; Landsbergen, D.; and Meyer, W. 1988. ALFA: Automated Load Forecasting Assistant. *IEEE Transactions on Power Apparatus and Systems* 3(3): 908–914.

Jantke, K. 1992. Case-Based Learning in Inductive Inference. In *Proceedings of the Fifth Annual ACM Workshop on Computational Learning Theory*, 218–223. New York: Association for Computing Machinery.

Johnson, W. L.; Benner, K. M.; and Harris, D. R. 1993. Developing Formal Specifications from Informal Requirements. *IEEE Expert* 8(4): 82–90.

Jona, M. Y. 1995. Representing and Applying Teaching Strategies in Computer-Based Learning-by-Doing tutors. Ph.D. diss., Dept. of Electrical Engineering and Computer Science, Northwestern University.

Jones, E. K. 1992. The Flexible Use of Abstract Knowledge in Planning. Technical Report, 28, Institute for the Learning Sciences, Northwestern University.

Kahn, C., and Anderson, G. 1994. Case-Based Reasoning and Imaging Procedure Selection. *Investigative Radiology* 29:643–647.

Kambhampati, S., and Chen, J. 1993. Relative Utility of EBG-Based Plan Reuse in Partial Ordering versus Total Ordering Planning. In Proceedings of the Eleventh National

Conference on Artificial Intelligence, 514–519. Menlo Park, Calif.: American Association for Artificial Intelligence.

Kambhampati, S, and Hendler, J. 1992. A Validation Structure-Based Theory of Plan Modification and Reuse. *Artificial Intelligence* 55(2–3): 193–258.

Kass, A. 1994a. The CASPER Project: Integrating Simulation, Case Presentation, and Socratic Tutoring to Teach Diagnostic Problem Solving in Complex Domains, Technical Report, 51, Institute for the Learning Sciences, Northwestern University.

Kass, A. 1994b. TWEAKER: Adapting Old Explanations to New Situations. In *Inside Case-Based Explanation*, eds. R. Schank, C. Riesbeck, and A. Kass, 263–295. Hillsdale, N.J.: Lawrence Erlbaum.

Kass, A. 1992. Question Asking, Artificial Intelligence, and Human Creativity. In *Questions and Information Systems*, eds. T. Lauer, E. Peacock, and A. Graesser, 303-360. Hillsdale, N.J.: Lawrence Erlbaum.

Kass, A. 1990. Developing Creative Hypotheses by Adapting Explanations. Ph.D. diss., Yale University. Also Technical Report, 6, Institute for the Learning Sciences, Northwestern University.

Kass, A., and Blevis, E. 1991. Learning through Experience: An Intelligent Learning-by-Doing Environment for Business Consultants. In Proceedings of the Conference on Intelligent Computer-Aided Training. Washington, D.C.: National Aeronautics and Space Administration.

Kass, A. M., and Leake, D. B. 1988. Case-Based Reasoning Applied to Constructing Explanations. In *Proceedings of the DARPA Case-Based Reasoning Workshop*, ed. J. Kolodner, 190–208. San Francisco, Calif.: Morgan Kaufmann.

Kass, A. M.; Leake, D. B.; and Owens, C. 1986. SWALE: A Program That Explains. In *Explanation Patterns: Understanding Mechanically and Creatively*, ed. R. Schank, 232–254. Hillsdale, N.J.: Lawrence Erlbaum.

Kass, A.; Burke, R.; Blevis, E.; and Williamson, M. 1994. Constructing Learning Environments for Complex Social Skills. *Journal of the Learning Sciences* 3(4): 387–427.

Keane, M. 1993. Analogical Asides on Case-Based Reasoning. In *Topics in Case-Based Reasoning*, eds. S. Wess, K.-D. Altoff, and M. Richter, 21–32. New York: Springer Verlag.

Kedar, S.; Burke, R.; and Kass, A. 1994. Acquiring Retrieval Knowledge for Multimedia Stories. In *Indexing and Reuse in Multimedia Systems*, 199–212. Menlo Park, Calif.: AAAI Press.

Kennedy, A. 1995. Using a Domain-Independent Introspection Mechanism to Improve Memory Search. In *Proceedings of the 1995 AAAI Spring Symposium on Representing Mental States and Mechanisms*, Technical Report WS-95-05, 72–78. Menlo Park, Calif. AAAI Press.

Kettler, B.; Hendler, J.; Andersen, W.; and Evett, M. 1994. Massively Parallel Support for Case-Based Planning. *IEEE Expert* 9(1): 8–14.

Kettler, B. P.; Hendler, J. A.; Andersen, W. A.; and Evett, M. P. 1993. Massively Parallel Support for Case-Based Planning. In Proceedings of the Ninth IEEE Conference on Artificial Intelligence Applications. Washington, D.C.: IEEE Computer Society.

Kibler D., and Langley, P. 1988. Machine Learning as an Experimental Science. In Proceedings of the Third European Working Session on Learning, 81–92. London: Pitman Publishing.

Kitano, H.; Shimazu, H.; and Shibata, A. 1993. Case-Method: A Methodology for Building Large-Scale Case-Based Systems. In *Proceedings of the Eleventh National Conference on Artificial Intelligence*, 303–308. Menlo Park, Calif.: AAAI Press.

Kitano, H.; Shibata, A.; Shimazu, H.; Kajihara, J.; and Sato, A. 1992. Building Large-Scale and Corporate-Wide Case-Based Systems. In Proceedings of the Tenth National Conference on Artificial Intelligence, 843–849. Menlo Park, Calif.: American Association for Artificial Intelligence.

Klein, G., and Calderwood, R. 1989. Decision Models: Some Lessons from the Field. *IEEE Transactions on Systems, Man, and Cybernetics* 21(5): 1018–1026.

Klein, G., and Calderwood, R. 1988. How Do People Use Analogues to Make Decisions? In *Proceedings of the DARPA Case-Based Reasoning Workshop*, ed. J. Kolodner, 209–223. San Francisco, Calif.: Morgan Kaufmann.

Klimesch, W. J. 1994. *The Structure of Long-Term Memory: A Connectivity Model of Semantic Processing*. Hillsdale, N.J.: Lawrence Erlbaum.

Kolodner, J. 1994a. Understanding Creativity: A Case-Based Approach. In *Topics in Case-Based Reasoning*, eds. S. Wess, K. Althoff, and M. Richter, 3–20. Berlin: Springer Verlag.

Kolodner, J. L. 1994b. From Natural Language Understanding to Case-Based Reasoning and Beyond: A Perspec tive on the Cognitive Model that Ties It all Together. In *Beliefs, Reasoning, and Decision Making: Psycho-Logic in Honor of Bob Abelson*, eds. R. Schank and E. Lanser, 55–110. Hillsdale, N.J.: Lawrence Erlbaum.

Kolodner, J. L. 1993. *Case-Based Reasoning*. San Francisco, Calif.: Morgan Kaufmann.

Kolodner, J. 1991. Improving Human Decision Making through Case-Based Decision Aiding. *AI Magazine* 12(2): 52–68.

Kolodner, J. 1989. Judging Which Is the "Best" Case for a Case-Based Reasoner. In *Proceedings of the DARPA Case-Based Reasoning Workshop*, 77–82. San Francisco: Morgan Kaufmann.

Kolodner, J., ed. 1988a. *Proceedings of the DARPA Case-Based Reasoning Workshop*. San Francisco, Calif.: Morgan Kaufmann.

Kolodner, J. 1988b. Retrieving Events from a Case Memory: A Parallel Implementation. In *Proceedings of the DARPA Case-Based Reasoning Workshop*, ed. J. Kolodner, 233–249. San Francisco, Calif.: Morgan Kaufmann.

Kolodner, J. L. 1987. Extending Problem Solving Capabilities through Case-Based Inference. In *Proceedings of the Fourth International Workshop on Machine Learning*, 167–178. San Francisco, Calif.: Morgan Kaufmann.

Kolodner, J. L. 1984. *Retrieval and Organizational Strategies in Conceptual Memory: A Computer Model*. Hillsdale, N.J.: Lawrence Erlbaum.

Kolodner, J. L. 1983a. Reconstructive Memory: A Computer Model. *Cognitive Science* 7(4): 281–328.

Kolodner, J. L. 1983b. Maintaining Organization in a Dynamic Long-Term Memory. *Cognitive Science* 7(4): 243–280.

Kolodner, J. L., and Jona M. 1992. Case-Based Reasoning. In *Encyclopedia of Artificial Intelligence* (2d ed.), ed. S. Shaprio. New York: Wiley.

Kolodner, J. L., and Penberthy, T. L. 1990. A Case-Based Approach to Creativity in Problem Solving. In *Proceedings of the Twelfth Annual Conference of the Cognitive Science Society*, 978–985. Hillsdale, N.J.: Lawrence Erlbaum.

Kolodner, J. L., and Simpson, R. 1989. The MEDIATOR: Analysis of an Early Case-Based Problem Solver. *Cognitive Science* 13(4): 507–549.

Kolodner, J. L., and Thau, R. 1988. Design and Implementation of a Case Memory, GIT-ICS-88/34, Department of Information and Computer Science, Georgia Institute of Technology.

Kolodner, J. L., and Wills, L. M. 1993. Case-Based Creative Design. In *Artificial Intelligence and Creativity: Papers from the 1993 Spring Symposium,* 95–102. Menlo Park, Calif.: AAAI Press.

Kolodner, J. L.; Hmelo, C.; and Narayanan, N. 1996. Problem-Based Learning Meets Case-Based Reasoning. In Proceedings of the Second International Conference on the Learning Sciences, Charlottesville, Va.: Association for the Advancement of Computing in Education. Forthcoming.

Korf, R. E. 1985. Macro-Operators: A Weak Method for Learning. *Artificial Intelligence* 26:35–77.

Koton, P. 1989. Evaluating Case-Based Problem Solving. In *Proceedings of the DARPA Case-Based Reasoning Workshop,* 173–175. San Francisco: Morgan Kaufmann.

Koton, P. 1988a. Integrating Case-Based and Causal Reasoning. In Proceedings of the Tenth Annual Conference of the Cognitive Science Society. Ann Arbor, Mich.: Cognitive Science Society.

Koton, P. 1988b. Reasoning about Evidence in Causal Explanation. In Proceedings of the Seventh National Conference on Artificial Intelligence, 256–261. Menlo Park, Calif.: American Association for Artificial Intelligence.

Koton, P. 1988c. Using Experience in Learning and Problem Solving. Ph.D. diss., Dept. of Computer Science, Massachusetts Institute of Technology.

Kriegsman, M., and Barletta, R. 1993. Building a Case-Based Help Desk Application. *IEEE Expert* 8(6): 18–26.

Laird, J. E.; Rosenbloom, P. S.; and Newell, A. 1986. Chunking in SOAR: The Anatomy of a General Learning Mechanism. *Machine Learning* 1:11–46. Also appears in *Readings in Machine Learning,* eds. J. W. Shavlik and T. Dietterich, 555–572. San Francisco, Calif.: Morgan Kaufmann.

Lancaster, J., and Kolodner, J. 1987. Problem Solving in a Natural Task as a Function of Experience. In *Proceedings of the Ninth Annual Conference of the Cognitive Science Society,* 727–736. Hillsdale, N.J.: Lawrence Erlbaum.

Larkin, J. H.; McDermott, J.; Simon D. P.; and Simon, H. A. 1980. Expert and Novice Performance in Solving Physics Problems. *Cognitive Science* 12:101–138.

Lave, J., and Wenger, E. 1991. *Situated Learning: Legitimate Peripheral Participation.* New York: Cambridge University Press.

Leake, D. 1996. Cognition as Case-Based Reasoning. In *The Blackwell Companion to Cognitive Science,* Eds. W. Bechtel and G. Graham. Oxford: Blackwell. Forthcoming.

Leake, D. 1995a. Abduction, Experience, and Goals: A Model of Everyday Abductive Explanation. *Journal of Experimental and Theoretical Artificial Intelligence* 7:407–428.

Leake, D. 1995b. Adaptive Similarity Assessment for Case-Based Explanation. *International Journal of Expert Systems* 8(2): 165–194.

Leake, D. 1995c. Combining Rules and Cases to Learn Case Adaptation. In Proceedings of the Seventeenth Annual Conference of the Cognitive Science Society, 84–89. Ann Arbor, Mich.: Cognitive Science Society.

Leake, D. 1995d. Representing Self-Knowledge for Introspection about Memory Search. In *Proceedings of the 1995 AAAI Spring Symposium on Representing Mental States and Mechanisms,* Technical Report WS-95-05, 84–88. Menlo Park, Calif.: AAAI Press.

Leake, D. 1994a. AAAI-93 Workshop on Case-Based Reasoning. *AI Magazine* 15(1): 63–64.

Leake, D. 1994b. Toward a Computer Model of Memory Search Strategy Learning. In *Proceedings of the Sixteenth Annual Conference of the Cognitive Science Society,* 549–554. Hillsdale, N.J.: Lawrence Erlbaum.

Leake, D., ed. 1993a. *Case-Based Reasoning: Papers from the 1993 Workshop.* Technical Report WS-93-01. Menlo Park, Calif.: AAAI Press.

Leake, D. 1993b. Learning Adaptation Strategies by Introspective Reasoning about Memory Search. In *Case-Based Reasoning: Papers from the 1993 Workshop,* Technical Report WS-93-01, 57–63. Menlo Park, Calif.: AAAI Press.

Leake, D. 1992a. Constructive Similarity Assessment: Using Stored Cases to Define New Situations. In *Proceedings of the Fourteenth Annual Conference of the Cognitive Science Society,* 313–318. Hillsdale, N.J.: Lawrence Erlbaum.

Leake, D. 1992b. *Evaluating Explanations: A Content Theory.* Hillsdale, N.J.: Lawrence Erlbaum.

Leake, D., and Ram, A. 1993. Goal-Driven Learning: Fundamental Issues. *AI Magazine* 14(4): 67–72.

Leake, D.; Kinley, A.; and Wilson, D. 1995. Learning to Improve Case Adaptation by Introspective Reasoning and CBR. In *Proceedings of the First International Conference on Case-Based Reasoning,* 229–240. Berlin: Springer Verlag.

Lehner, P. E. 1989. Toward an Empirical Approach to Evaluating the Knowledge Base of an Expert System. *IEEE Transactions on Systems, Man, and Cybernetics* 19(3): 658–662.

Lowry, M. 1987. The Abstraction-Implementation Model of Problem Reformulation. In Proceedings of the Tenth International Joint Conference on Artificial Intelligence, 1004–1010. Menlo Park, Calif.: International Joint Conferences on Artificial Intelligence.

Luger, G., and Stubblefield, W. 1993. *Artificial Intelligence: Structures and Strategies for Complex Problem Solving.* Redwood City, Calif.: Benjamin/Cummings Publishing Company.

McAllester, D., and Rosenblitt, D. 1991. Systematic Nonlinear Planning. In Proceedings of the Ninth National Conference on Artificial Intelligence, 634–639. Menlo Park, Calif.: American Association for Artificial Intelligence.

Macura, R., and Macura, K. 1995. MACRAD: Radiology Image Resource with a Case-Based Retrieval System. In *Proceedings of the First International Conference on Case-Based Reasoning,* 43–54. Berlin: Springer Verlag.

Maes, P. 1990. Situated Agents Can Have Goals. In *Designing Autonomous Agents: Theory and Practice from Biology and Engineering and Back,* ed. P. Maes. Cambridge, Mass.: MIT Press.

Marir, F. 1995. Representing and Indexing Building Refurbishment Cases for Multiple Retrieval of Adaptable Pieces of Cases. In *Proceedings of the First International Conference on Case-Based Reasoning,* 55–66. Berlin: Springer Verlag.

Mark, W. S. 1989. Case-Based Reasoning for Autoclave Management. In *Proceedings of the Second Case-Based Reasoning Workshop.* San Francisco, Calif.: Morgan Kaufmann.

Marks, M.; Hammond, K.; and Converse, T. 1989. Planning in an Open World: A Pluralistic Approach. In Proceedings of the Eleventh Annual Conference of the Cognitive Science Society, 749–756. Ann Arbor, Mich.: Cognitive Science Society.

Martin, C. E. 1993. Direct Memory Access Parsing, Technical Report, CS 93-07, Dept. of Computer Science, University of Chicago.

Martin, C. E. 1990. Direct Memory Access Parsing. Ph.D. diss., Dept. of Computer Science, Yale University.

Meen, D., and Keough, M. 1992. Creating the Learning Organization. *The McKinsey Quarterly* 1.

Minsky, M. 1986. *The Society of Mind.* New York: Simon and Schuster.

Minton, S. 1990. Quantitative Results Concerning the Utility of Explanation-Based Learning. *Artificial Intelligence* 42:363–391.

Minton, S. 1988. *Learning Effective Search Control Knowledge: An Explanation-Based Approach.* Norwell, Mass.: Kluwer.

Mitchell, M. 1993. *Analogy Making as Perception.* Cambridge, Mass.: MIT Press.

Mitchell, T. M.; Keller, R. M.; and Kedar-Cabelli, S. T. 1986. Explanation-Based Generalization: A Unifying View. *Machine Learning* 1:47–80.

Moorman, K., and Ram, A. 1994a. A Model of Creative Understanding. In Proceedings of the Twelfth National Conference on Artificial Intelligence, 74–79. Menlo Park, Calif.: American Association for Artificial Intelligence.

Moorman, K., and Ram, A. 1994b. Integrating Creativity and Reading: A Functional Approach. In Proceedings of the Sixteenth Annual Conference of the Cognitive Science Society, 646–651. Hillsdale, N.J.: Lawrence Erlbaum.

Mostow, J. 1989. Automated Replay of Design Plans: Some Issues in Derivational Analogy. *Artificial Intelligence* 40(1–3).

Munroe, M. E. 1963. *Modern Multidimensional Calculus.* Reading, Mass.: Addison-Wesley.

Navinchandra, D. 1992. Innovative Design Systems: Where Are We, and Where Do We Go from Here? Parts 1 and 2. *Knowledge Engineering Review* 7(3): 183–213, 7(4): 345–362.

Navinchandra, D. 1991. *Exploration and Innovation in Design: Toward a Computational Model.* New York: Springer Verlag.

Navinchandra, D. 1988. Case-Based Reasoning in CYCLOPS, a Design Problem Solver. In *Proceedings of the DARPA Case-Based Reasoning Workshop,* ed. J. Kolodner, 286–301. San Francisco, Calif.: Morgan Kaufmann.

Neter, J.; Wasserman, W.; and Kutner, M. H. 1989. Applied Regression Models. Homewood, Ill.: R. D. Irwin.

Newell, A. 1990. *Unified Theories of Cognition.* Cambridge, Mass.: Harvard University Press.

Nguyen, T.; Czerwinski, M.; and Lee, S. 1993. Compaq QUICKSOURCE: Providing the Consumer with the Power of Artificial Intelligence. In *Proceedings of Innovative Applications of Artificial Intelligence Conference 5,* 142–150. Menlo Park, Calif.: AAAI Press.

Nilsson, N. 1995. Eye on the Prize. *AI Magazine* 16(2): 9–17.

Nonaka, I. 1991. The Knowledge-Creating Company. *Harvard Business Review.*

Oehlmann, R. 1995. Metacognitive Adaptation: Regulating the Plan Transformation Process. Presented at the Fall Symposium on Adaptation of Knowledge for Reuse, 10–12 November, Cambridge, Massachusetts.

Oehlmann, R.; Sleeman, D.; and Edwards, P. 1993. Learning Plan Transformations from Self-Questions: A Memory-Based Approach. In Proceedings of the Eleventh National Conference on Artificial Intelligence, 520–525. Menlo Park, Calif.: American Association for Artificial Intelligence.

Ono, Y.; Tanimoto, I.; Matsudaira, T.; and Takeuchi, Y. 1988. Artificial Intelligence–Based Programmable Controller Software Designing. In Proceedings of the International Workshop on Artificial Intelligence for Industrial Applications, 85–91. Los Alamitos, Calif.: IEEE Computer Society.

Orasanu, J., and Connolly, T. 1993. The Reinvention of Decision Making. In *Decision Making in Action: Models and Methods,* eds. G. A. Klein, J. Orasanu, R. Calderwood, and C. E. Zsambok. Norwood, N.J.: Ablex.

Osgood, R., and Bareiss, R. 1993. Automated Index Generation for Constructing Large-Scale Conversational Hypermedia Systems. In Proceedings of the Eleventh National Conference on Artificial Intelligence, 309–314. Menlo Park, Calif.: American Association for Artificial Intelligence.

Owens, C. 1991. Indexing and Retrieving Abstract Planning Knowledge. Ph.D. diss., Yale University.

Owens, C. 1989. Integrating Feature Extraction and Memory Search. In *Proceedings of the Eleventh Annual Conference of the Cognitive Science Society.* Hillsdale, N.J.: Lawrence Erlbaum.

Owens, C. 1988. Domain-Independent Prototype Cases for Planning. In *Proceedings of the Case-Based Reasoning Workshop 1988,* 302–311. San Francisco, Calif.: Morgan Kaufmann.

Pfau-Wagenbauer, M., and Nejdl, W. 1993. Integrating Model-Based and Heuristic Features in a Real-Time Expert System. *IEEE Expert* 8(4): 12–18.

Pirolli, P., and Anderson, J. 1985. The Role of Learning from Examples in the Acquisition of Recursive Programming Skills. *Canadian Journal of Psychology* 39:240–272.

Pollock, J. L. 1995. *Cognitive Carpentry: A Blueprint for How to Build a Person.* Cambridge, Mass.: MIT Press.

Porter, B. W.; Bareiss, R.; and Holte, R. C. 1990. Concept Learning and Heuristic Classification in Weak-Theory Domains. *Artificial Intelligence* 45:229–263.

Portinale, L., and Torasso, P. 1995. ADAPtER: An Integrated Diagnostic System Combining Case-Based and Abductive Reasoning. In *Proceedings of the First International Conference on Case-Based Reasoning,* 277–288. Berlin: Springer Verlag.

Prabhakar, S., and Goel, A. 1992. Performance-Driven Creativity in Design: Constraint Discovery, Model Revision, and Case Composition. Presented at the Second International Conference on Computational Models of Creative Design, Heron Island, Australia.

Quinlan, R. 1992. *C4.5: Programs for Machine Learning.* San Francisco, Calif.: Morgan Kaufmann.

Ram, A. 1993. Indexing, Elaboration and Refinement: Incremental Learning of Explanatory Cases. *Machine Learning* 10:201–248.

Ram, A. 1991. A Theory of Questions and Question Asking. *Journal of the Learning Sciences* 1(3–4): 273–318.

Ram, A. 1987. AQUA: Asking Questions and Understanding Answers. In Proceedings of the Sixth National Conference on Artificial Intelligence, 312–316. Menlo Park, Calif.: American Association for Artificial Intelligence.

Ram, A., and Cox, M. T. 1994. Introspective Reasoning Using Meta-Explanations for Multistrategy Learning. In *Machine Learning: A Multistrategy Approach,* eds. R. Michalski and G. Tecuci, 349–377. San Francisco, Calif.: Morgan Kaufmann.

Ram, A., and Cox, M. T. 1993. Using Introspective Reasoning to Select Learning Strategies. In *Machine Learning: A Multistrategy Approach, Volume 4,* eds. R. S. Michalski and G. Tecuci. San Francisco, Calif.: Morgan Kaufmann.

Ram, A., and Santamaría, J. C. 1993a. Continuous Case-Based Reasoning. In *Case-Based Reasoning: Papers from the 1993 Workshop,* 86–93. Menlo Park, Calif.: AAAI Press.

Ram, A., and Santamaría, J. C. 1993b. Multistrategy Learning in Reactive Control Systems for Autonomous Robotic Navigation. *Informatica* 17(4): 347–369.

Read, S., and Cesa, I. 1991. This Reminds Me of the Time When...: Expectation Failures in Reminding and Explanation. *Journal of Experimental Social Psychology* 27:1–25.

Redmond, M. 1992. Learning by Observing and Understanding Expert Problem Solving. Ph.D. diss., Technical Report GIT-CC-92/43, College of Computing, Georgia Institute of Technology.

Redmond, M. A. 1991. Improving Case Retrieval through Observing Expert Problem Solving. In Proceedings of the Thirteenth Annual Conference of the Cognitive Science Society, 516–521. Ann Arbor, Mich.: Cognitive Science Society.

Redmond, M. A. 1990. Distributed Cases for Case-Based Reasoning: Facilitating the Use of Multiple Cases. In Proceedings of the Eighth National Conference on Artificial Intelligence, 304–309. Menlo Park, Calif.: American Association for Artificial Intelligence.

Reubenstein, H. B., and Waters, R. C. 1991. The Requirements Apprentice: Automated Assistance for Requirements Aquisition. *IEEE Transactions on Software Engineering* 17(3): 226–240.

Richter, M. 1995. The Knowledge Contained in Similarity Measures. Presented at the First International Conference on Case-Based Reasoning, 25 October, Sesimbra, Portugal.

Riesbeck, C. 1993. Replacing CBR: Now What? Presented at the Workshop on Case-Based Reasoning, 11–12 July, Washington, D.C.

Riesbeck, C. 1988. An Interface for Case-Based Knowledge Acquisition. In *Proceedings of the DARPA Case-Based Reasoning Workshop,* ed. J. Kolodner, 312–326. San Francisco, Calif.: Morgan Kaufmann.

Riesbeck, C. 1981. Failure-Driven Reminding for Incremental Learning. In Proceedings of the Seventh International Joint Conference on Artificial Intelligence, 115–120. Menlo Park, Calif.: International Joint Conferences on Artificial Intelligence.

Riesbeck, C., and Schank, R. 1989. *Inside Case-Based Reasoning.* Hillsdale, N.J.: Lawrence Erlbaum.

Rissland, E. L. 1990. Artificial Intelligence and Law: Stepping Stones to a Model of Legal Reasoning. *Yale Law Journal.* 99(8) (June 1990): 1957–1981.

Rissland, E. L. 1983. Examples in Legal Reasoning: Legal Hypotheticals. In Proceedings of the Eighth International Joint Conference on Artificial Intelligence, 90-93. Menlo Park, Calif.: International Joint Conferences on Artificial Intelligence.

Rissland, E. L., and Daniels, J. 1995. Using CBR to Drive IR. In Proceedings of the Thirteenth International Joint Conference on Artificial Intelligence, 400–407. Menlo Park, Calif.: International Joint Conferences on Artificial Intelligence.

Rissland, E. L., and Skalak, D. B. 1991. CABARET: Rule Interpretation in a Hybrid Architecture. *International Journal of Man-Machine Studies* 34:839–887.

Rissland, E. L.; Kolodner, J.; and Waltz, D. B. 1989. Case-Based Reasoning. In *Proceedings of the DARPA Case-Based Reasoning Workshop,* ed. K. Hammond, 1–13. San Francisco, Calif.: Morgan Kaufmann.

Rissland, E. L.; Skalak, D.; and Friedman, M. T. 1994. Heuristic Harvesting of Information for Case-Based Argument. In Proceedings of the Twelfth National Conference on Artificial Intelligence, 36–43. Menlo Park, Calif.: American Association for Artificial Intelligence.

Rissland, E. L.; Skalak, D. B.; and Friedman, M. T. 1993a. BANKXX: A Program to Generate Argument through Case-Based Search. In Proceedings of the Fourth International Conference on Artificial Intelligence and Law, 117–124. New York: Association for Computing Machinery.

Rissland, E. L.; Skalak, D. B.; and Friedman, M. T. 1993b. Case Retrieval through Multiple Indexing and Heuristic Search. In Proceedings of the Fourteenth International Joint Conference on Artificial Intelligence, 902–908. Menlo Park, Calif.: International Joint Conferences on Artificial Intelligence.

Rissland, E. L.; Valcarce, E. M.; and Ashley, K. D. 1984. Explaining and Arguing with Examples. In Proceedings of the Fourth National Conference on Artificial Intelligence, 288–294. Menlo Park, Calif.: American Association for Artificial Intelligence.

Robinson, S., and Kolodner, J. 1991. Indexing Cases for Planning and Acting in Dynamic Environments: Exploiting Hierarchical Goal Structures. In Proceedings of the Thirteenth Annual Conference of the Cognitive Science Society, 882–886. Ann Arbor, Mich.: Cognitive Science Society.

Rose, D. E., and Belew, R. K. 1991. A Connectionist and Symbolic Hybrid for Improving Legal Research. *International Journal of Man-Machine Studies* 35:1–33.

Rosenthal, U.; Charles, M.; and Hart, P., eds. 1989. *Coping with Crises: The Management of Disasters, Riots, and Terrorism.* Springfield, Ill.: Charles C. Thomas.

Ross, B. 1989a. Psychological Results on Case-Based Reasoning. In *Proceedings fo the DARPA Case-Based Reasoning Workshop,* 144–147. San Francisco: Morgan Kaufmann.

Ross, B. 1989b. Remindings in Learning and Instruction. In *Similarity and Analogical Reasoning,* eds. S. Vosniadau and A. Ortomp, 438-469. New York: Cambridge University Press.

Ross, B. 1984. Remindings and Their Effects in Learning a Cognitive Skill. *Cognitive Psychology* 16:371–416.

Ruby, D., and Kibler, D. 1988. Exploration of Case-Based Problem Solving. In *Proceedings of the Case-Based Reasoning Workshop 1988,* 345–356. San Francisco, Calif.: Morgan Kaufmann.

Russell, S., and Norvig, P. 1995. *Artificial Intelligence: A Modern Approach.* San Francisco, Calif.: Morgan Kaufmann.

Sakuri, T.; Shibagaki, T.; Shinbori, T.; and Itoh, M. 1990. An Automatic Programming System Based on Modular Integrated-Concept Architecture (MICA). In Proceedings of the Sixteenth Annual Conference of the IEEE Industrial Electronic Society, 1303–1308. Washington, D.C.: IEEE Computer Society.

Samuel, A. L. 1967. Some Studies in Machine Learning Using the Game of Checkers II—Recent Progress. *IBM Journal of Research and Development* 11:601–617.

Sanders, K. 1994. CHIRON: Planning in an Open-Textured Domain. Ph.D. diss., Technical Report 94-38, Computer Science Dept., Brown University.

Schank, R. C. 1991a. *The Connoisseur's Guide to the Mind.* New York: Simon and Schuster.

Schank, R. C. 1991b. *Tell Me a Story.* New York: Scribner's.

Schank, R. C. 1986. *Explanation Patterns: Understanding Mechanically and Creatively.* Hillsdale, N.J.: Lawrence Erlbaum.

Schank, R. C. 1982. *Dynamic Memory: A Theory of Learning in Computers and People.* New York: Cambridge University Press.

Schank R. C., and Abelson, R. 1977. *Scripts, Plans, Goals, and Understanding: An Inquiry into Human Knowledge Structures.* Hillsdale, N.J.: Lawrence Erlbaum.

Schank, R. C., and Kass, A. 1990. Explanations, Machine Learning, and Creativity. In *Machine Learning: An Artificial Intelligence Approach, Volume 3,* eds. Y. Kodratoff and R. Michalski, 31–60. San Francisco, Calif.: Morgan Kaufmann.

Schank, R. C., and Leake, D. 1989. Creativity and Learning in a Case-Based Explainer. *Artificial Intelligence* 40(1–3): 353–385. Also in 1990. Carbonell, J., ed., *Machine Learning: Paradigms and Methods.* Cambridge, Mass.: MIT Press.

Schank, R. C., and Leake, D. 1986. Computer Understanding and Creativity. In *Information Processing 86,* ed. H.-J. Kugler, 335–341. New York: North-Holland.

Schank, R. C., and Osgood, R. 1990. A Content Theory of Memory Indexing, Technical Report, 2, Institute for the Learning Sciences, Northwestern University.

Schank, R. C.; Fano, A.; Bell, B.; and Jona, M. 1993–1994. The Design of Goal-Based Scenarios. *Journal of the Learning Sciences* 3(4): 305–345.

Schank, R. C.; Ferguson, W.; Birnbaum, L.; Barger, J.; and Greising, M. 1991. ASK TOM: An Experimental Interface for Video Case Libraries, Computer Science Technical Report, 10, Institute for the Learning Sciences, Northwestern University.

Schank, R. C.; Kass, A.; and Riesbeck, C., eds. 1994. *Inside Case-Based Explanation.* Hillsdale N.J.: Lawrence Erlbaum.

Schmidt, H.; Norman, G.; and Boshuizen, H. 1990. A Cognitive Perspective on Medical Expertise: Theory and Implications. *Academic Medicine* 65(10): 611–621.

Segre, A. 1987. On the Operationality-Generality Tradeoff in Explanation-Based Learning. In Proceedings of the Tenth International Joint Conference on Artificial Intelligence, 242–247. Menlo Park, Calif.: International Joint Conferences on Artificial Intelligence.

Seifert, C.; Meyer, D.; Davidson, N.; Patalano, A.; and Yaniv, I. 1996. Demystification of Cognitive Insight: Opportunistic Assimilation and the Prepared-Mind Perspective. In *The Nature of Insight,* eds. R. J. Sternberg and J. E. Davidson. Cambridge, Mass.: MIT Press. Forthcoming.

Senge, P. 1990. *The Fifth Discipline: The Art Practice of the Learning Organization.* New York: Doubleday.

Shavlik, J. 1991. Finding Genes by Case-Based Reasoning in the Presence of Noisy Case Boundaries. Presented at the 1991 Case-Based Reasoning Workshop, May 8–10, Washington, D.C.

Shimazu, H.; Arita, S.; and Takashima, Y. 1992. Design Tool Combining Keyword Analyzer and Case-Based Parser for Developing Natural Language Database Interfaces. In Proceedings of COLING-92.

Shimazu, H.; Kitano, H.; and Shibata, A. 1993. Retrieving Cases from Relational Data-Base: Another Stride toward Corporate-Wide Case-Based Systems. In Proceedings of the Thirteenth International Joint Conference on Artificial Intelligence. Menlo Park, Calif.: International Joint Conferences on Artificial Intelligence.

Simina, M., and Kolodner, J. 1995. Opportunistic Reasoning: A Design Perspective. In Proceedings of the Seventeenth Annual Cognitive Science Conference. Ann Arbor, Mich.: Cognitive Science Society.

Simmon, H. 1976. *Administrative Behavior.* 3d ed. New York: Free Press.

Simoudis, E. 1992. Using Case-Based Retrieval for Customer Technical Support. *IEEE Expert* 7(5): 7–11.

Simoudis, E., and Miller P. 1993. Automated Support for Retrieve and Propose Applications. In *Case-Based Reasoning: Papers from the 1993 Workshop,* 147–152. Menlo Park, Calif.: AAAI Press.

Simoudis, E., and Miller, J. 1991. The Application of CBR to Help-Desk Applications. In *Proceedings of the DARPA Case-Based Reasoning Workshop,* ed. R. Bareiss, 25–36. San Francisco, Calif.: Morgan Kaufmann.

Simoudis, E., and Miller, J. 1990. Validated Retrieval in Case-Based Reasoning. In Proceedings of the Eighth National Conference on Artificial Intelligence, 310–315. Menlo Park, Calif.: American Association for Artificial Intelligence.

Simoudis, E., and Schutt, S. 1993. COPRA: Case-Based Computer Operations Problem Resolution Assistant. In Proceedings of the 1993 IEEE Conference on Artificial Intelligence Applications, 107–113. Washington, D.C.: IEEE Computer Society.

Sinha, A. 1994. Providing Design Assistance: A Case-Based Approach, PITT-AIM-47, Artificial Intelligence in Management Laboratory, University of Pittsburgh.

Skalak, D. B., and Rissland, E. L. 1992. Arguments and Cases: An Inevitable Intertwining. *Artificial Intelligence and Law: An International Journal* 1(1): 3–48.

Skalak, D., and Rissland, E. 1991. CABARET: Rule Interpretation in a Hybrid Architecture. *International Journal of Man-Machine Studies* 34(6): 839–887.

Smith, I.; Lottaz, C.; and Faltings, B. 1995. Spatial Composition Using Cases: IDIOM. In *Proceedings of the First International Conference on Case-Based Reasoning,* 88–97. Berlin: Springer Verlag.

Smyth, B., and Cunningham, P. 1992. Déjà Vu: A Hierarchical Case-Based Reasoning System for Software Design. In Proceedings of the Tenth European Conference on Artificial Intelligence, 587–589. London: John Wiley and Sons, Ltd.

Smyth, B., and Keane, M. 1995a. Experiments on Adaptation-Guided Retrieval in a Case-Based Design System. In *Case-Based Reasoning Research and Development,* eds. M. Veloso and A. Aamodt, 313–324. New York: Springer Verlag.

Smyth, B., and Keane, M. 1995b. Remembering to Forget: A Competence-Preserving

Case Deletion Policy for Case-Based Reasoning Systems. In Proceedings of the Thirteenth International Joint Conference on Artificial Intelligence, 377–382. Menlo Park, Calif.: International Joint Conferences on Artificial Intelligence.

Smyth, B., and Keane, M. 1994. Retrieving Adaptable Cases: The Role of Adaptation Knowledge in Case Retrieval. In *Topics in Case-Based Reasoning*, eds. S. Wess, K.-D. Altoff, and M. Richter, 209–220. New York: Springer Verlag.

Stanfill, C., and Waltz, D. 1986. Toward Memory-Based Reasoning. *Communications of the ACM* 29(12): 1213–1228.

Stefik, M. 1981. Planning with Constraints. *Artificial Intelligence* 16:111–140.

Sternberg, R. J. 1986. *Intelligence Applied: Understanding and Increasing Your Intellectual Skills.* New York: Harcourt, Brace, and Jovonovitch.

Sternberg, R. J. 1985. Teaching Critical Thinking: Are We Making Critical Mistakes? *Phi Delta Kappa*, 194–198.

Stevens, S. 1989. Intelligent Interactive Video Simulation of a Code Inspection. *Communications of the ACM* 32(7): 832–843.

Stone, R; Veloso, M.; and Blythe, J. 1994. The Need for Different Domain-Independent Heuristics. In *Proceedings of the Second International Conference on AI Planning Systems,* 164–169. Menlo Park, Calif.: AAAI Press.

Stroulia, E.; Shankar, M.; Goel, A.; and Penberthy, L. 1992. A Model-Based Approach to Blame Assignment in Design. In *Artificial Intelligence in Design,* ed. J. Gero, 519–537. Norwell, Mass.: Kluwer.

Sycara, K. 1988. Using Case-Based Reasoning for Plan Adaptation and Repair. In *Proceedings of the DARPA Case-Based Reasoning Workshop,* ed J. Kolodner, 425–434. San Francisco, Calif.: Morgan Kaufmann.

Sycara, K. P. 1987. Resolving Adversarial Conflicts: An Approach Integrating Case-Based and Analytic Methods. Ph.D. diss., School of Information and Computer Science, Georgia Institute of Technology.

Sycara, K. P., and Navinchandra, D. 1991. Influences: A Thematic Abstraction for Creative Use of Multiple Cases. In *Proceedings of the Case-Based Reasoning Workshop,* 133–144. San Francisco, Calif.: Morgan Kaufmann.

Sycara, K., and Navinchandra, D. 1989. Index Transformation and Generation for Case Retrieval. In *Proceedings of the DARPA Case-Based Reasoning Workshop,* ed. K. Hammond, 324–328. San Francisco, Calif.: Morgan Kaufmann.

Sycara, K.; Guttal, R.; Koning, J.; Narasimhan, S.; and Navinchandra, D. 1991. CADET: A Case-Based Synthesis Tool for Engineering Design. *International Journal of Expert Systems* 4(2): 157–188.

Thagard, P.; Holyoak, K.; Nelson, G.; and Gochfeld, D. 1990. Analog Retrieval by Constraint Satisfaction. *Artificial Intelligence* 46(3): 259–310.

Turner, R. M. 1994. *Adaptive Reasoning for Real-World Problems: A Schema-Based Approach.* Hillsdale, N.J.: Lawrence Erlbaum.

Turner, R. 1989. A Schema-Based Model of Adaptive Problem Solving. Ph.D. diss., GIT-ICS-89/42., Dept. of Information and Computer Science, Georgia Institute of Technology.

Turner, R. 1988. Organizing and Using Schematic Knowledge for Medical Diagnosis. In *Proceedings of the Case-Based Reasoning Workshop 1988,* 435–446. San Francisco, Calif.: Morgan Kaufmann.

Turner, S. R. 1996. *MINSTREL.* Hillsdale, N.J.: Lawrence Erlbaum. Forthcoming.

Turner, S. 1994. *The Creative Process: A Computer Model of Storytelling.* Hillsdale, N.J.: Lawrence Erlbaum.

Veloso, M. M. 1994. *Planning and Learning by Analogical Reasoning.* Berlin: Springer Verlag.

Veloso, M. M. 1992. Learning by Analogical Reasoning in General Problem Solving. Ph.D. diss., Technical Report CMU-CS-92-174, School of Computer Science, Carnegie Mellon University.

Veloso, M. M. 1989. Nonlinear Problem Solving Using Intelligent Casual-Commitment, Technical Report, CMU-CS-89-210, School of Computer Science, Carnegie Mellon University.

Veloso, M. M., and Aamodt, A., eds. 1995. *Case-Based Reasoning Research and Development: Proceedings of the First International Conference on Case-Based Reasoning.* Berlin: Springer Verlag.

Veloso, M. M., and Carbonell, J. G. 1991. Variable-Precision Case Retrieval in Analogical Problem Solving. In *Proceedings of the Case-Based Reasoning Workshop,* 93–106. San Francisco, Calif.: Morgan Kaufmann.

Veloso, M. M., and Carbonell, J. G. 1993a. Automatic Case Generation, Storage, and Retrieval in PRODIGY. In *Machine Learning: A Multistrategy Approach, Volume 4,* eds. R. S. Michalski and G. Tecuci. San Francisco, Calif.: Morgan Kaufmann.

Veloso, M. M., and Carbonell, J. G. 1993b. Derivational Analogy in PRODIGY: Automating Case Acquisition, Storage, and Utilization. *Machine Learning* 10:249–278.

Veloso, M. M., and Carbonell, J. G. 1993c. Toward Scaling Up Machine Learning: A Case Study with Derivational Analogy in PRODIGY. In *Machine Learning Methods for Planning,* ed. S. Minton, 233–272. San Francisco, Calif.: Morgan Kaufmann.

Voss, A. 1994. The Need for Knowledge Acquisition in Case-Based Reasoning—Some Experiences from an Architectural Domain. In *Proceedings of the Eleventh European Conference on Artificial Intelligence,* 463–467. New York: John Wiley and Sons, Publishers.

Waltz, D. L. 1989. Is Indexing Used for Retrieval? In *Proceedings of the DARPA Case-Based Reasoning Workshop,* ed. K. Hammond, 41–44. San Francisco, Calif.: Morgan Kaufmann.

Wasserman, A.; Freeman, P.; and Pacella, M. 1983. Characteristics of Software Development Methodologies. In *Information Systems Design Methodologies,* eds. T. Olle, H. Sol, and C. Tully. New York: North Holland.

Watson, I. 1995a. Case-Based Reasoning Development Tools: A Review. Available on the World Wide Web at http://www.salford.ac.uk/docs/depts/survey/staff/IWatson/cbrtools.htm.

Watson, I., ed. 1995b. *Progress in Case-Based Reasoning: First United Kingdom Workshop.* Berlin: Springer Verlag.

Weld, D. 1994. An Introduction to Least-Commitment Planning. *AI Magazine* 15(4): 27–61.

Weld, L. 1916. *Theory of Errors and Least Squares.* New York: Macmillan.

Wess, S.; Althoff, K.; and Richter, M., eds. 1994. *Topics in Case-Based Reasoning.* Berlin: Springer Verlag.

Wilensky, R. 1986a. Knowledge Representation—A Critique and a Proposal. In *Expe-*

rience, Memory, and Reasoning, eds. J. Kolodner and C. Riesbeck, 15–28. Hillsdale, N.J.: Lawrence Erlbaum.

Wilensky, R. 1986b. Some Problems and Proposals for Knowledge Representation, Technical Report, UCB/CSD 86/294, Dept. of Electrical Engineering and Computer Science, University of California at Berkeley.

Williams, S. M. 1993. Putting Case-Based Instruction into Context: Examples from Legal, Business, and Medical Education. *Journal of the Learning Sciences* 2(4): 367–427.

Williams, S. 1992. Putting Case-Based Learning into Context: Examples from Legal, Business, and Medical Education. *The Journal of the Learning Sciences* 2(4): 367–427.

Wills, L. M., and Kolodner, J. L. 1994. Toward More Creative Case-Based Design Systems. In Proceedings of the Twelfth National Conference on Artificial Intelligence, 50–55. Menlo Park, Calif.: American Association for Artificial Intelligence.

Wiseman, C. 1988. *Strategic Information Systems.* Homewood, Ill.: Richard D. Irwin.

Wolverton, M., and Hayes-Roth, B. Retrieving Semantically Distant Analogies with Knowledge-Directed Spreading Activation. In *Proceedings of the Twelfth National Conference on Artificial Intelligence,* 56–61. Menlo Park, Calif.: AAAI Press.

Wooldridge, M., and Jennings, N. 1996. Intelligent Agents: Theory and Practice. *Knowledge Engineering Review.* Forthcoming.

Yang, H., and Fisher, D. 1992. Similarity-Based Retrieval and Partial Reuse of Macro-Operators, Technical Report, CS-92-13, Dept. of Computer Science, Vanderbilt University.

Index